Building Business in Post-Communist Russia, Eastern Europe, and Eurasia

This book examines the development of business-interest representation in the post-communist countries of Eastern Europe and Eurasia. The central argument is that abusive regulatory regimes discourage the formation of business associations. At the same time, poor regulatory enforcement tends to encourage associational-membership growth. Academic research often treats special interest groups as vehicles of protectionism and non-productive collusion. This book challenges this perspective with evidence of market-friendly activities of industry associations as well as their benign influence on patterns of public governance. Careful analysis of cross-national quantitative data that spans more than twenty-five countries, as well as the qualitative examination of the development of business associations in Russia, Ukraine, Kazakhstan, and Croatia, shows that post-communist business associations function as substitutes for state and private mechanisms of economic governance. They challenge corrupt bureaucracy and contribute to the establishment of effective and predictable regulatory regimes. These arguments and empirical findings put the long-standing issues of economic regulations, public goods, and collective action in a new theoretical perspective.

Dinissa Duvanova is an assistant professor in the department of political science at the University at Buffalo. Her research explores business-state relations, state regulatory quality, and bureaucratic institutions. In 1998 she received the prestigious "Bolashak" Presidential Scholarship, awarded to the top graduates of universities in her native Kazakhstan. She was a recipient of the Foreign Language and Area Studies and the German Academic Exchange Service academic fellowships. After receiving her doctoral degree from The Ohio State University, she spent the 2007–08 academic year as a visiting scholar at the Princeton University Center for the Study of Democratic Politics. She was also awarded a post-doctoral fellowship by the Davis Center for Russian and Eurasian Studies at Harvard University. In 2008, Duvanova joined the department of political science at the University at Buffalo, where she researches the issues of regulatory intervention, bureaucratic discretion, civil-service reforms, and public accountability of state bureaucracy. Her work has been published in the *British Journal of Political Science*, *Comparative Politics*, *Post-Soviet Affairs*, and *Europe-Asia Studies*. Her current research projects are supported by the Baldy Center for Law and Social Policy at the University at Buffalo Law School.

Building Business in Post-Communist Russia, Eastern Europe, and Eurasia

Collective Goods, Selective Incentives, and Predatory States

DINISSA DUVANOVA
University at Buffalo, State University of New York

Shaftesbury Road, Cambridge CB2 8EA, United Kingdom

One Liberty Plaza, 20th Floor, New York, NY 10006, USA

477 Williamstown Road, Port Melbourne, VIC 3207, Australia

314–321, 3rd Floor, Plot 3, Splendor Forum, Jasola District Centre, New Delhi – 110025, India

103 Penang Road, #05–06/07, Visioncrest Commercial, Singapore 238467

Cambridge University Press is part of Cambridge University Press & Assessment, a department of the University of Cambridge.

We share the University's mission to contribute to society through the pursuit of education, learning and research at the highest international levels of excellence.

www.cambridge.org
Information on this title: www.cambridge.org/9781107030169

© Dinissa Duvanova 2013

This publication is in copyright. Subject to statutory exception and to the provisions of relevant collective licensing agreements, no reproduction of any part may take place without the written permission of Cambridge University Press & Assessment.

First published 2013
First paperback edition 2015

A catalogue record for this publication is available from the British Library

Library of Congress Cataloging-in-Publication data
Duvanova, Dinissa, 1977– author.
  Building business in post-communist Russia, eastern Europe, and Eurasia : collective goods, selective incentives, and predatory states / Dinissa Duvanova, State University of New York, Buffalo.
     pages   cm
  Includes bibliographical references and index.
  ISBN 978-1-107-03016-9
  1. Trade associations – Russia (Federation.)   2. Pressure groups – Russia (Federation.)
  3. Trade associations – Europe, Eastern.   4. Pressure groups – Europe, Eastern.
  5. Trade associations – Eurasia.   6. Pressure groups – Eurasia.   I. Title.
  HD2429.R8D88   2013
  381.06´047 – dc23   2012033219

ISBN   978-1-107-03016-9   Hardback
ISBN   978-1-107-45437-8   Paperback

Cambridge University Press & Assessment has no responsibility for the persistence or accuracy of URLs for external or third-party internet websites referred to in this publication and does not guarantee that any content on such websites is, or will remain, accurate or appropriate.

To my parents Svetlana and Sergey

Contents

List of Figures	*page* ix
List of Tables	x
Preface	xiii
Acknowledgments	xvii
List of Abbreviations	xxi
Note on Translation and Transliteration	xxiii

1.	Introduction	1
	1.1 *The Puzzle*	2
	1.2 *Theoretical Contributions*	5
	1.3 *Empirical Evidence*	10
	1.4 *Summary of Main Arguments*	10
	1.5 *A Roadmap*	12
2.	Collective Action in Adverse Business Environments	14
	2.1 *The Post-Communist Business Environment*	15
	2.2 *Defensive Organization*	20
	2.3 *A Formal Model*	23
	2.4 *Official and "Unofficial" Regulatory Costs*	31
	2.5 *Testable Hypotheses*	33
	2.6 *Conclusion*	35
3.	Post-Communist Business Representation in a Comparative Perspective	38
	3.1 *A Cross-National Comparison*	40
	3.2 *Qualitative Analysis of Business Representation in Four Countries*	54
	3.3 *Russian Business Associations: Sources and Consequences of Organizational Diversity*	54

vii

viii   *Contents*

    3.4 *Ukrainian Business Associations: A Case of Political Mobilization*   72
    3.5 *Kazakh Business Associations: High-Profile/Low-Impact versus*
         Low-Profile/High-Impact Organizations   80
    3.6 *Croatian Business Associations: From Corporatism to Pluralism*   84
    3.7 *The Main Features of Post-Communist Business Associations*   92

4. Business Environment and Business Organization: The
    Quantitative Approach   94
    4.1 *Micro- and Macrocorrelates of Organizational Participation: A*
         Hierarchical Model   96
    4.2 *Statistical Analysis and Results*   107
    4.3 *Robustness Checks*   117
    4.4 *Additional Quantitative Evidence*   120
    4.5 *Summary*   127

5. What You Do Is What You Are: Business Associations in Action   130
    5.1 *Advantages of Qualitative Data and Case Selection*   131
    5.2 *Against All Odds*   137
    5.3 *Changing Times – Changing Roles*   146
    5.4 *Selective Regulatory Relief*   150
    5.5 *Collective Goods*   155
    5.6 *The Lost Battles*   163
    5.7 *Dogs That Never Barked*   166
    5.8 *Tallying Up the Evidence*   170

6. Compulsory versus Voluntary Membership   172
    6.1 *Alternative Models of Business Representation*   173
    6.2 *Modeling Voluntarism in Compulsory Systems*   176
    6.3 *From Difference to Convergence*   180
    6.4 *Membership Rates*   189
    6.5 *Labor Relations and Business Organizations*   191
    6.6 *Beyond Corporatism*   194

7. Conclusions   196
    7.1 *Summary of Arguments and Findings*   196
    7.2 *Political and Socioeconomic Roles of Business Associations*   199
    7.3 *Broader Implications and Directions for Future Research*   206
    7.4 *Associations and Their Power*   210

Appendices
A. *Research Note on Qualitative Data Collection*   213
B. *Qualitative Research Instruments*   215
C. *Regional and Municipal Business Associations in Ukraine*   217
D. *Kazakh Business Associations*   218
E. *Relaxing Two Simplifying Assumptions*   223
F. *Estimating the EU and Non-EU Samples*   225

Bibliography   227

Index   241

Figures

2.1. Equilibrium outcomes under different values of exogenous parameters	*page* 27
3.1. Average number of trade associations per country (normalized by GDP)	41
3.2. Number of trade associations per firm, regional averages	42
3.3. Associations per registered firms by country, 2002	43
3.4. Membership density by country	44
3.5. Membership density in the former Soviet Union and Eastern Europe, 1999–2005	45
3.6. Assessing the influence of business associations	46
3.7. Member evaluations of associations' services (deviation from the mean)	47
3.8. Official regulatory burden	50
3.9. Corruption, red tape, and the rule of law across the world's regions	53
3.10. Number of and membership levels in Russian business associations, dynamics over time	59
4.1. Effects of regulations on membership in business associations	110
4.2. Effects of the rule of law on membership in business associations	111
4.3. Effects of regulations under constrained and unconstrained bureaucracy	113
4.4. Effects of bribery after instrumental variable probit estimation	116
4.5. Industry associations normalized by sector size	127

ix

Tables

3.1. Membership in Business Associations: Regional Density	*page* 44
3.2. Member Evaluations of Associational Services by Income Group	47
3.3. Major Obstacles Faced by Businesses (Survey Evidence)	49
3.4. Regulatory Burden by Country (Eastern Europe and the Former USSR)	52
3.5. Summary Indicators for Four Post-Communist Countries	55
3.6. Types of Russian Business Associations, with Examples	63
3.7. Member Services Listed by Russian Business Associations in Their Founding Charters	71
3.8. Organizational Structure of Croatian Business Associations	89
3.9. Member Satisfaction with Associational Services in Countries with Voluntary and Compulsory Membership	90
4.1. Summary of Theoretical Expectations	97
4.2. Bivariate and Partial Correlations Between Individual-Level Measures of Regulatory and Bureaucratic Environment and Membership in Business Associations	100
4.3. Firm-Level Variables: Summary Statistics	105
4.4. Aggregate-Level Variables: Sources and Descriptive Statistics	107
4.5. Estimation Results: Country-Level Fixed and Random Effects Logistic Regressions	109
4.6. Estimation Results: Instrumental Variables Regressions	115
4.7. Estimation Results: Robustness to Alternative Operationalization	119

Tables   xi

4.8. Members' Evaluation of Services Provided by Associations   122

4.9. Regulatory Burden and Member Benefits: Country-Level
     Mixed-Effect Linear Regression Estimates   123

4.10. Number of Industry Associations by Sector   126

4.11. Industry-Level Analysis   128

5.1. Member Services Provided by Business Associations (Based on
     Personal Interviews with Association Leaders and Analysis of
     Internal Documentation)   132

5.2. Summary of Analyzed Associational Services   135

6.1. Pluralist and Corporatist Models of Intermediation   175

6.2. National Chambers of Commerce: Type of Membership   182

6.3. Share of Participatory Firms in Compulsory- and
     Voluntary-Membership Systems   190

7.1. Assessment of Relative Political Influence of Business
     Associations   200

A.1. Business Associations Investigated Through Qualitative
     Research   214

C.1. Number of Registered Ukrainian Business Associations
     by Administrative Unit (According to the Ukrainian State
     Administration)   217

D.1. Kazakh Business Associations Active by the End of 2006
     (Data Gathered with the Assistance of the Kazakh Chamber
     of Trade and Industry)   218

F.1. Estimating EU and Non-EU Samples   225

Preface

The 2004 government takeover of Yukos, Russia's first fully privatized integrated oil company, "heralded a turn away from the liberalism of the 1990s towards an authoritarian corporatism" ("The Khodorkovsky Case" 2009). The takeover was neither a happy marriage between business and power nor a business-preserving bailout. It was preceded by the 2003 arrests of Yukos executives Platon Lebedev and Mikhail Khodorkovsky, who were later sentenced to eight-year prison terms, a legal battle over retroactive tax bills amounting to $34 billion, and an international bankruptcy dispute. In the meantime the company's shareholders' assets were frozen (BBC 2005; "The Khodorkovsky Case" 2009). The case culminated with the government auctioning off the company's major production facility to a private firm for a meager US$9.35 billion. Later, the state-owned corporate giant Rosneft acquired the company.[1]

The Yukos affair highlights aspects of the business environment that are central to this book. Perhaps the most crucial component of business operations in emerging markets, particularly post-communist economies, has been a general sense of uncertainty that goes beyond the risks that economic agents routinely face worldwide. In established capitalist economies such risks are associated with making decisions contingent on the anticipated actions of numerous economic actors whose circumstances and aspirations are coordinated by the market's "invisible hand" and the government's "visible hand," which provides law and order. In emerging markets, as the Yukos case demonstrates, the government's hand becomes less reliable and predictable. Also, the logic behind spontaneous economic coordination by the invisible hand becomes convoluted because property rights and contract enforcement cannot be taken for granted. Although Yukos is in no way a typical post-communist company, this example

---

[1] For a more detailed analysis of the Yukos affair and its consequences for Russian politics, see Hanson and Teague (2005), Tompson (2005), and Sixsmith (2010).

clearly demonstrates business's vulnerability vis-à-vis the state, insecure property rights, and feeble laws that are symptomatic of emerging markets.

Although the plight of Yukos and its executives attracted strong international and domestic attention, we often know too little about practices and conditions that structure an everyday environment of an average post-communist firm. Because of much attention to large-scale privatization, corruption scandals, and renationalization, the experience of oligarch firms have skewed our views of post-communist business. Such firms, although of much political and economic importance, are rather atypical examples of the post-communist business. This book is not about oligarch firms like Yukos but rather about everyday firms. Still, the Yukos case helps appreciate the extent of business vulnerability: when one of the largest and most well-governed companies cannot defend itself against the state, an average business has even less of a chance.

The Yukos affair is symptomatic not only of the business environment but also of the patterns of business representation developing in the region. The only Russian public organization that publicly defended Yukos executives and later opposed partitioning of the company was the Russian Union of Industrialists and Entrepreneurs (RUIE), of which Yukos was a member. Shortly after Khodorkovsky's arrest, the RUIE leadership petitioned President Putin to free Khodorkovsky. No liberal, proreform politicians or watchdog organizations joined the RUIE petition. Despite a rift among the RUIE leadership (only six of the twenty-seven board members went on record condemning the arrest), RUIE President Arkadii Volsky strongly criticized the government's handling of the case. In 2004 the office of the procurator general (public prosecutor) accused Volsky of pressuring the court (Netreba 2004). Still, the RUIE turned out to be powerless in defending Yukos. It eventually conceded to the government with regard to Yukos and refrained from criticizing other renationalization moves. Surprisingly, the RUIE's apparent failure to defend one of its members did not preclude the growth of membership and the continuing support from existing members, many of whom still believe that the RUIE remains a significant domestic force and stands by the private sector's interests.

The tale of Yukos and the RUIE points to the contradictory nature of formal organizations uniting business and industrial interests. On the one hand, business associations – voluntary-membership nonprofit organizations of businesses or their owners – appear to be important social institutions. On the other hand, their political influence is limited due to the nature of organizational structure, the diversity of members' interests, and the organizations' often overtly apolitical stance. Although some believe that business associations primarily protect particularistic moneyed interests at the expense of public interest, others cite such associations' socially and economically benign activities (e.g., resisting government encroachment on private business, compensating for underdeveloped mechanisms of economic coordination, and reducing transaction costs). This book demonstrates that although post-communist business associations engage in both kinds of behavior, lobbying for narrowly defined goals has not

Preface   xv

been the primary reason for associational formation. A more important reason for business associations' growth has been their ability to improve the business environment through self-regulation, information-sharing, and resistance to bureaucratic encroachment. This work helps unpack perplexing issues of business environment and business strategy by providing an integrated analysis of misunderstood, stereotyped organizations that I refer to collectively as "business associations."

Acknowledgments

This book would not have been possible without the outstanding intellectual guidance, kind encouragement, and constructive criticism of the mentors, colleagues, and assistants I was lucky to have over the years of working on this project. I first would like to thank my mentors at The Ohio State University for their advice, professional guidance, and, most importantly, for believing in my potential and stimulating my intellectual development. Professor Timothy Frye was my advisor during the years I spent at Ohio State and remained central to the development of my ideas after both of us left. I benefited tremendously from his insights, experience, and generous commitment to reading multiple drafts of this book.

Professors John (Jack) Wright and Marcus Kurtz provided indispensable support, taking a keen interest in this project. Without their insightful comments and intellectual support, I would not have been able to find inspiration to commence my writing. I want to thank Professor Wright for teaching me about topics that went beyond my comparative-politics training. Without his advice and expertise, I would never have been able to tackle many issues essential to this book. I thank Professor Kurtz for his stimulating discussions and thoughtful comments on my drafts. If not for his fresh ideas and encouragement to think outside of conventional disciplinary lines, my work would be less interesting and more narrowly focused.

I also thank other scholars at The Ohio State University department of political science who had crucial direct and indirect roles in developing the ideas of this book. Specifically, I would like to thank Sarah Brooks, Goldie Shabad, Anthony Mughan, William Liddle, Jakub Zielinski, Irfan Nooruddin, and Janet Box-Steffensmeier. Over the years of my work on this project, their vision of the discipline provided clear direction in navigating across relevant theoretical domains.

xvii

While researching and writing this book, I was fortunate to meet many outstanding scholars in other places as well. I want to thank Timothy Colton, Mark von Hagen, and Ferdinand Müller-Rommel, who have shown interest in my work and provided valuable feedback on different parts of this project. I thank participants in seminars at Ohio State, Harvard, Princeton, Columbia, and Buffalo.

I owe enormous gratitude to the Center for the Study of Democratic Politics at the Woodrow Wilson School of Public and International Affairs at Princeton University, specifically to Larry Bartels and Michele Demak Epstein, for giving me uninterrupted time to pursue this project. I am grateful for the opportunity to be a visiting Fellow in such a vibrant intellectual community. At Princeton I incurred many debts. Larry Bartels, Charles Cameron, Carles Boix, Mark Beissinger, Rodney Hero, Cesar Zucco Jr., Ismail K. White, and Thomas Sattler read parts of this book and shared their insightful comments on the core theoretical ideas of the book at the time I needed them most.

This book would have been much harder to complete if not for the congenial atmosphere I found at the University at Buffalo, my current academic home. I have benefited a great deal from the faculty and students there. Special thanks go to Charles M. Lamb, Harvey Palmer, Jason Sorens, Phillip Arena, Hongxing Yin, and Dan Kotlewski. One could not wish for better colleagues.

I owe enormous gratitude to all involved in the review process. I have been fortunate to work with Lewis Bateman at Cambridge University Press. Lewis skillfully guided the manuscript through the review and publication process. I would like to thank Errol Meidinger, Munroe Eagles, and Laura Wirth at the Baldy Center for Law and Social Policy for organizing a manuscript-development workshop to discuss the ideas of this book. I owe an important debt of gratitude to Scott Gehlbach and Peter Rutland for reading the entire manuscript and criticizing it in the most constructive and insightful manner. The manuscript was strengthened considerably by the comments and suggestions I received from Scott and Peter as well as other workshop participants. I also thank the anonymous reviewers for providing especially detailed and valuable comments. I am grateful to Eve Baker of Baker Editing Services for her skillful copyediting.

Empirical research presented in this book was made possible by generous financial support from The Ohio State University and the Phillis Krumm Memorial International Scholarship, which financed my field research in Russia and Ukraine. A Foreign Language and Area Studies fellowship from the U.S. Department of Education made it possible for me to travel to Croatia and add the country to my empirical exploration. I am grateful for the generous support from the Social Science Research Council; the German Academic Exchange Service; the European Consortium for Political Research; the Harriman Institute for Russian, Eurasian, and East European Studies at Columbia; the Munk Centre for International Studies at the University of Toronto; and the

Acknowledgments   xix

Baldy Center for Law and Social Policy at Buffalo – these institutions enabled me to present parts of this book at numerous locations.

This book would never have been completed without the support I received from the large number of individuals in Russia, Ukraine, Croatia, and Kazakhstan who showed ardent interest in my research and shared with me their valuable time, expertise, and resources. I am indebted to the business-association leaders, state officials, and academicians for sharing my passion for the subject of this project and supporting my enthusiasm. Most importantly, I want to thank Vladimir Volkov at the Russian Association for the Development of Small and Medium Size Entrepreneurship, Vladimir Bykov and Aleksander Alin at the Chambers of Commerce and Industry of the Russian Federation, and Dmitro Liapin at the Ukrainian Institute for Competitive Society, all of whom not only spent hours of their time answering my questions, but also provided me with valuable quantitative information.

Most importantly I want to thank my family for their emotional support. When I think about this book now, I can see that I wrote it for my parents Sergey and Svetlana, who always encouraged me to pursue high goals and achieve them. My husband Alexi deserves special thanks. He shared my ups and downs throughout the years I researched and wrote this book. I am grateful for his help, understanding, patience, and optimism, which made working on this project much less stressful.

I have previously published parts of the material presented in Chapters 2, 4, 5, and 6 in the following publications: "Bureaucratic Corruption and Collective Action: Business Associations in the Postcommunist Transition," *Comparative Politics* 39, no. 4 (July 2007): 441–62; "Business Representation in Eastern Europe: The Failure of Corporatism?" in *Interest Groups and Lobbying in Europe: Essays on Trade, Environment, Legislation, and Economic Development*, edited by Conor McGrath (Lewiston, NY: Edwin Mellen Press, 2009); and "Firm Lobbying versus Sectoral Organization: The Analysis of Business-State Relations in Postcommunist Russia," *Post-Soviet Affairs* 27, no. 4 (October–December 2011): 387–409. This material is reprinted here with permission from the original publishers.

Abbreviations

ACE	Association of Croatian Exporters
ADSMB	Association for the Development of Small and Medium-Size Business, Russia
ARB	Association of Russian Banks
AZZZ	Asociácia Zamestnávateľských Zväzov A Združení (Federation of Employers' Associations of The Slovak Republic)
BEEPS	Business Environment and Enterprise Performance Survey
CAC	Croatian Association of Cooperatives
CEA	Croatian Employers' Association
CEC	Coordinating Expert Center of Business Associations of Ukraine
CCE	Croatian Chamber of Economy
CCEO	Coordinating Council for Employers' Organizations, Russia
CCI	Chamber of Commerce and Industry, Russia
CIS	Commonwealth of Independent States
CPI	Corruption Perception Index
CTA	Council of Trade Associations, Ukraine
CTC	Chamber of Trades and Crafts, Croatia
CTI	Chamber of Trade and Industry, Kazakhstan
EBRD	European Bank for Reconstruction and Development
ECR	electronic cash registers
FCP	Federation of Commodity Producers, Russia
GDP	gross domestic product
GI	Global Integrity
IEI	Russian Institute for Entrepreneurship and Investment
IIPA	International Intellectual Property Alliance
IMF	International Monetary Fund

PARTAD	Professional Association of Registrars, Transfer Agents and Depositories, Russia
RAICP	Russian Association of Ice Cream Producers
RATEK	Association of Trade Companies and Producers of Consumer Electronics and Computers (Russian acronym)
RUIE	Russian Union of Industrialists and Entrepreneurs
SAA	Stabilization and Association Agreement
SIU	Scientific–Industrial Union, USSR
UALCE	Ukrainian Association of Leasing Companies and Entrepreneurs
UCCI	Ukrainian Chamber of Commerce and Industry
UEF	Ukrainian Employers' Federation
ULIE	Ukrainian League of Industrialists and Entrepreneurs
UNADTS	Ukrainian National Association for the Development of Trade and Services
USAID	United States Agency for International Development
USMPE	Ukrainian Union of Small, Medium, and Privatized Enterprises
VAT	value added tax
WB	World Bank

Note on Translation and Transliteration

I transliterated Russian and Ukrainian words using the simplified Library of Congress system (diacritics and two-letter tie characters are omitted), except for names of well-known people for whom a different spelling has become conventional, for example Yeltsin. I transliterated all Kazakh names from their Russian spelling. All translations from Russian, Ukrainian, and Croatian original documents and records are my own.

1

Introduction

People of the same trade seldom meet together ...

– Adam Smith

In 2005, on my second research trip to Russia, I visited a tiny but long-established association of small entrepreneurs in an administrative district of Moscow. As I walked through the door, a young male secretary greeted me and offered me the customary cup of tea while I waited for my appointment with the association's president. The office was small and neat. Newspapers and magazines filled the shelves. A map of Moscow hung on the wall. The suite comprised a conference room that could accommodate a dozen people, the president's office, and a room for two other staff members. The secretary smiled awkwardly at me. I was an unusual visitor, so he did not know how to start the conversation. I asked him not to mind my presence; I did not want to disturb whatever he had been doing before I arrived.

"It's a relatively slow day," he replied. "Summer, you know. Business is slow. The craziness will start in two weeks. Then you wouldn't have a chance to catch our president in the office."

Before I had arrived, he had been listening to the news on Nashe Radio, a popular Russian radio station. Now he changed the station. In a strong voice, a woman sang a lively tune: "They control our steps. They control our minds." I wondered if "they" referred to Russia's communist past or the currently emerging police state. It turned out that "they" referred to state regulators: *kontrolery*.

"I really like this song," the secretary said. "This is what we're dealing with here most of the time."

"How so?" I asked.

"You see, I'm the one who meets all our visitors and answers the phone here. For the most part, people contact us when they're in trouble. We rarely hear

1

from our happy members. So when they call, it's usually a complaint about yet another regulator who overstepped his limits or caused some other problems. I'm sick of hearing the same stories over and over."

That day I did not give much thought to my casual conversation with the secretary. Only later, after a couple dozen other meetings and endless phone conversations with industry leaders and functionaries, did I realize that the secretary's simplistic account of the association's role in dealing with state regulators provided the answer to the puzzle I was trying to crack.

1.1 The Puzzle

I went to Russia to study the formation and activities of business associations.[1] Prior to 1989, the post-communist countries of Eastern Europe and the former USSR lacked membership-based business associations.[2] After the collapse of communism, genuine membership-based business associations emerged as representative institutions of the private sector, surpassing other types of societal organizations in number, resources, and membership. The variation in membership rates across countries, however, is striking, ranging from 15 percent to 70 percent of business entities (European Bank for Reconstruction and Development and World Bank 2005). This prompts the question: why did some businesses in some countries join business associations while others did not?

Another important question is why these numerous, organizationally complex, and continuously expanding organizations are seldom implicated in rent-seeking or collusive behavior? As early as 1776, Adam Smith expressed a distrust of organized businesspeople, stating, "People of the same trade seldom meet together, even for merriment and diversion, but the conversation ends in a conspiracy against the public" (131). His two fundamental propositions, well known in modern scholarship as the collective-action problem and special interests' rent-seeking, have guided my study of business associations.

---

[1] Throughout this book I use the term *business association* rather than industry association because not all business associations are limited to particular industries. Many are based on region or on issues of concern. In the post-communist states, national legislation defines business associations as nonprofit organizations that unite companies or their managers on professional, geographical, sectoral, or other grounds. This definition legally restricts activities of business associations and clearly distinguishes them from industrial conglomerates, trusts, and firms (vertically and horizontally integrated commercial establishments). Although some countries' laws specify the permissible missions of such associations, most do not. My analysis of the charters and publicly stated objectives of more than 350 business associations revealed that most of these associations define their objectives broadly, declaring all types of activities permitted by law. The most commonly stated goals include growth within a particular industry or market, sharing of market-related information among members, protection and representation of members' professional interests in relation to the state, and harmonization of members' interests with regard to legislation, regulation, and strategic development.

[2] The Soviet-style associations often did not charge membership dues and were part of the state bureaucracy. They were not rooted in membership, as their official names would imply.

Introduction 3

According to the former concept, it is irrational for self-interested actors to join common-cause groups; instead, self-reliance and opportunism are their optimal strategies.[3] According to the latter, organized moneyed interests should always be suspect, as they tend to take advantage of disorganized consumers and short-sighted politicians.

Researching the origins of post-communist business associations, I wondered whether businesspeople were aware of the collective-action problem. Because the members of business associations often directly compete with one another for market share, why would they want to join a common-cause group, especially one that is open to public scrutiny and diverse membership? I was reluctant to conclude that post-communist businesspeople are simply irrational, wasting their time and resources on actions that are advantageous only in collective terms.

Both the public and academia tend to view post-communist business associations as having little influence over state policy and economic development (Kubicek 1996; Peregudov and Semenenko 1996; Fortescue 1997; Rutland 2001; McMenamin 2002; Lehmbruch 2003).[4] If associations are unimportant in lobbying for the business community's interests, however, it is unclear why firms across the post-communist world join them and why these associations grow in number and membership. Business associations' weak influence in post-communist societies contrasts with the enormous influence that individual companies have exercised; indeed, some scholars have concluded that such companies have managed to block economic reform in many post-communist states (Hellman 1998; Hellman, Jones, and Kaufmann 2000; Ganev 2001).

My puzzlement increased when I compared business associations' formation and membership across economic sectors and post-communist countries. Employer associations were numerous and prominent in highly fragmented small-business and retail-trade sectors as well as in sectors such as real estate and financial services, but not in metallurgy or coal industries. I was surprised

---

[3] Olson (1965) explained group formation as a product of club goods (selective incentives) and sanctions against free-riders. Because enforcing sanctions is costlier and the benefits are more dispersed in larger groups, business actors are easier to organize compared to more numerous labor groups. This logic, however, does not apply to a vast number of business sectors that are dominated by small and dispersed firms and heterogeneous interests. At the same time, firms with highly concentrated resources may have little incentive to act collectively but instead may pursue their interests through direct ties to public officials that crony capitalist arrangements offer. As documented in Chapters 3 and 5, the development of post-communist trade associations is not a simple product of groups' size and resource concentration, although both factors play an important role in explaining how and why some associations form whereas others fail.

[4] Remington (2004) describes the RUIE as "the single most powerful organized interest group in Russia" (153). Similarly, according to Fink-Hafner and Krasovec (2005), "Interest groups with more independent resources and greater power (especially economic interest groups) have succeeded in their pressure to create more institutionalized policy networks with an important influence on behalf of non-state actors" (414). However, such assessments are infrequent. Most scholars emphasize the weakness and disorganization of post-communist businesses.

to learn that some of Eastern Europe's most democratic countries with the strongest traditions of civic engagement, such as the Czech Republic and Poland, have *not* been leaders in the development of business associations; rather, their levels of participation in business associations were moderate during political and economic transition. This finding was hard to reconcile with scholars' predictions of greater organizational activity in countries with rational-bureaucratic legacies, deeper civic traditions that survived under communist regimes, and revitalized social activism that led to the peaceful anticommunist revolutions of the early 1990s (Jowitt 1992a; Schopflin 1994; Geddes 1995; Kitschelt 1999). From the standard perspective, post-communist business associations were forming in the wrong sectors and countries.

This book investigates the causes of the formation of business associations and their interaction with state institutions in the wake of the collapse of state socialism.[5] It advances a theory of the relationship between economic actors and the state, and contributes to ongoing debates in the study of post-communism as well as to more general studies of collective action, regulatory politics, and industrial organization. Several findings stand out. First, in contrast to popular wisdom, rates of membership in business associations are quite high in post-communist economies. Despite the purported flattened social landscape, high levels of social apathy, and incentives to work in the informal economy, people of the same trade frequently overcome the problem of collective action and come together in formal associations. Moreover, unlike accounts that declare post-communist business associations to be weak and inconsequential, this study demonstrates that these associations perform functions vital to their constituents – functions that have remained below the radar of transitional economy research.

Second, cross-national quantitative data from twenty-seven countries and qualitative data from Russia, Ukraine, Croatia, and Kazakhstan indicate that state regulatory institutions have a surprising effect on the formation of business associations. Counterintuitively, harsh regulations discourage the development of business associations, but lax enforcement of regulations, often linked to bureaucratic corruption, stimulates collective action.[6] Thus, it is critical to

---

[5] This research focuses on formal business associations, not business-interest groups broadly conceived. It thereby avoids the question of what constitutes an interest group. If one adopts the established view that "an interest arises from the conjunction between some private value held by a political actor – public officials or groups thereof as well as private sector operatives – and some authoritative action or proposed action by government" (Salisbury 1991, 12), civic associations that do not lobby the government are not interest groups. I find such exclusion unjustified. Unlike the literature on lobbying, this book concentrates on the organization of business communities rather than government's granting of private benefits. My approach excludes unorganized or individual demands and activities, does not require attempts to influence or lobby, and, when such attempts are present, does not specify the channels of influence.

[6] I define economic regulation as a direct state intervention in market decisions such as pricing, competition, and market entry or exit, regardless of whether it results in increased or hampered economic efficiency. Regulations may take different forms, ranging from trade protection and entry barriers to laws specifying property and consumer rights.

Introduction 5

differentiate between two distinct concepts that are often conflated: the extent of regulation and the enforcement of these regulations. Whereas the former weakens incentives to join business associations, the absence of the latter strengthens them. The logic here is straightforward but yields a counterintuitive insight. Corrupt bureaucrats often compete with business associations to provide regulatory relief. (In exchange for bribes, the bureaucrats overlook regulatory noncompliance.) To gain members, business associations must supply meaningful, cost-effective regulatory relief.[7] When regulations are particularly burdensome, business associations must work harder to make membership worthwhile; as a result, fewer of them are able to form and survive. However, when enforcement of harsh regulations is lax and corruption prevails, business associations can provide a valuable service to members by protecting them from corruption and, thus, can thrive as organizations.

Third, although a large body of literature on business-state interaction contends that interest groups make claims on the state and seek protection from market forces (Olson 1965; Stigler 1971; Peltzman 1976; Grossman and Helpman 1994; Groseclose and Snyder 1996; Rose-Ackerman 1999), I argue that business associations in the post-communist setting primarily protect firms from the state. This is not to say that post-communist businesses might not engage in collusion and rent-seeking. However, conspiracy against the public has not been the primary motivation behind the formation of business associations; instead, post-communist business associations have developed in large part to counter the arbitrariness, unpredictability, and injustice of state regulatory mechanisms. This study documents how the development of business associations improves the business environment, thereby making it more predictable and favorable to business activity. Thus, my findings stand in contrast to a large body of literature on the pernicious impact of interest groups.

1.2 Theoretical Contributions

Although the post-communist transition has provided fertile ground for studies of business-state interactions, few studies have focused on formal associations for business representation. Researchers have investigated reform of the state (Crawford 1995; Bunce 1999; Grzymala-Busse 2007; Pickles and Jenkins 2008; Frye 2010) and informal interactions between the state and private interests (Hellman 1998; Hellman, Jones, and Kaufmann 2000; Ganev 2001; Frye 2002a), but we know little about formal representation of non-state economic actors. A comprehensive analysis of the transitional processes that redefine the state's role in the economy must include the formation of formal associations representing the business community. This book is one

---

[7] Chapter 2 models the cost of membership as one of the parameters affecting association membership decisions.

of the first studies of business associations across sectors and countries in the post-communist world.

Business associations, which had a very limited role in the state-controlled socialist economy, mushroomed throughout East-Central Europe and Eurasia following communism's collapse. Business associations in the new member-states of the European Union (EU) have actively participated in Europe-wide industry federations and representative bodies, assisting harmonization with EU practices and institutions. Across the post-communist world some of these associations have become prominent actors in industrial relations, assuming functions that state institutions formerly performed (see Remington 2004; Fink-Hafner and Krasovec 2005). Others have attracted media attention for their public campaigns to exert pressure on national governments and international institutions.

Because associations representing business interests shape post-communist states and markets, the dynamics of group mobilization and the mechanisms of exerting influence warrant thorough investigation. By addressing business associations as crucial institutions linking civil society, the economy, and the state, this book fills a gap in the otherwise rich literature on the post-communist socioeconomic transition and contributes to theory on interest groups, institutional development, and capitalism. The primary theoretical focus on business-state relations and the structures of economic governance make this study highly relevant to post-communist politics and economics, regulatory politics, institutional development, and economic reform.[8]

Interest Groups, Rent-Seeking, and Governance

Special interest groups occupy a central place in the field of political economy (Olson 1965; Stigler 1971; Peltzman 1976). Traditionally, studies of organized producer interests have depicted business associations as rent-seeking vehicles of protectionism and unproductive collusion detrimental to social well-being (Grossman and Helpman 1994, 2000; Groseclose and Snyder 1996; Rose-Ackerman 1999). Recent studies of industrial relations in emerging markets have challenged this perspective with mounting evidence that business associations engage in market-friendly, efficiency-enhancing activities and benignly influence public governance (Recanatini and Ryterman 2001; Campos and Giovannoni 2005; Pyle 2006, 2011; Markus 2007; Yakovlev and Govorun 2011). This book contributes to this emerging intellectual tradition, highlighting formal business associations as nonmarket vehicles that improve business climate, efficiency, and growth. Specifically, it addresses the influence of the

---

[8] Theories of corporatism and, more recently, varieties of capitalism research are of specific relevance. Business associations are essential components of business-state-society relations. Better understanding of their economic, political, and social roles helps build a more comprehensive account of labor relations, economic policymaking, and capitalist development in post-communist countries.

Introduction

state regulatory environment on a company's decision to pursue one of two alternative strategies: opaque, direct transactions with regulators (i.e., bribery) or public collective action (i.e., participation in business associations).[9] This book's theoretical arguments and empirical evidence support the view that collective action by the business community is at least partly a response to malignant regulatory practices in emerging markets.

Post-Communist Political Economy and Civil Society

This study's primary empirical focus is on variations in the development of business associations across post-communist countries and economic sectors. Despite having much in common, these countries nevertheless vary in the number, strength, and characteristics of their emerging business associations.[10] Although scholars have examined the behavior and influence of business-interest groups, the reasons that business-interest groups do or do not form remains underinvestigated. What factors influence which businesses, economic sectors, and countries produce the most business associations? Post-communist comparative research has given this question little attention.

When political and economic reforms swept Eastern Europe in the early 1990s and shattered the remnants of the Soviet Union a few years later, scholars focused on the problems of democratic and economic transition. As liberal reforms in Eastern Europe and the Commonwealth of Independent States (CIS) proceeded, a twofold assessment of the development of interest groups emerged. Some scholars viewed post-communist business associations as having little influence on state policy and economic development (Kubicek 1996; Peregudov and Semenenko 1996; Fortescue 1997; Rutland 2001; McMenamin 2002; Lehmbruch 2003). Other scholars argued that mobilized business interests significantly influenced political and economic transition (Hellman 1998; Treisman 1998; Johnson, McMillan, and Woodruff 1999; Ganev 2001).[11] Although it emphasizes the importance of interest-group politics, this literature is silent with respect to the *causes* of group formation (or nonformation).

---

[9] A supplementary model relaxes this assumption and demonstrates that the major conclusions hold even if members or business associations can simultaneously engage in bribery.

[10] The early literature on the post-communist transition tends to emphasize Leninist legacies as a factor in the weakness of civil society in post-communist countries (Jowitt 1992a; Schopflin 1994; Geddes 1995). This emphasis seems to exaggerate similarities among Eastern European countries. These countries' experiences under communist rule substantially differed, yet the formal mechanisms of business-state relations followed similar patterns. This study investigates how diverse precommunist and communist legacies have shaped emerging business-state relations.

[11] A frequent argument is that business oligarchs have advanced their interests at the expense of the public interest (Shleifer and Treisman 2000). In Russia's case the banking sector (Johnson 2000) and energy sector (Lane 2001) have been identified as the most powerful business-interest groups. When such special interests gain access to political decision making, it is argued, they perpetuate the partial-transition stage that privileges their position. Frye (2002a) has critiqued this one-sided notion of state capture by business, showing that the state and business interests influence each other.

Scholars who underestimate the importance of business associations tend to doubt businesses' ability to overcome the collective-action problem, and those who emphasize strong economic interests concentrate on the effects of organized interests, ignoring how businesses overcome this problem. Consequently, neither approach has scrutinized business associations as a dependent variable. The question of which interests are represented in post-communist countries has important implications for the outcomes of political conflict and the general study of post-communism. Understanding why post-communist countries differ in the ways their social groups organize is an important element in identifying the trajectories of post-communist political and economic development.

Varieties of Capitalism

This study's primary goal is to chronicle one aspect of post-communist economic and social transformation: the formation and evolution of business representation. This book also places emerging business representation in a comparative perspective and highlights the importance of business associations in the market economy. Significantly, different types of capitalist economies can be traced to the different roles played by business-interest groups, especially employer/producer associations.[12] By exploring similarities and differences in the systems of representation of business interests across post-communist countries, this book contributes to research on the varieties of capitalism and on the ways different countries organize relations between business and the state.

Business associations are important social institutions that determine the type of a capitalist economy. They shape economic coordination, industrial relations, welfare systems, skill acquisition and certification, and public policy (Whitley and Kristensen 1997; Appelbaum and Schettkat 1998; Hodgson 1998; Hall and Soskice 2001, 2004). To understand the nature of capitalism, one must understand the roles, forms, and influence of business associations. Analysis of emerging systems of business representation also provides insights into what types of capitalism will develop in post-communist countries. Post-communist countries provide excellent cases for studying this topic because business-state relations are still in the process of forming.

State Bureaucracy

This book explores connections between society's economic domain and state bureaucratic structures. State institutions appear to play active roles in post-communist transitions, shaping the number, composition, functions, and, to

---

[12] Although primarily concerned with strictly economic aspects of business associations, the literature on varieties of capitalism points to these associations as the central nonmarket institutions of information transfer, standard setting, industrial-policy implementation, economic coordination, and public-policy formation (Whitley and Kristensen 1997; Appelbaum and Schettkat 1998; Hodgson 1998; Hall and Soskice 2001, 2004). Studies of the political economies of newly industrialized East Asian countries indicate that business associations are central to economic development (Johnson 1982; Lim 1983; Wade 1990; Morley 1999).

Introduction   9

some extent, demands of interest groups. This study addresses central questions of political economy: How does state authority shape the way markets work by changing the incentive structures of market agents? And how do these agents interact with the state in pursuit of economic gain? As Polanyi (1944) suggested, society's economic and political spheres are not separate entities. Markets are embedded in a web of social and political institutions that regulate their workings, and business associations are an important component of this web. By investigating the factors involved in business associations' formation and influence, this book advances a general theory of the relationships among economic actors, state institutions, and society (Evans 1995).

What This Book Is Not About

Although this book touches on lobbying for business interests as one aspect of associational development, it is not limited to the issue of direct influence on policy formation and implementation. Through their representative associations, businesses affect the state in important and subtle ways that would be missed if I focused solely on lobbying. This study elucidates such indirect but essential influences.

By addressing the formation of business associations, this research contributes to the study of interest groups in general and to that of their relations with state institutions in particular. However, business associations are probably not the most common type of interest group operating between the state and the market. Therefore, this study's findings do not necessarily apply to other types of civil associations (e.g., unions, civil-political groups, and religious organizations). Nevertheless, this research addresses a crucial aspect of state-society relations: interactions between economic elites and the state.

Unlike many influential works on business interests, this work does not start with the socioeconomic consequences of interest-group politics. Much of the research on interest groups' influence on the state examines the conditions under which these groups positively or negatively impact economic performance, accountability, fairness, and efficiency. Existing work on the consequences of business associations, however, misses a key selection process: business interests organize in some situations but not in others. This failure to problematize the selection process by which organized interests come into being opens possibilities of serious bias. By examining the causes of interest-group formation and growth, this study tackles the selection process, providing a foundation to link causes and consequences together. It shows that business-interest groups often form in response to state institutions' failure to provide collective goods, and it highlights such groups' positive effects: institution building that results in improved business climate, efficiency, and growth.[13] Although this research

---

[13] Although we cannot deduce the effects of group formation from its causes, we can better understand the socioeconomic consequences of business organizational development if we understand why groups form.

does not directly investigate the outcomes of interest-groups' politics, by implication it does help define the economic and political roles that business associations occupy in emerging markets.

1.3 Empirical Evidence

To account for the formation of business associations across countries and economic sectors, I analyzed data from (1) World Bank BEEPS surveys (1999, 2002, and 2005) of businesses in twenty-seven post-communist countries[14]; (2) a survey of Russian business associations; and (3) structured interviews and oral histories describing the development of business associations in post-communist Russia, Croatia, Ukraine, and Kazakhstan. This study includes large-N statistical analysis, comparative analyses of four countries, and in-depth case studies of business associations. The use of multiple research methods allowed me to derive hypotheses for different levels of analysis (firms, sectors, and countries) and, thereby, to cross-check the validity of my inferences.

Whereas the quantitative analysis is based on secondary data, I collected my qualitative data firsthand. In my field research I collected original data on the number of business associations, their estimated membership, and the economic sectors they represent. I also analyzed oral-history records and conducted more than eighty hours of structured interviews describing the development of twenty-four Russian, sixteen Ukrainian, and five Croatian business associations. Such data were not previously available. The interviewees were fifty-three officials representing business associations and state agencies in Russia, Ukraine, and Croatia. I also collected qualitative data on the development of Kazakh business associations. Appendices A and B provide the details of my fieldwork and research instruments.

1.4 Summary of Main Arguments

Although a number of theories illuminate the formation of interest groups, none adequately explains the development of post-communist business associations. As I pondered interviewees' accounts of the formation and evolution of dozens of business associations – small and large, local and national, poorly funded and resource rich, well established and disintegrating – I found no uniform answers as to why these associations emerge, why they fail or succeed, or why firms join them. Establishing an entrepreneurs' league, employers' union, or other business association is a complicated process that brings together

---

[14] Although the twenty-seven countries show increasingly divergent post-communist development, they share many preexisting traits. Pooling data on association membership in all twenty-seven countries allowed me to investigate the effects of different regulatory and macroeconomic variables, and examining data from three consecutive cross-national business surveys allowed me to investigate the temporal dimension of business participation.

Introduction

competing enterprises or individuals. There is no single reason to account for success or failure; rather, there are complex and mutually dependent reasons leading to the formation of business associations and members' decisions to join them. My research yielded the following primary findings.

Business associations form in response to unfavorable business environments. This finding accords with classical theories of group formation (Truman 1951; Olson 1982). With regard to post-communist business associations, the specific type of environmental disturbances is that of bureaucratic red tape and corruption. Unlike the interest groups analyzed in the literature on lobbying and influence, most post-communist business-interest groups organize primarily not to change regulatory legislation but more often to protect their members from its misapplication. They largely respond to, rather than create, bureaucratic corruption.

Business associations form and attract members when organizational entrepreneurs offer members strong selective benefits. In post-communist countries business associations help protect members from unpredictable, arbitrary regulations and predatory bureaucrats. Their attempts to bring about deregulation, predictable regulatory systems, and consistent, impartial enforcement, are often met with the free-rider problem. As a result, few associations succeed in lobbying. Instead, most post-communist business associations build their reputation by structuring and simplifying the process of regulatory compliance for their member companies. These benefits usually come in the form of excludable services.

Contrary to the classical theory of lobbying, stringent regulations discourage the formation of business associations. Corrupt bureaucrats often compete with business associations to provide regulatory relief. (In exchange for bribes, the bureaucrats overlook regulatory noncompliance.) Business associations must supply meaningful, cost-effective regulatory relief. When regulations are particularly burdensome, business associations must work harder to make membership worthwhile; therefore, fewer of them are able to form and survive.

Business associations evolve as regulatory substitutes for the state. Post-communist enterprises often lack nonmarket institutions of information transfer, quality control, and standard setting and enforcement. Economic sectors with characteristics essential to solving the collective-action problem – specific resources, homogenous interests, and relatively few participants – often develop business associations that act as mechanisms of self-regulation. These associations develop to compensate for an absence of state or private institutions of economic coordination.

Participation in corporatist-style compulsory-membership business associations does not substitute for voluntary membership in business associations. In some post-communist countries the state has created compulsory-membership business associations. Although such associations certainly solve the collective-action problem, membership in most post-communist business associations is voluntary. Voluntary associations form and attract sizable membership even in countries that also have compulsory-membership business associations. This finding challenges theories that emphasize the influence of institutional legacies on the formation of social organizations. Underlying social interests, not engineered formal institutions, emerge as the driving force behind organizational development.

1.5 A Roadmap

This book's central thesis, which I label the "defensive organization" theory, is that business associations emerge to protect their members from an unfavorable business environment. The book starts with the theory of business association development, provides an overview of currently available information, subjects the theory of defensive organization to a series of empirical tests, and concludes with a discussion of this research's major implications. Chapter 2 identifies the most compelling explanations for the formation of business associations and proposes the hypothesis of defensive organization. Integrating different approaches to the study of interest organizations and incorporating relevant features of post-communist transitional politics and economics, the chapter develops an original theoretical argument about the development of business associations in Eastern Europe and Eurasia. To illustrate the logic of defensive organization, I present a simple three-player game that models the choice of participation in business associations as a strategic interaction among the state, business associations, and firms. This framework offers a novel way to examine business association development.

Chapter 3 situates post-communist business representation in a large cross-national perspective, presents the history of post-communist business representation, introduces case studies of four countries, and provides descriptive analysis of business representation in Russia, Ukraine, Croatia, and Kazakhstan. The descriptive analysis explores the similarities and differences in business representation within these countries in terms of their respective political and economic transitions and diverse regulatory and political systems. The chapter focuses on the largest and most representative business associations, such as chambers of industry and commerce.

Chapter 4 tests a number of empirical propositions derived from the theory of defensive organization, focusing on the effects of regulatory environment and bureaucratic probity on firms' decisions to join business associations. The chapter analyzes aggregate, sector-level, and firm-level quantitative data. While macro-level data helps seeing a larger picture, firm-level data illuminates microlevel implications of defensive organization. Chapter 4 also analyzes macro factors, such as legal frameworks, the nature of political institutions, and the general quality of bureaucratic regulations and distinguishes the effects of corruption from the effects of firm and sector characteristics, political institutions, and macroeconomic conditions. Statistical analysis that controls for the effects of other correlates supports the defensive organization hypothesis.

Introduction 13

Most of the qualitative evidence presented in this book centers on case studies of business associations chosen to test the major hypotheses. Chapter 5 draws primarily on this qualitative evidence, comparing examples of the formation, development, and widely varied activities of business associations in post-communist Russia, Ukraine, Croatia, and Kazakhstan. I analyze thirteen case studies of business associations in different economic sectors in these four countries, in which business associations attempted to reduce business costs by reducing regulatory pressures or providing other benefits (collective and club goods) to their members.

Chapter 6 addresses compulsory membership. Although most post-communist countries have adopted a pluralist model of representation that relies on voluntary membership, some countries have compulsory-membership business associations. Despite institutional legacies, underlying legal frameworks, and official support for compulsory business associations, in the 1990s most such associations started incorporating elements of competition and voluntarism. In addition, voluntary-membership business associations have developed alongside compulsory-membership associations, casting doubt on the ability of state-sponsored methods to overcome the free-rider problem. Chapter 6 investigates the development of voluntary-membership business associations within compulsory-membership systems. I extend the formal model introduced in Chapter 2 to the analysis of compulsory-membership associations and analyze the development of business representation across compulsory-membership systems, paying special attention to Croatia as a representative case.

Although this book focuses primarily on the *causes* of the formation of business associations, the *effects* of business associations on the economic and political development of post-communist countries warrant further investigation. Chapter 7 summarizes this study's theoretical and empirical contributions and discusses how emergent systems of business representation affect post-communist countries' democratic and economic development. The chapter brings together the book's major arguments to create an integrated picture of emerging patterns of business representation. Chapter 7 also reviews evidence of business associations' important role in post-communist politics and discusses the implications of this work for theories of economic transition and business-state relations.

2

Collective Action in Adverse Business Environments

> What is the difference between a taxidermist and a tax collector? The taxidermist takes only your skin.
>
> – Mark Twain

Starting around the year 2000 the largest among the former Soviet cities underwent a construction boom. Against a backdrop of Soviet-style gray concrete architecture, new residential and office buildings with their flamboyant décor and space-age materials signaled the arrival of capitalism. This startling change was not limited to the buildings; the construction sites themselves looked rather different from familiar Soviet archetypes. Clean fences, warning signs, and safety nets guarded the public from construction debris, noise, and dust. One day I noticed something interesting at the construction site of a half-finished high-rise apartment building on a busy street in Almaty, Kazakhstan's largest city. Workers had replaced the decorative screen that had surrounded the site with a plain green rug. The screen had depicted the future building's façade. I soon noted that dull fences were replacing similar decorative screens on other Almaty streets. Puzzled, I mentioned my observation to someone in the Kazakh construction industry. I learned that Almaty officials were responsible for the installation of these mundane green and gray covers and dull fences, having decided that the images printed on the construction fences and screens, irrespective of their content, constituted advertisements. All ads displayed within the city limits were subject to regulation and approval by a special agency, and required high fees. Thus, by a stroke of the bureaucratic pen, fences and screens covering unsightly construction were turned into an expensive commodity. Rather than bear the costs and inconvenience, construction companies simply removed the images. Fighting the city's encroachment on the construction firms' interest in building their market reputation and the public's interest in living in a safe and beautiful city would have required collective action.

Collective Action in Adverse Business Environments 15

Some companies in post-communist countries _have_ responded to such situations with collective action, creating business associations intended to protect themselves from bureaucracy. This chapter presents a theoretical argument that specifies the conditions under which post-communist firms chose to organize and/or join business associations. It outlines the theoretical motivations and builds an analytical framework to guide subsequent empirical analysis.

Why do business associations form despite a legacy of social apathy and the pervasive collective action problem? I offer an explanation that considers the interplay between state bureaucracy, regulatory systems, and firms' interests as shaped by their business environments. I argue that abusive regulatory regimes and low-level bureaucratic corruption affect group formation. Contrary to much of the literature on interest-group formation, the theory developed here predicts that pervasive regulations discourage rather than encourage the formation of business associations. The theory also implies, in contrast to some existing arguments, that petty corruption increases the likelihood that firms will join business associations. Thus, it is important to distinguish between harsh regulation and petty corruption.

My theory of the formation of business associations starts with the assumption that they are the organizational means of interest representation – a standard definition of an interest group. I examine the institutional environment that affects the operation of post-communist businesses and propose a formal explanation of organizational dynamics that models firms' decisions to join business associations as a response to challenges that the bureaucratic environment presents. The chapter's central argument is that business associations arise as a defensive measure against regulatory pressures that corrupt enforcement practices often exacerbate. I further argue that protection from a hostile business environment can be provided in the form of selective incentives and thus is not subject to the collective action problem. This theoretical chapter sets the stage for the following chapters, which use quantitative and qualitative data to test my hypotheses and further investigate the causal mechanism behind the defensive organization argument.

2.1 The Post-Communist Business Environment

There are three major theories of interest-group politics that explain the formation of business associations. According to the modernization theory (Truman 1951; Peltzman 1976; Olson 1982; Becker 1983; Murrell 1984; Mueller and Murrell 1986), business associations form in response to changes in the socioeconomic environment. The social-choice tradition addresses group formation as a solution to the collective action problem (Olson 1965; Axelrod 1981; Levi 1990; Taylor 1990; Knight 1992). Within this framework, the characteristics of latent groups are the primary factors. According to the third theory, the industrial structure and the nature of production and exchange influence the organization of economic interest groups (Bates 1981; Frieden 1992; Hiscox 2001).

These theories of interest-group politics point to political and socioeconomic factors affecting the formation of organized interests. In addition to institutions shaping the political environment, state bureaucratic structures shape the regulatory environment in which firms operate. During profound socioeconomic transformation the state has a deep effect not only on the state-owned, but also private firms. The actions of state bureaucrats and the quality of state governance influence firms' economic viability, business strategies, costs, and opportunities. In many ways state bureaucratic agencies structure emerging markets by enforcing rules and regulations with varying degrees of consistency and precision.

Regulations were an integral part of the state (or bureaucratic) management of centrally planned economies. They were designed not to correct market inefficiencies but to replace the markets. When central planning collapsed and post-communist countries abandoned direct mechanisms of resource allocation, regulations regarding product standardization, labor management, use of machinery and equipment, and many other aspects of production and commerce were slow to change (European Bank for Reconstruction and Development 1999; Hellman et al. 2000; Kaufmann, Kraay, and Zoido-Lobaton 1999). Developed for the management of a centrally planned economy and with central planners' goals in mind, these regulations continued to impact the ways products were designed, produced, transported, and sold in post-communist transitional economies. As new market opportunities emerged after the dissolution of direct state controls, business managers started searching for ways to circumvent outdated regulations. Their attempts to reduce business costs associated with bureaucracy paved the way for bureaucratic corruption, which by the mid-1990s became the notorious companion of economic transition.

Corruption
Many of those who have lived, traveled, or done business in post-communist Eastern Europe have had at least one unpleasant encounter with a bureaucrat such as a customs official, police officer, fire inspector, or residency-registration officer. Confronted by officials enforcing a multitude of conflicting rules and regulations, most people feel lost; it appears that the rules are made to confuse the people who are supposed to follow them. At the same time, if you can show your gratitude, public servants – otherwise not very friendly – might go an extra mile to help you. Although navigating across the field of bureaucratic obstructions is difficult, offering bribes and giving into other forms of corruption frequently appears to be the path of least resistance when dealing with public servants. In this respect bureaucratic corruption – a distasteful practice nobody would want to defend – often provides the easiest way to do business. Businesspeople who need to obtain a registration, a license, or permission from state regulatory agencies often find that the path of least resistance is typically the only way to ensure the company functions

Collective Action in Adverse Business Environments 17

smoothly.[1] Because businesspeople generally can pay higher bribes than private citizens can, the former are often targeted by corrupt bureaucrats.

Much of the research on the post-communist transition focuses on corruption (Boycko, Shleifer, and Vishny 1995; Gaddy and Ickes 1999; Hellman, Jones, and Kaufmann 2000; Miller, Grodeland, and Koshechkina 2002). Corruption is generally considered a great impediment to the effective functioning of emerging markets and to businesses in transitional countries. In keeping with conventional usage, I intend *corruption* to mean abuse of public office for personal or group benefit that falls outside legal entitlements. The literature has identified two basic types of corruption: administrative (petty) corruption (also called bureaucratic corruption) and political corruption, or "state capture."[2] The former involves businesses, households, and low-level bureaucrats in their day-to-day economic and administrative functions. The latter involves industrial tycoons, financial magnates, and high-ranking public officials and impacts the allocation of public funds, large contracts, and property transfers. In state capture, businesses illegitimately influence the government's economic policies (Hellman, Jones, and Kaufmann 2000).

To better understand these two types of corruption, consider a stylized contrast between an imaginary baker and a banker (Webster 2002). As the owner of a small business, the baker interacts with the state primarily through routine encounters with local tax inspectors, police officers, registration officers, and fire and health department officials. The baker must obtain the incorporation documents, undergo inspections, file tax reports, apply for required licenses and permits, and so on. A baker who illegally pays inspectors or bureaucrats to expedite these administrative procedures and thus smooth out business operations is involved in administrative corruption. The baker's corruption most likely involves payments that allow business to keep running (Webster 2002, 11). These side payments to state inspectors and bureaucrats do not

---

[1] The number and power of regulatory agencies vary by country. Available data for post-communist states indicates great diversity. In 1998 Frye reported that, on average, Russian retailers were being inspected nineteen times a year by a total of four agencies, whereas Polish retailers were inspected nine times a year by an average of 2.6 agencies. According to a survey of Moldovan businesspeople, companies were inspected on average thirty-eight times a year (Transparency International 2002). According to the president of Almaty Entrepreneurs' Association (Yambaev 2005), thirty of Kazakhstan's state regulatory agencies seriously impeded small-business development. For worldwide comparative measures of bureaucratic regulations see Brunetti, Kisunko, and Wede (1997) and World Bank (2004–2010).

[2] Corruption has also been characterized as "ex ante" versus "ex post" (Guriev 2003) and as "corruption without theft" versus "corruption with theft" (Shleifer and Vishny 1993). In ex ante corruption the bribe recipient expedites the compliance procedure for both the compliant and noncompliant patrons. In ex post corruption the bribed bureaucrat colludes with the noncompliant briber, providing benefits to which the beneficiary is not legally entitled. Corruption without theft refers to the cases in which a business does not receive any additional transfers from the government. In corruption with theft a government official redistributes public resources in favor of the briber, thereby reducing social welfare.

purchase any advantages; the baker does not receive any services from the state bureaucrats in addition to the ones they are expected to provide by law. The baker's cost of doing business is reduced to an extent, but at the price of increased dependency in the future on those corrupt bureaucrats.

Now consider the head of a large bank. Such a person is likely to interact with local and national politicians and their staff members through formal channels (e.g., working groups, political functions, conferences, and round-tables) and informal channels (e.g., elite networks, business dinners, and social events). Corruption involving the banker is likely to be the high-level, political corruption often referred to as "state capture" (Hellman, Jones, and Kaufmann 2000) and characterized by close relationships between politicians and large businesses, who, through their influence over regulatory policy, secure continuing benefits at the expense of other (sometimes more efficient) economic actors. This produces socially undesirable outcomes. Payments by large businesses to politicians and high-ranking bureaucrats may purchase preferential treatment with respect to import-export operations, public procurement, and selective protectionism as well as other economic advantages over competitors (Webster 2002). Political corruption includes illegitimate privatization deals, private enrichment through government concessions, unfair awarding of lucrative contracts, and renationalization of private industries.[3] Economic benefits for the involved companies are usually immediate and substantial, whereas costs are often long term and dispensed across society at large.

Murky privatization deals, private enrichment through government concessions, and the scandalous renationalization of private industries might seem ubiquitous in large part because the press and public attention tend to follow big-ticket corruption. Although such corruption has long-term (and sometimes immediate) effects on a large number of businesses and households, the average businessperson is unlikely to experience it directly. This is in sharp contrast to the low-level administrative corruption economic agents feel in their daily activities. Even though administrative corruption is less likely to be the focus of mass media coverage, to portray petty administrative corruption as an insignificant phenomenon that has only a marginal effect on post-communist societies would be misleading. Although administrative bribes tend to be small, they occur with such frequency that they have a significant cumulative effect. Administrative corruption redistributes money from productive enterprises (that would otherwise be reinvested in the economy) to unproductive beneficiaries (bureaucrats likely to spend the money on private consumption). It also distorts state regulatory mechanisms, disrupts tax collection, undermines monitoring of public safety, impedes contract enforcement, and weakens the social safety net. Petty corruption, therefore, impinges on state capacity. Even if the central government is committed to a stable, efficient, and lawful environment,

---

[3] Sixsmith (2010) discusses at length despicable examples of these various forms of political corruption.

local corruption on the part of low-level bureaucrats entrusted with enforcing regulations can stall reform.

Russia's 1995 attempt at a tax law reform is a case in point. Open to multiple interpretations, the preexisting tax law contained loopholes for de facto tax reductions achieved in collusion with tax authorities. People justifiably complained that the tax system was overly complex and that it taxed not only profits and revenues but also transfers of goods and assets. In response, the federal government revised the law to allow small businesses to play a flat tax of 10 percent. Amid falling tax collection and a growing budget deficit, the Russian government hoped that the change would increase state revenue and stimulate domestic investment; however, local governments were entrusted with implementing the law, and considerable administrative abuse ensued. For example, St. Petersburg authorities imposed an US$8,500 fee on businesses desiring to switch to the simplified taxation (Murray 1999). For many small firms and self-employed individuals this fee often exceeded the tax break that the flat-tax law extended. It has clearly been a case of bureaucratic rule making that by attempting to preserve lucrative opportunities for bureaucratic enrichment undermined the central government's good intentions.

How does administrative corruption affect the formation of business associations? Researchers have argued that petty corruption debilitates businesses in transitional countries (Frye 1998; Murray 1999; Transparency International 2002; Webster 2002). Corruption increases uncertainty, undermines the institutional development, and decreases the provision of public goods that are important components of the business environment.[4] Businesses are affected by the regulatory and institutional environment in which they operate; therefore, administrative corruption should affect levels of business association membership.

The standard expectation developed in the literature is that businesses should be *less* likely to form legitimate associations in highly corrupt systems. In Leff's (1964) and Huntington's (1968) view, corruption reduces the need for collective action and formal associations because it allows individual firms to solve their problems by bribing public officials.[5] This notion that corruption reduces administrative rigidity is rooted in Coase's (1960) theory that, under costless transactions, any market-driven reallocation of resources leads to a more efficient social outcome. If the initial allocation of property rights and regulatory costs discriminates against the most efficient producers, under the

---

[4] Corruption may undermine the ability of state institutions to generate revenue and enforce regulatory frameworks (e.g., product safety, environmental regulations, and the labor code) and, hence, inhibit public-goods provision. Shleifer and Vishny (1993) contrast bribes paid in addition to official fees, taxes, and dues with those made instead of the official transfers. The former case represents corruption "without theft," which is not as detrimental to the provision of public goods as situations in which the bureaucrats pocket the entire amount of bribe and do not collect the official fees or enforce regulatory compliance.

[5] For similar treatment of corruption see Harstad and Svensson (2005).

20   *Building Business*

Coase theorem competitive bribery should allow those able to pay the highest bribes to gain access to otherwise unattainable markets and resources. As a means of allocating resources, corruption can promote productive activity, leading to Pareto-efficient outcomes in which bureaucrats receive bribes while entrepreneurs acquire opportunities to pursue profitable activities that state regulations prohibit. Because state interventions are largely less efficient than markets, the reasoning goes, society gains when corruption reduces the administrative barriers limiting economic activities. Corruption substitutes for other solutions (such as lobbying or self-regulation) to problems that require firms to organize.[6] According to this view, high levels of corruption in post-communist settings render the formation of business associations superfluous. If this is true, one should observe low levels of participation in business associations when corruption is widespread.

McChesney (1997) likewise reasons that corruption and stringent regulation should reduce membership in business associations. He sees corruption as a form of extortion by bureaucrats. In his view politicians and bureaucrats propose new regulations as a means of extorting payment from businesses that seek to prevent those regulations. According to McChesney, businesses become an easier target for extortion when they organize because business associations facilitate exchange of information about proposed regulations and promote lobbying. Therefore, where bureaucrats and politicians are corrupt, there is a disincentive to organize. If this logic is correct, corruption should negatively affect the formation of business associations.

In sum, researchers have proposed various theories regarding the possible effects of the state regulatory environment. Such an environment is of major importance to transitional firms because it affects their operating costs and how they do business. State bureaucratic institutions responsible for enforcing the regulations that directly affect economic activities are particularly relevant to post-communist countries. Characterized by unpredictability and, in many post-communist countries, corruption, these institutions warrant special attention because of their impact on business interests.

2.2 Defensive Organization

Regulatory rules affect production processes, relations with customers and suppliers, capital and labor-hiring decisions, and other important economic choices of post-communist enterprises. These and many other rules and regulations comprise the regulatory environment in which firms operate. Interest-group theories (Stigler 1971; Peltzman 1976, 1998; Keeler 1984; Weingast 1981; Noll and Owen 1983) that link regulations to activities of special interest

---

[6] Operating under the assumption that corruption is an alternative to lobbying, Campos and Giovannoni (2005), however, find that lobbying is more effective than bribery for individual firms in transitional countries.

Collective Action in Adverse Business Environments 21

groups (producers) predict that higher levels of collective action among producers coincides with more extensive regulatory activity by the government. This book's arguments and evidence support the opposite view. I take an approach that distinguishes official costs of economic regulations from those imposed through corrupt enforcement of the official regulatory norms. Although we often link corruption and extensive state regulatory involvement, treating regulations and corruption as two sides of the same coin obscures the analytical distinction between economic policy and its implementation and runs contrary to empirical evidence.[7] Taking into account the tremendous cost of corruption that may or may not accompany economic regulations, I argue that invasive regulatory systems discourage the formation of business associations by complicating their task of providing regulatory relief. At the same time, the business costs of bureaucratic red tape and corruption that arise in the context of implementing and enforcing state regulations encourage collective action.

Assertions that corruption discourages collective action have focused on either the opportunities that corruption offers businesses (e.g., reduction of red tape and avoidance of bureaucratic restrictions on business) (Leff 1964; Huntington 1968) or corrupt bureaucrats' victimization of businesses (McChesney 1997). The first type of assertion underemphasizes corruption's cost to businesses; the second overemphasizes bureaucratic extortion, depicting businesses as passive victims of predatory state behavior. I contend that both of these frameworks are one-sided and that a more balanced approach is needed.

As regulations and bureaucratic inefficiency increase, so does the pressure on individual businesses to bribe bureaucrats (Huntington 1968). As corruption spreads and the size of bribes increases, costs to businesses mount. At the same time, even in a predatory environment in which bureaucrats manipulate regulatory procedures to extort from firms, corrupt engagement provides some benefits to businesses. By paying bribes, firms avoid costlier regulatory compliance and gain an advantage over competitors who do not pay bribes. Therefore, the notion of corruption as an absolute loss for the business is also suspect.

My argument relies on two assumptions. First, businesses incur costs associated with regulatory compliance. Second, bureaucrats overlook noncompliance in exchange for bribes.[8] A regulatory environment is composed of regulations and enforcement mechanisms. The latter usually involve state agencies, courts,

---

[7] A comparison of the Transparency International Corruption Perception Index and the World Bank Doing Business data (World Bank 2006) shows that heavy regulatory burden does not necessarily coincide with corruption. The transitional economies of Poland and Slovenia, for instance, have "cleaner" bureaucracies compared to those of the Kyrgyz Republic and Georgia but almost three times the number of official regulatory procedures.

[8] The way it is formulated here, the argument captures the "corruption with theft" situation (Shleifer and Vishny 1993). Corruption in this formulation allows the bureaucrat to pocket the entire amount of the bribe and not collect the official fees, taxes, or other transfers to the state coffers. The proposed argument can be extended, however, to a "corruption without theft"

and the police. Regulations relevant to businesses may apply to business in general (e.g., accounting standards and labor laws) or to particular industries (e.g., licensing requirements, environmental regulations, safety regulations, and banking regulations). Compliance with regulations requires staff with special knowledge (e.g., accountants and attorneys). Also, managers must learn about the regulations and supervise their implementation, and thus the cost of managerial time should be considered. Regulations might mandate particular product specifications or production, transportation, and distribution practices that increase business costs.

In theory, equitable regulations protect property rights, make information-sharing more cost effective, make the business climate more predictable, and promote contract enforcement. Although such regulations benefit society and the overall economy, they come at a cost to firms.[9] Because regulatory compliance entails costs that are not directly linked to an immediate and noticeable increase in benefits to a firm, firms are interested in minimizing the cost of compliance.

The quality of institutions that enforce regulations affects the ways firms seek to minimize the costs of compliance. When dealing with grossly ineffective state bureaucracies and inconsistent enforcement, businesses are more likely to favor noncompliance.[10] When state bureaucracies are effective and honest, businesses are more likely to engage in organizational and technological innovations that reduce the costs of compliance.[11] In most post-communist countries, however, bureaucracies are capable of enforcing regulations but are not motivated to do so consistently and impartially. This lack of motivation often results from inadequate pay, inadequate political supervision, and the perverse incentive structure of poorly designed bureaucratic institutions. Under these conditions businesses are likely to avoid overt noncompliance but make corrupt deals with the bureaucrats entrusted with enforcing the regulations. In return for bribes or favors, corrupt bureaucrats will expedite processing of legitimate requests or ignore noncompliance.

Corrupt bureaucrats accept bribes as long as the benefits of supplementing their income outweigh the risks of job loss or prosecution. Businesses are willing to pay bribes as long as doing so costs them less than regulatory compliance. The equilibrium bribe will reflect the cost of regulatory compliance and the cost of corrupt behavior. Thus, the cost of corruption might increase or diminish as

---

situation by breaking down the cost of compliance into the official costs to be collected for the state coffers and the processing cost, which includes time, queuing, and external clerical service fees.

[9] The benefits of regulatory regimes, assuming the latter are well intentioned and not rigged in favor of particularistic interests, are classic public goods. Although beneficial to the group, their cost to individual businesses gives an incentive to free-ride.

[10] I am indebted to Marcus Kurtz for making this point with regard to some poorly governed Latin American countries.

[11] Businesses might also try to influence local and national authorities who determine regulatory practices and supervise bureaucrats; however, this approach is less rewarding when bureaucratic autonomy is high.

Collective Action in Adverse Business Environments

a result of better deterrence (anticorruption measures) or as the extent of regulatory intervention (and, thus, the cost of regulatory compliance) changes.

Confronted with an invasive regulatory environment and costly corruption, businesses generally benefit from finding legitimate ways to reduce regulatory costs. In such a situation the long-term benefits of engaging in corrupt behavior are diminishing because corruption increases businesses' vulnerability, heightens dependence on bureaucrats, and limits the availability of legal enforcement (so the bureaucrats can cheat with impunity). When corruption is costly, businesses are more likely to advance their economic interests by forming business associations, which allow firms to reduce regulatory costs and avoid predatory bureaucratic behavior. By joining business associations, individual firms might be better able to protect their economic interests without resorting to illegal and corrupt practices.

Business associations – organized groups of business owners or firms – are well equipped to act as agents, thereby reducing the cost of regulatory compliance for their members. They provide information on effective ways to deal with state regulatory systems, help develop legal protection, enable self-regulation that pre-empts bureaucratic intervention, and increase members' ability to inform politicians of bureaucratic inefficiency and abuse. By organizing into associations, firms can protect themselves from state regulatory intervention and bureaucratic predation. Associations can better navigate the complicated rules and regulations structuring the economic environment and may even play a role in creating more effective and beneficial regulatory systems. When state regulations are complicated and corrupt bureaucrats hold a monopoly over their implementation, self-regulating business associations capable of substituting for state regulatory regimes become much more attractive alternatives.

This argument suggests that business associations provide a selective benefit and thus compete with bureaucrats who might offer exemptions to noncompliant firms through corrupt transactions. The protection from a hostile regulatory environment that business associations supply for their members is better seen as a club good rather than as a purely collective good. As with other club goods, protection and self-regulation are excludable but nonrival, and their net benefit is an increasing function of associational membership. Business associations, however, do not directly reduce corruption, although their members are less likely to engage in corrupt transactions. Also, it seems reasonable to expect that corruption will become less attractive to bureaucrats when they have to compete with business associations for the provision of regulatory relief. In the following pages I formalize this argument.

2.3 A Formal Model

I have devised a formal model of businesses' decision to participate in business associations as a strategic interaction between businesses, state bureaucrats, and associations. Although this simple formal modeling exercise generally follows the intuition of the arguments presented above, the model helps highlight the counterintuitive relations between business organization, regulatory regimes, and corruption. It specifies conditions under which the formation of business associations is the optimal strategy for businesses.

Assumptions

As previously mentioned, I start with two plausible assumptions: (1) businesses seek to reduce the costs associated with regulatory compliance, and (2) in exchange for bribes, bureaucrats will overlook noncompliance. In the model the costs associated with regulatory compliance are factored into the business's profit-maximization function. The total cost of running a business can be divided into (1) the market cost of production and (2) the costs of regulatory compliance (including taxes, registration fees, licensing fees, inspection fees, and related managerial time). Firms maximize their profits by increasing revenues and reducing costs. If a firm cannot significantly reduce market-related costs and achieve sufficient revenue through market strategies and technological innovations – as might be the case for a firm in competitive market settings – reducing regulatory costs becomes the more feasible way to increase profits. As Huntington (1968) notes, corruption offers one way to reduce regulatory costs. "Speed fees" reduce processing and managerial time spent dealing with the state bureaucracy. "Blinders fees" that cause the recipient to ignore noncompliance allow businesses to skirt costly environmental and labor regulations, use unapproved equipment and production processes, and hide taxable transactions. As long as bribing is cheaper than compliance, a profit-maximizing firm will choose bribing. In other words, it will pay bribes up to the amount equal to the cost of regulatory compliance, subject to the total profit constraint.

Actors and Strategies

The model has three players: a firm (F), a bureaucrat (B), and an organization (O). All are assumed to be rational utility maximizers. The firm maximizes income (profit) or the difference between revenues and costs: $I_F = r - c$ where I_F is income, r is total revenue, and c is total cost. Businesses operate under the total budget constraint set by $0 \leq I_F = r - c$. The cost (c) is disaggregated into production cost (c_p) and regulatory cost (c_r). The bureaucrat maximizes his/her personal income rather than pursues public interest. The bureaucrat's income is derived from his/her salary and any bribe (b) he/she might receive as a "side payment" from the firm. Provision of such "additional" bureaucratic services does not entail any direct monetary costs.

The organization provides excludable particularistic goods, or selective incentives, to attract dues-paying members. Let g denote the value the firm

Collective Action in Adverse Business Environments

receives from the regulatory relief such selective incentives create. This can come from legal and professional help in complying with rules and regulations or informational assistance in dealing with regulatory frameworks.[12] Such a particularistic good is nonrival but perfectly excludable, and there is an economy of scale in providing g.[13] In order to provide member benefits, the association charges the firm membership dues. Let d denote dues charged for providing member-specific regulatory relief. Because of its specialization and the economy of scale, the association can provide g at the cost of αg, where $0 < \alpha < 1$. The association's utility from providing regulatory relief consists of the difference between dues (d) and the costs for providing particularistic goods (αg).

Although under this specification the organization is maximizing its profit, this formulation is also compatible with the members' surplus maximization objective.[14] Note that the model does not specify how the organizational profits are used. One might think of organizational profits as a common pool of resources that can be directed to meeting members' demands or be returned to the members in the form of collective or perfectly divisible goods (increasing members' surplus). Moreover, setting the organizational objective function to maximizing member surplus under minimum budget constraint does not change model predictions.

The firm chooses among three options for satisfying regulatory requirements: *comply* with existing regulations at a cost of c_r, *bribe* the bureaucrat, or *join* the organization and receive assistance in complying with existing regulations.[15] The bureaucrat chooses to be *honest* or *corrupt*; a corrupt bureaucrat must decide on the amount of a bribe (b) to charge the firm in exchange for overlooking regulatory violations. The organization decides on the level of dues (d) and on the amount of a particularistic good (g) that will be provided to the firm, subject to F paying d. If the firm engages in corrupt behavior, it

---

[12] Appendix E extends this framework by specifically modeling the value of nonregulatory relief services as part of firms' utility function. This does not alter the model's predictions.

[13] At this point the model includes one firm. Later in this chapter I discuss a multifirm extension.

[14] Gehlbach (2008) models organized-sector lobbies as maximizers of their members' joint welfare. However, in his analysis the state rather than business associations provides the collective benefits to the organized industry. According to Gehlbach, organized lobbies channel member contributions to politicians. In contrast, in my model of organizational dynamics, business associations use membership dues to create excludable benefits.

[15] Actually, a fourth strategy exists. If the cost of regulatory compliance exceeds a firm's revenue minus the cost of production and other strategies are unavailable, the firm might choose to operate illegally. If so, the firm risks prosecution; therefore, private protection mechanisms, including mafia-type organizations, must ensure that it can continue to operate. The firm's activities per se might be legal – that is, its products and services might be legal. However, the firm fails to comply fully with state requirements, such as paying taxes, obtaining required permits and licenses, and submitting its practices and products to state control and protection. This fourth strategy is beyond the scope of my investigation.

risks being prosecuted with probability (p) and paying a fine (f).[16] Under three strategies available to the firm, it maximizes income (I_F) as defined below.

$$I_F(comply) = r - c_p - c_r$$
$$I_F(bribe) = r - c_p - b - pf$$
$$I_F(join) = r - c_p - c_r - d + g$$

The bureaucrat maximizes income (I_B), where s is salary:

$$I_B(honest) = s$$
$$I_B(corrupt) = s + b$$

I further assume that the organization's payoff is an increasing function of membership and is greater when F joins than when F does not join. In offering the dues/benefits schedule, the organization, therefore, maximizes $d - \alpha g$. The organization's income, associated with F joining, is given by:

$$I_O(F) = d - \alpha g$$

When the firm does not join, the organization's utility is zero. All variables are assumed to be nonnegative, whereas p and α range from 0 to 1.

The bureaucrat and the organization make simultaneous proposals to the firm. The bureaucrat proposes a bribe (b), and the organization proposes dues (d) and a selective good (g). The firm then chooses *comply*, *bribe*, or *join*. The firm chooses *join* over *comply* if and only if $I_F(join) > I_F(comply)$ or, equivalently, $g > d$. Similarly, the firm chooses *join* over *bribe* if and only if $I_F(join) > I_F(bribe)$ or $g - d - c_r > b - pf$. Hence, in order to entice the firm into the organization, the organization must offer a combination of $g - d$ such that

$$g - d > c_r - b - pf. \tag{1}$$

The bureaucrat is corrupt whenever $I_B(corrupt) > I_B(honest)$, or

$$b > 0. \tag{2}$$

To entice the firm into corrupt behavior, the bureaucrat must offer a bribe such that $I_F(bribe) > I_F(join)$, or

$$b < c_r + d - g - pf.[17] \tag{3}$$

Notice from (3) that for any $c_r \leq pf$, the organization sets $g = d = c_r$, such that the firm is indifferent between joining and compliance, and the necessary and sufficient condition for the firm to bribe rather than join is $b < 0$. The bureaucrat, however, will be honest rather than offer a negative bribe and does not compete with the association for the provision of regulatory relief. The firm

---

[16] In this formulation the bureaucrat incurs no costs associated with bribery. Appendix E relaxes this assumption and models a symmetric corruption deterrence against both involved parties.

[17] The bribe should simultaneously satisfy $I_F(bribe) > I_F(comply)$, so that $b < c_r + pf$.

Collective Action in Adverse Business Environments

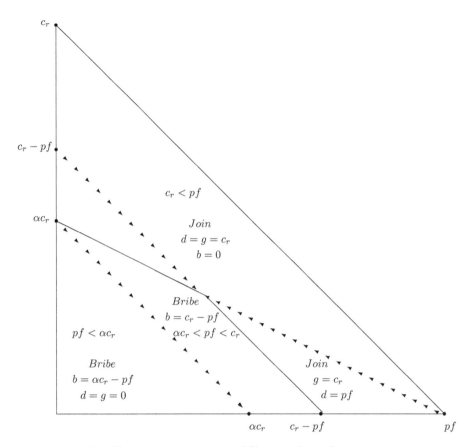

FIGURE 2.1. Equilibrium outcomes under different values of exogenous parameters.

joins rather than bribes, the bureaucrat chooses to be honest, and the organization earns $d - \alpha g = (1 - \alpha)c_r$, capturing the entire surplus.

When $\alpha c_r < pf < c_r$, however, the organization has to compete with the bureaucrat for the provision of regulatory relief. For any $g - d < c_r - pf$, the bureaucrat can offer $0 < b < (c_r - pf) - (g - d)$ that the firm accepts. The competition for membership drives down organizational rent. To beat the bureaucrat's offer, the organization sets $g = c_r$, $d = pf$ and earns $d - \alpha g = pf - \alpha c_r$. Note, however, that the organization cannot compete with the bureaucrat for the provision of regulatory relief when pf falls below αc_r. For any $\alpha c_r > pf$, the bureaucrat provides the service by setting $b = \alpha c_r - pf$.

Figure 2.1 summarizes the strategic space of the game under different values of pf and c_r. It can be seen from this graph that, all other things held constant, at higher levels of anticorruption (pf) organizations are easier to form because they can effectively compete with the bureaucrats for the provision of regulatory relief. When the cost of engaging in corruption exceeds the cost of regulatory compliance, the bureaucrat cannot entice firms into bribery. When anticorruption deterrence falls below the cost of compliance ($\alpha c_r < pf < c_r$), the association's payoff, all other things held constant, increases with pf: $\partial I_o / \partial(pf) > 0$. When pf falls below the organizational capacity to provide regulatory relief, firms will not join business associations but instead will obtain regulatory relief through corruption.

At the same time, the organization is more likely to gain membership when the cost of compliance (c_r) decreases. When compliance costs are low ($c_r \leq pf$), the association can attract members as a monopoly provider of regulatory relief. When the costs of compliance rise above the anticorruption deterrence, the organization has to compete with the bureaucrat for the provision of regulatory relief. For all $\alpha c_r < pf < c_r$, $\partial I_o / \partial c_r < 0$, meaning that higher regulatory costs, with all other parameters held constant, diminish organizational utility.

In addition, assuming that organizations are more likely to form when start-up costs are lower, organizational strategy should prevail at higher levels of bribery. Remember that F joins rather than bribes when condition (1) is satisfied. Because both sides of inequality (1) are positive, when b increases, the corresponding member benefits that secure participation ($g - d$) decrease. This means that, other things held constant, when bribery (b) is high, the organization does not have to offer high net benefits to its members to stay competitive. In the model, however, the competing bureaucrat and the organization set b, d, and g, and the firm's decisions to bribe, comply, or lobby are jointly determined, hence not independent from each other. It is easy to imagine, however, that when the new organization enters the competition, a period of coordination will follow. The bureaucrats will require time to realize lost utility and adjust bribery accordingly. If the bureaucrat fails to lower the bribe, the organization can derive higher rents from the difference in prices for its member services and the substitute (corruption). When bribery and organizational membership are substitutes, the firms that face a higher bribe schedule will likely pursue organizational strategies for obtaining regulatory relief.[18]

Implications

The following empirical predictions follow from the formal model. First, ceteris paribus, effective anticorruption measures should increase the attractiveness of business associations. Second, business associations should be less prevalent in systems with extensive regulation. A business association has an incentive to maximize the difference between total member contributions and the level of member benefits that guarantees participation. Therefore, establishing a business association is easier when the association can either charge firms higher

---

[18] Likewise, if an organization maximizes members' aggregate welfare, firms' net benefits of membership (and, thus, the probability that firms will become and remain members) increase as b increases.

dues or provide fewer benefits. Firms, however, will be reluctant to join such an association if alternative strategies (compliance or corruption) offer greater net benefits. When fines for corruption are large and the likelihood of prosecution is high, associations can persuade firms to join even when they offer lower particularistic goods or require higher dues. Still, when regulatory compliance is costly, business associations have to offer benefits that exceed in value the cost of compliance.

In sum, the model predicts that, ceteris paribus, business associations will form more easily and attract members in systems marked by effective anticorruption measures and liberal regulations. The first implication supports conventional wisdom. It is not surprising that firms are less likely to engage in corruption if doing so entails greater costs and risks. The second implication is somewhat counterintuitive. It is surprising that lower regulatory costs encourage the formation of business associations; one might suppose that *higher* regulatory costs would prompt associations to form in order to reduce regulatory pressures. According to the logic of defensive organization, however, when regulatory costs are high, business associations must work harder to provide cost-effective regulatory relief to attract members. Stringent regulatory regimes, therefore, make forming an association more difficult. Two forces are at play here. Although costly regulations may provide greater impetus for the firms to join, they simultaneously make it harder for business associations to provide regulatory relief. When regulatory pressures are high, existing associations must provide firms with greater benefits to attract their membership, and this condition makes forming business associations more difficult.

Although not directly derived from the comparative-statics results, three other implications follow. One of these extensions generates expectations in the sphere of organizational dynamics, and the other two in respect to bureaucratic probity. These extensions do not require additional assumptions and follow the basic intuition of the model. They also provide additional dimensions for thinking about business-state relations and the role that associations play in modifying them.

  a. *The Cost of Bribery.* According to prevailing opinion, there should be a negative relationship between corruption and legitimate collective action in business associations. If business associations provide an alternative to corrupt bureaucracy, corruption and collective action should be inversely related. The amount of rents the bureaucrats generate through misapplication of regulatory norms, however, may be indicative of the organizational opportunities to provide regulatory relief. Firms seeking to maximize profit will be willing to pay business associations as much as they otherwise would pay in bribes to avoid regulatory compliance.[19]

---

[19] In the absence of an associational alternative, the bribes bureaucrats charge will be $b < c_r + pf$. Thus, there is a relationship between the cost of regulatory compliance and bribes. However, the relationship changes once the associational strategy is available.

Thus, all other things held constant, as the costs of bribery increase, business associations should find it easier to attract members. This prediction contradicts the conventional arguments about the negative relation between corruption and legitimate collective action, but it is consistent with the notion that business associations provide protection against a corrupt bureaucratic environment.

b. *The Snowball Effect.* The model assumes the pre-existence of a business association that a firm can join. However, most post-communist systems lack pre-existing associations, so firms often must start associations from the ground up. Therefore, the first firm (F_1) that chooses participation actually establishes an association.[20] Initially (time t) this firm is the only contributor of dues $(d_{1t} = D)$ and the only recipient of benefits $(g_{1t} = G)$ that the association provides. Assuming that associational benefits are nonrival goods, when the second firm (F_2) joins an association at time $t + 1$ to receive the same level of benefits $(g_{1_{t+1}} = g_{2_{t+1}} = G)$, F_1 can contribute $d_{1_{t+1}} = D - d_{2_{t+1}}$ such that for constant benefits (g), $d_{1_{t+1}} \leq d_{1_t}$. This proposition captures the intuition that the start-up costs exceed the costs of subsequent membership.

Naturally, when a business association provides nonrival benefits, the associational strategy is more rewarding at higher levels of participation. Over time, associations mature and attract more members. One would expect the difference between benefits and costs of participation $(g - d)$ to increase over time. Equation (3), which solves the model in terms of participation, indicates that as d decreases or g increases with the addition of new members, $(g - d)$ goes up. The greater the difference $(g - d)$, the larger the corresponding term $(c_r - pf)$ can be in which firms still have an incentive to join. As $(g - d)$ goes up c_r, increases and p and f decrease, meaning that at higher participation levels, firms start joining associations under the otherwise restrictive conditions of extensive regulatory regimes and ineffective law enforcement. Thus, once multiple firms with relatively high regulatory and corruption costs choose the organizational strategy, other firms that had been benefiting from corruption are likely to follow suit. Assuming that associational benefits are an economy of scale and at least partly nonrival, increasing organizational membership makes participation more rewarding.

c. *Decreasing Corruption.* If by joining associations, businesses end their corrupt transactions with the bureaucrats, in the long run the development of business associations should lower the demand for corruption.

---

[20] Instead of a single firm, as discussed so far, suppose that the association vies for the membership of n firms. For a member firm i, the selective benefit $g_{(i)}$ is a function of the overall club good (G) that an association provides, $g_i = f(G)$, such that $g_i > \dfrac{G}{n}$, where n is membership. The association's utility from providing regulatory relief consists of the difference between dues $(D = \Sigma_{i=1}^{n} d_i)$ charged and the costs for providing particularistic goods $\alpha G(g_1, g_2, \ldots, g_n)$ to its n members.

Collective Action in Adverse Business Environments 31

To persuade firms to pay them bribes, bureaucrats must accept smaller bribe payments. If, as modeled in Appendix E, the bureaucrat faces any disutility from engaging in corruption, it will set the positive threshold for corruption. As demand for corruption decreases, a bureaucrat whose bribe level drops below his or her reservation value (0 in the current model and pf in Appendix E) chooses honesty over corruption. This leads to a decline in the overall levels of corruption and an improvement in bureaucratic quality. As more firms join associations – and this should happen because of the snowball effect described above – the supply of corruption and, hence, its occurrence, should decrease.

2.4 Official and "Unofficial" Regulatory Costs

So far I have treated regulatory costs in a way that implies the continuum from invasive to liberal regulation. In practice, however, the issue of regulatory costs is not as simplistic as having more or fewer rules or higher versus lower fees and taxes. Although the politicians draw the official regulatory policies, oftentimes bureaucratic agencies are responsible for designing an enforcement mechanism. They pass bylaws that specify details of regulatory activities and design specific procedures for monitoring compliance. Although such additional administrative costs are often necessary to ensure enforcement, from the standpoint of economic agents, these add up to an overall increase in the cost of regulatory compliance. A business paying 5 percent of its profit for an operating license and 1 percent of its profit in processing fees faces exactly the same regulatory cost as a business paying a 1-percent operating fee and a 5-percent processing fee. Business associations, however, might find that reducing one type of cost compared to the other is easier.[21]

According to the formal model presented earlier, the cost of regulatory compliance is given exogenously by state regulators; however, the regulatory environment is shaped not only by the state regulatory policy or the official regulatory regimes but also by street-level bureaucrats' discretionary application of rules and regulations (Huber and Shipan 2002; Frye 2004; Gordon and Hafer 2005; Bertelli and Whitford 2009). The 1995 Russian tax reform discussed earlier in this chapter illustrates this point. Although the official costs of compliance (tax rates) were lowered for small businesses, the bureaucrats enforcing the tax code imposed additional hurdles, which for many made the actual cost of compliance increase. In this section I consider regulatory costs imposed by the bureaucrats entrusted with the application of economic regulation; these costs stem from the bureaucrats' ability to freely interpret, inconsistently apply, and significantly alter official business regulations.

---

[21] As these costs benefit different distributional coalitions, reducing processing costs might be more feasible politically. At the same time, business associations might offer an organizational alternative to the state-provided regulatory enforcement and, hence, cut the "unofficial" regulatory costs.

When bureaucratic agencies are closely monitored and made accountable to their political masters and the public, their rule-enforcing authority is restricted to the consistent and predictable application of existing regulations. Political controls and accountability pressures are likely to work against the bureaucrats who alter regulatory procedure in a way that imposes additional regulatory costs. Such a constrained bureaucracy is not immune to corruption insofar as the bureaucrats may withdraw the enforcement of regulatory standards in exchange for bribes and favors. However, as modeled earlier, under a constrained bureaucracy the maximum bribe a corrupt bureaucrat can extract from a noncompliant firm cannot exceed the official cost of regulations less the probabilistic penalty. Political and legal limitations on the bureaucrats' ability to impose costly red tape make it impossible for the bureaucrat to manipulate the official regulatory environment to extort larger bribes. Bureaucratic power to interpret regulations and create bylaws, however, allows bureaucrats to increase the cost of doing business and, thus, extract more bribes from noncompliant firms (McChesney 1997; Shleifer and Vishny 1993).

When the bureaucrats are forced to applying rules and regulations in a consistent and predictable manner, official regulatory norms define the costs of doing business. The regulatory compliance game modeled earlier in this chapter applies to this situation. Conversely, when civil servants freely interpret regulatory norms and apply them in an unpredictable fashion, the actual cost of regulatory compliance to the firms reflects the official regulatory burden as well as "unofficial" costs associated with red tape, unpredictability, and inconsistency of enforcement. When bureaucrats create additional red tape, they alter firms' regulatory environments, leading to higher prices for bribery and compliance. By increasing the cost of regulatory compliance through generation of red tape, bureaucrats push up the upper limit of the bribe they can charge for overlooking regulatory noncompliance. When bribery is not effectively deterred and bureaucrats are free to interpret regulatory norms, they can increase the potential payoffs of corruption by the predatory practice of escalating the costs of regulatory burden. How do such "unofficial" regulatory compliance costs affect businesses' collective action?

Consider the following extension of the regulatory compliance game examined earlier. Suppose that through her power to interpret the content of regulatory norms, the bureaucrat augments the official costs of regulatory compliance (c_r) by creating red tape (τ) at zero cost to herself. The resulting cost of regulatory compliance amounts to:

$$c_r + \tau = c_r', c_r' \leq c_r \tag{4}$$

Now the bureaucrat chooses τ and. The firm and the organization observe c_r but not c_r'. They may invest ω to reveal the true c_r. Suppose also that by revealing the true c_r, the organization cuts the red tape, thereby reducing the firm's regulatory burden from c_r' to c_r. The bureaucrat's utility function is the same

Collective Action in Adverse Business Environments　　33

as in the previous model. The firm, however, now pays the augmented cost of compliance c_r' if $\omega = 0$ and receives the benefit $q = \tau$ when $\omega \neq 0$.

The bribe now should satisfy $b < c_r' + d - g - q - pf$, and in order to entice participation, the organization has to offer $g + q - d > (c_r + \tau) - b - pf)$. The bribery is not deterred by $c_r \leq pf$ because now the bureaucrat can set τ such that $c_r' \geq pf$. For the bureaucrat to stay honest, legal sanctions have to deter not only bribery but also the creation of red tape. This is achieved at $r - c_p \leq pf$ because any escalation of c_r' above $r - c_p$ drives the firm out of business. At such strict anticorruption measures, corruption is deterred and the bureaucrat is no longer interested in creating the red tape ($\tau = 0$). The association provides the regulatory relief by setting $g = d = c_r$, $\omega = 0$, and $q = 0$, and it captures $d - \alpha g = (1 - \alpha)c_r$; under those circumstances the firm joins.

When pf falls between $r - c_p$ and $\omega + ac_r$, the organization competes with the bureaucrat for the provision of regulatory relief. It spends ω to cut the red tape and provide benefits $q = \tau$, sets $g = c_r$, $d = pf$ and earns $pf - \omega - ac_r$. When pf falls below $\omega + ac_r$, the organization provides zero benefits, the bureaucrat sets $\tau = r - c_p$, and the firm pays $b' = r + c_p - pf$.

Two results follow. First, the model incorporating the bureaucracy-imposed regulatory costs shares one comparative-static result with the constrained-bureaucracy model: $\partial I_o / \partial (pt) > 0$. Ceteris paribus, collective action is easier to achieve in more orderly regimes (those with a high level of law enforcement). Thus, increasing the costs of anticorruption measures helps deter bribery in low- and high-discretion regimes. Second, when the bureaucrat creates the red tape, the official regulatory regime no longer directly affects the choice of organizational strategy. The red tape that takes away any organizational advantage in this sphere counters any decrease in the official costs of doing business that might make the organizational provision of regulatory relief easier. In respect to the bureaucrat's ability to generate red tape, predictions are mixed. On the one hand, bureaucratic red tape reduces an organization's expected utility (notice that ω enters organizational payoffs with the negative sign) and decreases its survival chances. On the other hand, if the size of ω is independent from the amount of red tape, the more red tape to be cut by investing ω, the more benefits the firm can derive from associational membership.[22]

2.5 Testable Hypotheses

One can generate testable hypotheses about the static and dynamic effects of the strategic interaction between firms, business associations, and bureaucrats.

---

[22] Although the size of τ does not affect the choice between corruption and organizational membership, it does affect the latter's attractiveness vis-à-vis regulatory compliance. When complying with the red tape, the firm receives $I_F(comply) = - c_r - \tau$, whereas organizational membership under the same conditions secures $I_F(join) = - c_r - \tau - d + q + g$. Under the cooperative equilibrium solution the organization secures $q = \tau$, making participation more attractive under higher τ. In fact, $\partial I_{F(comply)}/\partial \tau < 0$, which decreases the probability of compliance.

First, the formation of business associations should be inversely related to the official cost of complying with regulations. As the cost of regulatory compliance increases, associations should lower their dues and/or provide more benefits to attract members; otherwise, associational membership would not provide adequate regulatory relief. Under extensive regulation, firms' engagement in corruption is more advantageous; therefore, business associations must work harder to make participation worthwhile. An invasive regulatory system inflates an association's start-up costs and makes providing regulatory relief more difficult. We therefore arrive at the following hypotheses:

Hypothesis 1a: The greater the costs of complying with regulation, the lower the firms' propensity to join business associations.

Hypothesis 1b: Business associations operating within more-invasive regulatory systems provide greater benefits to their members.

Second, the models predict that firms are more likely to join business associations when bribery entails higher costs (f) and a higher probability (p) of prosecution:

Hypothesis 2: Effective anticorruption measures increase the likelihood that firms will participate in business associations.

Third, when bureaucrats face few restrictions on how they implement regulatory policy, unofficial hurdles are likely to become part of the regulatory environment. In the absence of bureaucratic constraint to apply regulations in fair, consistent, and predictable ways, the empirical link between the official cost of regulatory compliance and organizational participation should be obscured. This calls for a conditional hypothesis:

Hypothesis 3: When bureaucracy is constrained to apply economic regulations in a uniform and consistent manner, regulations should suppress collective action. When bureaucratic enforcement is capricious, the official regulatory burden should not affect collective action.

Hypotheses 1a through 3 are directly derived from the comparative-static results. However, as previously mentioned, three extensions logically follow from the model. As discussed above, the model implies that an association will more easily attract members if corruption (b) is costly:

Hypothesis 4: All other things held constant, the costlier the bribery, the more attractive is membership as a means of obtaining regulatory relief.

Note that in the theoretical model the cost of corruption is not independent from the costs of regulatory compliance and anticorruption efforts. This suggests that the empirical analysis should treat the cost of bribery as endogenous to other explanatory variables.

The dynamic extensions suggest that because of the economies of scale in providing regulatory relief, associations accumulate greater resources and

Collective Action in Adverse Business Environments 35

provide more benefits as their membership base increases. The following hypothesis captures this snowball effect:

Hypothesis 5: Over time, associations expand their resources and functions and offer greater benefits to members.

Lastly, the long-term implications of the declining demand for corruption are that the maturity of and increasing membership in associations should lead to the declining cost of bribery and supply of corruption.

Hypothesis 6: As organizational membership grows, corruption decreases. This effect should be observed in different countries and industries.

The above hypotheses operate at different levels of analysis and help answer two related but distinct questions: why business associations form and why firms join them. On the one hand, successful collective action is predicated on the individual incentives to participate. On the other hand, collective action cannot be reduced to the individual incentives and strategies, so the organizations should be treated as actors themselves. Hence, the theory of defensive organization takes into account individual-level incentives of economic actors as well as organizational-level opportunities of business associations. It is important, therefore, to consider testable implications that operate at these different levels. Hypotheses 1a, 2, 3, and 4 operate at the level of the firm; Hypotheses 1b and 5 operate at the level of business associations; and Hypothesis 6 at the levels of countries and industries. Testing the empirical implication of the model and its logical extensions at the multiple levels of analysis has the advantage of covering organizational formation from the standpoint of members and associations. Although the individual-level explanation is fundamental for understanding the growth of membership, the organizational-level behavior is of primary consequence and importance. Testing the theory of defensive organization with hypotheses operating at multiple levels subjects the theory to more rigorous testing and creates a more complete empirical account.

2.6 Conclusion

This chapter presented a theoretical argument about the effects of the regulatory environment on the formation of post-communist business associations. Many post-communist countries are characterized by (a) extensive regulation and (b) administrative corruption, both of which create opportunities as well as pitfalls for businesses. Although the regulatory burden does not directly result in corruption, the latter often functions as a mechanism of regulatory relief. My theory traced the roots of bureaucratic corruption to businesses' desire to reduce the costs of complying with state regulations. When states fail to provide a fair, effective, and predictable regulatory environment and instead harbor predatory bureaucrats, business associations offer members a way to bypass corruption and to reduce their regulatory costs through legitimate means.

Building a formal model of interactions among firms, bureaucrats, and business associations, I modeled participation in business associations as the firm's response to corrupt bureaucracy and intrusive regulation. By my analysis, firms organize to pool resources with the aim of obtaining regulatory relief, which the association supplies as a club good. Inadvertently, by providing member-specific regulatory relief, business associations strip bureaucratic rents and fight corruption.

Business associations can reduce the costs of regulatory compliance either by undermining the bureaucratic monopoly on regulation or by challenging regulatory practices. They might do the former through self-regulation that calls into question the necessity of state-provided regulatory-enforcement mechanisms and by cutting through the red tape. They might do the latter through litigation against state institutions, legal expertise, and other means that are usually too expensive for a single firm. By pooling their resources, member firms can better fight costly regulations by increasing public awareness, appealing to higher authorities, and taking legal action.

The model of the strategic interactions between firms, bureaucrats, and associations offers a new way of conceptualizing the effects of state regulatory systems and bureaucratic corruption on businesses' collective action. It does not, however, address political corruption, in which politicians and higher-level civil servants develop laws and regulations that favor special interests. In this analysis corruption entails bureaucrats' agreeing to ignore regulatory violations in exchange for bribes.

Building from a limited set of assumptions about firms' interests vis-à-vis state regulatory regimes, the model arrived at conclusions linking associational formation to regulatory regimes and the threat of anticorruption measures. Effective law enforcement that helps keep corruption at bay should promote participation in business associations. At the same time, other things being equal, intrusive regulatory systems should impede the formation of business associations. I modeled regulatory cost in two different ways. First, when regulatory authorities closely follow the official regulatory rules, the cost of compliance to the firms closely reflects the official regulatory policy. Second, when the bureaucrats fail to enforce regulations in a consistent and predictable manner, the cost of regulatory compliance reflects the official regulatory policy as well as unofficial hurdles that capricious regulators impose. Both kinds of costs are consequential to organizational membership, and they call for regulatory relief on the part of business associations.

Because business associations protect only their own members, the model does not imply that they immediately reduce regulatory burden and instances of bureaucratic corruption throughout an economy.[23] Instead, at least at the

---

[23] The theory of group formation constructed here cannot take for granted the ability of economic actors to overcome collective action. Therefore, groups' ability to provide a collective good is not part of the explanation of why they form.

initial stages of their formation, associations should attract firms who would otherwise pay higher bribes or, in economic terms, higher substitute prices. However, over time the growth of business associations should exhort competitive pressures on corrupt bureaucrats and reduce the price of bribery.

The success of the organizational strategy depends on the simultaneous actions of many individual firms and might become a subject of the collective action problem. Business associations bypass the collective action problem by providing concentrated private benefits to their dues-paying members; the firms participating in the organizations internalize the reduction of regulatory costs. In this formulation the development of business associations ceases to be a collective action problem in which goods are nonrival and nonexcludable. As the initial problem of organization is solved through the provision of selective benefits, opportunities for truly collective benefits and effective lobbying may arise.[24] Although small firms lack the bargaining power to change the cost of regulatory compliance or bribes, as a group they have more leverage over the official rules, regulations, and enforcement mechanisms. They may act as an interest group. Still, because of the free-rider problem, the interest groups seek to benefit their own members only and will pursue industry- or economy-wide benefits only if such efforts are costless by-products of promoting members' interests. Ironically, this inability to pursue collective interests of the reduced regulatory burden and orderly enforcement will undermine the very prospects of membership growth because lighter regulatory regimes enhance the groups' ability to provide membership-generating selective incentives. Based on the formal model, I identified six testable hypotheses that operate at different levels of analysis. The following chapters will evaluate these hypotheses in light of empirical evidence from post-communist countries.

---

[24] Once the initial task of securing stable membership is accomplished, business associations might become effective lobbyists. This role, however, is predicated on the continuing provision of club goods.

3

Post-Communist Business Representation in a Comparative Perspective

> No important institution is ever merely what the law makes it. It accumulates about itself traditions, conventions, ways of behavior, which are not less formidable in their influence.
>
> – Harold Laski

Depending on the region being considered, the term *business association* evokes varied images.[1] Casual or business encounters with industry associations range from local business directories and golden stars mounted on the Walk of Fame to wage controls and the composition of social packages resulting from tripartite negotiations.[2] Business associations in Latin America may conjure thoughts of clandestine clubs conspiring with right-wing politicians; those in continental Europe may be associated with more transparent, harmonious relations with government and unions; and those in East Asia may be considered direct extensions of ministerial bureaucracy.

Regional differences alone cannot account for the dissimilarities in our experiences with business associations. At the first mention of business associations, some people picture high-profile organizations that negotiate with foreign donors and national governments. Those interested in the development of the small-business sector picture a small chamber preoccupied with local issues. What kinds of organizations are the subjects of this book? How do Eastern European business–interest organizations compare to their counterparts in other parts of the world? And how do they differ within the region?

---

[1] Although these are often called industry associations, I employ the term business association to signify the fact that not all of these groups are organizations unifying firms in particular industries. A large number of these are organized on cross-industry, regional, or issue bases.

[2] The Hollywood Chambers of Commerce created and manages the well-known Walk of Fame along Hollywood Boulevard to commemorate outstanding contributions to the entertainment industry.

Post-Communist Business Representation

This chapter introduces essential descriptive information that highlights important characteristics of Eastern European industry associations and places them in a broader comparative perspective. First, the chapter descriptively analyzes available cross-national data demonstrating that, collectively, post-communist countries differ from other regions of the world in terms of business representation and regulatory environments. Second, it documents a high degree of cross-national variation within the post-communist group in terms of regulatory burden and organizational development of the business community. Third, it further explores cross-national and subnational variation by analyzing the diverse trajectories of business-state relations in Russia, Ukraine, Croatia, and Kazakhstan.

This chapter shows that although they are numerous, post-communist business associations enjoy less political influence and member esteem than do their counterparts in other parts of the world. Expectedly, the membership in business associations remains low by all comparative standards. Consistent with the arguments presented in the previous chapter, low membership coincides with a much more difficult regulatory climate and relatively unobstructed opportunities to engage in corruption. At the same time – and this further supports the defensive organization theory – membership density increases in response to economic reforms and improved governance.

A detailed description of the number, organizational bases, structural forms, membership, functions, and general patterns of creation of business associations in four post-communist countries reveals that despite the increasing institutional and economic diversity of the countries in which they operate, business associations are profoundly affected by the regulatory environment. The analyzed cases are characterized by a high degree of pluralism and competition among numerous business associations. Business associations are able to sustain themselves under different political regimes, but democratic politics makes their influence more visible and increases the attractiveness of membership. Despite the high visibility of large umbrella groups, typical post-communist business associations are local, regional, or sector-based rather than centralized peak organizations. The analysis shows that due to both internal and external constraints, post-communist business associations do not form strong lobbies. Whereas only a few associations provide collective benefits, the vast majority concentrate on the provision of selective incentives. Such benefits differ from the typical mixture of member benefits found in other parts of the world. Much of what post-communist business associations do is shaped by the challenges and opportunities presented by the transitional regulatory environment.

This chapter is organized in the following way. The next section offers a brief survey of the essential features of post-communist business associations, situating them in global comparative settings. Then I introduce four country cases and describe the number and types of associations and their membership, functions, and activities in Russia, Ukraine, Kazakhstan, and Croatia. Each of the country cases illustrates different features of post-communist associations.

40   *Building Business*

The Russian case explores the origins and causes of organizational pluralism, the Ukrainian and Kazakh cases contrast the influences of political environment on the development of business associations, and the Croatian case illustrates the evolution of compulsory and voluntary-membership organizations. Associations' ability to provide selective incentives emerges as the key precondition to successful collective action across all analyzed cases.

3.1 A Cross-National Comparison

How can we start assessing the size, coverage, influence, and activities of post-communist business associations? Against what benchmarks should we compare them? Associational landscape in other parts of the world is instrumental for establishing some baseline expectations. This section establishes comparative reference points that facilitate descriptive analysis of the post-communist organizational landscape and provide essential background for the empirical research that will follow.

Cross-national data on interest associations are scarce and often unreliable. Official national statistics tend to use incompatible methodologies, which invalidates direct cross-national comparisons. Further, most cross-national research either limits itself to the high-income OECD countries for which reliable data exist (e.g., Bischoff 2003) or relies on the World Guide to Trade Associations (WGTA) data (Zils 1980, 1999; Saur 2003; Coates, Heckelman, and Wilson 2007, 2010; Coates and Wilson 2007).[3] Because of its worldwide coverage, the WGTA allows us to compare post-communist business-interest groups to those found in other developed and developing countries.

When comparing across different regions of the world, post-communist countries have among the lowest number of business associations per country.[4] By 1999 Eastern European countries surpassed only Sub-Saharan Africa in terms of national averages. Although between 1973 and 2002 the total number of industry groups more than quadrupled in the region, the average number of groups in a country is thirty. The rest of the world experienced a decline in the average number of associations, yet on average it had 183 associations per country in 2002. Although the number of post-communist business associations grew, the average number of chambers of commerce declined from 20 to 14. This development appears to be part of a worldwide trend; in the rest

---

[3] The WGTA is an international reference source on trade associations and chambers of commerce around the world. Six editions of the WGTA were published between 1973 and 2002. The publication identifies business associations and chambers of commerce from a mailed questionnaire as well as national publications and electronic sources.

[4] Communist and post-communist countries in other parts of the world (Mongolia, the People's Republic of China, and the Socialist Republic of Vietnam) share many features of Eastern European business representation. Unless stated otherwise, this section includes these countries in the post-communist category. Results and conclusions are similar when the category includes only Eastern European and former USSR countries.

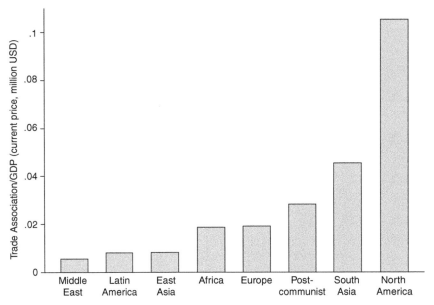

Source: The Word Guide to Trade Associations, 2002. Penn World Tables.

FIGURE 3.1. Average number of trade associations per country (normalized by GDP).

of the world the number of chambers declined from 160 to 124 per country.[5] Country averages, however, are rather misleading because they do not take into account the underlying size of the economy or the diversity of economic interests. Western Europe, for instance, has three times the number of North American business associations, but its national average is only a quarter of what is found in North America.

Figures 3.1 and 3.2 normalize the total number of associations by the size of the regional economy and the number of registered firms. When economy size is taken into account, post-communist business associations outnumber their Western European and Latin American counterparts, coming second only to North America and South Asia. After normalizing by the number of firms, post-communist associations are few but comparable to the levels found in North America and South Asia.

Aggregate differences mask variation within the post-communist group. Figure 3.3 plots associational coverage of businesses by country. It reveals, for

---

[5] A number of authors attribute this decline to the diminishing competitiveness of the neocorporatist model of business-state relations that heavily relies on the compulsory-membership chambers (Hassel 1999; Lash and Urry 1987; Beyer and Hopner 2003). Later in this chapter I discuss the development of post-communist chambers of commerce. The Croatian case demonstrates that the compulsory-membership chamber systems have not been particularly effective in representing business interests in Eastern Europe.

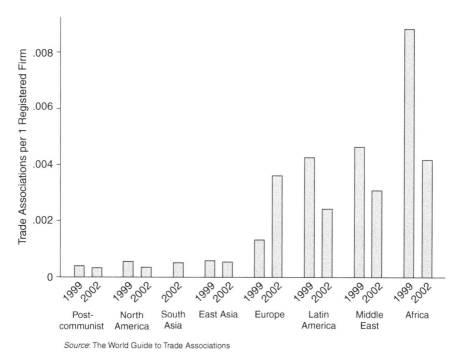

FIGURE 3.2. Number of trade associations per firm, regional averages.

instance, that in Albania there are more associations per firm than in France or Denmark, whereas Lithuania and Czech Republic outperform the Netherlands and South Africa. At the same time, eight out of ten countries with the lowest associational coverage belong to the post-communist group. Although representative of the extent of organizational diversity, these figures do not distinguish between countries that have larger encompassing associations uniting many businesses and countries with small associations representing few firms. Knowing the size of associational membership and its concentration is indispensible in making an informed comparison.

The associational-membership figures are customarily obtained firsthand from associations. These, however, are often unreliable because of the conflict of interest that associations face. Most organized groups tend to exaggerate their membership because larger membership boosts their legitimacy and attractiveness. Clearly, obtaining cross-national data is even more difficult. Luckily, the World Bank (WB) and the European Bank for Reconstruction and Development (EBRD) conducted a cross-national business survey that provides reliable microlevel data on the rate of participation in business associations.[6]

---

[6] The World Business Environment Survey (WBES) is a survey of firm owners and managers conducted in 125 countries. It was first launched in 1999 in Eastern Europe, Eurasia, and Turkey under the name of Business Environment and Enterprise Performance Survey (BEEPS). In the

Post-Communist Business Representation

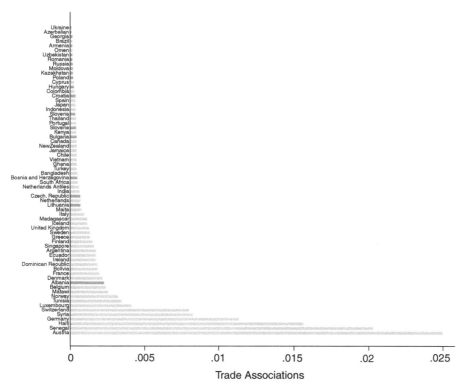

Source: World Bank and the World Guide to Trade Associations

FIGURE 3.3. Associations per registered firms by country, 2002.

The survey data covers 125 countries but falls short of providing worldwide coverage. Cross-regional comparison (Table 3.1) shows that post-communist businesses have the lowest rates of participation in business associations. On average 35 percent of post-communist businesses participate in industry associations, compared to the 66 percent rate in the rest of the world. At the same time, as further detailed in Figure 3.4, membership density has a very large variance across post-communist countries, with Azerbaijan, Belarus, and Tajikistan occupying the bottom of the distribution, and Slovenia, Albania, and Croatia by far exceeding the average.

2000s it included other developing markets as well as many advanced industrialized countries. WBES examines a wide range of interactions between firms and the state. The firms participating in the survey represent different sectors and industries and are of different sizes and ownership types. Based on face-to-face interviews with firm managers and owners, WBES was designed to generate comparative measurements in such areas as corruption, state capture, lobbying, and quality of the business environment. WBES data and questionnaires are available at Enterprise Surveys, http://www.enterprisesurveys.org/. Until 2006 the survey included a question about membership in business associations, though this query was subsequently dropped.

TABLE 3.1. *Membership in Business Associations: Regional Density*

Region	Average Membership Rate	Standard Deviation
South Asia	.776	.417
Europe	.772	.420
Middle East and North Africa	.652	.477
Africa	.648	.478
Latin America	.614	.487
East Asia and Pacific	.603	.489
Post-Communist	.402	.490

Source: Enterprise Surveys, http://www.enterprisesurveys.org, 2002–2006.

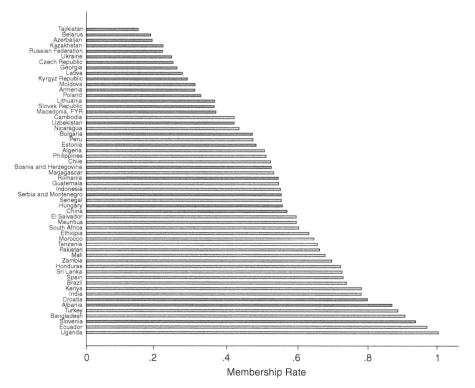

Source: BEEPS 2002–2006 (Average Levels)

FIGURE 3.4. Membership density by country.

In addition to cross-national variation, post-communist cases demonstrate variation over time. On average, between 1999 and 2005, their membership rates grew from 24 to 37 percent. Although the majority of post-communist countries experienced associational-membership growth, some witnessed

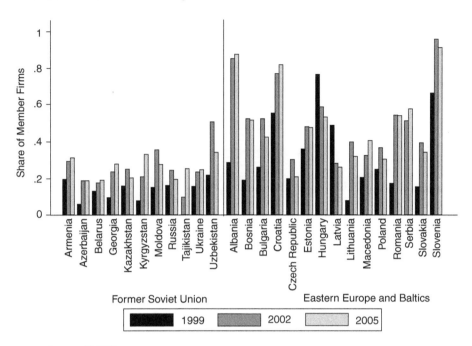

Source: BEEPS

FIGURE 3.5. Membership density in the former Soviet Union and Eastern Europe, 1999–2005.

a decline over the entire period (Hungary and Latvia) or in the mid-2000s (Kazakhstan, Russia, Bulgaria, Czech Republic, Lithuania, Poland, Slovakia, and Slovenia). Figure 3.5 shows that the former Soviet Republics (excluding three Baltic states) have much lower membership rates compared to the East-Central European countries. At the same time, no clear pattern can be observed in terms of different membership trends in consolidated democracies versus autocracies, EU member states versus nonmembers, and fast versus slow reformers. Although Eastern European countries might not be much different from many developed and developing economies in terms of the number of business associations (relative to the size of the economy and the number of businesses), they generally have lower rates of participation in business associations.

Low participation rates may not necessarily be symptomatic of organizational weakness. If business associations are exclusive clubs of powerful corporations or monopolistic cartels of well-connected firms, low participation should not reflect on their political influence and economic importance. How influential are post-communist business associations? No standard measure of influence has been devised in the comparative literature. Here I turn to survey evidence based on the WBES question that asked members and nonmembers of business associations to evaluate the degree of influence associations have

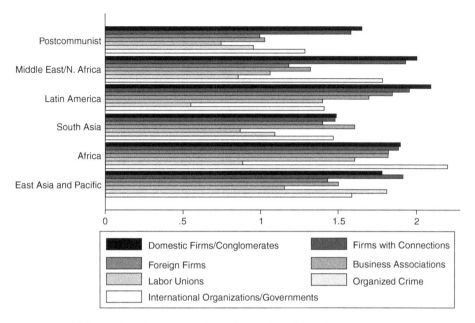

How much influence the following groups had on laws and regulations that impact your business? 0 = No Impact; 4 = Decisive Influence

FIGURE 3.6. Assessing the influence of business associations.

over their regulatory environments. The influence of other societal forces provides a reference frame. Figure 3.6 plots average responses for post-communist countries and countries in other regions. Within the post-communist group the influence of business associations surpasses that of labor unions, foreign organizations, and organized crime, but it is ranked far below the influence of well-connected firms and large conglomerates. Post-communist associations receive the lowest rating compared to business associations in other parts of the world. Low membership levels and low levels of influence are undoubtedly interconnected. It is not clear, though, whether low membership leads to low influence or whether low levels of influence diminish the attractiveness of membership. Qualitative analysis of country cases discussed later in this chapter suggests that causality runs in both directions.

Do post-communist businesses have different experiences with their associations? Does membership entail different things in different parts of the world? Several installments of WBES contained a question about the overall levels of member satisfaction with services and benefits business associations provide in six distinct service domains. These include (1) lobbying; (2) assistance in resolving disputes with government officials, unions, and other firms; (3) provision of domestic market information; (4) international market information; (5) product certification and reputational benefits; and (6) information

Post-Communist Business Representation 47

TABLE 3.2. *Member Evaluations of Associational Services by Income Group*

Countries	Average Satisfaction with Associations' Services*
All post-communist	1.28
Upper middle income (excluding post-communist)	1.35
High-income OECD	1.4
Lower middle income (excluding post-communist)	1.67
Low income	1.71

* Evaluations range from 0 – "no value" – to 4 – "critical value to the firm."

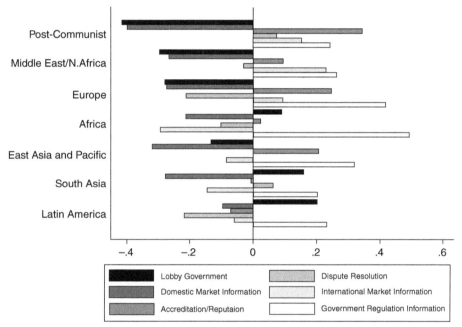

FIGURE 3.7. Member evaluations of associations' services (deviation from the mean).

on government regulations. These are ranked on a five-point scale ranging from "no value" to "critical value to the firm." When comparing across different income groups, firms in high- and upper-middle-income countries tend to value their associational membership lower than do firms in low- and lower-middle-income countries (Table 3.2). On average, compared to other regions and income groups, post-communist membership receives the lowest evaluations. Satisfaction levels, however, are not much different from the levels found in the comparable income group.

When considering different types of associational services, post-communist patterns diverge considerably from other countries. Figure 3.7 plots the average differences from the mean level of member satisfaction, with positive bars indicating above-average values for a given service and negative bars corresponding to below-average values. The first striking difference of post-communist cases is that associations appear to be quite ineffective in lobbying the government and resolving disputes. Second, the most valuable services of post-communist business associations involve providing information on domestic markets and government regulations; somewhat lower values are placed on international market information and reputational services. Although the value of domestic information that post-communist member firms receive by far exceeds the value of similar services provided by associations in other parts of the world, their ability to provide information on government regulations is more limited than in the high-income OECD countries, Africa, East Asia, and the Middle East. This, perhaps, stems from the unique challenges that the post-communist regulatory environment presents.

When judged by companies's subjective assessments, on average, post-communist business environments present as many constraints as in other countries, but the nature of these constraints is very different in the post-communist settings. Table 3.3 contrasts subjective assessments of business constraints reported by post-communist firms with the noncommunist reference group. Firms in the reference group on average report more problems with telecommunications, energy sources, high interest rates, and macroeconomic instability.[7] Conversely, post-communist firms are most pressured by high taxes, regulatory uncertainty, cumbersome tax administration, an ineffective legal system, and, perhaps as a result, anticompetitive practices. Post-communist firms are also more likely to complain about regulations on trade, land use, and licensing than non-post-communist firms. In general, the business environment of the post-communist businesses features a heavier and much less predictable regulatory burden on firms. Labor regulations are the only type of regulations that present a smaller obstacle to post-communist firms than they do to firms in the rest of the world.

Do subjective assessments reflect the actual differences in the regulatory environment in post-communist countries, or do they simply reveal shared beliefs and expectations derived from cultural predispositions? In order to answer this question, I turn to the "hard" data reflecting the actual number of regulatory procedures specified by law and other binding documents. The Doing Business Dataset compiled by the World Bank contains information on regulatory procedures involved in starting a business, dealing with construction

---

[7] In addition to twenty-six post-communist countries, between 2002 and 2006 WBES was administered in Algeria, Bangladesh, Brazil, Cambodia, Chile, China, Ecuador, Egypt, El Salvador, Eritrea, Ethiopia, Guatemala, Honduras, India, Indonesia, Kenya, Madagascar, Mali, Mauritius, Morocco, Nicaragua, Oman, Pakistan, Peru, Philippines, Senegal, South Africa, Spain, Sri Lanka, Syria, Tanzania, Turkey, Uganda, and Zambia.

Post-Communist Business Representation

TABLE 3.3. *Major Obstacles Faced by Businesses (Survey Evidence)*

How Problematic are these Different Factors for the Operation and Growth of Your Business? No Obstacle (0) ... Major Obstacle (3)	Non-Post-Communist Countries' Mean	Post-Communist Countries' Mean
Macroeconomic instability	1.783	1.620
Interest rates	1.713	1.561
Tax rates	1.320	1.731
Regulatory policy uncertainty	1.161	1.674
Corruption	1.160	1.217
Tax administration	1.105	1.467
Access to finance	1.055	1.370
Anticompetitive practices	1.039	1.327
Electricity	1.026	.632
Labor skills	.923	1.000
Crime, theft, disorder	.891	.921
Labor regulations	.849	.848
Customs and trade regulations	.779	.999
Licensing and operating permits	.702	.959
Legal system/conflict resolution	.659	1.070
Telecommunications	.638	.480
Transport	.632	.598
Access to land	.616	.676

permits, registering property, paying taxes, trading across borders, enforcing contracts, protecting investment, hiring and laying off workers, and liquidating a business.[8] This information is collected from official government publications, reports of development agencies, and government web pages and verified by experts in 183 countries. According to these data, post-communist businesses face an average of 140 regulatory procedures, which exceeds the world average by 15 percent. On average, it takes 495 days for post-communist businesses to fulfill these regulatory requirements, compared to the world average of 435.[9] Figure 3.8 breaks down different regulatory categories and shows the over-time trends between 2006 and 2010 in post-communist and non-post-communist countries.

Although the post-communist regulatory burden is rather heavy by comparative standards, the downward trend toward reducing the number of regulations is much more pronounced in the post-communist sample. Figure 3.8

[8] Data are available from Doing Business, http://www.doingbusiness.org.

[9] These averages exclude contract-enforcement time and procedures since a low number in this area usually indicates underdeveloped contract law rather than regulatory constraints.

50   Building Business

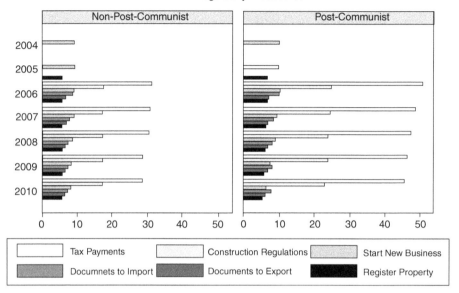

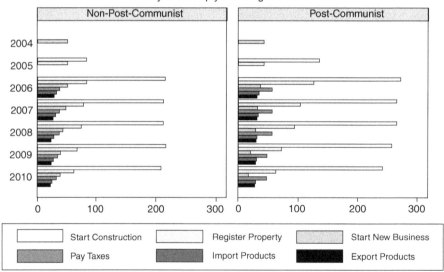

Source: Doing Business Dataset, WB

FIGURE 3.8. Official regulatory burden.

clearly illustrates that in the 2000s, post-communist countries made substantial progress by slashing the number of business-entry requirements and the tax burden. It shows that in less than a decade the Eastern European regulatory environment was profoundly transformed, making it comparable to the world's average levels on several dimensions. For instance, post-communist countries reduced the number of entry and property registration procedures by nearly 40 percent and 20 percent respectively, whereas the rest of the world slashed their entry and registration regulations by 16 and 3 percent, respectively. Post-communist countries also made considerable progress in terms of reducing other types of official regulatory costs, cutting construction regulations by 7 percent and the number of tax payments by 10 percent. Nonetheless, these figures continue to exceed the world's average significantly.[10]

Some post-communist countries are more successful in reducing their official regulatory burden compared to others. Table 3.4 gives the average number of all regulatory procedures for the countries of Eastern Europe and the former USSR from 2004 through 2010. Ukraine had the most regulatory procedures, with 247, whereas Lithuania had only 74, the fewest in the post-communist sample. EU member states tend to have a lighter regulatory burden than non-members, and East-Central European countries fare better than the former Soviet Republics. Still, geography does not explain all variation. Romania, for instance, on average had a heavier regulatory burden than Russia, whereas Kazakhstan had a lighter regulatory burden than Poland. Such profound variation shows that Eastern European countries create vastly different regulatory environments for their businesses. These, according to the defensive organization theory outlined in the previous chapter, create different conditions for establishing business associations.

Chapter 2 speculated that not only the nature of the official regulatory environment but also the unofficial regulatory burden and the costs of engaging in bureaucratic corruption drive the development of post-communist business associations. How do post-communist countries fare in these respects? Figure 3.9 plots the average survey responses to questions aimed at identifying the cost of corruption ("unofficial payments" and "gifts"), red tape, and the strength of legal institutions. It shows that post-communist businesses face low corruption costs, have intermediate levels of red tape, and are not confident in the strength of their legal systems. These in fact can explain low levels of associational membership. According to the defensive organization theory developed in Chapter 2, a high regulatory burden coupled with affordable unofficial ways to avoid regulatory compliance should suppress business organization. Relatively low costs of bribery, together with a legal system that cannot prosecute corruption effectively, may in fact make participation in business associations a less attractive option for post-communist businesses.

---

[10] At the same time, in the 2000s the total average tax rates declined in Eastern Europe from 2 percent above the world average to 3 percent below.

TABLE 3.4. *Regulatory Burden by Country (Eastern Europe and the Former USSR)*

Country	Average Number of Procedures
Estonia	75
Lithuania	81.6
Latvia	88.4
Slovenia	95.8
Hungary	98.8
Slovak Republic	99.4
Czech Republic	103
Georgia	107.2
Croatia	113.6
Bulgaria	113.8
Kazakhstan	123.4
Macedonia FYR	129.8
Poland	133.2
Bosnia and Herzegovina	137
Albania	138.8
Azerbaijan	139.8
Russian Federation	139.8
Armenia	144.4
Serbia	152.8
Tajikistan	159.75
Kyrgyz Republic	168.8
Romania	185.4
Montenegro	194
Belarus	195.8
Uzbekistan	213.8
Ukraine	243.4

Source: World Bank Doing Business reports, 2004–2010.

Using the available quantitative data, this section described the general features of business associations and their institutional environment, putting post-communist countries in a broader comparative perspective. Descriptive analysis shows that when judged by their total number and influence, post-communist business associations are rather insignificant. The number of post-communist business associations relative to the size of the economy and the number of firms, however, is comparable to the developed capitalist economies. Analysis also shows that fewer firms participate in business associations in the post-communist countries than in any other region. Several features of post-communist business environments help explain such low levels of participation. For instance, Eastern European businesses on average face heavier official regulatory burden, which, according to the defensive organization theory,

Post-Communist Business Representation

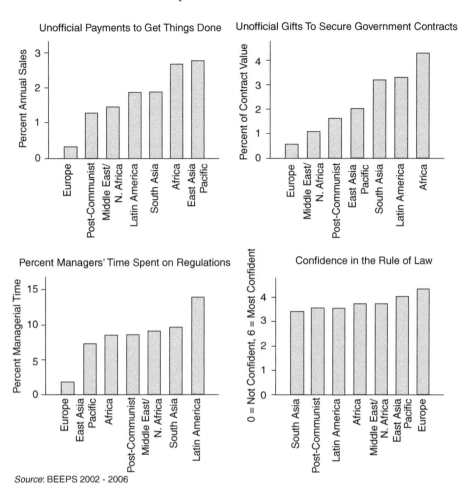

FIGURE 3.9. Corruption, red tape, and the rule of law across the world's regions.

makes attracting members harder for associations. Post-communist cases also feature relatively "cheap" corruption, as reflected in the comparatively low costs of bribery and ineffective legal deterrence against bureaucratic graft. These, according to the defensive organization theory, make the unofficial ways of coping with the regulatory burden more attractive than participation in industry associations. Members of post-communist business associations value different types of associational services than do firms in other parts of the world. Consistent with the logic of the defensive organization, firms enjoy domestic market services and information about their regulatory environment but see only a limited capacity on the part of business associations to engage in lobbying and interest intermediation.

3.2 Qualitative Analysis of Business Representation in Four Countries

The rest of the chapter details the major features of business associations in four post-communist countries. It analyzes the central characteristics of post-communist business representation and business climate as well as explicates the extent of cross-national and subnational variation in the development of business associations. Russia, Ukraine, Croatia, and Kazakhstan are pivotal cases. They differ on dependent and independent variables as well as on the number of other political, economic, institutional, and historical influences that make them appropriate candidates for process-tracing, qualitative research.

Russia, Ukraine, and Kazakhstan feature low levels of membership. Croatia, however, has one of the highest levels of participation in business associations in the region. Croatia and Kazakhstan have a more favorable official regulatory environment compared to Russia and Ukraine. The over-time variation creates an additional comparative dimension. Although membership levels continued to grow in the mid-2000s in Croatia and Ukraine, they experienced a slight drop in Russia and Kazakhstan. Corruption opportunities also vary across these cases; Croatia features the least corrupt environment, followed by Ukraine and Russia. Kazakhstan's record in terms of combating corruption deteriorated progressively in the examined period. (Table 3.5 contains summary indicators for the four countries.) Different dynamics of regulatory changes, the quality of civil administration, and associational development found in the four country cases present a fertile ground for analyzing the development of post-communist business-interest organizations.

Furthermore, the four countries represent different trajectories of political and economic development, and this enables us to consider the ways in which these trajectories affect business-state relations. Specifically, Croatia is an example of a compulsory-membership chamber of commerce system, Russia is an example of impressive organizational diversity and uneasy relations between business and the state, Ukraine features a dedicated business party, and Kazakhstan is profoundly shaped by authoritarian politics. Comparison across these country cases illuminates the effects of different legal and political frameworks as well as historical legacies on the formation of business associations.

3.3 Russian Business Associations: Sources and Consequences of Organizational Diversity

Russia's large economy and its political, economic, military, and cultural influence in the region make it a crucial case for investigating post-communist business-state relations and business representation. In the 1990s Russia was a textbook example of a state captured by moneyed interests; in the 2000s it developed into a strong statist economy. One would expect that the logic of defensive organization would be least applicable to Russia, yet analysis of

Post-Communist Business Representation

TABLE 3.5. *Summary Indicators for Four Post-Communist Countries*

Indicator	Russia			Ukraine		
	1992	2000	2006	1992	2002	2006
Freedom House Ranking	PF	NF	NF	PF	PF	F
Political Rights (FH)	3	5	6	3	4	3
Civil Liberties (FH)	3	5	5	3	4	2
Capture Index (Hellman)	...	32	...	...	32	...
Regulatory Quality	...	−.3	...	...	−.62	...
Corruption (CPI Rank)	...	82	121	...	87	99
Corruption (CPI Score)	...	2.1	2.5	...	1.5	2.8
Entry Procedures (Number)	...	20	10	...	13	15
GNI/Capita (current US$)	3,070	1,710	5,800	1,420	700	1,950
	Croatia			Kazakhstan		
Freedom House Ranking	PF	F	F	PF	NF	NF
Political Rights (FH)	3	2	2	5	6	6
Civil Liberties (FH)	4	3	2	4	5	5
Capture Index (Hellman)	...	27	...	...	12	...
Regulatory Quality	...	.19	...	...	−.74	...
Corruption (CPI Rank)	...	51	69	...	65	111
Corruption (CPI Score)	...	3.7	3.4	...	3.0	2.6
Entry Procedures (Number)	...	12	11	...	12	8
GNI/Capita ($) 2005	3,150	4,430	9,300	1,480	1,270	3,870

Note: Freedom House Nations in Transit ranks countries as F = free (1 to 2.5), PF = partly free (3 to 4.5), and NF = not free (5 to 7) (http://www.freedomehouse.org). Transparency International's Corruption Perception Index ranks countries' degree of corruption from 1 (most corrupt) to 10 (least corrupt) (http://www.transparency.org). The state-capture index (Hellman et al. 2002) reflects the proportion of surveyed firms that reported being directly affected by bribes to public officials. Regulatory quality (Kaufmann, Kraay, and Mastruzzi 2003) ranges from −2.5 to 2.5, with higher values indicating better governance.

the historical origins, organizational structures, membership, and functions of Russian business associations shows that for the most part they have not been the source nor the instrument of oligarchical interests. Instead, they have remained organizationally or functionally fragmented and have been more successful in member-service provision than in collective lobbying.

As a case of low-intermediate levels of business association membership (16 percent, 25 percent, and 20 percent in 1999, 2002, and 2005, respectively), Russia is representative of a large group of post-communist countries. After an initial period of democratization, Russia consolidated a peculiar type of electoral authoritarianism, featuring intra-elite competition and curtailed civil liberties.[11] Post-transitional economic recovery and major reforms of regulatory

---

[11] Russia's retreat from democratic principles followed the rise to power of Russia's second president, Vladimir Putin, in 2000. During Putin's two terms in office the government has reduced

Building Business

framework, commercial law, and civil administration came during the democratic slide back and resulted in some improvement in regulatory quality. At the same time, the country's ability to combat corruption worsened during the mid-2000s, which coincided with declining associational-membership rates.

Although this is generally consistent with the defensive organization argument, simultaneous changes in Russian politics might have contributed to the declining membership rates. President Putin's campaign to curtail political and economic ambitions of powerful business interests might have weakened business representation. This section shows, however, that due to organizational, strategic, and functional reasons, Russian business associations had been marginal political players well before the consolidation of competitive authoritarianism. Instead, their major efforts were directed toward the provision of club goods. To show this, I first discuss the origins of Russian business associations, their number, and organizational principles, and then I turn to analyzing membership and the member services business associations provide.

Formation

Although the oldest existing associations in Russia were established after 1991, it would be misleading to assume that in the early 1990s the Russian civic landscape was a tabula rasa. Institutional continuity from Soviet ministries, agencies, and trusts or *perestroika*-era civic organizations should not be discounted. For example, the Chamber of Commerce and Industry (CCI) and the National Association of International Auto Trackers both trace their origins to Soviet state-controlled organizations.[12] Of the 325 Russian business associations that participated in the 1999–2000 national survey of business associations conducted by the Russian Institute for Entrepreneurship and Investment (IEI) (Kaganov and Rutkovskaia 2001),[13] one traces its existence to a Soviet

freedom of the press, replaced democratically elected local authorities with presidential appointees, and eliminated opposition parties from national politics. The regime, however, moved in the direction of institutionalization rather than personification of power with the rise of the United Russia party and the election of Russia's third president, Dmitry Medvedev.

[12] The CCI is a unique example of rapid adaptation to the post-communist environment. In the USSR the Chamber of Commerce, created as a counterpart to similar foreign institutions, specialized in international economic relations. It was the primary organization responsible for expositions, accreditation of foreign trade missions, arbitration, certification, some technical standard setting, and quality control. A 1993 presidential decree established the CCI as a public (nonstate) association with independent financing and a wider range of functions. International trade expertise that the Chamber of Commerce developed during Soviet times was expanded to include the domestic economy. In the mid-1990s it developed a system of regional chambers so that services offered by the national chamber could be extended to local businesses.

[13] According to official records (which include inactive and defunct associations), Russia had more than 1,500 business associations in 1999. The IEI contacted these associations, and 325 (about 22 percent) participated in its survey. Participants reported total membership of 401,972 firms – 14 percent of all Russian firms, according to official statistics. This percentage is close to the estimated participation level based on BEEPS data. The survey also elicited information about

Post-Communist Business Representation

international economic-cooperation organization established in 1974, and twelve were formed in the 1980s during *perestroika*, when independent professional and interest organizations were officially allowed to form. Associations of cooperatives, leaseholders, entrepreneurs, and farmers were created alongside independent trade unions. Some of the top national associations are successors to all-Soviet associations. For example, the Russian Union of Industrialists and Entrepreneurs (RUIE) is the successor to the Scientific-Industrial Union, and the Association for the Development of Small and Medium-Size Business (ADSMB) is the successor to the Leaseholders' Association.

Many Russian business associations were built on the ruins of the all-Union ministerial system. Upon its independence in 1991, Russia inherited two governmental systems: that of the Russian Federation and that of the USSR. The USSR system was dissolved, and its major resources and personnel were incorporated into all-Russian institutions. The ministerial bureaucrats who lost their positions possessed important knowledge about enterprises that their agencies formerly supervised. They had developed lasting personal connections with the managers of state enterprises in the corresponding sectors. These bureaucrats usually had professional backgrounds in the industry their agencies formerly supervised and had deep understanding of technological processes, supply chains, and other important elements of industrial relations. In sum, they were especially suited to organizing business associations. Some sectoral associations, especially in manufacturing, were established with the help of former ministerial bureaucrats.

Russian legislation stipulates requirements for regional and national status of business associations. An association can claim provincial (*oblast/republic/autonomous-republic*) status if its founding members reside within one province and file an incorporating charter with the province's authorities. Associations with members representing more than half of Russia's eighty-nine regions are granted national status (Civic Code).[14] To attain national status, many Moscow-based associations opened regional chapters. At the same time, local businesses independently created other regional associations, some of which later joined national associations. The development of many regional associations involved simultaneous efforts on the part of local organizers and organizational work by political entrepreneurs from Moscow.

The Number of Associations

Although Russian legislation requires that all business associations register with the state, estimating the number of business-interest groups that function

---

the business associations' size, scope, activities, goals, and legal forms as well as the dates they were founded and the sectoral composition of their membership.

[14] The Ministry of Justice and local authorities are responsible for legally validating the business associations within a given territory. Associations must officially register in order to open a bank account, collect dues, or rent office space.

at any given point in time is difficult.[15] Russian legislation makes incorporating a civic group easier than officially liquidating it. As a result, many officially registered Russian business associations exist only de jure. Also, many local and regional associations register with local authorities rather than the federal Ministry of Justice, making it harder for national statisticians and researchers to trace the records of their establishment. Using federal and regional incorporation records, the IEI identified over 11,500 business associations that existed in Russia in 2001. Organizational activists who coordinate business-interest organizations, however, can trace the activity of only about 300 business associations and chambers of commerce (Volkov 2005). This gives the most conservative estimate of how many business associations actively participate in Russia's public life.

The IEI provides data on growth in the number of business associations in Russia. These are based on the dates of incorporation of business associations surveyed in 2001. As is evident in Figure 3.10, about one-third of all associations were established shortly after the dissolution of the Soviet Union, with another third entering the public space in 1996. By 1997 the number of business associations stabilized at about 300, which, according to my interviews with the leaders of prominent Russian associations, is close to the number of groups that actively participated in Russia's public life in 2005.

Even by the most conservative estimates, Russia has an impressive number of business associations, by far exceeding the world's average. This is in drastic contrast to scholarly accounts mainly focusing on a few high-profile, top national associations (Kubicek 1996; Peregudov and Semenenko 1996; Fortescue 1997; Remington 2004; Markus 2007). In fact, peak national associations – the "megalevel associations" in Cawson's (1985) terms – constitute only a small portion of business associations existing in Russia. Most Russian firms that join a business association join a regional or sector-based association that may or may not be part of a national umbrella group. Of the 357 business associations that participated in the IEI survey (Kaganov and Rutkovskaia 2001), 125 (35 percent) operate at the local level, 159 (44.5 percent) at the regional level, 24 (6.7 percent) at the interregional level, 43 (12 percent) at the national level, and 5 (1.4 percent) at the international level.[16] Sixty-five percent have fewer than 100 members; only 9.7 percent have more than 1,000

---

[15] Russian business associations may register with state authorities as an association/union, a civic organization, or a nonprofit partnership. All civic organizations register using the same legal forms. Statistics on the number of Russian civic associations do not include separate figures on the number of business associations. The names of business associations listed in Ministry of Justice registries often do not identify them as business associations. For example, the name "Opora Rossii" (Russia's Support) does not reveal that this association represents small and medium-size businesses.

[16] Regional and local associations are most likely to be omitted from the IEI survey due to an absence of data on their incorporation. Therefore, the reported figures likely underestimate their numbers.

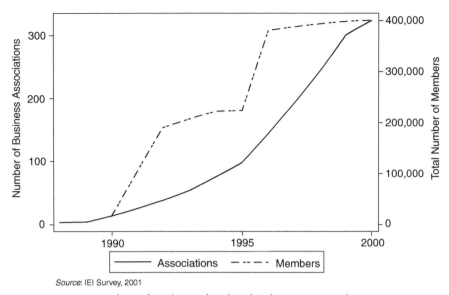

FIGURE 3.10. Number of and membership levels in Russian business associations, dynamics over time.

members. The regional and local associations combined have 215,423 members, and the national associations have 107,383 altogether. Based on four different studies, Yakovlev and Govorun (2011) report that between 2003 and 2009 the average size of associations ranged from 168 to 617 firms. It should be taken into account, though, that most of the national associations estimate their membership based on figures reported by their regional and local branches, making the national associations' actual direct membership figures substantially lower than reported. By all accounts, national high-profile associations constitute only a small portion of Russian business associations. In the interest of conducting a balanced analysis, this study draws from a large representative sample of business associations, including smaller, sectoral, professional, and issue-specific organizations.

The Structure of Associations

Many of Russia's national business associations are vertically integrated structures with regional and local branches. For example, the CCI has regional organizations in all of Russia's eighty-nine territories as well as in a number of localities. The regional and local CCIs are largely independent of the national CCI in their operations and financing. Their membership, activities, and influence vary considerably from region to region. Loose, national-level umbrella associations present a different type of vertical integration. In the sphere of labor relations, for instance, the Coordinating Council for Employers' Organizations (CCEO) represents Russian employer organizations. RUIE created the CCEO

60   *Building Business*

in 1994 as a designated representative of employers in tripartite negotiations. Because of the low priority of labor relations – during economic transition labor demands were directed at the state rather than at employers (Clarke 2006) – CCEO has not become a central player in business representation. Organizational fragmentation at the national level, with the CCEO, CCI, and RUIE occupying different representative roles, in many ways contributed to employer organizations' inability to impose binding agreements on the businesses, which reinforced labor-state rather than labor-employers conflict.[17]

Most Russian business associations are integrated in horizontal networks. For instance, the Russian Franchising Association, ADSMB, and Russian Shareholders Association have overlapping memberships. Similarly, the RUIE is a member of CCEO, and the CCEO leaders occupy important positions in the RUIE. Therefore, a mix of vertical and horizontal integration characterizes the Russian system of business representation.

Lehmbruch (2003) has investigated firms' memberships in multiple business associations, tracing this phenomenon to associations' organizational weakness and to firms' desire to spread risks and maximize their access to political decision making. The causes for the horizontal and vertical integration among Russian associations, however, differ from those responsible for the firms' decisions to join multiple associations. As discussed earlier, Russian law prescribes a territorial basis for the formation of business associations. Thus, the legal framework encourages vertical integration in that business associations open offices in regional centers or co-opt regional associations in order to attain a more prestigious national status. The legal framework is also responsible for a peculiar pattern of horizontal integration when one association becomes a member in another association while retaining its autonomy. Before 1995 registering a new business association was easier if its founders were civic organizations (other business associations) rather than corporations or individuals.[18] This fact largely explains overlapping organizational memberships.

---

[17] In fact, the absence of conflict with organized labor is a peculiar characteristic of post-communist business representation. Research shows that post-communist transition has put labor organizations in a paradoxical position. In order to prevent declining living standards these organizations had to support the transitional agenda. This, however, meant abandoning the "labor agenda" and allying with employers' interests (Allio 1997; Crowley and Ost 2001; Kubicek 2004; Clarke 2006). Symptomatically, long-time president of the Russian Federation of Independent Trade Unions Mikhail Shmakov noted that "in preparing the tripartite General Agreement we find that we have much more in common with the employers than with the government" (quoted from Clarke 2006, 81).

[18] According to Russian law, a business association may take one of three forms: civic organization (Law on Civic Organizations, May 1995, amended in 1997 and 1998), association/union (Law on State Support for Small Entrepreneurship, June 1995, amended in 1998), or nonprofit organization (Law on Non-Profit Organizations, November 1996, amended in 1998 and 1999). Only civic organizations permit individual or other civil associations' membership. A union/association, on the contrary, cannot accept personal membership; only corporate membership is permitted. IEI estimates that 48 percent of Russian business associations are registered as civic

Post-Communist Business Representation 61

An important issue in analyzing the Russian system of interest representation is to assess the degree of autonomy member associations enjoy within national umbrella associations. Do the latter organizations tightly control the former, resulting in a vertically integrated system of the neocorporatist type? In Russia this seems not to be the case. Business associations frequently affiliate with multiple umbrella groups. For example, the Association of Russian Banks (ARB), which has 543 members, and the Russian Association of Wood-Processing and Furniture Industries, which has 40 members, belong to the CCI, the RUIE, and other groups. Such overlapping membership makes it impossible for the CCI, the RUIE, and other umbrella groups to control the activities of member associations effectively.

According to Aleksandr Onischuk, president of the Association of Trade Companies and Producers of Consumer Electronics and Computers (Russian acronym RATEK), when RATEK first formed, it decided to join all major associations, advisory councils, and working groups active in Moscow. This strategy gave RATEK access to informational and organizational resources and helped it attract members and gain influence with state agencies and other interest groups. It was worth paying dues to umbrella groups to make RATEK's position and activities known to politicians and industry participants. Once RATEK had established itself, Aleksandr Onischuk told me, there was no need to continue participating in most other associations. Thus, RATEK withdrew from many organizations but remained in the CCI, which, in Onischuk's words, offers "an indispensable informational advantage." This example suggests that mutual cross-membership in Russian business associations is a method of networking rather than a form of organizational dependency and hierarchy. It also shows that even the large peak associations are more valued for their informational functions than for their ability to influence policy.

Contrary to prevailing opinion, many Russian business associations do not seek to encompass diverse business interests. Unlike large peak associations that represent business in general, a growing number of Russian business associations organize on sectoral, professional, or issue-specific principles. Sectoral and regional divisions have been the primary bases for business organization in the developed capitalist economies. The Russian organizational landscape is much different in this respect. According to the IEI (2001), few sectoral associations formed in Russia in the early and mid-1990s. Sector-based associations became more prominent in the late 1990s, and 40 percent of Russian business associations were organized on sectoral principles by 2001.[19]

---

organizations, 30.4 percent as unions/associations, and 21.6 percent as nonprofit partnerships (Kaganov and Rutkovskaia 2001).

[19] Some authors argue that many major Russian associations, such as the RUIE and the Federation of Commodity Producers (FCP), represent particular economic sectors. They variously contend that the RUIE represents defense industries (Hanson and Teague 1992), automobile and machinery producers (Lohr 1993; McFaul 1995), or the financial sector (Fortescue 1997). In reality, since at least 1992 the RUIE has represented a range of diverse business interests. The

Apart from the typical sectoral, regional, and professional groups, many Russian business associations unite firms involved in the production of a particular product or around a specific issue. For example, the Association of Ice Cream Producers includes milk-processing plants, ice-cream makers, producers of refrigerators, and retailers. The Association of Trademark Holders serves law firms, large domestic and foreign producers, and trading companies in diverse lines of business by protecting intellectual-property rights associated with trademarks. As its name indicates, the ADSMB represents the interests of small and medium-size businesses, including retailers, subcontractors, bakeries, taxi companies, and private dentists. Although it is not a sector-based association, it focuses on a much narrower range of issues (specific to small businesses) than do general associations such as the CCI or the RUIE. Such issue-driven business associations are rather atypical by Western standards; in developed capitalist economies that protect property rights and enforce contracts, such associations would not find enough shared interest to unite firms from different industries. Their development in Russia, however, is a logical response to the lack of secure property rights and an unpredictable regulatory environment that similarly affect very diverse firms.

Like cross-sector associations, sector- and issue-based associations have vertical and horizontal relationships with other associations. For example, the National Farmers Union and the ADSMB have regional offices in over half of Russia's regions. Sector- and issue-based associations also join general associations organized on a territorial basis. Table 3.6 presents a typology of Russian business and employer associations in respect to their structural forms and organizational bases. Examples of real-world associations that fall into each of these types are given in parentheses.

Membership

With the exception of professional and sectoral groups, all-Russian business associations have open membership for all business entities. Even those organizations that require members to have professional or industry-related credentials usually offer affiliated membership to firms or businesspeople who do not satisfy their requirements. Open membership allows many Russian associations to boost enrollment while also preventing them from acting as cartel-type arrangements that discriminate against nonmembers.

When the RUIE formed in 1992, it already had over 2,000 member firms that jointly produced 65 percent of Russia's GDP. In 2006 the RUIE claimed 328,000 members (corporations and individuals). Businesses that belong to the RUIE currently produce 85 percent of Russia's GDP.[20] The CCI reports

---

most important factor that signifies the cross-sectoral orientation of this association is its leadership's commitment to bringing diverse business interests into its organizational base. This interest is particularly evident in the diversity of RUIE's services that target different economic sectors and types of firms (Markus 2007).

[20] See Russian Union of Industrialists and Entrepreneurs, http://www.rspp.ru.

Post-Communist Business Representation   63

TABLE 3.6. *Types of Russian Business Associations, with Examples*

	Multisector	Sectoral/Professional
National	**Peak Associations/Umbrella Groups** (RUIE; CCI; CCEO) **National Issue-specific** (ADSMB)	**National Sectoral** (ARB; RATEK; Realtor's Guild; Association of Confectioners)
Interregional	**Umbrella Organizations for Regional, General, or Issue-specific Groups** (Far East Confederation of Businesswomen; Moscow International Business Association)	
Regional	**General** (CCI of Perm Oblast') **Issue-specific** (Tambov Association of Small Entrepreneurs)	**Sectoral/Professional** (Novosibirsk Producers of Scientific-Industrial Products; Pharmaceutical Association of Krivoi Rog)
Local	**General** (Union of Entrepreneurs of Arhari Village, Amur Oblast) **Issue-specific** (Center for Development and Protection of Small Business, Krasnodarskii Krai)	**Sectoral/Professional** (Rostov Organization of Private Taxi Owners; Kostroma Guild of Realtors)

membership of approximately 20,000 corporations.[21] Focusing on such large national business associations, Kubicek (1996) has regarded Russia's emerging system of business representation as neocorporatist. Yet the vast majority of Russian businesses associations have fewer than 100 members (Kaganov and Rutkovskaia 2001). Moreover, membership in large national umbrella associations is calculated from the membership in regional branches or affiliated groups. Over 100 sectoral and issue-specific associations operating at the national or regional level are under the RUIE's umbrella. The CCI's membership comprises 169 regional chambers and 178 sectoral and issue-specific associations. Only 38 corporations directly joined the CCI. Because of cross-cutting membership and the low levels of control that the national umbrella associations have over regional and sectoral organizations, this system is hardly consistent with the corporatist patterns.

According to the ISI data, in the 1990s Russia experienced a steady growth of associational membership. Figure 3.10 shows that the growth of membership accelerated in 1995 and continued through the late 1990s. The BEEPS data, which provide a much more reliable measurement, document a 9 percentage

---

[21] See Chamber of Commerce and Industry of the Russian Federation, http://www.tpprf.ru.

64 *Building Business*

points increase in membership rates between 1999 and 2002 but a 5 percentage points decline by 2005. Membership growth and decline coincided with two important developments during President Putin's first term in office. First, as part of his campaign against undue influence of private-sector "oligarchs," Putin designated RUIE, Delovaya Rossiya (Business Russia), and Opora the top representative associations of large, medium, and small businesses. During his first meeting with business leaders in July 2000 the president expressed a desire to routinize and institutionalize business-state relations and declared that the government will engage in conversation with businesses only through their top representative organizations. Although Putin's promotion of the organizational channels was advantageous to business associations, their leadership grew increasingly wary over the government's treatment of the Yukos case and the threat emanating from the statist direction of Putin's policies. A failed attempt of RUIE, Delovaya Rossiya, and Opora to defend Yukos in 2003 (Rossiya and Opora 2003) demonstrated the associations' weakness. This in part might explain members' decreased enthusiasm and declining membership.

At the same time, Putin accelerated the pace of institutional reforms, forcing through the government the overdue financial, tax, legal, and pension reforms as well as foreign exchange liberalization and anticorruption legislation. These reforms were aimed at reducing regulatory burden, and doing so, according to the defensive organization theory, should stimulate membership growth. However, the mid-2000s brought about cheaper (per the BEEPS data) and even more widespread corruption. As reflected in the country's climbing corruption scores, reforms failed to deter bureaucratic graft effectively, perhaps making it a more attractive option for businesses seeking regulatory relief. Indeed, we observed somewhat declining rates of participation in business associations in 2005. A more recent study, however, estimated that participation in business associations rose to 39 percent in 2009, suggesting that the reforms of the mid-2000s took several years to produce improvements in the business climate and bureaucratic environment. Once these effects were realized, businesses' collective action was enhanced.

A hotly debated aspect of associational membership are the questions of who joins Russian business associations and whose interests do the associations represent.[22] The literature concerned with the top national associations, such as the RUIE, does not provide a conclusive answer to the latter question. The RUIE is often described as an association of "red directors," financial tycoons, and oligarchs. The biggest irony of such assessments is that the interests of "red directors" conflict with those of tycoons and oligarchs: managers

---

[22] One might argue that membership does not necessarily indicate whose interests an association represents, because a rather narrow group could advance its own interests at the expense of other members. However, it is unlikely that such a hijacked association would be able to retain and expand its membership over time. When businesses join an association voluntarily and at a cost, they expect certain benefits in return. If an association fails to provide such benefits, there is no reason to expect that it will sustain its membership.

Post-Communist Business Representation 65

of state-controlled enterprises have advocated retaining state subsidies and trade barriers, whereas tycoons and oligarchs have championed fewer export controls and state withdrawal from the economy.

Analysts who view umbrella associations such as the RUIE, CCI, and the Federation of Commodity Producers (FCP) as representing narrowly defined interests usually overlook or downplay these associations' multisectoral nature.[23] Broad constituencies, programs of action, and interest areas characterize Russia's top national business associations (Primakov 2002; Volsky 2005). Although the political and economic significance of the red directors in the early and mid-1990s and private-sector oligarchs in the late 1990s to early 2000s should not be denied, equating the interests of these groups with those of national umbrella associations such as the RUIE, CCI, FCP, and CCEO is misleading.

According to a number of empirical studies, members of business associations tend to rely more on market mechanisms in dealing with business partners, more frequently use commercial courts, and more actively invest, innovate, and assist subnational governments (Frye 2002; Pyle 2006, 2011; Yakovlev and Govorun 2011). Enterprises with nontransparent ownership structure and subsidiaries of large holding companies, however, are less likely to join business associations (Yakovlev and Govorun 2011). Although business associations' members are more likely to interact with the state through various advisory institutions (Pyle 2006, 2011) and receive organizational and financial assistance from authorities (Golikova 2009; Yakovlev and Govorun 2011), these effects are observed only at the local and regional, not national, level. This offers little support for seeing members of business associations as market-hostile red directors and state-capturing business oligarchs.

The absence of a clearly defined, narrow constituency, however, is not a universal feature of Russian associations. Regional, sectoral, and issue-specific associations have smaller potential memberships but attract firms with much in common: sectoral membership, professional orientation, ownership, scale, and specific-issue focus. Although Russian business associations representing homogenous groups have recently grown in number, there is still a great degree of variation across economic sectors. According to BEEPS (European Bank for Reconstruction and Development [EBRD] and World Bank 1999–2005) data, the rate of association membership is 19.4 percent for the Russian secondary sector, 17.8 percent for service industries, and only 10.2 percent for the primary sector (excluding agriculture).[24] Data from the 2001 IEI survey show

---

[23] Fortescue (1997), however, acknowledges this diversity of interests but sees the diverse membership and goals of the RUIE and other umbrella groups as limiting their success: "The RUIE has tried to please everybody [industry, the financial sector, and the new private sector] and has ended up pleasing nobody" (138).

[24] Percentages are computed using a weighted sample. I thank Yuriy Gorodnichenko for pointing out potential problems arising from the BEEPS sampling method and for sharing a Russian sample frame for computing probability weights. Other studies conducted in Russia between 2003

66 *Building Business*

that different business sectors differ considerably with respect to associations' development (see Figure 4.5 and Table 4.10).

Individual versus firm membership is another controversial issue. In reporting their membership some Russian sources include only corporate members; others also include individual entrepreneurs. Although formal requirements imposed by the law largely dictate individual versus corporate membership, my interviews with representatives of business associations indicate that associations usually do not distinguish between individual and corporate membership. Most Russian business associations require the same dues for individual and corporate members. At the same time, many associations price-differentiate between full and associate members, allowing associations to attract some members who might be deterred by large amounts of required contributions.

Lobbying and Interest Representation

Operating under the assumption that business associations organize to lobby for their members' interests, many authors conclude that Russian business associations are ineffectual because they rarely lobby successfully (Kubicek 1996; Peregudov and Semenenko 1996; Fortescue 1997; Rutland 2001; McMenamin 2002; Lehmbruch 2003).[25] Some scholars contend that individual corporations and financial-industrial groups lobby more effectively than do formal business associations (Peregudov and Semenenko 1996; Fortescue 1997; Chaisty 2006).[26] These assessments are generally consistent with the logic of defensive organization, suggesting that lobbying cannot be the primary source of organizational development.

Perhaps the most successful lobbying by business associations has been credited to the RUIE. Peregudov and Semenenko (1996) cite Russia's 1991 privatization law as an important accomplishment of the RUIE's predecessor, the Scientific-Industrial Union (SIU).[27] The law allowed for the "insider" privatization scheme that resulted in transferring the ownership of large state enterprises into the hands of their managers. According to Fortescue (1997)

---

and 2009 estimate secondary-sector membership levels between 25 and 43 percent (Yakovlev and Govorun 2011). In addition to the actual growth of membership these differences reflect different sampling techniques in identifying subject enterprises.

[25] Lobbying the government is often included in the definition of an interest group (Salisbury 1991).

[26] For a detailed analysis of Russian financial-industrial groups, consult Rutland (2001).

[27] Arkadii Volsky, a former top-level CPSU technocrat with ties to state manufacturing giants, organized SIU in 1987. As a leader of RUIE, Volsky often stressed his industry background. Between 1955 and 1969 Volsky worked at Likhachev Automobile Plant (ZIL) as the head of the plant's communist party organization and the foundry manager. His ties to the manufacturing sector were strengthened in the 1970s and 1980s through positions he held at the CC CPSU car manufacturing section and its mechanical engineering division. After the collapse of the USSR, Volsky reorganized SIU as the RUIE and served as its president until 2005. Alexander Shokhin then replaced him. Shokhin has been the minister of economy, was the first deputy prime minister in the mid-1990s, and later held leading positions in the federal Duma.

Post-Communist Business Representation

and Remington (2004), another victory for the RUIE's red directors was the 1992 replacement of reformist Prime Minister Yegor Gaidar by centrist Viktor Chernomyrdin. In 2000 President Putin held a number of closed-door meetings with RUIE leaders and recommended that the RUIE expand its ranks and play a more assertive role in Russian economic policymaking. After that, the RUIE actively promoted government-backed pension reform in 2002, the new customs code, which incorporated internationally recognized practices in 2003, and the Law on Protection of Competition, which transferred authority over antimonopoly sanctions from a specialized state agency to the courts in 2006 (Markus 2007). An important question is whether the RUIE's lobbying history is representative of other Russian business associations: Do different types of associations have different lobbying records?

According to available quantitative data, about 90 percent of Russian business associations' founding documents list lobbying as one of their primary purposes (Kaganov and Rutkovskaia 2001).[28] This, however, may be a result of following the standardized language required for an official registration of civic organizations. In the open-ended interviews that I conducted, only 20 percent of interviewees mentioned being involved in lobbying. When I asked interviewees if their association's main goal is to lobby for members' interests, most referred to their founding documents and said that their association occasionally lobbies. However, only a few could remember specific issues or state institutions they have lobbied in the past.[29]

When asked about lobbying, the majority of my respondents admitted that business associations are not the most effective means of lobbying.[30] ADSMB president Aleksandr Ioffe stated, "We cannot help each of our members to solve specific issues plaguing their individual business. Instead, we try to influence the government by educating them about problems common to all our members."[31] Leaders of other associations expressed similar views, saying that they lobby but usually with respect to issues that are not the focus of lobbying by corporations. The executive director of the Association of Ice Cream

---

[28] The most widely used statement of organizational goals is "protection of members' rights and interests." The second most frequently indicated purpose is lobbying.

[29] To ensure that interviewees' responses did not reflect a negative perception of lobbying, I asked how the Russian public perceives lobbying. Only two interviewees answered that the public's perception of lobbying is negative.

[30] It is important to keep in mind that lobbying in the contemporary Russian usage usually entails solving a specific issue through noninstitutionalized channels. Lobbying in Russia is done behind closed doors. None of my respondents referred to using media, petitioning the government and the legislators, or participating in state advisory bodies as lobbying. Hence, lobbying here is not synonymous with influence.

[31] The fact that lobbying is viewed as seeking relief for a particular firm rather than a favorable change in the content of regulations that would affect many firms highlights unique experiences of post-communist firms and their associations. On the one hand, it suggests that the official regulations are often irrelevant for the operation of business. On the other, it reflects the customary ways of informal parochial business influence.

Producers Valerii Elhov told me, "It makes little sense for an association to promote the narrow interests of a few members; we lobby for our sector, and these are the legitimate concerns."

I also asked representatives of twenty-four business associations about the mechanisms of their interactions with state institutions (ministries, legislators, local government, and executive authorities). The answers indicated that seventeen of the associations interacted with state authorities through advisory institutions such as councils, working groups, committees, and think tanks. The association representatives were usually permanent members of these institutions. Some associations had helped create these institutions, and some had been invited to join by state authorities. Participation in such advisory institutions offers business associations varying degrees of access to politicians and higher-level bureaucrats, though the degree of influence of the consultative institutions varies. The Entrepreneurs' Council of Moscow's city government, for instance, has the right to veto any city bill that affects the operation of businesses in virtually all spheres of economic activity. In sharp contrast, an advisory entrepreneurial council to the Russian president that includes representatives of the RUIE, Delovaya Rossiya, the ARB, and other national associations has little formal authority and is largely perceived as a rubber stamp for all major government initiatives.

According to the interviews, leaders of business associations do not regard their participation in permanent or special advisory institutions as a form of lobbying but rather as a form of communication and cooperation. This closely corresponds to what Frye (2002a) calls "exchange," distinguishing it from one-sided lobbying in which one party seeks favors from the other. The benefits of such exchange vary, but generally are limited to information-sharing, coordination of social and infrastructure-related initiatives, and execution of federal-development programs.[32]

Besides the consultative institutions that advise executive and legislative authorities, the Russian political system offers multiple access points. Perhaps the most accessible are the regional and local media. Peregudov and Semenenko (1996) and Fortescue (1997) describe influencing public opinion as one form of lobbying by business associations. Although not directly aimed at political authorities, associations' publications, conferences, statements to the press, and expert commentary advance associations' agendas. Associations can further influence policy makers by conducting expert evaluation of proposed economic and regulatory policies' expected effects. Many business associations – whether general (e.g., the RUIE and CCI), issue specific (e.g., the CCEO), or sectoral (e.g., the ARB and Guild for the Development of Audio-Video Trade) – have research departments that monitor the legislative and regulatory environment. The RUIE's Expert Institute has more than 100 researchers. Such departments periodically release expert analyses and special reports on issues and events

---

[32] Yakovlev and Govorun (2011) corroborate my assessment.

Post-Communist Business Representation

of concern to the members of their respective association. These analyses and reports often reach the corridors of power and inform political decision makers about particular issues or industries.

Before the consolidation of the country's superpresidentialism in the early 2000s, the Russian federal legislature was relatively open to lobbying. In Russia no special legislation regulates lobbying or political contributions, although legislators are required to report all income, including funds received from lobbyists. *Novye Izvestiia* reported in 2003 that average contributions paid to deputies for introducing a bill were US$50,000–US$70,000, and average sums paid to a parliamentary group (*fraktsiia*) for supporting a bill were US$250,000–US$300,000 ("Tsena Zaprosa" 2003).[33] Verifying these sums is of course difficult, but there is a wide belief that bribes in fact speed the introduction of many bills. With the rise of United Russia as the dominant parliamentary force, the importance of national legislature in regard to lobbying declined progressively. The government now initiates most bills that the federal Duma considers, evidencing a limited scope of parliamentary influence. The government institutions at the ministerial and regional levels, however, remain frequent targets of lobbying efforts. The focus here, however, is on the application of rules and regulations rather than the introduction of new laws. Individual firms often engage in such lobbying to obtain exemptions or other special treatment from bureaucrats.

Although all attempts to organize a Russian business party failed in the early 1990s, some businesspeople have been elected to regional or national legislatures. In place until 2007, the single-member district system contributed to the election of most of the businesspeople in the federal Duma, the lower house of the Russian parliament ("Tsena Zaprosa" 2003). After the 2003 elections, about one-fourth of the Duma' s deputies had business backgrounds. In their 2010 article, Gehlbach, Sonin, and Zhuravskaya question the influence-driven motivations of such parliamentarians, reflecting on the widespread belief that their runs for public office might serve as a means to secure parliamentary immunity and protection from prosecution.

The limited lobbying efforts on the part of associations is likely related to the abundant lobbying opportunities for individual firms (Chaisty 2006), who most often lobby for private rather than collective goods. Not all corporations, however, can gain direct access to the legislators and ministerial staff to benefit from such informal contacts. Associations, however, especially those that have established themselves as serious players, are better positioned to shape public opinion, engage in informational lobbying, and promote industry-wide interests. Much of the influence business associations exert is achieved through consultations, advisory meetings, and information-sharing that do not involve bribes or other financial favors.

---

[33] In Russia a committee or any deputy can introduce a bill, which can become law if approved by Parliament within three readings.

Member Services

Although only a few Russian business associations are actively engaged in lobbying, virtually all organizations provide various services to their members. One can group such services and member-oriented activities into two categories: some are directed specifically at the association members, whereas others benefit the associations' constituency without discriminating between members and nonmembers. Differences can be traced to the nature of provided services; some services cannot be provided to the members without benefiting nonmembers. In the language of the collective action literature, these are nonexcludable goods. Other services can be provided exclusively to association members to create incentives to join.[34] However, some associations make strategic decisions to offer perfectly excludable goods to nonmembers at an extra charge in order to raise money.[35] Russian legislation restricts the commercial activity of business associations registered as associations/unions; however, civic organizations and nonprofit partnerships are legally entitled to supplement their budgets through commercial activities, including provision of services. Such legal restrictions, together with the specific needs of constituencies, affect the types of services associations provide.

Table 3.7 summarizes the member services that Russian business associations offer. The most frequently provided services are business information, legal support, and consulting, closely followed by marketing and investment assistance. The least frequently mentioned are specialized professional services, expositions, and targeted financial assistance. Only a few specialized associations offer the latter group of services. The CCI, for instance, had organized international expositions in Soviet times and has continued by specializing in this sphere of activity. A number of specialized associations known as business incubators provide a wide range of targeted assistance for fledgling small businesses. Business incubators therefore, resemble the charitable institutions of civil society dedicated to the task of private-sector development.

The types of services listed in Table 3.7 are often provided in combination. The League of Trade Merchants, for example, publishes a subscription-based information bulletin that reviews recent changes in regulations affecting retail

---

[34] Information provision is a peculiar service. On the one hand, some information – for example, a business's reputation – is valuable precisely because it is public. On the other hand, a better informed business has an advantage over an uninformed competitor when privately held information helps to design a better business strategy. Once made public, information is a nonexcludable good. However, many means of sharing information (private correspondence, subscription-based access, password-protected Web pages, etc.) allow associations to effectively exclude nonmembers from informational benefits. In what follows I refer to privately beneficial information.

[35] Another reason is a purely strategic market behavior. Six associations whose leaders I interviewed extend perfectly excludable goods, such as access to their online databases, newsletters, and seminars, to nonmembers at no cost. After firms begin using the services, the associations start discriminating between members and nonmembers in an expectation that firms will join associations to secure continuing access to services and information.

Post-Communist Business Representation

TABLE 3.7. *Member Services Listed by Russian Business Associations in Their Founding Charters*

Services	Percentage of Associations
Information services (publications, Web sites, special request)	100
Legal support	100
Consulting	73
Marketing services	65
Assistance in attracting investments	61
Education/training	55
Assistance in developing business plans	30
Targeted business assistance (office space, transportation services, etc.)	6
Facilitating the search for business partners	5
Auditing/accounting services	5
Specialized/professional services (e.g., advertising, obtaining patents)	1
Expositions	<1

Note: Data are from the IEI survey (2001).

trade. The association also offers regular seminars in which legal experts familiarize participants with such changes and offer consulting on specific issues. These activities combine informational, legal, and educational services. Most of the member services listed in Table 3.7 (e.g., legal support, consulting, education, professional services, targeted business assistance, and assistance with developing business plans) are excludable goods. Other services, such as expositions, assistance with finding business partners, arbitration, quality certification, and setting of technical standards, are not purely excludable; if nonmembers were denied access to such goods, the overall benefits to the members and nonmembers alike would decline.

By providing services crucial to business operation and development, associations are able not only to expand their membership but also to facilitate dues collection from the existing members. About 60 percent of my interviewees reported that only 20 to 40 percent of new members pay dues regularly. Although collecting dues is the most pressing problem for Russian business associations, the usual way to encourage membership renewals has been to develop differential fee schedules for dues-paying members and nonmembers. By charging nonmembers for services, business associations not only reduce their reliance on membership dues but also facilitate dues collection.

My interviews confirmed that Russian business associations offer their members and constituents a great variety of services. BEEPS data show that, on average, association members in Russia are somewhat more satisfied with these services than are businesses in other countries, whereas satisfaction with Russian associations' lobbying efforts is much lower compared to the reference group. Markus (2009) has found that in Russia and Ukraine, membership in business associations helps improve the security of firms' property rights vis-à-vis the state and business partners. According to my interviews, such security is achieved through legal advice, information-sharing, professional and business training, and reputational benefits.

Contrary to many earlier accounts, a descriptive analysis of Russian business-interest groups shows considerable pluralism and diversity. National peak organizations have the most visibility and political clout but are not the most typical business associations. Most Russian businesses participate in local, regional, or sectoral groups that concentrate on providing benefits specific to their members and rarely influence state institutions in pursuit of collective interests. When they do lobby, it is mostly in the form of consultation with state authorities. Although associations are many, membership levels remain low in Russia. The lack of membership growth coincides with associations' limited political influence as well as high regulatory costs and widespread and affordable bribery, all of which complicate the task of providing regulatory relief to attract new members.

3.4 Ukrainian Business Associations: A Case of Political Mobilization

Ukraine is similar to Russia in many respects. Both countries are presidential and post-Soviet and, for most of the post-communist period, have had comparable levels of civil liberties and political competition.[36] However, compared to Russia, Ukraine has less prohibitive legislation regulating the formation of social organizations. Ukraine also gives citizens' groups more room for expression and influence. In Ukraine greater political competition has allowed business elites to have a more transparent and active role in politics. The most striking difference from all other country cases analyzed here is that Ukraine has an active political party of entrepreneurs, thereby allowing business interests a more direct access to politics. Does that affect the business community's position vis-à-vis the state? Do the party and Ukrainian business associations divide responsibilities of serving their constituents? Does direct representation in parliament through a political party discourage or promote the formation of business associations? The following analysis addresses these questions.

---

[36] Following the economic mismanagement and political corruption of Ukraine's first two presidents, Leonid Kravchuk and Leonid Kuchma, Ukraine showed reinvigorated competition and political freedom during the Orange Revolution of November–December 2004. The years since have been marked by acute political confrontation, active political participation, and repeated attempts at reform.

Post-Communist Business Representation 73

The analysis demonstrates that although Ukraine's business associations are much more engaged in politics than are their Russian counterparts, they still attract a small fraction of businesses. Political activism and visibility, therefore, do not make associational membership more attractive to potential members. Similarly to the Russian case, Ukrainian business associations strive to provide members with regulatory relief. According to the defensive organization theory, having one of the worst regulatory climates in the region should strongly impact their ability to do so. As discussed earlier in this chapter, Ukraine's business environment involves heavy official regulatory pressures, high levels of red tape and unofficial burden, and ineffective anticorruption measures. All these features, according to the defensive organization theory, should retard businesses' collective action.

Formation

The first Ukrainian nongovernmental, nonprofit organizations to represent the emerging nonstate (cooperative) sector were the Union of Ukrainian Cooperators and Entrepreneurs (1989), the Federation of Professional Unions of Cooperatives and Enterprises of Alternative Forms of Property (1990), the Ukrainian Union of Small, Medium, and Privatized Enterprises (USMPE) (1990), and the Ukrainian Association of Leasing Companies and Entrepreneurs (UALCE) (1990). The words "union" and "cooperative" in these associations' names reflect the post-communist economic transition, which featured cooperative property in the emerging private sector and no clear distinction between employers and employees in small family businesses and production collectives. However, the USMPE and UALCE adapted to new economic realities and, in 2006, were among the most stable and reputable organizations representing the Ukrainian small-business sector.

The Ukrainian Association of Enterprises in Industry, Construction, Transport, Communication, and Science, whose members included the giants of Ukrainian industry, formed in 1990. This association was modeled after the SIU of the USSR[37] and was reorganized in 1992 as the Ukrainian League of Industrialists and Entrepreneurs (ULIE).[38] Ukraine's greatest surge of

---

[37] The influence of Russian-style organizational forms can be seen in many Ukrainian associations. Business Incubators, the Franchising Association, the Association of Manufacturers and Consumers of Packaging Products, and many other Ukrainian associations closely resemble their Russian counterparts in organization, agenda, and activities. Due to their shared communist legacy, business associations in the two countries have faced similar problems during economic transition.

[38] From the beginning the ULIE represented large, state-owned, and privatized enterprises mainly located in Central and Eastern Ukraine. Since 1997 Anatolii Kinakh has served as its president. Kinakh's important positions in government considerably strengthened the ULIE. He played a central role in the parliamentary commission on economic reform (1990), was governor of Mykolaiv (1992), was Ukraine's vice premier for industrial policy (1995), served in the presidential administration (1996), headed the parliamentary commission for industrial policy (1998), was Ukraine's first vice premier (1999), founded and led the Ukrainian Party of Industrialists

74   *Building Business*

association formation was in the mid- to late 1990s, when most sectoral and regional associations were established. According to a survey conducted by the Coordinating Expert Center of Business Associations of Ukraine (CEC), about 10 percent of Ukraine's existing business associations were established before 1995, about 50 percent between 1995 and 2000, and about 25 percent after 2000 (Liapin 2005b).

An important question in understanding the causes of business association formation is the issue of foreign-donor assistance. At the outset of economic transition a number of international organizations introduced programs to assist the development of nascent private businesses in Ukraine. Some Ukrainian business associations benefited from such programs as either direct recipients or fund-distributing agencies. According to one study, three of the nineteen associations in the study indicated donor contributions as the primary source of their financing, twelve reported relying primarily on membership dues, and four indicated private and corporate donations as the primary sources of financing (Bilych et al. 2005).

My interviews revealed that many Ukrainian business associations have at some point participated in foreign-sponsored programs. I learned about multiple cases in which business associations were established solely to obtain foreign-donor money or execute donor-sponsored programs. According to my interviewees, such associations rarely survived. One of them said, "Everybody knew that these were well-financed façades with no local initiative behind them. Serious businessmen never took them seriously." Therefore, donor programs cannot be seen as the primary reason for the formation of Ukrainian business associations. The emergence and development of most associations has been largely a response to domestic demands and conditions rather than an outside influence.

The Number of Associations

According to the Ukrainian state administration, 858 national, regional, and municipal business associations officially existed in the country in 2005 (Bilych et al. 2005). However, the number of functioning business associations is believed to be considerably smaller; according to one report, there were only 200 in 2005 (Bilych et al. 2005), though according to another report, there were about 500 in the same year (Liapin 2005b). The complex procedure of legalizing and liquidating a civic organization explains the disparity between the number of officially registered business associations and the number of functioning associations. As in Russia, disbanded organizations are not easily removed from official records.

and Entrepreneurs (1999), and was Ukraine's prime minister (2001). According to ULIE documents, the ULIE now unites large and small businesses that jointly produce more than 80 percent of Ukraine's GDP.

The Organizational Structure

In Ukraine two laws regulate the formation of business associations and their legal rights. The 1992 Law on Civic Organizations stipulates that civic associations can be legalized either by notification through public media or by official registration with municipal and regional authorities and the Ministry of Justice. Organizations that the state has not recognized are considered illegal. In official registration, which takes up to two months, state authorities review the association's founding documents. The incorporation by notification is simpler and less time-consuming, but the 1992 law is vague regarding eligibility and the process. Business associations established after 2001 can legalize by satisfying the requirements of the 2001 Law on Employer Associations. Whereas the 1992 law recognized only individuals and non-commercial civic organizations as founding entities and potential members, the 2001 law allows corporate entities and individuals to organize and participate in business associations. Both laws require official registration for legality and allow state authorities to reject an application. In Ukraine the formation of a business association also entails registration with the office of statistics, the social security office, the state pension fund, the tax administration, and other state authorities. Many Ukrainian business associations registered as for-profit entities (Liapin 2005b). This legal status allows associations to conduct economic activities such as providing services on a commercial basis and renting out equipment and premises to members and nonmembers.

By law, Ukrainian business associations can be established at the municipal, provincial, or national level. Enterprises or businesspeople located in one municipal unit form municipal associations. Provincial and national organizations unite lower-level territorial organizations or individual employers from different municipalities or provinces. The 2001 law also recognizes sector-based business associations, although it does not accord them any special status. Appendix C supplies data on the regional distribution of officially recognized business associations. Compared to Ukraine's western regions, central and eastern regions have a higher concentration of industrial production and, on average, more associations per 1,000 privately owned firms.

Some Ukrainian business associations have overlapping organizational structures and membership, although such overlapping is not as widespread as in Russia. Ukrainian business associations maintain organizational independence, and there is little horizontal integration. One exception is a loosely organized group established in 1998 for strategic coordination, the Coordinating Expert Center of Business Associations of Ukraine (CEC), founded as a permanent coalition of business associations. The CEC is the largest and most significant horizontally integrated group uniting Ukrainian business associations. Its organizational structure is fluid. The CEC emphasizes partnership and cooperation among its members and does not advocate protectionism or restrictions on a free market (Liapin 2005a).[39] Although the CEC has permanent staff and regional offices and has established a think tank (Institute for Competitive Society), it does not see itself as a hierarchical umbrella organization but instead as a coalition.

Although a Ukrainian business association can have regional or national status without being vertically integrated, several vertically integrated business associations have emerged in Ukraine. The ULIE, Ukrainian Chamber of Commerce and Industry (UCCI),[40] and the Ukrainian Employers' Federation (UEF) are the major associations with a strictly hierarchical organization. The national-level ULIE and UCCI unite territorial organizations from all of Ukraine's provinces and federal cities as well as from the Republic of Crimea. Whereas other hierarchically organized associations function as cross-sector, general-purpose organizations, the UEF was created in 1998 specifically to participate in tripartite negotiations.[41] The UEF is organized based on territory and business sector, uniting 29 regional, 121 sectoral, and 246 local chapters.

Membership

Although the ULIE has nearly 38,000 members and the UCCI has 7,000 members, most Ukrainian business associations have small memberships. In the study of nineteen Ukrainian business associations (all members of the CEC), roughly half of the associations had fewer than 100 members, one-third had between 100 and 1,000 members, and one-fifth had more than 1,000 members (Liapin 2005b).[42] Unfortunately, I could not verify the accuracy of these estimates. Many associations do not publicly disclose their membership, and those who do are rarely consistent in their reports. Some associations disclose only the number of firms who recently paid their dues, whereas others never remove prior members from their databases and include them in membership estimates.

Ukrainian business associations rarely differentiate between individual and enterprise membership. Business leaders are assumed to represent their respective firms. The leaders of Ukrainian business associations seem to value actively involved individuals more than influential enterprises as members. As expressed by Volodymyr Gryschenko, first deputy chairman of the Federation of Employers of Ukraine, "People are everything! It is not the Zaporozhstal

---

[39] See http://www.ics.org.ua.

[40] The UCCI was created in 1972 as a branch of the Chamber of Commerce and Industry of the USSR. Starting in 1992 it functioned as a state institution of the independent Ukraine. In 1997 the Ukrainian Parliament passed a law that transformed the Chamber into a nongovernmental, nonprofit, self-governing, voluntary-membership organization of Ukrainian businesses, entrepreneurs, and their associations. The UCCI inherited staff, buildings, and equipment from its state predecessor and thus had a head start in providing services to existing and new members.

[41] Similarly to the CCEO in Russia, UEF was established to represent employers during the tripartite negotiations. As its Russian counterpart, UEF often allies with the unions and does not have the authority to enforce collective agreements.

[42] Because these figures are based on membership data reported by business associations, they likely overestimate membership.

Post-Communist Business Representation 77

[Ukraine's largest steel-producing corporation] that sits at the meetings and battles our opponents. It is the people who represent it" (Gryschenko 2006).

The personalities of an association's leaders play a large role in establishing its reputation and popularity. In their quest for influential members Ukrainian business associations compete with other institutions that directly represent large businesses. From 1993 to 2005 large businesses had direct access to Ukraine's top executive institutions through the Entrepreneurs' Council under the Cabinet of Ministers (Bilych et al. 2005; Liapin 2005a). Because the process of selecting members for the Entrepreneur's Council was not transparent, its claims that it represented Ukrainian business interests were never considered fully legitimate. The national legislature was another venue for direct political influence of businesspeople. Throughout the 1990s Ukraine was a leader in the post-communist world in terms of the number of businesspeople elected to its national legislature. The direct influence of medium- and large-sized businesses on the executive and legislative branches has diminished the attractiveness of Ukrainian business associations as instruments of business representation and influence.

Since the early 2000s, however, business associations have become more attractive as institutional mechanisms of representing business interests (primarily of small and medium-size businesses, previously all but excluded from business-state interactions). More businesspeople and political leaders have become active in existing associations, and others have established new associations. Yuri Yehanurov (CEC, USMPE), Anatolii Kinakh (UEF, ULIE), and Ksen'ia Liapina (CEC) have actively led business associations while holding high government office. A number of public campaigns organized by Ukrainian business associations in the late 1990s and early 2000s brought greater recognition of business associations' legitimacy and led to the development of formal mechanisms of interactions between the state and business organizations.

In 2006 the Council of Trade Associations (CTA), the first Ukrainian advisory board consisting solely of business association representatives, was established under the State Committee for Economic Development. The CTA was created as an alternative to the Entrepreneurs' Council under the Cabinet of Ministers, which traditionally consisted of high-profile businesspeople rather than representatives of business associations. More transparent than the Entrepreneurs' Council, the CTA represented the interests of diverse groups of entrepreneurs and emphasized business development, particularly in the private sector. Viktor Yanukovich liquidated the CTA in 2004, but Yulia Tymoshenko revived it in 2005 in response to street protests organized by small entrepreneurs in the aftermath of the Orange Revolution.

In 2000 a presidential decree established other formal venues for interaction between associations and the state in the form of (1) the Civic Collegium under the State Committee for Regulatory Policy and Entrepreneurship and (2) the Commissions (Coordinating Councils) for Enterprise Development under municipal and regional authorities. These institutions did not consist exclusively of representatives of business associations; they included other civic organizations, media, academicians, and representatives of large corporations. Also, although both institutions had only consultative powers, they signified official recognition of business associations as legitimate representatives of business interests.

Functions and Activities

The statutes of the overwhelming majority of Ukrainian business associations declare "defense of the legitimate rights of the association's members" as the associations' primary objective. Other declared goals include lobbying for members' interests, facilitating business contacts, promoting market and industry development, and providing informational, business, and professional-development services. The statutes of Ukrainian business associations often include the same (or virtually the same) list of objectives, in keeping with a blueprint established by legislation. The use of standardized language seems to ease the registration of new associations.

The functions that Ukrainian business associations actually perform largely depend on an association's size, leadership, resources, and membership base. Associations' functions also evolve in response to challenges and opportunities presented by the economic and political environment. As in Russia, in Ukraine the vast majority of business associations perform multiple functions. According to the 2005 CEC study, 20 percent of Ukrainian business associations offer their members legal protection and organizational support, 17 percent lobby on behalf of their members, 14 percent organize meetings and roundtable sessions to discuss shared problems, 14 percent provide business information, 12 percent organize training seminars, 8 percent help in the search for potential business partners, and 7 percent organize informal member meetings (Liapin 2005b).

In the course of interviews with leaders of business associations I was particularly interested in the services that associations provide to their members and in their other activities, the nature of which are usually hidden under a vague "protection of members' rights" label. Such services often included "legal protection" in the form of class-action lawsuits, professional legal advice, or various information and training opportunities that help businesspeople defend their property rights and make informed legal decisions. In addition to these legal services, "protection" usually implies lobbying for collective interests and representing business interests in state institutions.[43]

Almost all of the Ukrainian business associations that I visited provide services tailored to their members. The only associations that seem to disregard

---

[43] It should be noted that until the early 2000s there were few legitimate methods of business representation in state institutions. "Representation," therefore, involved establishing personal contacts with local and national politicians who could promote companies' interests. As a result, business associations have not been important instruments in lobbying and representation, with most such activities carried out through direct contacts between businesspeople and politicians.

Post-Communist Business Representation   79

this sphere of activity are the hierarchically organized umbrella groups. (Although an umbrella association, the UCCI has an outstanding record of providing a variety of services relevant to many different spheres of economic activity.) Informational services are perhaps the most popular services, but most Ukrainian business associations do not provide information exclusively to their members; rather, they sell their publications and data to generate additional revenue. The oldest and best-known association publications are the USMPE's *The Bulletin* and the UALCE's *The Employer*. In addition to such publications, informational services include databases that facilitate business contacts (the USMPE) or help establish business reputation (the UCCI). Such services are particularly valued by provincial enterprises who are isolated from vibrant urban business environments and cannot rely on informal networking to gather valuable information about potential business partners.

Another sphere of business association activities includes exhibitions, fairs, and other public events that bring public attention to goods and services available from local businesses. The UCCI specializes in organizing international trade shows in Kyiv and abroad. Regional associations organize local events. For example, the Ukrainian Bakers' Association organizes an annual Bread Festival in the city of Khmelnytski. Since 1997 the Association for the Development of International Business in Kremenchutsy has managed an annual international fair in that provincial city.

Many Ukrainian business associations organize official meetings, conferences, and seminars that bring together businesspeople, bureaucrats, politicians, and media. Most members of the association New Formation are attracted by its well-publicized regular meetings with high-ranking public officials. Covered by the media and open only to the association's members, such meetings give members current information on government economic initiatives, new appointments, and the government's position on industry-related issues. The Ukrainian European Business Association, whose membership is open to foreign and domestic firms, often organizes roundtable discussions of economic reform and state policy with state officials and politicians. Since 2000 the municipal Union of Entrepreneurs has organized an annual business forum in Zhytomyr that brings together representatives of the local business community, the provincial administration, and international guests.

Unlike Russian business associations, many Ukrainian associations have successfully defended business interests through public campaigns. In sharp contrast to the pro-establishmentarianism and political neutrality of their Russian counterparts, many Ukrainian associations representing new small businesses boldly participated in the street protests of the late 1990s and early 2000s and formed strong alliances with the political forces behind the 2005 Orange Revolution. Sometimes spontaneous but often led by business associations, the street protests attracted owners of family businesses, open-market traders, taxi drivers, and other "micro" businesspeople. The protests took place in front of the Parliament building as well as near the seat of the Cabinet and

80   *Building Business*

the Kyiv city administration in 1999, 2000, and 2001 and in the aftermath of the 2005 Orange Revolution. Many business associations (including the USMPE and UALCE) participated in these protests (some business associations even planned them) as part of larger advocacy campaigns (see the Ukrainian case studies in Chapter 5). Consistent presence in Ukraine's public space, active political participation, and frequent appeals to the general public are the distinguishing features of Ukrainian business associations.

The analysis of Ukrainian business representation shows that the existence of a business political party and other direct political participation of influential businesspeople does not preclude the formation of business associations. Although Ukraine has high levels of direct business representation and its business associations are well integrated in the political process, it continues to have low levels of business association membership. This further supports the view that the main function of post-communist business associations is not lobbying or otherwise gaining access to policy formation but rather subtler representation, such as providing information, offering expert opinions, maintaining a positive public image, and providing member-oriented services. I will explain in further detail in Chapter 5 how bureaucratic abuse and bribery often hastened Ukrainian businesspeople's collective action and also how associations' inability to tackle the root cause of discontent – burdensome regulations and bureaucratic red tape – have led to members' disillusionment and associations' failure.

3.5 Kazakh Business Associations: High-Profile/Low-Impact versus Low-Profile/High-Impact Organizations

Kazakhstan's situation is marked by stagnant political reform coupled with solid economic transformation. It introduces two comparative dimensions: authoritarianism and corruption. As a society with very limited opportunities for expression, Kazakhstan presents an important case by which to examine the effects of civil liberties and political freedoms (or the lack thereof) on the development of business representation. Despite profound political differences from the other country cases, levels of participation in Kazakh business associations closely resemble those found in Russia and Ukraine. This fact rules out politics as the primary explanation for businesses' collective action. As the following discussion will demonstrate, this does not mean, however, that political developments are inconsequential to business representation.

Unlike the other countries selected for study, Kazakhstan ranks low on the state-capture index (Table 3.1); the authoritarian government apparently dominates private interests. At the same time, the state, which the country's president and his family tightly control, made considerable progress in reforming the economy and reducing official regulatory burden to below the regional average. This, according to the defensive organization theory, should promote collective action. Instead, similarly to Russia, Kazakhstan experienced a decline in associational membership in the mid-2000s.

Post-Communist Business Representation 81

Notorious for its administrative and political corruption (Henderson 2000; Werner 2000; Nichols 2001; Miller, Grodeland, and Koshechkina 2002; Kaser 2003), the country is a perfect case by which to examine corruption's effect on business-state relations.[44] Although the costs of corruption in Ukraine rival those in Kazakhstan, the latter's regulatory bureaucracy has less autonomy in applying state regulations. This means that when providing regulatory relief, Kazakh business associations more often have to tackle official regulatory norms. At the same time, high costs of bribery diminish the attractiveness of corruption as a means of regulatory relief and stimulate collective action despite the highly repressive political environment.

If, as Huntington (1968) suggested, corruption opens informal channels of interaction between individual firms and state bureaucrats, one might expect that fewer legitimate business associations would emerge in such a corrupt political system; however, since the mid-1990s the number of national, sectoral, and regional business associations in Kazakhstan has increased. Among Kazakh firms surveyed in the BEEPS, 15.6 percent belonged to business associations in 1999, about 25 percent in 2002, and 20 percent in 2005. By some estimates Kazakhstan now has more than 100 business associations, which is a large number for a country of 15 million residents (Batalov 2005). In a comprehensive search of the literature I came across sixty-eight active business associations: thirty-six were sectoral and thirty-two were general (see Appendix D).[45] The large number of Kazakh business associations and their low membership figures suggest competition among associations, duplication of functions, and organizational weakness.

Kazakh business representation closely resembles Russian and Ukrainian business representation in terms of membership, legal foundations, organizational forms, and activities. As in other examined countries, Kazakh business

---

[44] The corruption scandal that Western media and the dissident Kazakh press labeled "Kazakhgate" started with a 1997 lawsuit in the United Kingdom against three U.S. businessmen and Kazakhstan's prime minister. The investigation of illegal oil deals led to the freezing of Swiss bank accounts opened in the names of high-ranking Kazakh officials, including President Nazarbayev. Nazarbayev claimed that the frozen assets were part of Kazakhstan's secret oil fund rather than his personal wealth accumulated through oil concessions. In 2001 the U.S. State Department opened its own investigation of violations by U.S. businesspeople of the 1977 Foreign Corrupt Practices Act (FCPA). The investigation and the resulting indictments implicated high-ranking Kazakh officials in corruption (Stodghill 2006; Fidler and Chung 2006; Economist Intelligence Unit 2003).

[45] There are no precise data on the number of Kazakh business associations. Although Kazakh legislation strictly regulates the process of establishing civic associations and requires all organized groups to apply for official registration by state authorities, the registries are not particularly useful in identifying the number of business associations. Once registered, an association may stay on the books after it ceases to exist. Also, the names of Kazakh business associations often refer to them as unions, foundations, or civil organizations. To determine whether a civil association in fact represents business interests, one must examine the organization's statute, membership, and current activities. My analysis of Kazakh business associations is based on a sample of active rather than officially registered associations.

associations vary in their organizational bases and structures. As Appendix D shows, about half (thirty) are regional, and about half (thirty-six) are national. Many of the local and regional associations are integrated into larger national associations. Vertical integration characterizes such associations as the Chamber of Trade and Industry (CTI, functioning since 1965),[46] the Kazakh Business Forum (created in 1992), and the Employers' Confederation of the Republic of Kazakhstan (1999). However, many Kazakh business associations are integrated into horizontal networks rather than vertical structures, and some associations are both vertically and horizontally integrated. For example, the Kazakh Business Forum comprises regional offices (vertical integration) as well as member associations that maintain organizational and financial independence (horizontal integration). As in Russia, the Kazakh civil code allows for public entities – noncommercial associations – to be founded by other "legal entities," including other business associations. Partly for this reason, Kazakh business associations show overlapping memberships and organizational interlocking.

Another similarity among systems of business representation in Kazakhstan, Russia, and Ukraine are the bases on which associations form. Many Kazakh business associations do not seek to encompass diverse business interests. Unlike large cross-sector associations that claim to represent business in general, a growing number of Kazakh business associations are organized based on particular business sectors, professions, or issues. The Kazakh Bar Association and the National Association of Freight Forwarders are professionally based groups. The Association of Milk and Dairy Producers, the Tourism and Hotel Industry Association, and the Association of Construction Industry are sectoral groups. The Eurasian Industrial Association represents businesses in ore mining and metallurgy. The Association for the Development of Small and Medium Business focuses on issues common to all small and medium-sized businesses.

The composition of membership in Kazakh business associations depends on the type of association. Firms that join national umbrella associations tend to be large and resource-rich. Regional associations as well as many professional and sectoral groups are often joined by medium-size and small businesses, with the primary exceptions of such sectoral organizations being the Kazakh Energy Association and the Kazakh Banking Association. Although large companies make up a sizable portion of membership of the national umbrella associations, due to horizontal and vertical integration, small and medium-size companies constitute most of the membership of these associations. Thus, Kazakh business associations are not the exclusive "clubs of industry tycoons"

---

[46] The Soviet structure was reorganized as the CTI of the Republic of Kazakhstan in 1995 as a public (nonstate) nonprofit association with independent financing and a wider range of functions. International trade expertise that the chamber developed during Soviet times was expanded to include domestically oriented activities. In 1999 a number of regional chambers were formed to facilitate member recruitment and regional coverage.

Post-Communist Business Representation 83

as the media frequently portrays them ("Uspeshnyi Predprinimatel" 2005; Shahnazarov 2005).

Like Russian and Ukrainian business associations, Kazakh business associations attempt to lobby on behalf of their constituents. However, unlike in Ukraine where, over time, business associations have found expanding institutionalized methods of influence, Kazakh business associations are faced with shrinking institutional opportunities for lobbying. In the 1990s Kazakh business associations were participants in high-profile advisory bodies, and some of them enjoyed the support of the executive branch. President Nazarbayev regularly attended Business Forum congresses and frequently had closed-door meetings with business leaders. Although there is little evidence that such channels of representation led to any substantive collective benefits to the Kazakh business community as a whole, they provided opportunities to complain about bureaucrats' actions and the absence of business-friendly legislation (Batalov 2005; Yambaev 2005).

Executive-branch favoritism to Kazakh business associations ended in the late 1990s. The frequency of high-level meetings diminished, whereas formally business associations continued membership in advisory commissions and working groups under the president, central government, ministries, state agencies, and local administrations. Although business associations fell out of favor with the all-powerful executive branch, this did not prevent the growth of associational membership in subsequent years. In fact, according to the World Bank survey data, membership rates increased from 16 to 25 percent between 1999 and 2002.

For the most part, Kazakh business associations' lobbying is ineffective, especially when their demands clash with the economic interests of the ruling family and its cronies. Business interests aligned with interests of the ruling elite usually receive direct protection in the patron-client network outside institutionalized channels.[47] Those outside the inner power circle, however, frequently resort to organizational strategy for protection against direct or hidden expropriation.

In Kazakhstan the political and economic elite is so powerful and so shielded from accountability that lobbying by even the most resource-rich business associations tends to be ineffective. Consider the case of the Casino Association. In 2006 a new regulation was promulgated that would prohibit gambling in Almaty. The regulation designated a resort area on Lake Kapshagai as a casino park, a move that the casino industry welcomed. However, shortly before the regulation took effect, a powerful corporation with close ties to the ruling elite bought the land designated for the casino park. The Casino Association then campaigned against new zoning restrictions on gambling. Despite its attempts to shape public opinion and its lobbying at local and national levels, the

---

[47] Recent political assassinations and government reshuffles in Kazakhstan suggest that such client-based frameworks provide, at best, unreliable property rights and political influence.

84 *Building Business*

association failed to defend the gambling industry against the well-connected land speculator (Mikhailova 2006).

Due to the high concentration of political authority and strong insulation of the political elite from society, many highly visible associations that bring together prosperous businesses in rapidly developing sectors are ineffective at organizing successful lobbying efforts. Thus, rather than concentrating on lobbying or using other legitimate channels of influence, many Kazakh business associations focus on providing particularistic benefits to their members. As in the cases of Russian and Ukrainian business associations, their services include legal and technical consulting, assistance in finding new business partners, help developing business plans, marketing advice, and professional training. Kazakh business associations seem most effective in helping firms deal with low-level regulatory officials. Sharing information and expertise and building networks and reputation appear to better protect members' property rights than do sporadic lobbying campaigns. Low-profile local business associations often provide more consequential benefit to their members than do high-profile large associations.

Kazakhstan's severe authoritarianism has not prevented the formation of business associations, but it does severely limit the extent to which business associations can exert political influence and protect their members' interests. Compared to Russian, Ukrainian, and Croatian business associations, Kazakh business associations are much more limited in their use of public space. No Kazakh business association has organized or participated in a public protest against the government. Although Kazakh business associations use the media and participate in government-sponsored events, officially recognized public forums, and conventions, these activities do not appear to have any significant impact. Nevertheless, activities undertaken by the Almaty Association of Entrepreneurs and the Business Forum (discussed in Chapter 5) demonstrate that Kazakh business associations can help alleviate regulatory burden. The low degree of regulatory autonomy on the part of Kazakh street-level bureaucrats facilitates associations' success in providing member-directed regulatory relief.

3.6 Croatian Business Associations: From Corporatism to Pluralism

Croatia is an example of a highly participatory country. Its system of business representation was patterned after the "continental European" chamber systems. Such systems, based on compulsory membership in hierarchical peak associations, were adopted by a few post-communist countries, including Hungary, Slovakia, Albania, Moldova, and all successor states to the former Yugoslavia.[48] Croatian institutions and developments in respect to business

---

[48] Although initially a compulsory-membership system, Hungary, Slovakia, Slovenia, and Macedonia subsequently abandoned compulsory requirements.

Post-Communist Business Representation 85

representation exhibit strong similarities to other countries in this group and serve as a representative case of compulsory-membership systems. Croatia's system of business representation differs considerably from those of Russia, Ukraine, and Kazakhstan not only because of compulsory membership but also because this Balkan country has drastically different economic and institutional legacies stemming from the Yugoslav model of socialism widely regarded as the most liberal of all socialist economies. Croatia experienced early, fast economic reform, and, after an initial transitional setback, succeeded in building a democratic political system.[49] The system of Croatian interest representation deserves special attention because its different structure might have provided different challenges and opportunities for addressing business demands. The following analysis suggests that although Croatian business representation was initially different from the forms developing in Russia, Ukraine, and Kazakhstan, it later converged with the other analyzed countries in many respects.

Membership Levels

Among post-communist countries Croatia has the third-highest rate of participation in business associations (neighboring Slovenia has the highest rate, but it abandoned compulsory membership in 2006; Albania has the second-highest rate) (World Bank BEEPS 2005). In 1999, some 55 percent of the representative sample of Croatian businesses were members; that number grew to 77 percent by 2002; and 82 percent by 2005. Hungary had higher membership rates in 1999, but membership levels declined after compulsory participation was abolished. Such enthusiastic participation in business associations is linked to the compulsory chambers system. In the early 1990s Croatia adopted legislation that seemingly put business representation on a neocorporatist path. The major associations – the Croatian Chamber of Economy (CCE), Chamber of Trades and Crafts (CTC), and the Croatian Association of Cooperatives (CAC) – were created on the basis of compulsory membership for businesses satisfying the requirements of size, official registration, sector, and location.

Given the peak associations' claims for universal membership and representation, why the membership rates detected by the BEEP survey fall short of 100 percent seems puzzling. However, the explanation lies in the mechanisms of official enrollment in the compulsory associations. For the most part, membership in corresponding associations is automatic upon the official incorporation of an enterprise or licensing of entrepreneurial activity. Thus, many businesspeople are unaware of their membership status. Awareness about membership

---

[49] As a successor state to Yugoslavia, Croatia experienced a transition initially marked by war, ethnic violence, and political exclusion. Xenophobic politics and restrictions on political expression characterized the rule of its first president, Franjo Tudjman. Throughout the 1990s Freedom House rated Croatia as partially free. After Tudjman's death in 1999, power peacefully transferred to Stjepan Mesić. Competition between nationalistic and liberal parties has dominated post-2000 Croatian politics.

in associations usually comes as a result of a firm's joining a local or sectoral organization of the corresponding chamber, and these are the businesses' voluntary decisions (see below). Additionally, some spheres of economic activities that do not require special operation certificates, particularly in sectors dominated by small businesses, are exempt from the official membership requirement.

Compulsory-Membership Associations

The central peak organization of Croatian industry and commerce is the Croatian Chamber of Economy. The CCE traces its history to the nineteenth century. The Chamber was established in 1852 following the European tradition of chambers of commerce. With somewhat modified functions, it continued operating after Croatia was integrated into Yugoslavia. The CCE survived the socialist period as part of the Yugoslav chamber system. After Croatian independence from Yugoslavia, the Croatian Parliament enacted the Chamber of Economy Act (1991), which established the CCE as a business association independent of the government. At that time the CCE was designated as the only business association that represents all economic entities in Croatia. Every Croatian company that has at least fifty employees and is registered with the Commercial Court automatically becomes a CCE member.

The CCE's highest governing body is the assembly, whose members elect management and supervisory boards, the president, and five vice presidents responsible for different CCE activities. Local chambers appoint assembly members. Seven of the CCE's departments cover different economic sectors. The CCE has two centers responsible for education and statistics; five business centers that implement specialized programs; a permanent arbitration court; a conciliation center, which mediates in minor business conflicts; and a court of honor, which enforces the Responsible Business Practice Code, a code of business ethics that goes beyond rules enforceable through the court of law.

Croatian legislation provides the CCE with institutionalized channels of access to political decision makers. CCE participation in government institutions, including the ministries and cabinet, is organized on either a permanent basis or upon invitation to working sessions and meetings. The CCE is required to prepare position statements for parliamentary committees on economic, budgetary, financial, labor, and social-policy issues (Croatian Chamber of Economy 2006). The CCE also routinely provides economic information to parliamentary committees and individual legislators. Written reports, position statements, proposals, and other materials the CCE issues are known as "joint proposals of the business community." The CCE also commissions studies by research institutions. Its official status as the representative body of Croatian industry has allowed the CCE direct participation in international negotiations, including negotiations regarding (1) Croatia's accession to the World Trade Organization, (2) signing of the Stabilization and Association Agreement with the European Union (EU), and (3) joining the Central European Free Trade Association and the European Free Trade Agreement.

The CCE's central office traditionally focuses on economic relations with other countries. It organizes international fairs and exhibitions as well as facilitates information-sharing and collaboration between Croatian firms and foreign partners. The CCE functions as a designated agency to enforce the implementation of the Agreement on Trade in Textiles between Croatia and the EU. The CCE also represents Croatia in several regional agreements, including the Stability Pact, Central European Adriatic-Ionian, and Southeast European Cooperative Initiatives.

Further, the CCE performs regulatory and certifying functions in various fields of international commerce and transportation. For example, in 2004 special government regulations authorized the CCE to issue and validate import-export documentation such as certificates of origin and export permits. The Road Transportation Act (NN 178/04) authorized the CCE to issue transport permits for international goods, coordinate passenger transportation schedules, harmonize bus fares, and participate in occupational certification exams.

In the sphere of domestic market regulation, in 1997, the CCE began voluntary quality-control programs in which Croatian products that meet CCE quality, environmental, and ergonomic standards are labeled "Croatian Quality" or "Croatian Creation." The labeling encourages informational accuracy, reduces transaction costs, and builds producers' reputations. The CCE tries to ensure impartial, professional evaluation of products.

Growing Pluralism and Alternative Organizations
The CCE's representative and regulatory functions were expected to integrate the business community into political processes and lead to beneficial self-regulation. However, as soon as the CCE formed, businesses voiced dissatisfaction with the compulsory-membership requirement and its inability to protect and promote the interests of diverse business sectors adequately. This dissatisfaction has led to spontaneous self-organization of rival business associations. A number of sector-specific (the Association of Travel Agencies, Association of Croatian Exporters) and cross-sector (the Croatian Employers' Association) organizations emerged to represent businesses that felt the CCE was ignoring their interests and goals.

The CCE was criticized for giving little recognition and virtually no representation to the small-business sector and emerging industries. In response, in 1994 the CCE established forty professional associations and eighty-seven specialized groups as semiautonomous subdivisions. Membership in such groups is voluntary and requires additional dues. Sector-specific subdivisions are governed by their own charters, which the members can amend, although the law provided for a compulsory membership of such sectoral groups in the CCE.

County chambers of commerce heavily rely on activities of voluntary-membership business associations that focus on particular business sectors or professions. Many CCE activities, such as developing business proposals, providing information on local economic conditions, and monitoring the effects of government policies, are conducted through such associations. In cooperation with the central CCE office, trade associations organize sectoral fairs, monitor economic trends within sectors, develop specific regulatory propositions, and directly participate in advisory bodies of various government agencies.

In addition to the elaborate organizational structure of the CCE, special legislation established two alternative compulsory-membership organizations to represent businesses with cooperative property, small businesses, and crafts. Membership in these associations substitutes for CCE membership. The staffs, budgets, and organizational structures of these associations are separate from those of the CCE, although in many ways their organizational principles parallel those of the CCE.

The 1993 Trade Law, which outlined regulations for entrepreneurial activities of physical entities in service industries and various spheres of production, created the CTC, a compulsory-membership association of craftspeople who become members when they register through the county's crafts registries.[50] The law restricts local and sectoral associations of craftspeople to one per geographical location and sphere of commercial activity. The law prescribes these associations' internal structures and governance mechanisms and broadly outlines their spheres of activities. The Ministry of Craft, Small, and Medium Entrepreneurship ensures that the CTC complies with the law, and the CTC in turn ensures that the statutes of local and sectoral associations do so. In 1994 the CTC convened its assembly and took over the property of the socialist-era Union of Craft Organizations in Zagreb and provincial cities.

In keeping with provisions of the Law on Cooperatives, the CAC was established in 1995 as a compulsory-membership association of Croatian cooperatives and sectoral and territorial cooperative associations. All cooperatives registered in the Court Register automatically become CAC members.

---

[50] The CTC dates back to 1879, when Zagreb craftspeople and merchants organized a crafts convention. The Crafts Union, the first union of Croatian craftspeople, was organized in the 1906 struggle for formal recognition from state authorities. In the interwar period the Crafts Union strengthened its base by founding a crafts museum, local crafts schools, and philanthropic and credit organizations. With the establishment of a socialist economy, the Crafts Union's operations were banned and its property nationalized. Private economic activity of small scope was not completely outlawed in Yugoslavia, but starting in the late 1940s most artisan production was transferred to the social (primarily cooperative) sector. Occupational chambers, which favored state and cooperative enterprises, were established. Chambers of economy replaced them in 1962. In 1980 an association of craftspeople was revived in the form of the Union of Craft Organizations. In 1992 this association inherited the property that had belonged to the first Croatian Crafts Union and that had been nationalized in 1947 (see Croatian Chamber of Trades and Crafts, http://www.hok.hr/hok/).

Post-Communist Business Representation

TABLE 3.8. *Organizational Structure of Croatian Business Associations*

	Hierarchical Membership Structure	Directs Membership	Hierarchical Membership Structure
Compulsory membership	Croatian Chamber of Economy; Chamber of Trades and Crafts; Croatian Association of Cooperatives	Croatian Chamber of Economy; Chamber of Trades and Crafts; Croatian Association of Cooperatives	Croatian Chamber of Economy; Chamber of Trades and Crafts; Croatian Association of Cooperatives
	↑	↑	↑
Voluntary membership	Territorial associations (chambers)		Sectoral associations (chambers)
	↑		↑
	Firms and individual entrepreneurs registered in the court or crafts registers		

The CAC encompasses twelve regional and sectoral associations, such as the Croatian Union of Housing Cooperatives, the Cooperative Union of Slavonia, and the Croatian Association of Credit Cooperatives (Bartolić 2006). Table 3.8 shows the organizational structure of three Croatian peak associations that incorporate compulsory and voluntary membership.

Voluntary Tier

Croatian businesspeople have complained that a top-down, compulsory-membership organizational structure is unwieldy, does not adequately represent the business community or meet its needs, and allows little room for businesses to challenge the official state position. In the early 2000s, as compared to the post-communist levels, Croatian businesspeople were 30 percent less satisfied with the quality of services their associations provided. This reflects an overall trend found across all compulsory-membership systems, in which member satisfaction is considerably lower compared to voluntary-membership regimes (Table 3.9).

Those dissatisfied with the official peak organizations have developed voluntary-membership associations that, over time, became formidable rivals to the top-down official associations. Despite the introduction of formal institutions of the compulsory-membership system, voluntary organizations of business representations emerged in Croatia as early as 1992 to serve different sectors and focus on various issues that range from lobbying for the EU import quotas to building web-based business contacts databases. Some of these associations have found competing with the compulsory chamber system to be difficult because business participation in voluntary organizations would

90   *Building Business*

TABLE 3.9. *Member Satisfaction with Associational Services in Countries with Voluntary and Compulsory Membership*

Type of Service*	Voluntary Membership**	Compulsory Membership
Lobbying government	1.34	.917
Dispute resolution (with state officials, workers, business partners)	1.37	.853
Foreign-markets information	1.66	1.26
Accreditation, standardization, reputational benefits	1.86	1.32
Information on government regulations	1.84	1.46
Domestic market information	1.9	1.46

* *Source:* World Bank, BEEPS 2002, 2005.
** Evaluations range from 0 ("no value") to 4 ("critical value to the firm").

double businesses' annual contributions. Also, legislation that resulted from the 1994 organizational reform within the CCE mandated that voluntary-membership, sector-based business associations join the CCE. In effect, many voluntary-membership associations formed through business-community initiative have become absorbed into the official CCE system.

Nevertheless, a number of independently developed voluntary-membership associations have been quite successful in maintaining their autonomy from the CCE and expanding their membership.[51] In 1992 newly established travel agencies organized the Croatian Association of Travel Agencies. The association grew and expanded its activities to include a travel database, recommended quality-standards control, a mandatory members' code of business ethics, a customer-oriented database of services and facilities, and a range of research and lobbying initiatives. In an interview Executive Director Maja Stanić indicated that the association attracts members because it creates a space of shared information and combats unfair competition within the travel industry (Stanić 2006). The official chamber system failed to provide valuable member benefits to meet the industry's needs. Instead of relying on the CCE bureaucracy, travel agencies created a bottom-up alternative.

Perhaps one of the most significant voluntary-membership Croatian business associations is the Croatian Employers' Association (CEA). In 1993 a German investor and a few prominent Croatian businesspeople founded the CEA as a voluntary, nonprofit, independent organization. Ivica Todorić served as the first president. Through his networking, the CEA attracted a large

---

[51] Unfortunately, there are no reliable estimates of the number of voluntary associations. Officially, Croatia has over 500 industry groups. Most of these are affiliates of the official chamber system. The official figures, however, do not allow one to distinguish between compulsory and voluntary-membership groups.

Post-Communist Business Representation

number of entrepreneurs. In 2006 the CEA' s membership comprised more than 5,000 businesses employing in excess of 400,000 workers from all parts of Croatia.

Organized as a confederation of individual businesses and twenty-three voluntary, sector-based associations, the CEA has democratic internal governance.[52] Its statute declares its primary goals as representing members' interests and protecting private property. Since the 1994 establishment of the National Economic and Social Council, the CEA has been the only employers' association that the government and trade unions have included in tripartite negotiations and agreements. The CEA' s participation in collective bargaining has been mainly in the areas of labor and social legislation.[53]

The CEA is an active player in the sphere of industrial relations. It conducts studies, makes proposals, and organizes conventions on protection of private property, economic development, and regulation of the market economy. Since the EU accession negotiations opened up a possibility for Croatian integration in the EU, the CEA has prioritized issues relating to harmonizing Croatian industrial legislation with EU practices and creating a favorable investment climate. The association maintains a center for EU pre-accession programs; disseminates information including *Eukonomist* magazine and specialized reports through its Web site; conducts expert studies; and maintains a dispute-mediation center. In 2004 the CEA launched a specialized project that focuses on developing best-practice recommendations in the sphere of corporate governance.

The system of business representation that developed in Croatia after its independence from Yugoslavia seemingly presents a drastically different model of representation. Still, many similarities in strategies, organizational forms, and activities business associations have undertaken can be seen in Croatia, Ukraine, Russia, and Kazakhstan. Based on nearly universal business participation, large compulsory-membership business associations have promised greater participation, cohesion, and representation that would all translate into a stronger position for the business community vis-à-vis the state. This, however, did not preclude the grass-roots organizational development on the part of the business community. As the official compulsory system was shaping up, alternative voluntary associations took on the roles that the official peak organizations forsook or did not perform adequately. Self-organization of rival associations and the creation of alternative associations to represent small businesses and cooperatives brought about a de facto annulment of the CCE monopoly on business representation and introduced principles of voluntarism and competition.

---

[52] A new CEA member may join a sector-based association in his or her industry. The sectoral associations have independent charters, specialized functions, and differing membership fees.

[53] Similarly to other analyzed cases, in Croatia the national organization that represents employers in tripartite negotiations is a voluntary association that possesses few institutional mechanisms for enforcing collective agreements.

92   *Building Business*

Chapter 6 offers an explanation as to why compulsory-membership organizations in many post-communist countries fail to meet the demands of their constituents, thereby giving rise to voluntary-membership groups.

3.7 The Main Features of Post-Communist Business Associations

This chapter descriptively analyzed post-communist systems of business representation. It used quantitative data to put the post-communist business associations and regulatory regimes in a larger comparative perspective. It also demonstrated that there is a considerable degree of variation across post-communist countries that makes them suitable for cross-national quantitative research. Business associations also vary within countries. To illustrate important sources of cross-national and subnational variation, this chapter presented a qualitative analysis of four country cases that were strategically chosen to capture important differences in the institutional, political, and economic milieu. Country cases demonstrate that although political institutions affect business-state relations in a profound way, they do not provide convincing explanations for the differential rate of membership in business associations; instead, features of the post-communist business environment line up well with the observed variations.

Analysis has shown that although countries' politics, legal institutions, and economic challenges differentially influenced the development of business associations, post-communist business associations have much in common. They are numerous, in most cases are open to any business who wants to join, often have cross-cutting membership, organize on geographical and sectoral bases, and provide similar types of benefits to their members. These features justify comparing them across national borders. The next chapter will engage in such cross-national quantitative comparative research and will treat firms' membership in business associations as meaning the same thing across different countries.

Because of their high visibility and political clout, national peak organizations (e.g., chambers of commerce) have attracted the most scholarly analysis and journalistic curiosity. Such selective attention, however, generally distorts the image of typical post-communist business associations. Oftentimes, business associations are portrayed as detrimental oligarchies, large hierarchical organizations, or collusive industry arrangements. The descriptive analysis of origins, organizational structures, membership, and activities of business associations in four post-communist countries dispels these myths. Each of the studied countries shows considerable pluralism and competition among numerous business associations. This is true even in compulsory-membership systems in which the law requires firms to join officially designated groups, as in Croatia. Even there, businesspeople have developed multiple and competing business groups that present organizational alternatives to the official chambers. The vast majority of post-communist business associations are

Post-Communist Business Representation 93

local, regional, or sector-based. The analysis points to the existence of business associations in sectors rarely associated with powerful economic interests. Although rent-seeking cannot be ruled out as one of the areas of their activities, post-communist business associations oftentimes defend legitimate interests, promote economic competition and efficiency, and provide valuable resources to firms in a wide range of business sectors.

Most importantly, the country cases analyzed in this chapter showed that although only a few associations are able to secure collective benefits to firms in a particular locality, region, or business sector, the vast majority concentrates on the provision of benefits specific to their members. These benefits consist of networking, information, training, and other assistance that best fits the definition of club goods. Moreover, associations' political influence does not seem to ensure stable membership growth. This piece of information is central to the defensive organization theory. According to its logic, provision of particularistic benefits helps overcome the problem of collective action and promotes organizational survival. The analysis of the country cases in this chapter provides evidence to support this notion. By concentrating their activities on selective incentives, business associations can form and expand their membership despite competition from the officially organized compulsory-membership institutions and direct (nonassociational) channels of business influence, and they can also expand in political systems unreceptive to business demands. The qualitative analysis has supported the notion that the main function of post-communist business associations is not lobbying or otherwise gaining access to policy formation but rather subtler representation by providing information, offering expert opinion, maintaining a positive public image, and providing member-oriented services. This notion is crucial for the explanation of businesses' collective action advanced in this book.

4

Business Environment and Business Organization

The Quantitative Approach

In the new capitalist economies under study, the regulatory power of the state remains quite heavy. Clearly, regulation does not completely wither away during the transition to a market economy. In fact, virtually all capitalist economies are regulated in one form or another by nonmarket forces. In the post-communist world, though, the subject, mechanisms, and objectives of state regulation often were blindly transferred from the socialist past with little recognition of the new capitalist realities. In many countries the state regulatory machine has bestowed enormous power on its officials, who use it to their personal advantage. Those officials who have the most power vis-à-vis economic actors subjected to regulatory restrictions often resort to corruption, graft, and outright expropriation of enterprises' resources.

Chapter 2 argued that when the state fails to defend businesses against economic uncertainties, unstructured markets, and bureaucratic extortion, business associations emerge as institutions of private protection and governance. In other words, business associations are forming in post-communist Eastern Europe and Eurasia as defense mechanisms against predatory bureaucrats and the major uncertainties associated with underprovision of essential collective goods. This chapter substantiates this claim with empirical evidence. Through a cross-national quantitative analysis that spans from the late 1990s to the mid-2000s, I evaluate the effect of regulatory pressure, corruption, and anti-corruption measures as well as industry and country characteristics related to the nature of regulation.

Both corruption and interest-group influence are among the toughest subjects for quantitative analysis. The difficulty with corruption is that, because it is an illegal and shameful activity, people are reluctant to admit their involvement. This becomes particularly problematic in the large-N studies that traditionally rely on empirical measures of behavior and attitude. Because we are usually most interested in actual participation in and attitudes toward corrupt transactions, the risk is that subjects will underreport their engagement in or exaggerate their repugnance for corrupt behavior. Although we have a good sense of the direction of the bias in the responses, we have less confidence in the magnitudes of this response bias across different types of respondents. These problems are less detrimental to qualitative analyses that rely on media coverage, corruption scandals, records of prosecution of corrupt officials, and direct observation.

Interest groups present another challenge for quantitative research. Although case studies are often criticized for offering too small a basis for inference and providing little evidence for the support of theoretical arguments (Salisbury 1994), the lack of clear operational definitions for capturing the nature of the interest-groups' activities in different institutional and social contexts often precludes the development of large-N analysis. Organized interests are particularly hard to study cross-nationally because the drastically different institutional and legal environments that shape their composition, organizational forms, and venues of influence often make identifying relevant comparative categories difficult. As a result, case studies remain "virtually the only way to do research in this realm" (Salisbury 1994, 13). Of course, qualitative case studies of particular interest groups do not lend themselves to more general claims about other groups. The problem of quantitative analysis is further exacerbated in many post-communist countries because of high rates of organizational attrition, ambiguous incorporation records, and de jure continuation of the de facto nonexistent associations. Realizing the limitations of a quantitative approach, this chapter presents cross-national quantitative evidence based on a survey of business elites. Other chapters of this book rely on qualitative analysis. Although each empirical approach taken in this study – large-N statistical model, country-level descriptive analysis, and case studies of interest groups – has its problems, finding consistent evidence across all approaches will reinforce our confidence in the validity of inference.

Recognizing the difficulties associated with applying quantitative methodology to this subject matter, this chapter relies on the best available cross-national data to investigate the effects of regulatory bureaucratic environments on the development of business associations. I have developed statistical tests of the propositions outlined in Chapter 2. In a hierarchical model I bring together microlevel and macrolevel factors often cited as promoting successful collective action and evaluate them against the key variables capturing the effects of a regulatory and bureaucratic environment. Next, I address one of the most pervasive but frequently ignored problems of the social sciences – the problem of endogeneity that arises from the fact that treatment (the independent variable) cannot be randomly assigned to the subject population; that is, the firms that decide to join business associations may differ systematically from other firms in ways that also make them likely to experience different levels of corruption, thereby biasing the statistical analysis. In what follows, the chapter presents additional evidence on the over-time dynamics of business

96 *Building Business*

participation in associations, member satisfaction with associational services, and cross-sectoral patterns of associational development in Russia. These provide auxiliary support for the defensive organization argument. Chapter 5 will further investigate the causal mechanism behind defensive organization by examining qualitative evidence on how post-communist business associations are able to provide protection from stringent and corrupt state regulations.

4.1 Micro- and Macrocorrelates of Organizational Participation: A Hierarchical Model

To test the effects of the institutional business environment on group formation, I evaluate a series of statistical models using different estimation methods and data. Table 4.1 summarizes the testable hypotheses developed in Chapter 2 and identifies the level of analysis at which they operate. In what follows, I subject Hypotheses 1a, 2, 3, and 4 to statistical tests. Testing Hypotheses 1b, 5, and 6 requires detailed association-level data and longer cross-national time series that do not exist at this point. Still, with the quantitative data at hand, later in the chapter I discuss the indirect evidence that generally supports the hypotheses operating at the aggregate level or pertaining to the behavior of business associations.

Data

To capture business participation in associations, I use the Business Environment and Enterprise Performance Survey (BEEPS) data.[1] A number of questions in the survey address the issues of organizational membership; a wide array of questions specifically target regulatory environment and corruption.[2] The question

---

[1] The 1999 survey covered 4,104 firms in twenty-four post-communist countries (Albania, Armenia, Azerbaijan, Belarus, Bosnia (including Republika Srpska), Bulgaria, Croatia, Czech Republic, Estonia, Macedonia, Georgia, Hungary, Kazakhstan, Kyrgyz Republic, Latvia, Lithuania, Moldova, Poland, Romania, Russia, Slovak Republic, Slovenia, Ukraine, and Uzbekistan). In 2002, a total of 6,667 firms were surveyed followed by 9,655 enterprises in 2005. These firms were located in twenty-six countries – Serbia and Montenegro and Tajikistan in addition to the twenty-four countries listed in the BEEPS 1999 survey.

[2] Although on the country level, BEEPS was designed as a self-weighted sample, enterprise quotas for large, state-owned, and foreign enterprises were imposed to meet the research objectives of the conducting institution. The sample size of various parameters resulting from the self-weighted universe was often outside the BEEPS minimum quotas for state-owned, foreign, and large firms. In cases in which quotas were applied, latitudinal parameters (i.e., subsector, size, or location) had to be reweighted with the revised total samples, but the proportions of the original self-weighted universe were preserved. As a result, the representativeness of the sample to the population of firms was distorted. Therefore large, state-, and foreign-owned enterprises are overrepresented in respect to the population of enterprises. Additionally, firms in small countries have the same probability weight as the firms in larger countries. See discussion on BEEPS sampling at "The Business Environment and Enterprise Performance Survey (BEEPS) 2005: A Brief Report on Observations, Experiences and Methodology from the Survey," Synovate, July 2005, http://siteresources.worldbank.org/INTECAREGTOPANTCOR/Resources/beeps05r.pdf.

Business Environment and Business Organization

TABLE 4.1. *Summary of Theoretical Expectations*

Hypotheses	Level of analysis	Operationalization of IDV	DV	Effect
H1a: The greater the costs of complying with regulation, the lower firms' propensity to join business associations.	Firm	Regulations of entry (number)	Membership	–
H1b: Business associations operating in more-invasive regulatory systems provide greater benefits to their members.	Association	Regulations of entry (number)	Member benefits	+
H2: Effective anticorruption measures increase the likelihood that firms will participate in business associations.	Firm	Confidence in the rule of law	Membership	+
H3: When bureaucracy is constrained to apply economic regulations in a uniform and consistent manner, regulations should suppress collective action. When bureaucratic enforcement is capricious, the official regulatory burden should not affect collective action.	Firm	Agency Audit Institutions × Regulations of entry (number)	Membership	– /0
H4: All other things held constant, the costlier the bribery, the more attractive is membership as a means of obtaining regulatory relief.	Firm	Average bribe (% sales)	Membership	+
H5: Over time, associations expand their resources and functions and offer greater benefits to members.	Association	Time after transition	Member benefits	+
H6: As organizational membership grows, corruption decreases.	Country	Membership density	Levels of corruption	–

98   *Building Business*

about membership in business organizations reveals that 38.2 percent of firms participating in the survey belonged to at least one association. Membership figures increased from 26.5 percent in 1999 to 42.8 percent in 2002, followed by a slight drop to 40 percent in 2005, which is within the margin of error.[3] The survey also reveals a vast divergence among levels of organizational membership in different countries. Figure 3.5 in Chapter 3 illustrates the extent of cross-national variation and dynamics over time.

Although the BEEPS survey offers a diachronic perspective on the post-communist business environment of the late 1990s to early 2000s, it does not trace the experiences of specific firms over this period.[4] Testing hypotheses about the effects of the bureaucratic environment on participation in business associations with such snapshot data is not a straightforward exercise. The theory of defensive organization (see also the empirical case studies assembled in Chapter 5) suggests that successful industry associations provide particularistic benefits of protection from corruption as well as legal and logistical assistance with regulatory compliance. In other words, they alter the business environment: once a firm joins a business association, a range of member services available through membership makes running the business easier. As a result, particularistic benefits provided by the association to attract new members later influence the individual experience of firm managers and owners. In methodological terms we are dealing with a feedback effect or the case of endogeneity.[5]

A glance at the correlates of associational membership (Table 4.2) illustrates the point. The table reports bivariate and partial correlations between associational membership and managerial responses to the survey questions addressing regulatory environment (A) and bureaucratic corruption (B). The first conclusion to be drawn from the table is that the relationships among individual-level measures of corruption, regulatory burden, and organizational membership are not constant across different survey questions. Some are consistent, whereas others are contradictory to Hypotheses 1a, 2, and 4.

---

[3] The means are computed using country-level base weights. Due to the unavailability of detailed sampling frames across all countries, I was unable to construct comprehensive weighting schemes. Still, for the country samples for which I did have the sample frames, the application of weights resulted in a negligible change of statistics. To avoid potential problems associated with the deviation from strict randomization, in the multivariate analysis I employ customary remedies.

[4] Although repeated at three-year intervals, the subsequent rounds of the survey do not form a true panel, making it impossible to trace firms' membership status over time. Still, one can compare the responses to the similarly worded questions across the three installments.

[5] On the more granular conceptual level, however, the relationship is not totally circular. Although the perceptions of the business environment in general (often formed by the actual experiences of dealing with the regulatory institutions) may precipitate the decision to join business associations, it is not the membership per se but rather the quality and extent of member services that might alter the managerial experience of complying with the rules and regulations as well as encounters with bureaucratic corruption later on. Thus, the feedback effect is conditional on business associations' actual ability to reduce the costs of regulatory compliance.

Business Environment and Business Organization 99

As Table 4.2 suggests, there is a strong empirical link between regulatory burden and associational membership, as measured by various instruments. The members of business associations, on average, experience a more favorable rather than more obstructive regulatory environment. They are less likely to report taxation as being a burden to their business and find obtaining information about regulatory requirements to be easier. These relationships are generally consistent with theoretical expectations. At the same time, contrary to the defensive organization hypotheses, associational membership is correlated with more managerial time spent dealing with rules and regulations and greater overall levels of regulatory pressure. Table 4.1 also shows that members of business associations are less likely to report bureaucratic extortion and less aware of the current bribe schedule, and they believe that bribe amounts are significantly lower than nonmembers report. However, they are more likely to report a higher frequency of bribery in their environment. How does one make sense of these contradictory perceptions?

To dissect this interlocking web of correlates of associational membership, we have to examine the multidirectional causal linkage between the business environment and associational membership and, more specifically, the feedback effect of associational membership on a firm's experiences with the regulatory environment. The problem with using the individual-level measures of regulatory burden is that we do not know when a firm joined an association or whether its perceptions of regulatory burden were formed before or after that event. If the decision to join an industry organization is a relatively recent event (for the most part it is, because associational membership is drawn predominantly from new enterprises), managerial perceptions of regulatory burden are likely to reflect pre-membership experience as well as the current state of affairs. If the change in membership status is a distant event, managerial assessment of regulatory environment should be a function of membership (more specifically, member benefits) to a greater extent.

It would be logical to expect that at least some individual-level measures of regulatory burden reflect a firm's membership status, making them the outcome rather than the causal factors. Some correlations in Table 4.2 reflect this reverse causal link between associational membership and bureaucratic environment, mediated by particularistic member benefits associations provide. The positive relationship between organizational membership and managerial time spent on dealing with regulations, for instance, squares well with the incentive-driven membership theory: the information-sharing, training, and consultative functions of business associations are targeted at enterprise managers, making them more involved (and thus spending more time) in ensuring regulatory compliance. The observations that members of business associations find obtaining information about regulations to be easier, see tax administration as less problematic, and on average pay fewer bribes are also consistent with the idea that particularistic benefits provided by associations help enterprises navigate through regulatory regimes and make them more immune to bureaucratic extortion.

100   *Building Business*

TABLE 4.2. *Bivariate and Partial Correlations Between Individual-Level Measures of Regulatory and Bureaucratic Environment and Membership in Business Associations*

A. Regulatory environment	Bivariate correlation	Partial correlation^
Information on the laws and regulations affecting my firm is easy to obtain.	.0876***	.0992***
Interpretations of regulations affecting my firm are consistent and predictable.	.0111	−.0298*
Tax regulations/administration are problematic for operation and growth of my business.	−.0473***	−.0454***
On a four-point scale, how problematic are the following for the operation and growth of your business: business licensing, customs/foreign trade regulations in your country, labor regulations, foreign currency/exchange regulations, environmental regulations, fire/safety regulations, tax regulations/ administration?	.0470***	.0735***
Percentage of senior management's time per year spent in dealing with government officials about the application and interpretation of laws and regulations.	.0254***	.0365**

B. Bureaucratic Environment		
It is common for firms in my line of business to have to pay some irregular "additional payments" to public officials to get things done.	−.0306***	−.0264
Firms in my line of business usually know in advance about how much this "additional payment" is.	−.0304***	−.0103
On average, what percent of revenues do firms like yours typically pay per annum in unofficial payments to public officials?	−.0640***	−.0594***
How often do firms like yours nowadays need to make extra, unofficial payments to public officials for any of the following: to get connected to public services, electricity, and telephone; to get licenses and permits; to deal with taxes and tax collection; to gain government contracts; when dealing with customs/ imports; when dealing with courts; to influence the content of new laws, decrees, or regulations; other?	.0268***	.029*
When firms in your industry do business with the government, how much of the contract value would they typically offer in addition to official payments to secure the contract?	−.0082	.0101

Note: ^with respect to all other variables presented in the table; * = p <.05, ** = p <.01, *** = p <.001(two-tailed significance test).

Business Environment and Business Organization 101

Another methodologically relevant point is the difference in wording between questions in groups A and B, Table 4.1. Because of the sensitivity of the subject of corruption (its illegality and social stigma), all corruption-related questions in the BEEPS survey refer to experiences of "firms like yours," rather than ask for a first-person response. The survey questions about regulatory environment, however, target the individual experiences of interviewed firm managers. Corruption-related questions, therefore, solicit impressionistic responses that rely on beliefs about corruption. Such questions are more likely to gauge the overall bureaucratic climate as perceived by industry practitioners. In contrast, questions about regulatory environment target firms' specific experiences. The differences between these impressionistic and experiential categories are fundamental: the former reflect beliefs whereas the latter reflect the actual practices surrounding the regulatory and bureaucratic environment. It is logical to expect that although impressionistic, belief-based responses are more likely to capture the overall bureaucratic climate experienced by members and nonmembers alike, experience-based instruments are more likely to suffer from the feedback effect of member benefits on the business environment and capture the outcome rather than the cause of membership.

Distinguishing between the aggregate-level measures of regulatory pressure and the experience of individual firms offers a way out of the endogeneity problem. In testing Hypothesis 1a, stating that high regulatory pressures suppress organizational membership, aggregate-level rather than individual-level data on the severity of business regulation are more appropriate.[6] In what follows, the stringency of regulatory regimes is operationalized by the "hard" data on the number of business regulations on market entry. These data come from the World Bank's Doing Business Project.[7] Although the Bank has recently started publishing the data on the number of procedures involved in dealing with construction permits, registering property, paying taxes, trading across borders, and enforcing contracts, these data are not available for the period covered by the earlier BEEPS surveys. For 1999 I use the data from Djankov et al. (2002), who pioneered the Doing Business methodology and collected their data on the number of entry procedures in the late 1990s. For 2002 and 2005 I use the World Bank data on the number of entry procedures. These procedures are identified from official government publications, reports of development agencies, and government Web pages, making the data reflect the official rather than unofficial regulatory practices. As a robustness check, I also use a count of regulatory procedures across all available categories for 2002 and 2005 only as

---

[6] Chapter 2 argued that extensive regulations generally impede the formation and entrenchment of associations because regulatory relief is more difficult to provide in a high-cost regulatory regime. In essence, when the regulatory environment is harsh, there should be fewer associations offering commensurate selective incentives, and thus, membership levels should be suppressed.

[7] Doing Business data are available at http://www.doingbusiness.org.

well as the measures of time and monetary costs of regulatory compliance from the 2006 Doing Business database, and I obtain similar results.[8]

In addition to being independent from any regulatory relief provided by business associations, the Doing Business data have another important advantage. Hypothesis 3 reflects the theoretical distinction between official regulatory costs and bureaucracy-imposed "unofficial" burden, both of which shape the business environment but in dissimilar ways. Survey responses of business leaders and country experts are designed to reflect the actual level of regulatory burden businesses experience. This, according to the argument advanced in Chapter 2, comprises the official costs of regulatory policy (the variable of interest) as well as the unofficial costs, including the cost of the red tape that bureaucrats create in order to extort more bribes. Most perception-based measures of regulatory burden do not allow one to differentiate between these official and unofficial costs; the methodology behind the Doing Business data ensures that they reflect only the official costs of regulatory compliance that state regulations impose.

Hypothesis 2 suggests a positive relationship between effective and certain punishment for corrupt transactions and the propensity to engage in collective action. The survey (individual-level) measure of the rule of law is used to capture the underlying concept of the effective legal deterrence against corruption.[9]

To test Hypothesis 4, postulating a positive relationship between the cost of bureaucratic graft and firms' propensity to join associations, I operationalize corruption in terms of its reported cost (as a percentage of firm's sales). This allows me to capture the extent of firm-specific bureaucratic burden. Because of the sensitivity of corruption-related questions (few respondents would be likely to admit personal engagement in corrupt transactions), again the survey question asks participants to evaluate the experience of "firms like yours" rather than report their actual encounters with corrupt officials.[10] Because the cost of bribery is endogenous to other characteristics of business environment – in the formal model it depends on the level of anticorruption efforts as well as the extent of regulatory intervention – I follow the instrumental variable approach.

With respect to Hypothesis 3, suggesting that the official costs of regulatory compliance should have a weaker effect on collective action when the bureaucrats are free to alter the regulatory burden, the model includes an interaction

---

[8] These do not vary across time and are temporally posterior to the survey observations. Hence, in this chapter I use the number of regulatory procedures as the primary way to operationalize official regulatory costs.

[9] The survey question reads, *To what degree do you agree with this statement? 'I am confident that the legal system will uphold my contract and property rights in business disputes.'* The responses range from 1 (strongly disagree) to 6 (fully agree).

[10] The survey question reads: *On average, what percent of revenues do firms like yours typically pay per annum in unofficial payments to public officials?*

Business Environment and Business Organization 103

between country-level measures of bureaucratic constraint and the official regulatory burden. Because both concepts are defined in terms of the state policy and institutions, country-level measures are most appropriate. Bureaucratic constraint to apply regulations in the way specified by the law is assessed through the Global Integrity (GI) country-level ranking of the effectiveness of government oversight institutions (Global Integrity 2006) and the Governance Matters voice and accountability score.[11]

The GI ranking for "Government Oversight and Controls" category is based on the country-expert assessments of the strength and effectiveness of national ombudsman and supreme audit institutions as well as the fairness and capacity of customs, tax, licensing, and financial sector regulatory authorities. The GI aggregates across these components and produces an overall oversight score, which serves as a proxy for institutional constraints on bureaucratic ability to impose additional regulatory burden. The original measure of audit effectiveness was collected in 2004, but only Russia and Ukraine were included in the worldwide sample. In what follows, I use the 2006 data, as it has wider coverage. For countries not covered in 2006, I use later reports. One limitation of these data is that they are measured after the surveys were conducted and do not vary over time. I also employ a one-year lag on the Worldwide Governance Indicators measure of Voice and Accountability as an alternative operational definition of bureaucratic constraint.

Firm-Level Controls

A number of firm and sector characteristics are believed to make some enterprises more likely to overcome the problem of collective action involved in forming business associations. In explaining why some firms join business associations whereas others do not, it is important to consider a firm's size, ownership structure, and prior experiences with regulatory state agencies. Another important aspect is to examine characteristics of the groups of firms in particular sectors and industries.

One can expect a firm's type of ownership and experience under a state-controlled economy to affect its participation in business organizations. Managers of enterprises formed after the collapse of central planning might have better incentives to join business associations. State-owned enterprise managers have well-established relationships with state agencies, ministries, and traditional trading partners (Huber and Worgotter 1998) and thus should be less interested in seeking new institutional venues for networking, political and bureaucratic connections, information-sharing, and reputation building. One can also expect that foreign-owned firms have a greater propensity to join associations. Foreign managers might have a greater cultural predisposition to join associations and a greater need for publicly legitimating their businesses.

---

[11] The latter data are available from the World Bank (1996–2010) at Worldwide Governance Indicators, http://info.worldbank.org/governance/wgi/index.asp.

It can also be supposed that large firms in stable economic standing are more likely to participate in associations; the costs firms incur in joining associations might be prohibitive to small firms, but large firms can be expected to have more readily available resources to support their organizations.

Firms also vary considerably across different sectors of the economy. One characteristic, factor (capital) mobility, is an essential aspect that potentially has important consequences for collective action.[12] The standard expectation in the literature is that high asset specificity (immobility of capital across industries) should stimulate collective action. Resource mobility reflects the costs of moving assets between different uses (across industries or national borders). High levels of investment in fixed capital suggest lower mobility because such fixed capital, as opposed to financial assets, is much harder to convert to other uses. This implies that firms with highly specific assets should organize interest groups, whereas mobile asset enterprises should be less likely to participate in such groups. If resources are not easily transferable to another use, a business is more dependent on the conditions in a particular industry. When conditions in a given industry deteriorate, business is reluctant to move to other sectors but instead lobbies for protection. As a result, more firms in asset-specific industries join interest groups (associations).

Unfortunately, measuring resource specificity at the microlevel is difficult. Mobility of a firm's assets is conditional upon many factors, including institutional, financial, and technological constraints that often have different consequences in different countries and industries. It has been customary in the politico-economic analysis, however, to ascribe different levels of specificity to different factors of production or industrial sectors. This analysis uses a firm's sector as a proxy for resource specificity. I rank sectors according to a priori expectations about their specificity from the most to the least resource-specific in the following order: mining, power generation, manufacturing and repair, hotel and real-estate industry, retail trade, personal services, business services, and finance. As a validity check, I also use the self-reported level of investment in fixed capital over total sales. Unfortunately, this survey item was not available in the 1999 survey and the 2002 and 2005 data sets had few valid observations, resulting in a substantially reduced sample; thus, I do not report this control in the main analysis.

In the statistical analysis I control for the type of ownership, firms' origin, size, longevity, and asset specificity. The ownership effects are captured by the dummy variables that equal one if the state (national or local government) or a foreign private entity has a financial stake in the enterprise. The extent of resource endowment is captured by a cardinal measure based on the midpoint

---

[12] Although sometimes the terms *specificity* and *mobility* of resources refer to different aspects of resource use (specificity indicates strictly technological aspects of physical capital, whereas mobility indicates institutional constraints), here I will use mobility as the opposite of specificity (Hiscox and Rickard 2002).

Business Environment and Business Organization 105

TABLE 4.3. *Firm-Level Variables: Summary Statistics*

Variable	Range	Count		Mean	St. Dev.	Min	Max
		0	1				
Association member	Binary	12,456	6,748	...	...	0	1
Employment size	Cardinal	...	...	190.844	721.237	0	5,500
Foreign-owned	Binary	16,603	2,595	...	...	0	1
State-owned	Binary	16,299	2,873	...	...	0	1
Longevity	Numeric	...	...	1988	18.168	1800	2001
Privately created	Binary	6,829	12,376	...	...	0	1
Resource specificity	Ordinal	...	...	4.146	1.769	0	8
Bribe (% sales)	Percentage	...	...	1.704	3.975	0	50
Rule of law	Ordinal	...	...	3.481	1.372	1	6
Regulatory time	Percentage	...	...	7.075	12.040	0	95
Clear rules	Ordinal	...	...	3.303	1.441	1	6
Fixed assets/ sales	Cardinal	...	...	3.715	74.380	0	4,167

value of the full-time employment categories.[13] The date of firm incorporation and the dummy for de novo firms capture the arguments about past experiences under state socialism and long-lasting relations with the state agencies. Asset specificity is captured by an ordinal scale variable ranging from 1 to 8 (Table 4.3).

Country-Level Controls

In addition to the microlevel controls, the model includes country-level variables that are expected to affect the formation of and membership in industry associations. A number of theories of interest-group politics point to political and socioeconomic factors affecting the emergence of organized interests. Variants of the modernization theory link group formation to the challenges and opportunities created by the rise of industrialized societies (Truman 1951; Olson 1982). When extending these theoretical arguments about the effects of socioeconomic modernization and growth to the post-communist cases, one can expect that in countries with more advanced economic organization – diversified

---

[13] The BEEPS does not report the actual size of firms' employment but rather classifies the firms into seven categories based on the number of full-time employees.

economies, high trade flows, efficient corporate governance, and, in general, higher levels of wealth – the resources available to invest in organizational activities and the potential gains from such activities would be higher. This should lead to higher levels of business associational activities. The overall levels of economic development, according to these arguments, should have a positive effect on groups' propensity to organize.

A cursory look at some of the data on the formation of business-interest groups seems to support the development theory. The levels of business organization in the wealthier, more economically developed post-communist countries are generally higher than in their poorer, less developed neighboring countries. In 1999 the mean percentage of associational membership in the region's higher-income countries (Poland, Slovakia, Slovenia, Hungary, Estonia, Lithuania, Croatia, Czech Republic, and Latvia) was 38 percent, whereas the mean for the region's lower-income countries (GDP per capita below US$2,000) was only 16 percent. If wealth (measured as per capita GDP) is a good indicator of the overall level of development, the dynamics of post-communist group-formation seem to support the development theory.

Another potential contributing factor suggested by the development theory as well as the neoliberal approach to post-communist economic transition is the size of the private sector in the national economy. As the privatization of formerly state-owned enterprises went on, a greater number of businesses lost insider access to the state. This should make formal business organization and collective action directed at the state more likely. The growth of private start-up companies is likely to accelerate this trend.

The study of interest groups cannot ignore the institutional structures within which interest groups have to operate in order to achieve their goals. Deductively, one could expect that the degree of organizational success of business-interest groups should increase as post-communist political systems become more democratic. Democratization should aid the process of interest articulation and should ease interest-group organization. The expectation is that liberal political regimes that do not suppress societal activism or political expression should lower the official barriers for civic engagement that might exist in authoritarian regimes. As such, protection of political rights and civil liberties should aid in businesses' collective action. Political pluralism and access to independent media may also reinforce institutionalized mechanisms of groups' influence. Because authoritarian regimes often deny freedoms of association and expression and undermine political competition, special interest groups might seek alternative mechanisms of expression, for example, patron-client relationships. I capture the extent of political liberalism with the combined Freedom House political rights and civil liberties scores. As a validity check, I also use the Polity IV measure of political regime institutionalization.

As discussed in Chapter 3, in the successor states to the former Yugoslavia, Albania, Hungary, and Slovakia, formerly state-controlled chambers gained compulsory membership similar to the "corporatist" continental European

Business Environment and Business Organization

107

TABLE 4.4. *Aggregate-Level Variables: Sources and Descriptive Statistics*

Variable name	Description	Source	Mean	St. Dev.
Log (GDP/capita)	GDP per capita (constant prices USD), t–1	Penn Table	8.772	.736
Entry procedures	Number of procedures to open business, t–1	World Bank, Doing Business Reports	10.538	3.274
Private GDP	GDP share produced in private sector, t–1	EBRD	63.667	13.273
Compulsory chamber system	Compulsory-membership chamber of commerce (dummy)	Self-Coded	.177	.381
Freedom House	Political rights and civil liberties score(1–6), average, t–1	Freedom House	3.274	1.772
Polity score	21-point regime authority score (–10–10), t–1	Polity IV	4.829	5.987
Public oversight	Government Oversight & Controls (0–100), 2004–2009	Global Integrity	80.403	10.703
Voice and accountability	Citizens' control of the government (–2.5–2.5), t–1	World Bank, Governance Matters	–.016	.854
CPI	Corruption Perception Index, recoded (0–100) from the least to the most corruption control, t–1	Transparency International	31.401	12.553
Transition index	EBRD transition indicator (1–4.33), t–1	EBRD	2.985	.555

model (Ingleby 1996; Luksic 2003). To account for the organizational advantage created by the state-backed compulsory-membership institutions, the following analysis includes the *Compulsory* dummy that takes the value of 1 for firms in Albania, Bosnia, Croatia, Macedonia, Serbia, Slovenia, and Hungary in 1999. Summary statistics for the aggregate-level measures can be found in Table 4.4.

4.2 Statistical Analysis and Results

To investigate the effects of bureaucratic environment on firms' decisions to join business associations, controlling for a number of firm characteristics and country-level variables, I estimate a series of variance component models that are best suited for the pooled cross-sectional data with firm-level observations nested in countries and three survey installments. Because of the simultaneous inclusion of the firm- and country-level variables, *within*-country observations are not independent from one another. Pooling observations across twenty-six economies assumes homogeneity among firms in different countries and is likely to suffer from the specification (omitted variables) problem. A customary way of accounting for such omitted (unobservable) country-level effects in political science applications has been to use fixed effects or dummy-variable models. Fixed effects error correction models have additional advantages of removing endogeneity originating from panel settings. The fixed effects models, however, cannot estimate country-invariant variables, because *within*- transformation wipes out any country-invariant effects. When the estimated variables exhibit temporal variation, I use fixed effects models. When the country-level variables are invariant across surveys, I use hierarchical random effects estimation. Unlike the fixed effects models, the random coefficient hierarchical (or variance component) models treat country-level effects as random variables.[14]

I start with Hypothesis 1a. To evaluate the theoretical expectation that stringent official regulations should suppress collective action, I first estimate a logistic regression that includes only country-level variables with country- and survey-level fixed effects. Table 4.5 has the results. I reject the null hypothesis with 99.99 percent confidence and find that the marginal effects of entry procedures are given by dy/dx= −.015. Holding all control variables at their means and averaging across fixed effects, a move from the lowest levels of regulatory procedures (5) to the highest level (20) cuts the probability of positive outcome in more than half, from 45 to 21 percent. When the firm-level controls are introduced in the model (column 2 in Table 4.5), negative influence persists, and the marginal effects remain virtually unchanged. With control variables set at their means or modal categories and averaging across country- and survey-level fixed effects, a move from the minimum to the maximum number of regulatory procedures reduces the probability of organizational membership from 46 to 20 percent.

To evaluate Hypothesis 2, postulating the positive effects of the corruption-inhibiting legal environment, the second regression model also includes the firm-level *Rule-of-Law* variable. The results are consistent with prior expectations. Legal deterrence against corruption makes firms more likely to participate in business associations. Holding other regressors at their means or modes and averaging across fixed effects, one standard deviation increase in the confidence in the rule of law increases the probability of membership by .013 points. Moving from the least confident to the most confident respondent increases the likelihood of membership from to 37 to 42 percent.

---

[14] I use a country-level random intercept specification. See Raudenbush and Bryk (2002) and Luke (2004) for details on estimation. Survey-level random effects are not statistically significant from zero. The estimates of random intercept and random trend models of the form $Y_{ij} = \alpha + \Sigma\beta_k X_{kitj} + u_{0jt} + u_{1i}(Country)_t + u_{2i}(Time)_j + e_{itj}$ are not different from the ones reported for the random timetrend specification. Because trend estimates are not of interest here, I omit these models.

Business Environment and Business Organization

TABLE 4.5. *Estimation Results: Country-Level Fixed and Random Effects Logistic Regressions*

	FE Logit (1)	FE Logit (2)	RE Logit (3)	RE Logit (4)	RE Logit (5)
Entry procedures	–.076 (.017)***	–.083 (.018)***	–.046 (.015)***	.125 (.078)	–.044 (.015)***
Public oversight				1.992 (.958)***	–.091 (.330)
Entry × procedures Public oversight				–.178 (.079)**	
Freedom House	–.156 (.062)**	–.224 (.066)***	–.180 (.050)***	–.182 (.049)***	–.166 (.052)***
Private GDP	.076 (.009)***	.077 (.010)***	034 (.008)***	.039 (.008)***	.034 (.008)***
Log (GDP/capita)	–.364 (.248)	–.459 (.265)*	–.306 (.156)**	–.314 (.154)**	-197 (.164)
Compulsory			1.758 (.180)***	1.779 (.177)***	1.753 (.182)***
Rule of law		.038 (.013)***	.034 (.013)**	.033 (.013)**	.045 (.014)***
Employees (100)		.030 (.003)***	.029 (.003)***	.029 (.003)***	.029 (.003)***
Foreign-owned		.694 (.051)***	.694 (.051)***	.695 (.051)***	.689 (.052)***
State-owned		–.205 (.063)***	–.217 (.063)***	–.218 (.063)***	–.231 (.064)***
Longevity		–.011 (.001)***	–.011 (.001)***	–.011 (.001)***	–.011 (.001)***
Privately created		–.403 (.048)***	–.403 (.048)***	–.414 (.048)***	–.412 (.049)***
Specificity		.072 (.011)***	.075 (.011)***	.076 (.011)***	.073 (.011)***
Regulatory time					.018 (.003)***
Reg. time × oversight					–.004 (.004)
$\beta_1+\beta_3$				–.053 (.015)***	.013 (.002)***
Const.	1.016 (1.930)	24.565 (3.114)***	22.648 (2.708)***	20.453 (2.840)***	20.358 (2.760)***
Obs.	17872	16926	16926	16926	16395

Dependent Variable: Pr (Member = 1).

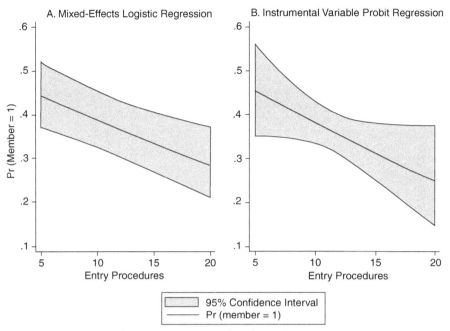

FIGURE 4.1. Effects of regulations on membership in business associations.

These results hold when I re-estimate the model with a country-level random effects specification and a dummy for compulsory-membership chamber systems. Estimated coefficients on *Entry Procedures* and *Rule of Law* remain statistically significant, but the magnitude of their effects somewhat diminishes. Still, they continue to have substantively significant effects on membership. To illustrate these effects, Figures 4.1.A and 4.2.A plot the predicted probabilities of membership against changes in the corresponding explanatory variables. The figures present the results after setting fixed effects at their 2002 level,[15] ignoring country-level random effects, and holding the effects of other variables at their means/modes. Figure 4.1.A shows that at the level of regulatory costs found in Latvia in 2002 (five entry procedures) the probability of membership amounts to 44 percent. This compares to 33 percent at fifteen entry procedures, which is the level of regulatory burden found in Russia in 2002. In 2002 firms that were most confident that the legal system upholds contracts and property rights were 11 percent more likely to participate in business associations compared to those who lacked this confidence.

---

[15] The magnitude of the substantive effects of regulatory procedures somewhat increases over time, whereas the substantive effects of the rule of law somewhat diminish. Hence, for the graphical presentation I chose the 2002 survey sample, as those estimates fall in the middle.

Business Environment and Business Organization

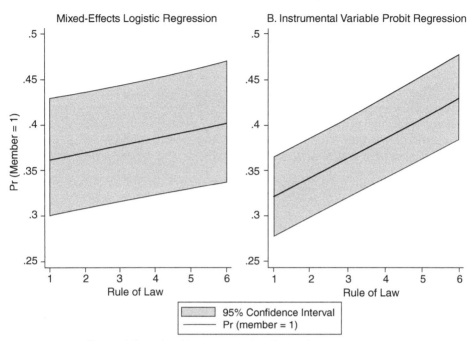

FIGURE 4.2. Effects of the rule of law on membership in business associations.

Table 4.5 shows that most control variables have the expected statistically significant effects on the firms' propensity to organize. Firm size, foreign ownership, resource specificity, and the size of the private sector have a positive impact on membership, whereas enterprise age, de novo status, and state ownership make firms less likely to join. The coefficient on the Freedom House scores is negative, meaning that chances of membership improve together with civil liberties and political rights. The negative effect of the level of development runs contrary to the conventional theories. One interpretation is that GDP per capita may capture the extent of institutional sophistication. Well-developed economic institutions may substitute for the need to join business associations.

Hypothesis 3 states that the effect of the official regulatory policy on the firm's propensity to organize is conditional on bureaucratic constraint in applying regulatory procedures. To test this proposition, I include a multiplicative interaction between regulatory procedures and public oversight over state bureaucracy. For the ease of interpretation, I constructed a binary variable coded 1 if a country's rating exceeded the regional mean of 80.4 points (high values correspond to more institutional constraints) and 0 otherwise. Substantive results do not change when an ordinal scale is used instead. Because this measure of public oversight does not vary over time, I estimate the pooled sample

112 *Building Business*

containing the 1999, 2002, and 2005 surveys with a random effects estimation. Theoretical arguments suggest the following regression specification:

$$Y_{ijt} = \beta_0 + \beta_1 X_{1jt} + \beta_2 X_{2j} + \beta_3(X_{1jt} + X_{2j}) + \Sigma\beta k_{(i)jt} X k_{(i)jt} + a_t + \mu_j + e_{ijt}$$

Where Y_{ijt} is the dependent variable for i firms across j countries and t surveys, X_{1jt} stands for the number of official regulations for market entry, X_{2j} is a dummy for high public oversight, $\Sigma\beta k_{(i)jt} XK_{(i)jt}$ contains firm- and country-level controls, a_t are time fixed effects, μ_j are country-level random effects, and e_{ijt} is a stochastic element. Note that if $X_{2j} = 0$, then

$$Y_{ijt} = \beta_0 + \beta_1 X_{1jt} + \Sigma\beta k_{(i)jt} X k_{(i)jt} + a_t + \mu_j + e_{ijt}$$

If $X_{2j} = 1$,

$$Y_{ijt} = \beta_0 + (\beta_1 + \beta_3)X_{1jt} + \beta_2 X_{2j} + \Sigma\beta k_{(i)jt} X k_{(i)jt} + a_t + \mu_j + e_{ijt}$$

Column 3 in Table 4.5 presents the results of the baseline model, omitting the interaction term, and column 4 shows the results of the above regression specification. In a multiplicative interaction model, *Public Oversight* as well as the interaction term are statistically different from zero. The oversight variable has a positive effect on membership. When public oversight of bureaucracy is low ($X_{2j} = 0$), the official number of regulatory procedures has no statistically significant effect on the probability of membership. When the public oversight is above average, however, the official number of regulatory procedures has a positive and statistically significant effect, as given by $\beta_1 + \beta_3 = -.053$, s.e. =.015. These terms are jointly significant at conventional levels, meaning that under high levels of oversight, official regulations directly affect membership. Figure 4.3 plots the predicted probabilities of membership for high- and low-oversight regimes.[16] When public oversight of bureaucracy is high, one standard deviation increase above the mean number of official regulatory procedures reduces the probability of membership from 23 to 20 percent in 1999, from 37 to 33 percent in 2002, and from 37 to 33 percent in 2005. At the same time, when the public oversight over regulatory bureaucracy is low, the effects of any additional regulatory procedures are not distinguishable from zero. This is consistent with the notion that bureaucratic power to freely interpret regulatory norms, apply them in a haphazard manner, and impose additional "unofficial" regulatory hurdles makes the official regulatory environment irrelevant.

To check whether these relationships hold for unofficial regulatory costs, I interact public oversight with the amount of managerial time spent on applying rules and regulations. This is a subjective firm-level measure of regulatory burden that reflects not only the official regulatory requirements but also bureaucracy-imposed hurdles. In fact, this often serves as the primary measure

---

[16] Figure 4.3 plots reflect only the fixed portion of the model, ignoring the country-level random effects.

Business Environment and Business Organization

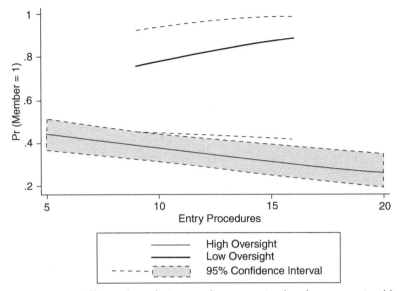

FIGURE 4.3. Effects of regulations under constrained and unconstrained bureaucracy.

of the amount of red tape in the cross-national assessments of business climate (Schwab 2010). The theory suggests that the effects of unofficial regulatory costs originating in bureaucratic red tape should not be conditional on bureaucratic constraint nor should they make it harder for business associations to provide regulatory relief. The unconstrained bureaucracy may have greater proclivity to produce the red tape, but once the "unofficial" burden is generated, its effect should hold, ceteris paribus. Furthermore, business associations might have a similar capacity to cut the red tape irrespective of the amount of burden it imposes, producing the scale economy that might entice higher-cost members to join.

The last column in Table 4.5 shows that the effect of red tape is independent from levels of public control of bureaucracy. The interactive term is not statistically significant, and the effects of red tape under unconstrained bureaucracy are not substantively different from its effects under strong public oversight. The regression coefficients are .018 and .013 respectively, both significant at the .001 level, showing that the actual costs of doing business affect membership irrespective of the institutional features of regulatory bureaucracy. The positive coefficients suggest that unlike the official regulatory costs, which suppress membership, bureaucratic red tape, other things held constant, makes firms more likely to join associations. This is consistent with the notion that the *official* regulatory burden and bureaucracy-imposed regulatory costs have substantively different effects on membership and brings us to the subject of corruption.

To test the hypothesized effects of bribery (Hypothesis 4), I proceed with the instrumental variable approach. As discussed earlier, the cost of corruption is theoretically expected to be endogenous. In addition to the theoretical reasons, because the firm-level analysis uses perception-based measures of corruption, the same explanatory factors may influence both the membership in associations and the perception of the business environment. One could hypothesize that participation in associations may increase a firm's awareness of corruption. To model these endogenous relationships, I use the instrumental variable (IV) two-stage least squares (2SLS) fixed effects model and Newey's two-step IV probit model, with robust standard errors clustered in country (Borjas and Sueyoshi 1994). Both models include fixed effects for three installments of BEEPS. Although the probit model is better suited for analyzing the dichotomous dependent variable, the mixed-effect 2SLS better captures the hierarchical nature of the data. The two estimation methods, however, yield similar results.

The excluded instruments are the clarity and consistency of interpretation of economic rules and regulations (*Clear Rules*) and the percentage of managerial time spent in ensuring regulatory compliance (*Regulatory Time*). These two can be interpreted as measures of bureaucratic red tape and are theoretically linked to corruption. According to the argument advanced in Chapter 2, bureaucrats create red tape in order to extort more bribes, and this justifies using *Clear Rules* and *Regulatory Time* to identify the corruption equation. The perception-based measure of bureaucratic red tape, however, should not have a direct effect on membership in business associations. The effects of the official costs of regulatory policy (c_r) are captured instead by the "hard" data on the number of entry procedures.[17] Exclusion of the perception-based measures of bureaucratic red tape, therefore, reflects the theoretical logic developed in Chapter 2.

Table 4.6 reports the results of the first and the second stage 2SLS and IV probit regressions. The Sargan-Hansen test of over-identifying restrictions does not reject the null hypothesis that all instruments are uncorrelated with e_{ijt}, indicating that instruments are appropriately independent of the error process. In the second stage of the fixed effects 2SLS regression the coefficient on the instrumented *Bribes* variable is in the expected direction and is significantly different from zero.

Columns 3 and 4 report the results of the IV probit model with the survey-level fixed effects and country-clustered robust standard errors. The excluded instruments are statistically significant predictors of bribery. At the same time, the Ameniya-Lee-Newey χ^2 is sufficiently small to maintain the null hypothesis of instruments' independence from the error structure. The

---

[17] Elsewhere (Duvanova 2012) I discuss the theoretical importance of distinguishing between the official costs of regulatory compliance and unofficial, bureaucracy-generated costs, empirically investigating their distinct economic effects.

Business Environment and Business Organization 115

TABLE 4.6. *Estimation Results: Instrumental Variables Regressions*

	Mixed effects 2SLS		IV probit	
	1*st* stage	2*nd* stage	1*st* stage	2*nd* stage
	Bribe %	Member	Bribe %	Member
	(1)	(2)	(3)	(4)
Entry procedures	−.137	−.011	−.011	−.038
	(.030)***	(.004)**	(.026)	(.020)*
Public oversight			.028	−.005
			(.010)**	(.010)
Freedom House	−.488	−.031	.121	−.088
	(.119)***	(.017)*	(.061)*	(.019)***
Private GDP	−.0008	.014	−.0004	.006
	(.016)	(.002)***	(.009)	(.007)
Log(GDP/capita)	−1.387	.025	−.945	.064
	(.462)***	(.065)	(.156)***	(.107)
Compulsory			−.458	.845
			(.313)	(.172)***
Bribes *(% sales)*		.052		.140
		(.007)***		(.018)***
Rule of law	−.216	.022	−.203	.058
	(.023)***	(.004)***	(.031)***	(.006)***
Employees (100)	−.010	.006	−.010	.017
	(.004)**	(.0006)***	(.004)**	(.002)***
Foreign-owned	−.337	.152	−.320	.422
	(.087)***	(.012)**	(.111)***	(.057)***
State-owned	−.598	−.028	−.570	−.068
	(.105)***	(.015)*	(.110)***	(.045)
Longevity	.005	−.003	.004	−.007
	(.002)**	(.0003)***	(.002)*	(.0009)***
Privately created	.276	−.091	.388	−.275
	(.079)***	(.011)***	(.105)***	(.046)***
Specificity	.014	.013	.022	.043
	(.017)	(.002)***	(.026)	(.015)***
Regulatory time	.051		.052	
	(.003)***		(.006)***	
Clear rules	−.121		−.117	
	(.022)***		(.037)***	
Const.	11.222	4.242	2.351	12.199
	(5.332)**	(.747)***	(4.158)	(1.921)***
Overidentification $\chi2$		.384		2.280
		(.535)		(.131)
Survey year	Fixed effects		Fixed effects	
Country	Random effects		Robust standard errors	
Obs.	13588	13588	11649	11649

Dependent Variable: Pr (Member = 1).

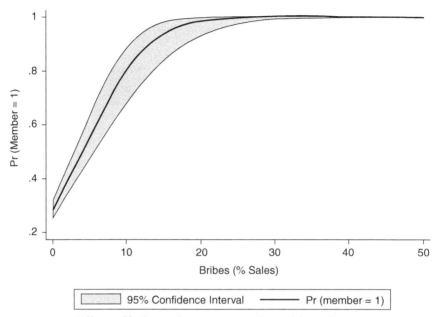

FIGURE 4.4. Effects of bribery after instrumental variable probit estimation.

instrumented corruption variable has a positive and statistically significant effect on membership in business associations.

Graphical representation of the substantive effects of corruption, holding all other regressors at their means/modes, can be found in Figure 4.4, which plots predicted probabilities of membership for the 2002 survey sample. Effects are virtually indistinguishable from those found in the 1999 and 2005 samples. The graphs reveal a positive, substantively significant relationship between the cost of corruption and the likelihood that a firm is a member of a business association. Controlling for the influence of other factors and accounting for the endogenous nature of this variable one standard deviation from the mean cost of corruption raises the probability of associational membership from 35 percent to almost 50 percent.

The estimates also fail to reject hypotheses regarding the effects of regulatory pressure and anticorruption, as measured by the number of entry regulations and the respondents' confidence in the rule of law. In the 2SLS and instrumental variables probit models, the coefficients on *Entry Procedures* and *Rule-of-Law* variables have the expected signs and are statistically significant. Figures 4.1.B and 4.2.B illustrate the magnitude of these effects in the IV probit models. The effects of the key explanatory variables appear to be substantial and robust to different estimation methods. The next section discusses additional robustness checks that help improve the overall confidence in the statistical inference.

4.3 Robustness Checks

To ensure that the empirical results are robust to the alternative operationalization of independent variables and are not driven by the inclusion of specific countries, I conduct the following validity checks. As a check on construct validity, I use other independently generated data that capture the concepts of control of corruption and official regulatory burden. I re-evaluate Hypothesis 2 with a country-level indicator of the central government's effort to combat corruption – the Transparency International Corruption Perception Index (CPI). CPI is developed by Transparency International and is one of the most widely used indicators of government probity. CPI is well suited to serve as an indicator of the central government's effort to combat corruption because it reflects the overall levels across different forms of corruption, including grand political, bureaucratic, and private sector corruption.[18]

I operationalize the stringency of regulatory regimes by the European Bank for Reconstruction and Development composite transition indicators score (ranges from 1 to 4.33, with higher scores corresponding to greater progress in transition). The EBRD assesses progress in transition against the standards of industrialized market economies, with lower scores representing little change from a rigid centrally planned economy and high scores representing the standards of industrial capitalism. Among other aspects of economic change, the transition indicators reflect the extent of state intervention and the degree of regulatory transformation. Although these do not directly capture the costs of compliance, it is generally safe to assume that unreformed command-style regulations are ill-suited to contemporary market conditions and impose greater costs than market-friendly regimes. Unlike the individual-level measures, the EBRD experts' ratings tend to take into account the official cost of regulatory intervention.

In addition, I check the robustness of empirical findings against the alternative measure of political environment. Whereas the Freedom House score is based on the assessment of countries'political rights and liberties, Polity IV offers an institutional approach for distinguishing among different political regimes. If politics is implicated in organizational dynamics, we should see the institutional features of democratic regimes having a positive effect on membership.

Column 1 in Table 4.6 presents the results of fixed effects logistic regression using the alternative measures of regulatory compliance, corruption control, and political regime. The positive coefficient on the *Business Freedom* variable

---

[18] Note that on the flipside of anticorruption this variable captures the frequency, or pervasiveness, of corruption, and this is conceptually different from the notion of corruption costs discussed earlier. Corruption might be widespread but not costly to businesses, or vice versa; bribes might be rare, but their amounts may be substantial.

is consistent with the hypothesis that heavy state involvement in the economy suppresses organizational development. The probability of a firm being a member of a business association at the mean value of the EBRD index is 33 percent. One standard deviation increase from the mean raises this probability to 44 percent, and one standard deviation increase from the mean value of the reversed CPI index increases the probability of positive outcome from 34 to 40 percent.

To check the validity of Hypothesis 3, I operationalize bureaucratic constraint with the World Bank's *Voice and Accountability* index, which captures the extent to which citizens are able to hold their government accountable through elections as well as their level of freedom of expression, freedom of association, and free media. Similarly to the previous estimation, I dichotomize this variable to facilitate interpretation of the results. The expectation is that the pressures of democratic accountability constrain bureaucrats' whims in regulatory policy interpretation. The index is produced by aggregating various survey- and expert-based rankings of political and civil institutions and is available for the same years as the enterprise survey. When a bureaucrat freely interprets the rules and increases compliance costs, greater democratic accountability should ease the process of complaining and redressing the problem.

Column 2 in Table 4.7 contains the results of re-estimating the multiplicative interaction term model found in Table 4.5, column 3. Results are in line with the theoretical expectations and the previous estimation. The explanatory variables and the interactive term are statistically significant, and the coefficient on the regulatory burden under high *Voice and Accountability* is positive and statistically significant. Holding all other variables at their means/modes and accounting for the fixed effects, one standard deviation increase in the EBRD transition index improves membership chances from 30 to 36 percent. When *Voice and Accountability* is low (and bureaucracy is poorly constrained), regulatory burden no longer has a statistically significant effect on membership. The coefficient $\beta_1 + \beta_3 = .448$, and the standard error equals .345. Columns 1 and 2 also reveal that the Polity IV political regime score has a positive effect on membership, meaning that under democratic political regimes, firms are more likely to participate in business associations. In fact, setting all other variables at their means/modes, businesses in consolidated democracies are three times more likely to join industry associations than they are in consolidated dictatorships. Both *Voice and Accountability* and *Polity IV* variables are statistically significant when they appear on the right-hand side of the membership equation.

Columns 3 and 4 in Table 4.7 post the results of the re-estimation of the instrumental variable probit model with the alternative measures of regulatory burden and the rule of law. The Ameniya-Lee-Newey overidentification test does not reject the null hypothesis of instruments' independence from the error structure, and the second-stage shows positive, statistically significant effects of corruption costs. At the same time, regulatory-burden and the rule-of-law

Business Environment and Business Organization

TABLE 4.7. *Estimation Results: Robustness to Alternative Operationalization*

| | Fixed effects logit | Fixed effects logit | IV probit | |
| | | | 1st stage | 2nd stage |
	(1)	(2)	(3)	(4)
Transition index	.824	1.428	–1.383	.557
	(.332)**	(.420)***	(.788)	(.173)***
Voice &		2.297	1.308	.011
accountability		(.989)**	(.413)***	(.120)
Transition index		–.980		
× voice &		(.334)***		
accountability				
$\beta_2 + \beta_3$		.448		
		(.345)		
CPI (reversed)	.020	.019		
	(.004)***	(.022)***		
Polity IV	.055	.087	–.103	.0003
	(.017)***	(.022)***	(.036)**	(.017)
Private GDP	.068	.073	.032	–.009
	(.009)***	(.009)***	(.017)*	(.005)*
Log(GDP/capita)	–1.401	–1.557	–1.262	.060
	(.359)***	(.386)***	(.005)***	(.080)
Compulsory			.015	.953
			(.356)	(.182)***
Bribes (% sales)				.077
				(.024)***
Rule of law			–.319	.067
			(.004)***	(.009)***
Employees (100)	.030	.029	–.013	.017
	(.003)***	(.003)***	(.004)***	(.002)***
Foreign-owned	.705	.700	.369	.408
	(.050)***	(.051)***	(.110)***	(.068)***
State-owned	–.233	–.245	.560	–.158
	(.061)***	(.062)***	(.110)***	(.064)**
Longevity	–.010	–.009	.008	–.007
	(.001)***	(.001)***	(.002)***	(.0009)***
Privately created	–.347	–.352	.348	–.251
	(.047)***	(.047)***	(.118)***	(.052)***
Specificity	.062	.063	.061	.026
	(.010)***	(.011)***	(.025)**	(.017)
Regulatory time		.070	.017	
		(.009)***	(.001)***	
Clear rules			–.061	
			(.034)*	
Const.	23.356	18.795	.846	10.886
	(3.444)***	(3.189)***	(5.448)	(2.139)***
Overidentification χ^2				1.061
				(.303)
Obs.	17781	17266	13944	13944

Dependent Variable: Pr (Member = 1). Models 1 and 2 include country-level fixed effects.

variables remain statistically significant predictors of associational membership. The effects of the official regulatory burden, corruption control, and corruption costs hold across different installments of the BEEPS survey when the sample is divided into EU member/candidate and non-EU countries, and also when countries are dropped from the estimated sample one at a time.[19]

The application of different model specifications and estimation techniques establishes that, controlling for the effects of other variables, regulatory pressures, anticorruption measures, and costs of bribery are strong predictors of associational membership. The statistical tests developed above reveal that business associations' membership is statistically related to characteristics of the regulatory environment when controlling for other factors, such as country-level and time effects, resource specificity, enterprise characteristics, and macroeconomic and political factors. The results of applying alternative statistical techniques and different model specifications all suggest a positive, statistically and substantively significant relationship between corruption-limiting measures and firms' likelihood of being a member of business associations. The severity of regulatory pressure has a negative effect on membership. Such an effect is more consistent in countries that have institutional constraints on the power of bureaucracy to impose red tape and heighten regulatory costs. These results support the intuition behind Hypotheses 1a, 2, and 3 developed in Chapter 2. The results also show that costly corrupt transactions, though endogenous to regulatory pressures and anticorruption, make firms more likely to participate. This supports Hypothesis 4, suggesting that as corruption becomes costlier, firms become more likely to join interest associations.

4.4 Additional Quantitative Evidence

Dynamic Extensions

As the dynamic extension of the theoretical model suggests, the temporal effects of organizational development should affect systemic corruption. According to the theory, the increased availability of business associations for coping with regulatory costs should reduce the supplementary income derived from bureaucratic corruption. When such income falls below the costs associated with bureaucratic graft, corruption should subside. The long-term implication of this argument is that as associational membership grows, corruption should become less frequent (Hypothesis 6).

A simple check on the plausibility of this prediction is to see whether associational membership predicts subsequent levels of corruption. By aggregating the BEEPS responses, I estimate the *Membership Density* as a proportion of enterprises that report membership in business associations across participating countries. This reflects the extent to which businesses – regardless of

---

[19] The EU dummy variable in the random effects models does not change the results either. See Appendix F for additional robustness checks.

Business Environment and Business Organization

their ownership, sector, or size – are organized in a given country. The correlation between corruption at time t and associational membership at $t+1$ is .12, whereas there is a negative .13 correlation between corruption and participation at $t-1$:

Membership Density at $_{t-1}$	$\rightarrow$	Mean Corruption Score	$\rightarrow$	Membership Density $_{t+1}$
	(r=−.133)		(r=.119)	

Moreover, regressing the membership density at time t on the aggregated responses about frequency of corrupt transactions in firms' environment at $t+1$[20] and controlling for the average perceptions of the rule of law, compulsory-membership system, and a time trend, I find that past density is a strong, statistically significant predictor of the subsequent corruption frequency. A twenty percentage points increase in membership density results in a .2 point reduction in corruption frequency. At the same time, in a similar regression model, corruption frequency is not a statistically significant predictor of the subsequent levels of membership. The negative effect of preceding membership on the extent of corrupt encounters is consistent with the dynamic implications of the analytical model discussed in Chapter 2. Hypothesis 6, which postulates that organizational membership in the long run should result in the gradual decline of corruption, finds tentative support.

Member Satisfaction

Another way to establish the causation implied in the defensive organization argument is to work through causal mechanisms through which corruption affects participation in interest groups. For the most part, qualitative process-tracing evidence is needed to track causal linkage. Chapter 5 offers such evidence through a number of case studies of association development in different countries and industries. Here, some indirect quantitative evidence supporting the causal mechanisms implied by the defensive organization argument can be presented without sacrificing much space. The defensive organization argument rests on the notion of member benefits that make organizational strategy superior to corruption and passive compliance. Implicit in this mechanism is the idea that, once established, the associations should excel in providing club goods. According to Hypothesis 5, organizational capacity to provide club goods should increase over time.

The BEEPS 2002 and 2005 surveys provide information on the overall levels of member satisfaction with services and benefits that business associations provide. Table 4.8 summarizes firms' evaluations of six distinct service

---

[20] I use the survey question that asks, *How common is it for firms in your line of business to have to pay some irregular "additional payments" to public officials to get things done?* Responses are given on a six-point scale ranging from "never" to "always."

TABLE 4.8. *Members' Evaluation of Services Provided by Associations*

Services	Mean value in 2002 0="no value"; 4="critical value"	Mean value in 2005 0="no value"; 4="critical value"
Lobbying	.83	.95
Dispute resolution	.89	.97
International markets information	1.33	1.46
Standardization, reputation building	1.46	1.60
Government regulations information	1.56	1.62
Domestic market information	1.63	1.74

Source: BEEPS 2002, 2005.

domains. The table demonstrates the across-the-board increase in members' ratings of associations' activities, supporting the expectation that as organizational resources accumulate over time, associations become more effective in providing selective benefits. In three years, from 2002 to 2005, the average member satisfaction with associational services increased from 1.2 to 1.4 points, as measured on a 0- to 4-point scale. It is important to note that association members rate lobbying lowest, corroborating the Chapter 3 finding that business associations in general are poorly equipped to lobby for the interests of their members and rarely engage in rent-seeking via lobbying.

A closer look at member satisfaction with associational services also sheds light on Hypothesis 1b, which links extensive regulatory burden to higher levels of the provision of selective benefits. Because heavier regulatory burden makes it harder for associations to compete with corrupt bureaucrats for the provision of regulatory relief, they have to offer greater selective incentives to entice member participation. This suggests that higher official regulatory burden should lead to more member benefits and, by implication, higher levels of member satisfaction. I evaluate this proposition by regressing two measures of regulatory burden – the number of entry procedures and the time officially required to open a new business – on the level of member satisfaction with associational services averaged across six different categories. Both explanatory variables come from the World Bank Doing Business dataset. The model contains the same controls as used in the analysis of firms' membership status. Table 4.9 shows the results. The estimation reveals that in fact, regulatory burden has a positive effect on member satisfaction. Other things held constant, four additional regulatory procedures increase member satisfaction by one standard deviation, whereas a move from the minimum to the maximum number of days required to open a new business would increase member satisfaction by .3 point. Although Hypothesis 1b calls for association-level analysis, available membership-level evidence is consistent with the expectation that regulatory costs put pressure on business associations to provide more member benefits.

Business Environment and Business Organization

TABLE 4.9. *Regulatory Burden and Member Benefits: Country-Level Mixed-Effects Linear Regression Estimates*

	Entry procedures, number	Entry time, days
	(1)	(2)
Regulatory burden	.025	.003
	(.011)**	(.001)**
Private GDP	.005	.005
	(.003)	(.003)
Log(GDP/capita)	−.026	−.052
	(.047)	(.048)
Compulsory	−.386	−.363
	(.072)***	(.074)***
Rule of law	.075	.073
	(.010)***	(.010)***
Employees (100)	.006	.005
	(.001)***	(.001)***
Foreign-owned	.107	.108
	(.034)***	(.034)***
State-owned	−.006	−.007
	(.044)	(.044)
Longevity	−.0003	−.0003
	(.0007)	(.0007)
Privately created	.063	−.066
	(.034)	(.034)
Regulatory time	.003	.003
	(.001)***	(.001)***
Specificity	.002	.001
	(.008)	(.008)
Const.	1.262	1.668
	(1.459)	(1.445)
Obs.	4134	4134

DV: Member satisfaction with services provided by business associations, average across six categories. Time-level fixed effects and country-level random effects estimation.

Crony Capitalism and Sectoral Analysis of Membership

An interesting finding that emerged from the firm-level analyses presented earlier in this chapter is that larger, private firms that underwent privatization and operate in resource-specific sectors are more likely to participate in business associations. Does it mean that business associations represent the interests of influential industry actors who benefit from post-communist crony capitalism? Influence-centered theories can offer a strong alternative explanation for the findings of this chapter. The dominant firms that concentrate vast amounts of resources in highly monopolized settings may become the patrons of industry associations and use them to meet company-specific objectives (Walker 1983). If this is the case, it will cast doubts on the defensive organization argument.

Interest fragmentation/homogeneity and levels of industrial concentration have long been identified as the "usual suspects" in the formation of special interest groups. Industries that have fewer actors who share similar interests are more likely to coordinate and engage in collective action than are industries with fragmented, heterogeneous establishments. Large firms operating in highly concentrated sectors, therefore, may seem good candidates for collective action. Conversely, large, resource-abundant firms are well positioned to act as solitary-actor lobbies; they often can achieve their goals without engaging in collective action. Other research has argued that large firms' ability to lobby their interest directly jeopardizes collective action (Duvanova 2011). Will the defensive organization hypothesis hold against alternative explanations emphasizing dominant, highly concentrated interests as the driving forces behind associational formation?

Here I evaluate the central implication of the defensive organization theory – the expected negative effect of regulatory burden on organizational formation – against alternative explanations that see associations as collusive industry arrangements. Subnational, sector-level variation in the levels of industrial concentration, resource specificity, and regulatory burden found in the Russian Federation serves to illustrate my argument. The defensive organization theory postulates that industry associations are more likely to form in a low-cost regulatory environment that eases the provision of selective benefits. The influence-centered explanation leads to the opposite prediction. If associations are the agents of crony capitalists, the heavy regulatory burden should be either unrelated to or aid their emergence.[21] Furthermore, if associations are part of crony capitalism, we should see more of them in highly monopolized industries. If, however, associations act as alternatives to crony capitalism, highly monopolized industries should have fewer associations because the dominant firms may rely on noninstitutional channels of protection and influence.

In evaluating the effects of sector-level regulatory pressures I rely on the data that come from the databases of *Garant*, a prominent Russian legal information service. The database is a comprehensive collection of legal documents that were issued by Russia's federal and regional authorities starting in 1991. It was assembled from the archives of the Federal Ministry of Justice and regional governments, covering 145 thematic sections of federal and regional legislation as well as the decisions of the Federal Arbitration Courts of Circuits. *Garant* indexed over 4 million documents, of which 116,377 were sector-specific

---

[21] Two scenarios are possible. First, if regulatory burden equally affects the dominant firm and the marginal players, the dominant firm will use an association to act as an antiregulation lobby. Second, if the dominant firm is exempt from regulations through the crony capitalist arrangements, the official regulatory burden should be irrelevant to its decision to become the association's patron.

Business Environment and Business Organization   125

legislative statutes, executive decrees, or regulatory directives. The number of regulatory documents ranges from 115 for the pharmaceutical industry to 18,680 for the construction sector. To account for the possible heterogeneity of regulated firms and activities, I normalize these data by the size of the sector.

The dependent variable – number of industry associations normalized by the sector's size – comes from a survey of business associations conducted in 2000 by the Russian Institute of Entrepreneurship and Investment (Kaganov and Rutkovskaia 2001). Out of 1,500 business associations officially registered with Russian local authorities or with the Ministry of Justice by the end of 1999, IEI was able to gather data on 325 associations. These cover all of the country's largest and most politically active business organizations. Despite a modest response rate of 20 percent, the sample covered over 85 percent of the associations recorded in the database of the federal Chamber of Trade and Industry. The surveyed associations reported 401,972 firms as members, which amounts to 14 percent of all firms officially registered by Russian authorities (Sokolin 2001). These membership figures are close to the estimated levels of participation in business associations (around 16 percent) according to the World Bank BEEPS figures.

Of the 325 associations IEI surveyed, 161 define their membership along sectoral lines. Such sector-specific associations reported 41,839 firms as members. Because of missing data and suspect reliability of self-reported membership figures (see Chapter 3 for related discussion), I operationalize the dependent variable by the number of sectoral associations normalized by the size of the sector. Such operationalization reflects the theoretical priors of the influence-centered explanation. If large monopolistic firms form, sustain, and dominate industry associations, sectoral membership rates will be misleading. Measuring collective action with the number of associations per firm, however, does not stack the deck against finding support for alternative explanations. Table 4.10 and Figure 4.5 give the total count of industry associations and the associational density across sectors. Together these reveal drastic differences across sectors in respect to associational formation.

Lacking a more direct measure, I approximate industrial concentration by (1) the share of the sector's total production that firms employing more than 200 full-time employees generate and (2) the logged employment in an average firm.[22] Both measures reflect the extent to which large businesses dominate a sector. Because resource specificity is theoretically linked to collective action and varies considerably across economic sectors, in the statistical analysis I control for the average fixed-capital investment. According to the logic of the resource specificity argument, collective action should be more rewarding in

---

[22] Unfortunately, more conventional measures of industrial concentration and market shares are unavailable for a number of service sectors (e.g., banking, insurance) and sectors dominated by companies of small size (e.g., restaurants), where statistics are often based on economy-wide projections rather than actual enterprise-level data. Because the analyzed sectors include trade and services, other sectoral characteristics – for example, exposure to imports and reliance on exports – could not be integrated into the model.

126   *Building Business*

TABLE 4.10. *Number of Industry Associations by Sector*

Industry	Number of associations	Industry	Number of associations
Coal mining	0	Advertising	3
Nonferous metallurgy	0	Audit	3
Power generation	0	Fishing	3
Chemical industry	1	Communication	4
Construction materials	1	Construction	5
Exchange	1	Finance (all categories)	5
Ferrous metallurgy	1	Lumber processing	5
Information technology	1	Light manufacturing	6
Insurance	1	Oil and natural gas	6
Property management	1	Pharmaceuticals	6
Research and innovation	2	Real-estate services	8
Banking	2	Wholesale trade	8
Credit organizations	2	Retail trade	9
Forestry	2	Communal and personal services	15
Machinery	2	Transportation	16
Restaurants	2	Food processing	21

sectors with greater amounts of fixed-capital stock. Resource concentration and specificity data come from *Rosstat*, the Russian state statistical agency.

Cross-sectional OLS regression estimates the effect of sectoral regulations, concentration, and specificity on organizational density – the number of sectoral associations per thousand firms. All right-hand-side variables are lagged by one year. If business associations organize to represent powerful economic interests, measures of concentration should have a positive effect on organizational density, whereas regulatory burden should have either a positive or no effect. The opposite result would be consistent with the defensive organization argument. The standard expectation about the effects of factor specificity is that we should observe positive signs on fixed-capital investment.

Consistent with firm-level analysis presented earlier in this chapter, higher levels of investment in fixed capital are associated with the development of industry associations. Factor specificity, however, is not the only force driving sectoral variation in the development of industry associations. As evidenced by Table 4.11, controlling for the effects of resource specificity, sectors with higher industrial concentration tend to have fewer associations per thousand firms. Contrary to the notion that the large and influential firms drive the development of business associations, two alternative measures of resource concentration have a negative effect on associational density. One plausible explanation is that single-company influence in sectors with highly concentrated economic power dampens demand for associational services and retards collective action.

Business Environment and Business Organization

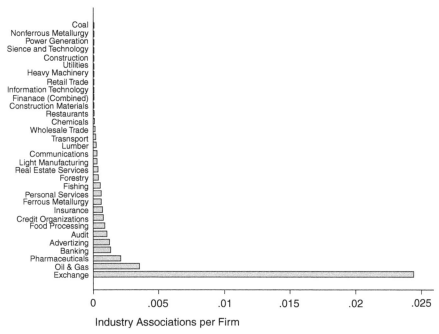

FIGURE 4.5. Industry associations normalized by sector size.

The empirical findings in respect to resource concentration are consistent with the theoretical treatment of industry associations as antithetical to rent-seeking and collusion by powerful economic interests.

More importantly, Table 4.11 shows that, taking into account the effects of resource specificity and concentration, sectors with a higher number of official rules and regulations have fewer associations per thousand firms. This effect holds for the raw number of regulations and when regulations are normalized by the number of firms in a sector. Substantive effects range from a .24- to 4-point drop in associational density per one standard deviation increase in regulatory burden. This result supports the defensive organization argument but is inconsistent with the notion that industry associations arise as collusive arrangements between dominant firms.

4.5 Summary

This chapter evaluated the defensive organization argument against firm-level survey, aggregate, and sectoral data. The theory developed in Chapter 2 has linked participation in business associations with firms' responses to corrupt bureaucracy and intrusive regulatory regimes. In this formulation associations attract firms by providing members with regulatory relief. Business associations, therefore, can be seen as a private mechanism to protect businesses against

TABLE 4.11. *Industry-Level Analysis*

DV: Associations/1000 firms	Regulations/firm	Regulations
	(1)	(2)
Sectoral regulations	−3.875	−.00006
	(1.397)***	(.00003)**
Fixed-capital investment/firm	.150	.122
	(.023)***	(.012)***
Production concentration	−3.150	
	(.681)***	
Log (average employment)		−.686
		(.094)***
Const.	3.219	3.029
	(.601)***	(.424)***
Obs.	23	24

corruption and extensive regulation. They can help reduce the regulatory burden through a form of selective benefits. These targeted club goods allow the firms to escape the pitfalls of the collective action problem. The model predicted that, other things being equal, business associations should find organizing firms in an environment marked by lax deterrence against bureaucratic corruption to be easier. Another prediction is that more intrusive regulatory regimes, in fact, make it harder for associations to form and provide meaningful regulatory relief. I predicted that as business associations mature and attain larger membership, they would become more efficient in satisfying the demands of their members. I also expected that effective institutional constraints on the bureaucratic agencies enforcing regulations should condition the effects of regulatory regimes. Liberal regulations make it easier for associations to provide regulatory relief and attract members only if bureaucrats enforce them the way they are formally designed. When the bureaucrats entrusted with regulatory enforcement are able to impose costly red tape, official costs of doing business no longer reflect the actual regulatory burden and no longer correspond to associations' ability to provide regulatory relief. Lastly, I expected that, all other things being equal, higher costs of bribery would make the associational route for obtaining regulatory relief more attractive, hence boosting membership. Empirical analysis provided general support for these hypotheses.

One of the most consequential long-term predictions, based on the dynamic extensions of the model, has been that, at some point, associations should out-compete corrupt bureaucrats in providing regulatory relief. Thus, as associational membership grows, instances of bureaucratic graft should decrease. Although the lack of long-term data prevents putting this hypothesis to a direct test, available evidence is generally consistent with this long-term implication.

Business Environment and Business Organization 129

Overall, the empirical findings of this chapter support the expectations derived from the formal model.

The most important findings of this chapter concern the effects of the state regulatory environment. Extensive state intervention characterizes the regulatory environment in many post-communist countries. The statistical analysis of cross-national survey data on 17,872 firms in twenty-seven countries of Eastern Europe and the former USSR as well as of the aggregate socioeconomic indicators is consistent with many competing theories about the causes of interest-group formation. Still, the statistical tests presented in this chapter support the overall logic of the defensive organization argument: controlling for a number of firm-, industry-, and country-specific factors implicated in successful solutions to the collective action problem, features of regulatory regimes emerge as strong predictors of business participation in associations. Both the survey and aggregate data are congruent with the notion that business associations emerge and expand their membership in response to the state's failure to provide a beneficial and predictable regulatory environment. My analysis established that costly bureaucratic corruption has a positive effect on membership in business associations, whereas the failure to control systemic corruption and pervasive regulations impedes participation. Firm-level indicators of low-level bureaucratic corruption have a positive effect on membership. This suggests that an interesting pattern of relationships between economic agents and state structures is emerging in the post-communist context. Higher levels of bureaucratic corruption associated with "unofficial" regulatory burden stimulate collective action on the part of post-communist firms, whereas restrictive official regulatory policy suppresses the formation of business associations.

5

What You Do Is What You Are

Business Associations in Action

> The first business association I joined sent me a Christmas card, the second association sent me an invitation to the dinner with the mayor, and the third association sent me an official manual on banking regulations. I stick with the third.
>
> – Anotolii Fedianin, director general of the Perm Branch of RosBank

By joining associations, businesses gain access to member benefits. Naturally, the value of organizational membership is directly linked to what businesses get in return for membership dues. The services and benefits the associations provide to attract members and keep them satisfied should, therefore, directly address businesses' needs and demands. The ways to address them, however, largely depend on the associations' resources, connections, expertise, and management. In order to offer their members benefits that cannot be obtained elsewhere (e.g., from private markets or state agencies) at competitive costs, the associations have to invent ways of directing information flows, exhorting influence, and managing resources to effectively and efficiently address firms' demands. They have to seek new opportunities in a changing environment. In other words, they have to innovate.

This chapter examines the ways in which business associations interact with state regulators, facilitate information exchange, and build the mechanisms of self-regulation. All of these constitute innovative responses to the demands of associations' constituents. This chapter builds on the case studies of business associations in Russia, Ukraine, Croatia, and Kazakhstan. These cases illustrate different approaches business leaders have undertaken to combat the problems of a suffocating regulatory environment and corrupt bureaucracy.[1] I examine

---

[1] The research design and analyzed data do not allow for causal inferences about associations' effect on the regulatory environment. These go beyond the purpose of this chapter and the focus

What You Do Is What You Are 131

the functions performed by business associations that act as organizational entrepreneurs seeking innovative solutions to some of the problems that an adverse business environment creates. The analysis shows that in many cases associations' services and activities are specifically directed to reduce bureaucratic intervention, businesses' vulnerability, and transaction and regulatory costs. The case studies demonstrate that protection from corruption and reduction of bureaucratic barriers are provided in the form of selective incentives and, in some cases, as industry-wide collective benefits.

5.1 Advantages of Qualitative Data and Case Selection

Although the quantitative analysis developed in Chapter 4 supports the argument linking participation in business associations to features of the regulatory environment, the best available quantitative data do not allow us to understand *how* corruption and regulations affect the formation of business associations. Case studies are essential to understanding the mechanisms through which associations respond to regulatory burden and corruption. Demonstrating the mechanisms through which corrupt regulatory practices are factored into the process of associational development is essential to establishing the validity of the defensive organization argument.

To trace the causal mechanisms behind the defensive organization hypothesis, this chapter presents thirteen case studies of business associations. Some cases illustrate the ways in which associations provide protection from corruption in the form of selective incentives, and some present examples of collective benefits of regulatory relief that are a common good for the entire business community. The case studies do not cover all types of activities that business associations undertake, but they are representative of the most typical activities of business associations. In order to serve the interests of their members, associations interact with the state bureaucracy and political elites; thus, the adopted strategies are shaped not only by the demands of the business community and resources available to associations but also by the constraints and opportunities presented by state institutions and markets. I followed a nested analysis research strategy advocated by Lieberman (2005). The results of the quantitative analysis guided my selection of comparative cases for in-depth, process-tracing, qualitative analysis. This analysis compares business organizations across sectors (sometimes in the same country, sometimes in different ones) and across countries (sometimes in the same sector). By choosing cases based on country and sector, this approach controls for a variety of political and economic factors, ruling out concerns that the results are due to the idiosyncrasies of political regimes or economic conditions in a particular sector.

of the book. Instead, this chapter investigates causal mechanisms that are implicit in the causal argument about sources of business organization.

132 — Building Business

TABLE 5.1. *Member Services Provided by Business Associations (Based on Personal Interviews with Association Leaders and Analysis of Internal Documentation)*

Type of Service	Number	%
Information on business-promoting and cost-saving strategies:	27	61
Selective (club) goods	21	48
Collective	16	36
Legal advice and paperwork processing	26	59
Training in accounting, tax preparation, licensing, and certification	16	36
Legal action on behalf of members[a]	12	27
Total number of associations	44	100

[a] Although only 27 percent of analyzed associations have acted on behalf of their members in court (class-action suits), about a quarter of the associations provided other legal support. These two categories in fact are very close but are separated here to distinguish among continuous service provisions, for example, legal advising and sporadic actions such as court cases. Overall, legal protection, either by filing class-action suits or by advising enterprises in other litigations, is characteristic of a large number of business associations.

In order to ensure that the cases are not idiosyncratic but do in fact reflect general trends in the development of associational functions, I first analyzed detailed qualitative data on forty-four business associations. Table 5.1 summarizes the distribution of different types of member services across the sample. It shows that of the forty-four associations I closely studied while researching this topic, more than half provide their members with information on market-related and regulatory issues. I classify these informational services into collective or selective benefits based on the modes of delivering the information. When information was provided through club channels (e.g., subscription-based publications, mailed newsletters, password-protected websites, closed seminars), I identified these as selective incentives. Cases of mass media and publicly distributed publications, open-access databases, and public conferences were classified as collective benefits.

Information is a type of commodity that has spillover effects and hence is hard to keep exclusive to dues-paying members. However, most of the value associated with information comes from its timing and relevance and the transaction costs in obtaining it. Although the associations generate some types of information (e.g., expert reports, databases, technical recommendations), the majority of informational services fall into the information-transmission type. Associational publications, newsletters, and Web sites often digest public information that is available through other sources. The transaction costs of obtaining such information from public sources, however, are often high. Most of the value of informational services provided by business associations is derived from the reduction in the transaction costs of obtaining relevant, timely, and accurate (e.g., verified) information. Transaction costs associated

What You Do Is What You Are

with information transmission make it possible to provide informational services in the form of club goods or selective incentives.[2]

Some associations have undertaken legal action on behalf of their members, and many others offer legal advice and clerical help in complying with rules and regulations. Additionally, a number of associations educate their members about regulations in their corresponding industry and/or the legal rights of entrepreneurs. Other associations organize training in accounting practices, tax preparation, licensing, and certification procedures that, in many cases, minimizes the cost of regulatory compliance.

Although 70 percent of the association leaders I talked to had a favorable opinion of the prospects for industry self-regulation, over half of these respondents admitted that their members were not yet ready for self-regulation or doubted that bureaucrats would ever relinquish their regulatory monopoly. Only six associations were successful in demanding such delegation of bureaucratic tasks.[3] In cases in which this form of delegation has not happened, associations have been active in lobbying to reduce bureaucratic barriers and change regulatory regimes in a way that would make regulations more transparent and less costly.

Knowing the overall frequency of these service categories helped me select representative cases. Three principles guided the case selection. First, the cases had to represent the most common spheres of activities that associations undertake. Although each association presents a distinctive combination of goals and ways to accomplish them, I attempted to sample the kinds of activities most characteristic of a wide range of associations. The second criterion in the selection of cases was to cover a wide range of different strategies available to associations in advancing their agenda; therefore, I tried to select cases as diverse as possible in the kinds of instruments and strategies business associations choose. In selecting the cases on which to perform a detailed, descriptive analysis, I considered the associations' size and resources and selected associations operating in different countries and sectors under different institutional and market constraints. The third criterion was verifiability. Representatives

---

[2] In the quote that opens this chapter, the manual in question is an official publication by the Russian Finance Ministry and the Central Bank. Obtaining this manual in the mid-1990s in the provincial city of Perm was a complicated business. The provincial ministry was not in the habit of providing a copy of this manual to banks, even upon request. Obtaining a copy usually meant a trip to the ministry and pleading for the use of the Xerox machine to make a photocopy. By mailing a copy of an official manual to its regional members, the Russian Banking Association (not to be confused with ARB) reduced transaction costs. Although the information per se (the manual) is a public good, the transaction costs of obtaining such information are clearly private and hence constitute a selective incentive.

[3] Sectors that require highly specialized regulatory expertise – often "new" sectors that did not exist in the command economy – have been more successful at self-regulating. Realtors, accountants, bankers, and consulting firms of various sorts have imposed much stricter self-regulations than the existing bureaucratic policy.

of business associations have an incentive to exaggerate their organization's indispensability to the members and to portray themselves in a good light. Aware of this bias, I tried to verify all information obtained in the course of my interviews by consulting internal and public documents, third-party assessments, and media coverage. As a result, the case studies collected in this chapter for the most part reflect well-publicized issues and campaigns that attracted public attention.

Table 5.2 summarizes types of benefits I analyzed across thirteen cases. It shows a mixture of selective incentive and collective benefits business associations provide on both ongoing and sporadic bases. These different types of activities reflect different strategies by which associations cater to the interests of their members. In many cases, however, judging how effective associations are in satisfying members' demands is very difficult.[4] I present cases that allow for the evaluation of the extent to which associations are able to provide regulatory relief through some objective measures (e.g., whether or not a demanded change in regulation was implemented, a lawsuit decided in an association's favor, or the state authorities changed the implementation policies). Nevertheless, judging how much of the success or the failure is to be attributed to associations' actions is still difficult. The discussed cases are not meant to demonstrate that all associations through their actions are able to lower the cost of doing business and fight corruption; instead, I attempt to walk the reader through possible mechanisms of how activities of business associations (if successful) can lead to regulatory relief and reduced corruption.

My examination of associational services is primarily driven by the desire to understand why businesses join existing associations. In some sectors and locations, however, these associations had to be created before they could start providing benefits. Several cases discussed in this chapter examine business mobilization that led to the establishment of business associations. The question of initial mobilization is closely related to the issue of why businesses join associations. On the one hand, the firms that establish an association are simultaneously solving the question of their own membership. On the other hand, pressures responsible for business mobilization, if not immediately resolved through collective goods provision, are likely to motivate other firms to engage in collective action and join existing business organizations. Although the questions of group membership and initial mobilization are separate, they are closely related in theory and by the empirical realities of the post-communist organizational landscape. The initial mobilization efforts are particularly

---

[4] In order to address this question, we need to examine member-level rather than association-level data. The cross-regional comparisons discussed in Chapter 3 in fact demonstrate that post-communist business associations are quite effective in satisfying member demands for market-related and regulatory information. A number of recent studies corroborate this evidence (Golikova 2009; Markus 2009; Yakovlev and Govorun 2011; Pyle 2006, 2011).

What You Do Is What You Are

TABLE 5.2. *Summary of Analyzed Associational Services*

Association	Selective Benefits	Collective Benefits
Guild for the Audio-Video Trade Development, Russia	One-time: legalization of inventory held by the members prior to the new licensing scheme (successful)	One-time: participated in the development of implementation schemes for new licensing regulation (successful)
Federation of Restaurants and Hotels, Russia	Ongoing: voluntary quality certification, professional training, market and regulation information	Ongoing: participation in the development of new state regulations One-time: developed and lobbied for new state standard (GOST) (successful)
Ukrainian Association of Leasing Companies and Entrepreneurs	Ongoing: legal consulting, collective complaints to the regulating state institutions, market and regulation information, class-action lawsuits	Ongoing: member to the National Council on Social Partnership, legislative lobbying
League of Trade Merchants, Russia	Ongoing: legal consulting, market and regulation information, professional training One-time: class-action suit against state bureaucracy (successful)	Ongoing: member of advising and consulting groups under state institutions
Ukrainian Chamber of Commerce and Industry	Ongoing: quality inspection, arbitration, marine and forwarding agents, customs brokers, research and testing facilities, certification, market information, regulatory information, legal consulting and assistance	Ongoing: fee-based provision of some member services to nonmembers, positive externalities
Professional Association of Registrars, Transfer Agents, and Depositories, Russia	Ongoing: enforcement of professional rules of conduct for its members, self-regulation	One-time: lobbied in favor of the law on self-regulation (successful)
Almaty Association of Entrepreneurs, Kazakhstan	Ongoing: mobile legal service team	Ongoing: public advocacy, conferences and open seminars One-time: temporary suspension of unannounced state inspections (successful)

(continued)

136   *Building Business*

TABLE 5.2. *(continued)*

Association	Selective Benefits	Collective Benefits
Association of Trading Companies and Producers of Appliances and Electronics, Russia	Ongoing: voluntary product certification, marketing and technical databases, discounts on services provided by the association's affiliates One-time: prevented legal actions against member companies in relation to import machinations (successful)	Ongoing: business forums, seminars, joint advertising campaigns, market research (some results are published, while others are provided exclusively to the members), industry magazine publication One-time: facilitated legalization of confiscated imports for the purchase by the industry (successful)
Association of Croatian Exporters	Ongoing: regulatory and market information (newsletter and password-protected website)	One-time: lobbied for extending working hours of the customs offices (successful), lobbied for EU sugar quota increase (successful)
Coordinating Expert Center of Business Associations of Ukraine	None observed	Ongoing: monitors regulatory legislation, develops joint proposals, media campaigns, legislative lobbying, picketing One-time: lobbied against the Stamp Duty (successful) and electronic cash registers (unsuccessful)
Russian Association of Ice Cream Producers	Ongoing: certifies production facilities of its members, regulatory and market information through member-only newsletter, professional training	Ongoing: informational (monthly magazine and annual pamphlet), annual expositions, regional expos, research, member of the Expert Council on Food Regulation under the parliamentary committee One-time: lobbied for new GOST, the reduction of the VAT, and reduction of import tariffs (all successful)
Kazakh Business Forum	Ongoing: media campaigns in support of individual members	One-time: lobbied against tobacco-advertising regulation (unsuccessful)
Ukrainian National Association for the Development of Trade and Services	Ongoing: targeted market and regulatory information, legal counseling and assistance	One-time: advocacy campaigns against food-safety permits for baked goods (successful) and plastic-card-processing terminals regulations (unsuccessful)

What You Do Is What You Are   137

interesting because they present the opportunity to examine the most difficult steps in associational development – overcoming the start-up costs.[5]

Business associations that exist in any given country at any given time are a subset of all possible associations that could have emerged there if conditions were right. We do not know about associations that never came into existence. A closer look at the cases in which associations failed to emerge, however, is necessary to avoid selection bias. At the end of this chapter I offer a discussion about "dogs that did not bark" – industries that failed to develop associations despite some strong reasons to expect associational formation. Naturally, cases of failed collective action are hard to study due to the lack of data; few records, if any, are kept on organizations that do not survive or are not even initiated. Still, by identifying economic interests that fail to organize, I put the association-formation theory to an additional test. Most important, these cases of nonformation are consistent with the argument made above.

5.2 Against All Odds

The analysis of microlevel data in Chapter 4 points to the importance of firm size, ownership structure, and resource specificity as strong predictors of firms' associational membership. The highest levels of participation in business and employer associations across the post-communist space are observed in industries characterized by a small number of firms, considerable concentration of resources, large number of foreign-owned businesses, and, in some instances, large firm size. Associational development and membership growth in the above-mentioned sectors, however, cannot serve as valid evidence in favor of the defensive organization argument because enterprises in such industries possess characteristics that act as important facilitators of business participation. To examine the mechanisms implied in the explanation based on characteristics of the regulatory environment, one should consider sectors lacking those important factors. In the following pages I investigate two sectors that lack factors facilitating collective action. In fact, group characteristics make the industries analyzed below the least likely places for the development of business associations. These are the crucial cases for evaluating the plausibility of causal mechanisms behind the effects of the regulatory environment because the potential effects of other factors implicated in successful collective action are effectively minimized.

Below I closely examine two sectors – the audio-video trade and the hospitality industry. Both are dominated by small, locally-based, new, and formerly-state-owned privatized businesses with little investment in fixed

---

[5] As the theoretical extension developed in Chapter 2 points out, the costs of membership should be highest (and the net benefits lowest) at the early stages of organizational formation. As the organizations mature and their membership grows, the net benefits of organizational membership should grow, thereby easing the membership decisions.

capital. A crucial piece of information lies in the circumstances surrounding the emergence of associations representing the interests of firms operating in these lines of business. An examination of benefits extended by business associations to their first members should suggest the reasons firms join these associations. These two case studies show how the regulatory environment and the anticorruption measures shape the associations' ability to provide member services and enhance the attractiveness of organizations as a means of regulatory relief.

"Guys from the Street Corner"

The story of the Guild for the Audio-Video Trade Development (the Guild) is an interesting example of business mobilization. In Russia small enterprises that surfaced in the early stages of economic liberalization dominate the audio-video retail trade as well as trade in computer software. This "new" sector of the Russian economy is highly fragmented and resource-poor, aggravating the problem of start-up costs for a business organization. The sector developed virtually from scratch after the Soviet-era music-recording labels lost their distribution networks to the new, smaller entities that were able to satisfy consumer demands for cheap entertainment. Russia inherited the Soviet legal system, which had little recognition of copyrights. The complete absence of a working system of copyright protection has precipitated the decline of the Soviet-era audio industry. General economic hardship stalled domestic film and audio production while foreign counterfeit products came to dominate the market. The video and computer software industry did not have any roots in the Soviet economy; naturally, foreign-pirated products flooded the market.

Trade in pirated audio and video products, initially imported from Bulgaria and China and later produced at home, burgeoned by the mid-1990s. The 1993 law on Copyright and Neighboring Rights created a legal basis for copyright protection, and the norms of international conventions on copyrights were incorporated into Russia's legislation. The enforcement mechanisms, however, were weak. The law did not stipulate the mechanisms through which holders of the copyrights were to be compensated. Copyright violations were classified as an administrative or economic crime, and no criminal charges could be brought against pirates. In 1996 the International Intellectual Property Alliance (IIPA) reported that a complete absence of any effective enforcement has meant that in Russia "piracy rates approached 100 percent in most sectors" (IIPA 1996).

In 1995 the introduction of administrative and procedural changes to the legislation opened new channels for copyright law enforcement.[6] Nevertheless, the presidential veto on amendments to the criminal code (some of which

---

[6] The move came after Russia opened the WTO accession negotiations in 1993. The talks highlighted intellectual property as one of its weakest links. All regulatory changes in the sphere of copyright protection undertaken by the Russian governments thereafter were driven by the external pressures of the WTO accession demands.

What You Do Is What You Are 139

would make copyright violations criminal offenses) delayed the implementation of effective enforcement until 2002. The only available venues for copyright protection were civil damage remedies and administrative control by state authorities, who were given the right to seize counterfeit products ex officio. The former mechanism resulted in meager compensations; thus, the holders of copyrights would rarely revert to legal action. The latter mechanism consisted of police raids by the Ministry of Interior on street vendors and at other locations where counterfeit products were suspected, resulting in the confiscation of pirated products. The producers of pirated video, audio, and software products were also subject to raids, during which their equipment was confiscated.

Because the legitimate holders of the copyrights and legitimate producers lacked established legal mechanisms to fight counterfeit retailers, the major threat to the pirated audio-video trade came from the coercive and inconsistently applied power of state agencies that wielded this power at their discretion. Throughout the late 1990s there were a number of crackdowns carried out against retail traders. However, those crackdowns were sporadic and targeted few retail locations; they would hurt some traders but left others unaffected. Multiple reports suggest that authorities often patronized the pirated trade and harassed legitimate traders with arbitrary inspections (CNews.ru 2003; Vorontsov 2003). According to IIRA, such raiding by the police and municipal authorities was rarely followed up by prosecution and the court system (IIPA 2002). This indicates that oftentimes regulatory and enforcement agencies struck deals with the pirates to share the proceeds from their continuing violation of the law. At the same time, the firms that chose compliance with copyright regulations were not only losing in market competition with pirates but were also suffering from raids and bureaucratic inspections that interrupted their commerce. A large portion of the market participants who were willing to "play by the rules" suffered from the nonenforcement of standards and procedures and from the increasing insecurity associated with unclear regulations. Because confiscations did not seem to make any noticeable difference, high-level authorities tried to implement other mechanisms of control that would make collusion harder for bureaucrats and pirates. In 2002 the ban on street-vendor video and audio trade was put in place in Moscow and some other cities (Liubavina and Nagibin 2003). Again, enforcement was sporadic, and multiple mechanisms for avoiding confiscations and subsequent legal actions existed. Needless to say, the only way this industry could exist was by sharing its profits with bureaucrats who refrained from enforcing the copyright law in exchange for bribes.

This wild pirate market has prevailed for a decade, allowing the establishment of specialization, competition, and product-promotion strategies. In this new branch of commerce, few prerequisites for collective action existed. A large number of small competing firms or individual traders, operating in isolated locations, dominated the sector. By the mid-1990s, a number of larger production facilities established themselves, with a few big plants producing CDs and

140   *Building Business*

DVDs. At the same time, small, usually financially unstable firms employing a small number of people continued to dominate the retail trade. Balancing on the fine line of legality, enterprises in the audio-video trade were especially vulnerable to corruption, albeit often using it to stay in business (Dorohov and Krampets 2003).

If, as suggested by the defensive organization hypothesis, businesses join associations as an alternative to illegitimate means of easing their operations, the situation that developed in the Russian audio-video trade sector by the mid-1990s was not very conducive to group formation. The state was failing to fulfill its functions of contract enforcement, property rights protection, and corruption deterrence. Legislative loopholes rewarded pirating while putting legitimate business in a disadvantageous situation. Bureaucrats entrusted with regulatory enforcement were inconsistent and unaccountable and often colluded with the violators. No association to unite enterprises in the audio-video sector emerged in the 1990s; instead, firms relied on corruption as a means of solving their problems.

The event that tipped the situation in favor of collective action was the introduction of new licensing procedures in 2002 that ensured more consistent and accountable enforcement.[7] The new regulation gave entrepreneurs a means to legalize their trade while at the same time increasing the penalties for illegal operations and collusive behavior. Following the changes to the criminal code that made copyright infringement a criminal offense, the October 2003 raids on the Gorbunova market and Moscow Expo Center evoked a strong reaction from market participants. The 2003 crackdown on the largest concentration of audio-video commerce put the entire audio-video trade in danger. Moscow authorities began enforcing property rights by closing down enterprises that failed to prove that they sold licensed products. The criminalization of pirating also made patronizing the pirates much costlier for regulating agencies.

The actions of the Moscow authorities brought together entrepreneurs who formed a hastily organized group. In a meeting instituting the Guild, they designed a program of reconciliation for the existing situation and made an effort to contact Moscow authorities. "We were not sure if the authorities would even talk to us," said Iurii Sorokin, the director general of the Guild. "In the end, we were just guys from the street corner" (Sorokin 2005). However, Moscow's city government not only opened communication but was also eager to invite representatives of the association to the working group that developed new regulations. Despite the fact that the association did not have a long-established membership base, it became the primary channel for voicing

---

[7] Although the new licensing regulations were an important step against pirating, copyright infringements continue to plague the sector to this day. Part of the problem is that Russian legislation does not require explicit contracts between the sellers and the holders of the copyrighted material but instead stipulates a compensation mechanism. In addition, the burden of prosecuting copyright violators rests with the owners, who have to initiate lawsuits against the pirates.

What You Do Is What You Are 141

the interests of the audio-video market traders in the emerging situation. Authorities were eager to win private-sector allies in their fight against corrupt enforcers. The Guild pushed for the legalization of products its members held prior to the introduction of the new licensing scheme. It advocated against repressive crackdowns and corrupt inspections, arguing that clear licensing procedures and improved transparency would eradicate pirating more effectively. The association declared the formation of a "civilized" market, guided by consistent and fair regulations that are developed in consultation with the industry as its major goal.

By increasing the punishment for illegal trade and cover-ups on the part of regulating agencies and enforcement officials, the 2002 law raised the cost of engaging in corruption for both the businesses and bureaucrats. The higher costs of corruption closed up informal channels of regulatory relief and brought together an otherwise disorganized and fragmented group in the search for a legitimate alternative to the corrupt bureaucratic solution. This is an example of how increasing the threat of persecution for corruption stimulated group formation. The exogenous (mostly international) pressures pushing toward stringent antipirating measures, which increased the penalty for engaging in corrupt cover-ups of illegal trade, provided the stimulus for collective action among small, financially unstable, and, for the most part, competing firms in the video-audio retail sector.

The Federation of Restaurants and Hotels

The Federation of Restaurants and Hotels (the Federation) presents an example of collective action in the dining and hotel sectors, which were largely underdeveloped under state socialism. Few restaurants and hotels were oriented toward foreign tourists, and the majority of enterprises offered cheap, low-quality services for domestic consumers. Before the transition, most demand for public dining was satisfied through *vedomstvennye* [departmental] cafeterias that served industrial enterprises and public organizations. The cooperative movement in the late 1980s hardly had an impact on the sector; only privatization during the early 1990s allowed for the establishment of the majority of new enterprises. In the process of privatization, vedomstvennye cafeterias, restaurants, and hotels were among the first enterprises to undergo privatization, which removed state control in the sector. Until the 1998 default, small restaurants were growing as side businesses for the new entrepreneurial class, accommodating the emerging demand for dining and entertainment. The economic difficulties that followed Russia's shock therapy and resulting falling incomes and demand, however, slowed the development of such new enterprises.

The sector got a strong impetus for development when the Russian economy underwent recovery after the 1998 collapse, and an improving economic situation put more disposable income in the hands of the middle class. Class differentiation created customers who demanded higher quality services in the sphere of public dining and hotel accommodations. By the late 1990s a large

142   *Building Business*

number of restaurants and cafeterias oriented to middle-class customers opened in major Russian cities. In the most economically prosperous regions, in the sphere of public dining, to this date the industry has not been able to accommodate the rapidly growing demand; the shortage of restaurants is particularly felt during lunch hour in Moscow and other large cities. To some extent such shortages can explain the fact that the McDonald's restaurant on Pushkin Square in Moscow daily serves the largest number of customers in the world.[8] At the same time, the construction boom in Moscow and St. Petersburg has accelerated development in the hotel industry. Given the large size of Russia's potential internal market, the hotel and restaurant sector remains small, with about 3,700 enterprises employing 189,000 individuals (Sokolin 2006).

In terms of the ownership structure and average size of businesses, the sector falls into the category for which one would not expect successful collective action. Most firms are domestically owned and small. Following economic liberalization, some major foreign hotel chains have entered the Russian market, though they are confined to the major cities of Moscow and St. Petersburg. Starting in the late 1990s the hotel industry grew predominantly in the "microhotel" sector, which required less capital investment and allowed greater flexibility. Optional hotel certification schemes that remained in place until 2010 promoted the development of small and microhotels. Larger hotels, according to the Russian classification, fall in the category of medium-sized businesses, whereas small, locally owned enterprises dominate the restaurant and microhotel businesses. The average firm in the sector employs fifty people; the modal enterprise, however, employs fewer than half of this number. Although franchising schemes have been introduced in Russia, the number of franchised brands is still limited, with the major ones – Shokoladnitsa, Country Chicken, and Grill Master – jointly accounting for about fifty franchised operations.[9]

The industry, dominated by numerous, small, largely locally owned and geographically dispersed enterprises, should, theoretically, face strong impediments to collective action. Despite this, in August 2003 leading Moscow restaurants founded the Federation of Restaurants and Hotels (the Federation). The main purpose of the Federation, according to its founding documents, is the "development of the dining and hospitality industry by means of consolidation of its enterprises and unification of efforts of Russian restaurants into one powerful force to overcome obstacles for development" (Federation of Restaurants and Hotels 2003, 4). The major tasks of the Federation, as formulated by its

---

[8] According to the official McDonald's Asia Web site, http://i-am-asian.com/, Pushkin Square restaurant serves 40,000 people every day and is the busiest McDonald's in the world. The restaurant opened in January 1990 to become Russia's first McDonald's. With a maximum occupancy of 900 customers, the restaurant served 30,000 guests on its first day of operation. This record remains unchallenged (Golloher 2010). The world's largest McDonald's restaurants, located in Vinita, Oklahoma, and Beijing, China (30,000 and 28,000 square feet, respectively), occupy larger premises but serve fewer guests.

[9] See www.franchisinguniverse.ru.

What You Do Is What You Are 143

leadership, include representing the industry's interests in the state agencies, participating in the development of normative documents regulating the industry, facilitating the development of markets for restaurant and related services, and organizing training centers for the industry's personnel.

In 2006 the Federation united 980 enterprises in the hospitality industry, including large and small hotels, haute cuisine and fast food restaurants, clubs, and entertaining venues. In the three years since its formation, the Federation has opened branches (regional associations) in at least half of Russia's provinces and established contacts with related international (International Association of Restaurants and Hotels) and domestic (Opora, the CCI) associations. The Federation made its way into a number of state working committees, including the advisory councils under the administration of the president of the Russian Federation and the Ministry of Economic Development and Trade. To pursue its task of facilitating professional recruitment and training, the Federation established contacts with the Ministry of Education and Federal Migration Service. The Federation also supports active contacts with the Federal Service on Supervision in the Sphere of Consumer Rights Protection.

Unlike the case of business association formation in the sphere of the audio-video trade, in which a changing regulatory environment stimulated collective action, few regulatory changes have been made in the restaurant and hotel industry since the transition. In fact, by the turn of the century, regulatory state institutions were still enforcing sanitary, consumer safety, and quality standards that had been developed as early as the mid-1950s. Indeed, Aleksandr Kindeev, the executive director of the Federation, linked the formation of the association to the growing desire of its participants to modernize outdated practices and regulations that retarded their businesses' development.

Outdated standards and Soviet-era norms has greatly slowed the development of the sector. Although the overall number of regulatory guidelines is not particularly high – with 3,735 federal, regional, and local regulations, the sector has an average number of regulatory documents among Russian industries[10] – restaurants often have to comply with outdated sanitary and safety regulations. They also have to develop their menus under Soviet-era guidelines. Industry regulations prescribe the types and capacity of equipment to be employed in the kitchens, establish norms of handling and use of ingredients, and regulate standards of quality of raw products and output. Because, for the most part, these regulations have not been updated for a long time, they fail to recognize and establish standards for handling new ingredients, usage of modern kitchen equipment, and greatly changed service practices. This situation led to increasing bureaucratic discretion in applying the existing norms and more opportunities for bureaucratic extortion.

---

[10] The number of regulatory procedures is obtained from *Garant*. See Chapter 3 for a detailed description.

144 *Building Business*

The outdated regulations gave the regulating agencies greater room in interpreting existing standards and procedures when applying them to new products and equipment. This practice increases firms' dependency on bureaucratic judgment and discourages the introduction of new products, equipment, menus, and services. As an example, the storage standards for produce and partially processed food, developed in the 1960s, make it impossible to utilize new refrigeration equipment to its full capacity. Although manufacturers' specifications would allow much longer storage time, existing storage norms, developed for the old equipment, could not be extended. Novel, often imported produce presents additional difficulties because quality, storage, and use regulations are nonexistent. One high-cuisine restaurant complained about the difficulty in classifying artichokes for the purpose of storage and processing. Until somewhat recently, Russian chefs only rarely used artichokes, so they were not listed in the vegetable regulation guidelines. When visited by an inspector, one restaurant was fined for storing artichokes as a vegetable. After the restaurant started storing artichokes with the greens, the same inspector issued another fine, arguing that an artichoke is clearly a vegetable (Kindeev 2005).

The lack of contemporary standards makes restaurants that introduce novel produce and equipment particularly vulnerable vis-à-vis regulatory state agencies. The major complaint voiced by the restaurants and the hotels was not that the standards were too hard to meet – in fact new equipment and technology often made it possible to significantly exceed the prescribed quality standards – but rather that they were inconsistently enforced. For example, standards for five-star-hotel certification that replaced the Soviet-era classification in 1994 resembled the Western classification only in name, setting suboptimal standards for the industry. The real problem was their inconsistent application across the country's regions and over time.[11] In the restaurant sector, official regulations did not stipulate any norms to be followed in serving customers, making it more difficult to position restaurants that adhere to different standards of etiquette on the same market (e.g., differentiating among cafeterias as well as self-service and full-service restaurants).

The Federation seeks to become a self-regulating association that develops norms and standards for the industry at large and enforces such norms among its members. Although Russian legislation has not yet extended the self-regulation schemes to the hospitality sector, the Federation developed and enforced alternative quality standards for its members, allowing them to use their membership status as a marker, thus conveying information about the quality of their services to customers. In order to facilitate the application of its quality standards, the Federation runs a number of vocational training venues where members enjoy preferential fee schedules. To solve the collective-reputation

---

[11] In 2003 the tourist law was amended to clarify five-star classification standards, and a more reasonable centralized classification system was put in place in 2006. However, quality certification, which created room for industry-provided quality standards, was optional until 2010.

What You Do Is What You Are 145

problem and modernize outdated regulatory standards, the Federation actively engages state authorities. It made its way to the ministerial working groups that designed new state standards (GOSTs) for the food industry, facilitated the adoption of new federal laws that separated restaurant regulations from those enforced in the retail sector, and developed a new curriculum for state-run professional education institutions. This shows that the Federation has made much progress in serving its members through selective incentives and has helped reshape the industry's regulatory environment through its advocacy.

If inadequate and inconsistently enforced regulations were the major catalyst of the association's development, why had the businesses waited to establish an association until 2003, after an entire decade of the sector's existence outside state control? The reasons can be traced to the internal development of the sector. Although initially there were many "random people" trying out the sphere of the restaurant business, by the turn of the century there emerged entrepreneurs who had accumulated the experience and expertise specific to the market for restaurant and hotel services. Their ability to provide better services, increasing demand, and growing competition played a great role in bringing enterprises together in search of better standards. The restaurants of the mid-1990s neither had the vision nor the need for alternative standards or regulatory practices. The demands for associational services emerged after the post-communist transformation produced a more structured market in the sphere of dining services.

In terms of the formal model developed in Chapter 2, Russia's hospitality sector experiences a combination of moderate official regulatory burden,[12] high bureaucratic discretion,[13] and costly corruption. The latter originates from the inadequacy of the regulatory framework, giving the bureaucrats the power to interpret regulations freely and extort bribes. As a result, the industry's dissatisfaction with the regulations and push for self-regulation reflected not the high official regulatory burden but rather the unofficial impediments created by unaccountable and corrupt street-level bureaucrats. The combination of underdeveloped regulatory frameworks and corrupt enforcement mechanisms made it possible for the association to establish itself as an appealing alternative to corrupt behavior. The association has offered its members more adequate self-regulation mechanisms and a collective-advocacy venue that might have increased the cost of compliance but significantly decreased vulnerability, transaction costs, and bureaucratic dependence.

These case studies of business associations representing business interests in two sectors of the Russian economy point to the connection among regulatory regimes, corrupt enforcement mechanisms, and the development of associational services. In the course of my field research in Russia I came across many

---

[12] As mentioned earlier, the sector has an average level of official regulatory procedures.

[13] In fact, discretionary bureaucratic enforcement accounts for much of the regulatory cost.

examples in which, similar to the audio-video and restaurant-sector examples, business associations were formed in an attempt to counter regulations and corruption. Although the two case studies presented above reflect recently established associations, I also came across sectoral associations formed as early as 1991. Qualitative research suggests that the goals, strategies, and activities of such associations changed along with the changing membership and economic conditions. These changes in organizational priorities provide additional evidence that associations are actively searching for ways to provide regulatory relief and countervail corruption. The next section presents case studies that speak to this point.

5.3 Changing Times – Changing Roles

The Ukrainian Association of Leasing Companies and Entrepreneurs (UALCE)

As one of the oldest Ukrainian business associations (see the description of Ukrainian business representation in Chapter 3), the UALCE underwent a profound transformation of its membership, functions, and prioritized activities. Established as a part of the All-Soviet organization in 1990, the UALCE pioneered the representation of the first nonstate proprietors: over 1,000 formerly state-owned enterprises that were privatized or leased into private operation at the outset of the economic transition. The UALCE defined its primary goal as protecting emerging private property through legal assistance, leadership development, training, and lobbying for changes in legal frameworks that would guarantee the property rights of private and leased companies. Starting in 1993, the UALCE participated in the process of tripartite negotiations through the National Council on Social Partnership under the president of Ukraine and became one of three employer associations to sign the annual General Tripartite Agreements.

Initially, from 1990 to 1996, the UALCE's activities concentrated on the process of privatization and the development of a legal foundation for private property. The UALCE advocated long-term leases with buyouts as a mechanism for privatization. This mechanism allowed for small and medium-size enterprises to develop on the basis of state-owned land, equipment, production facilities, and premises without any initial capital required for a buyout but with a constant stream of benefits flowing to the state coffers. The low-ranking managers of state-owned enterprises, cooperators, and de novo start-ups favored this plan. In 1991 the UALCE was able to propose its draft bill, "On Entrepreneurship," to the Parliament; in 1992 it made its proposal of the draft laws, "On Leasing the Property of State Enterprises and Organizations"; in 1994 "On Privatization"; and in 1996 "On the Specifics of Privatization in the Agro-Industrial Sector."

Starting in the early 1990s, representing the legal interests of association members in a court of law became the major selective benefit provided to

What You Do Is What You Are 147

association members.[14] Legal assistance includes providing information, legal consulting, and class-action suits as well as coordinating collective complaints against regulating state institutions. As early as 1990 the association put together an informational publication on the taxation of nonstate enterprises. The publication was distributed to the association members to educate them about their rights vis-à-vis state authorities.

As new start-up companies, which had no connections to the state, joined the initial members, the UALCE opened a legal department that offered individual consultations regarding taxation, enterprise incorporation and registration, licensing, and other aspects of conducting business in Ukraine. Corruption in state regulatory agencies has gradually become one of the most frequent issues the UALCE members raise. In the late 1990s, to facilitate its anticorruption actions, the UALCE established a telephone hotline and a dedicated mailbox where members are instructed to direct their complaints about corrupt officials. Below are excerpts from one of the letters sent to the "anticorruption mailbox" followed by the association's response, as reprinted in the UALCE monthly magazine.

> When I started my business, I came across the problem of corruption.... The most profitable business opportunities and contracts were taken by the close associates of key bureaucrats at the Kyiv city administration, police, and other official institutions.... Whenever I come up with a new business idea, I find myself confronted with all kinds of "inquiries" from the controlling state organizations. Only later do I realize that my ideas have been put into practice by someone else without any licenses, permissions, or control from the state institutions. I even know the rates of bribes paid to the representatives of state agencies and organizations.... I'm not alone in this situation. What should be done when my rights are clearly violated? What else can I do in addition to going to court? Is bribing the easiest way to get things done?

The UALCE gave the following response in its monthly magazine:

> Unfortunately, many businessmen find themselves in similar situations. There are multiple ways to fight corruption. In addition to going to court, you can file complaints against actions of state officials, or report instances of corruption to the special investigating agencies. If you have concrete evidence of corruption, we recommend, either individually or with our assistance, that you report it to the investigating agencies.... You are right that giving bribes seems to be the most rational way.... But, it is also true that legal action is the most efficient and civilized way to confront corruption that has ever been invented.... Understandably, it is hard to do so alone: you have to find an attorney, spend time in consultation, and come up with strong arguments for your litigation – all these at the expense of time needed for

---

[14] By 2005 the UALCE united 1,020 direct members (firms); 4 all-Ukrainian associations, including the Association of Employers in Trade and Commerce, Barber's Union, All-Ukrainian Union of Trade and Services, and the Association of Ukrainian Glass Producers; 36 regional organizations; and 19 local offices. The ALCE estimates that over 40 percent of its members are microbusinesses (*Rabotodavets'* February 2004, December 2005).

148   *Building Business*

> your business. But for that, there are business associations like the UALCE. We exist, among other reasons, to help defend entrepreneurs' rights. *Rabotodavets'* magazine for two years has been working towards our main goal of uniting employers into one civil force. Although individually, businesspeople like you can do nothing but pay bribes (and if you don't pay enough, you lose!), when we unite into a socially important force, everybody – and the corrupt officials in particular – has to take us into account. (*Rabotodavets,* November 2005)

This selection from *Rabotodavets* highlights two important aspects of the UALCE mission. First, the association routinely offers legal support to defend property rights against bureaucratic predation. It pays special attention to protection from corruption, and the association's legal specialists can reduce managerial time and effort spent in litigation. Second, the UALCE clearly recognizes its protective function in firms' relations with regulating authorities. The association's response clearly identifies bureaucratic predation as a common threat to businesses and proposes collective action as an effective response to this common enemy. Evidently, the legal assistance and benefits of protection in this case are available exclusively to the organization's members. Although the ultimate goal might be the complete eradication of corruption, which is a collective good, the mechanisms the association uses imply selective benefits.

Initially established to represent the interests of private businesses that leased their equipment or land from the state, over the years the association added many functions to the list of its activities. As the market transformation proceeded, the association's membership base changed from the leasing companies and cooperatives to the privately owned start-ups operating predominantly in the small-business sector. The association had to find ways to attract these businesses. Because the legislative protection of private property, which had been the first priority in the early 1990s, was no longer relevant, the association discovered other ways to secure the property rights of its changing constituents. By providing legal advice and coordinating anticorruption efforts, the association has offered protection against the adverse regulatory environment.

The League of Trade Merchants, Russia

The League of Trade Merchants (the League) also provides the selective benefits of reducing the cost of regulatory compliance and corruption to its members. The association was established in the early 1990s, when vast economic changes were sweeping Russia. The League dates its existence to the price liberalization of 1992. The shocks of newly liberalized prices, inflation, and, more importantly, the breakdown of the Soviet-style, state-controlled retail trade left Moscow's grocery stores in complete disarray. Initially, the League brought large supermarkets and grocery stores together in an attempt to cope with the challenges of building new markets. Organizational stimulus came from the former Ministry of Trade and its Moscow branch. However, in the following years the association's membership composition, personnel, and

What You Do Is What You Are 149

activities changed dramatically. The privatization of the retail trade enterprises and mushrooming of small de novo stores have resulted in the demise of traditional large retailers. Small firms came to dominate the sector. The League found itself poorly equipped for the task of attracting new members whose interests were quite different from those of its initial membership base. Firms that emerged on the new economic landscape were no longer interested in an association taking over the functions of coordination formerly performed by the state agencies.

To attract new members, the League changed the focus of its activities. The association had to offer its constituents member services they could not obtain elsewhere. Starting in the mid-1990s, the League realized that the most important service it could offer to its constituents was intermediation between firms and the state bureaucracy. The activities undertaken by the association included educating the firms about the best strategies for confronting corruption, informing them about their legal rights with respect to inspections and regulations, and providing legal advice and assistance to the firms coping with new regulations on trade. The kinds of mechanisms the League uses to serve its constituents include lawsuits against regulatory agencies, informational support to keep the firms updated on new regulations and legal mechanisms of safeguarding their interests, and active attempts to influence new legislation and regulations at both the formulation and implementation stages. According to the association officials, association members appreciate these services most, and although association membership rates remain low in the sector – estimated at about 15 to 20 percent – the firms that find themselves in legal disputes or experiencing continuing harassment from regulating authorities constitute a sizable portion of the new members.

The following example illustrates how the League's activities benefited small retail stores whose operations were burdened by low-level bureaucratic abuse. A new regulation that came into effect in 2004 demanded that all retail traders install electronic cash registers (ECRs) that would make auditing and control more effective. Firms had to purchase the new registers and dispose of the old ones, and small firms found complying with the new regulation particularly expensive. The firms that purchased registers of the old type shortly before the regulation came into effect incurred particularly heavy losses. According to the enterprise law, the firms actually had the right to keep their old equipment to settle its depreciation value, but when such firms were inspected, they were given a large fine for not complying with the regulation. Most firms were unaware of their right to keep their old registers in use. The League used the newsletter to educate its members about their rights and advised them to report all unlawful fines to the League. Due to time and resource limitations, small firms that were fined were unlikely to dispute fines with the authorities. The League, however, collected the reported instances of unlawful fines and disputed them in court on behalf of the firms, and the judge overturned most of these fines. Other examples of issues in which the League was involved

150 *Building Business*

include fees and regulations on trash disposal, city regulations on signboards, and appraisal of store premises.[15]

Although the League had initially assumed the role of a self-regulating organization that concentrated on providing market-related information, the subsequent changes in the composition of the sector led to the transformation of the association's functions toward "defensive" selective incentives. The association discovered that by providing defense mechanisms against bureaucratic pressures to its members, it could attract new firms when its old tactic of pursuing a coordinating role in the industry began to fail. This case study demonstrates that business associations actively search for ways to serve the evolving interests of their constituents. By finding new ways to relieve the regulatory pressure of the corrupt bureaucratic machine, the League was able to continue its existence and increase its membership.

5.4 Selective Regulatory Relief

Here I consider further examples of business associations providing regulatory relief and protection from corruption in the form of selective incentives or particularistic services directed specifically to dues-paying members. Such services and activities undertaken by business associations provide firms with strong incentives for joining and maintaining membership in these organizations. Below I consider three ways in which business associations can be instrumental in keeping the state regulatory institutions in check: continuous provision of services, periodic activities, and immediate responses to changes in regulatory environment that increase instances of predatory bureaucratic behavior. These mechanisms help ensure that the state regulatory apparatus is not abusing its power to regulate the industry.

Self-Regulation on a Large Scale (The Ukrainian Chamber of Commerce and Industry)

Perhaps the most effective form of relief from state regulatory pressure is achieved through the delegation of some state functions to business associations. This is best accomplished when a business association does not become the instrument of state regulatory policy but rather a voluntary alternative to the existing state control mechanisms.[16] The Ukrainian Chamber of Commerce and Industry (UCCI), since its reformation in 1998 as an entity independent from the government organization, has acquired many functions instrumental in providing regulatory relief and defending its members against bureaucratic predation.

Building on its legacy of regulating foreign economic relations, the Chamber has extended its quality inspection services and arbitration services in

---

[15] Based on numerous personal interviews with staff members in Moscow, August 2005.

[16] When business associations become the only providers of the regulatory control formerly

commercial disputes to its domestic members.[17] The Chamber's surveyor and inspection services guarantee that the quality and quantity of all kinds of goods in various trade operations correspond to contractual obligations. The association offers the services of marine agents, forwarding agents, and customs brokers to facilitate the fulfillment of contracts. This also puts the authority of a reputable association behind the businesspeople in their interactions with the state. The Chamber acts as a more powerful agent in these interactions. International and domestic arbitration courts and the Maritime Arbitration Commission are governed by the New York Convention on the Recognition and Enforcement of Foreign Arbitral Awards (1958), providing for a greater protection of firms' economic rights compared to the national legal code.[18]

The Chamber's legal department offers standard templates of legal documents used to conclude contracts and interact with state institutions. The department surveys Ukrainian legislation and updates information on regulations specific to member operations. A special resolution of the Ukrainian Cabinet of Ministers (April 1, 1999, #529) requires all government agencies periodically to submit their regulatory documentation and statistics to the Chamber. The Chamber regularly updates its members on the important regulatory changes affecting their sectors. Its legal department offers support in formulating claims and complaints against unlawful or unethical actions of business partners and state authorities.

In 2001 the Chamber's Central Test Laboratory of Quality Surveillance received accreditation from the State Certification System. The laboratory specializes in testing the quality of foodstuffs and raw materials used in the food industry. The laboratory carries out complex testing and certifies the health safety of foodstuffs. This service is particularly valuable to companies importing new products and raw materials and introducing new transportation, storage, and processing in the sphere of food production. Independent certification reduces companies' dependency on bureaucratic controls and guards against predatory bureaucratic behavior that thrives when certification and control functions are fused in one state organization.

The Chamber's Norma certification agency provides additional certification services. Norma issues quality certificates for consumer products, raw materials, and equipment that go beyond compulsory state certification. In some sectors the lack of compulsory certification requirements results in suboptimal information and high transaction costs. To reduce transaction costs and signal valuable information to potential customers, some producers voluntarily

---

exercised by the state, opportunities for abuse (e.g., entrance barriers, favoritism, negative externalities) multiply.

[17] Some services discussed here are free to the Chamber's members, whereas others are provided for a fee. Nonmembers can receive many Chamber-provided services at substantially higher fees.

[18] See International Commercial Arbitration Court at the Ukrainian CCI, http://www.ucci.org.ua/arb/icac/en/icac.html.

undergo UCCI certification. The Chamber's reputation serves as a measure of its reliability (Yanovsky 2006).

These services do not directly target state predation. Still, by providing institutional alternatives to the state agencies, the Chamber facilitates contract enforcement, reduces transaction costs, and provides valuable legal information instrumental in protecting property rights in an environment of complex and frequently changing rules and regulations. Such alternative institutional solutions reduce a business's vulnerability and curtail areas in which state regulators exercise unchecked authority over the private sector.

Sectoral Self-Regulation in Russia

In the late 1990s and early 2000s, a number of professional and sectoral organizations in Russia's construction, financial, and other sectors voiced demands for regulatory changes that would remove opportunities for bureaucratic predation without sacrificing high regulatory standards (e.g., reduce the red tape but retain the official regulations). Sectoral (the Association of Russian Banks, the All-Russian Insurance Association, and the Russian Franchising Association) and general-purpose umbrella associations (Opora, ADSMB, and CCI) have championed the issue of self-regulation. Industry self-regulation was advocated as a mechanism of debureaucratization that would not sacrifice environmental or consumer protection or public safety.

The Professional Association of Registrars, Transfer Agents, and Depositories (PARTAD), one of the first self-regulated organizations in Russia, played a key role in promoting the idea of self-regulation. Starting in 1994 it united professionals operating on the securities market; in 1997 it adopted a set of binding professional rules of conduct for its members. The Russian law, however, did not recognize this regulatory initiative, thereby limiting its benefits. Viktor Pleskachevskii, the chair of the association's governing council since 2000, was one of PARTAD's best assets in the organization's quest for official recognition. Mr. Pleskachevskii's long experience in securities trading (his executive positions in investment companies date back to 1988) and his leadership role in the federal parliamentary committee overseeing property relations (Pleskachevskii was elected to the Federal State Duma in 1999 under the Unity party ticket) made him the most energetic and well-positioned spokesperson for self-regulation.

In 2002 the parliamentary committee on property, privatization, and economic activities, in close cooperation with the representatives of business associations, developed and introduced to the State Duma a bill that would open the way for the official recognition of noncommercial organizations promoting industry self-regulation. The bill's long-term objective was to gradually phase out some of the most cumbersome practices of state regulation (e.g., licensing, technical regulations, product standardization in certain industries). Not surprisingly, the bill met strong opposition in the Duma and the government and several times was returned to the committee (Pleshanova 2008).

After five years of rigorous lobbying by business associations, the Duma approved the amended bill in November 2007. The core criterion for the establishment of public alternatives to the state regulatory bureaucracy supervising real estate, construction, the financial industry, and related sectors was that the regulatory standards developed and enforced by such nonstate organizations uniting industry participants had to adhere to existing official regulatory norms. Self-regulating organizations may, however, impose restrictions that go beyond the official regulations. The law opens up channels for transferring a number of state regulatory functions (e.g., licensing, technical regulation) to authorized industry organizations. Although self-regulation is proclaimed to be the ultimate goal, with a complete retrieval of the state bureaucracy from direct regulatory oversight, the law stipulates the transitional period in which the state- and self-regulatory options would coexist.

Since the law was passed, a large number of noncommercial organizations have applied to receive self-regulating status. According to the networking website of self-regulated organizations (http://sro.su), there are currently about fifty such organizations in Russia's construction and financial sectors. This rapid growth reflects the fact that many business associations in the affected sectors – the PARTAD being a good example – have engaged in self-regulatory practices for a long time. Naturally, they have developed the membership, infrastructure, and expertise necessary to engage in legally binding self-regulation and were able to offer their members an alternative mechanism of regulatory compliance. It remains to be seen whether the self-regulatory experiment undertaken by Russia in the construction, real estate, and financial sectors will be extended to other sectors and whether it would result in the overall reduction of bureaucratic corruption. What appears to be clear at this point, however, is that business associations have become important institutions that have shaped business practices in the real estate, finance, and construction sectors of Russia's emerging market. They have altered their members' business practices and influenced the reforms of the state (Frye 2000).

Inspection Emergency Call (the Almaty Association of Entrepreneurs, Kazakhstan)

One of the most proactive solutions in providing protection from bureaucratic extortion comes from the Almaty Association of Entrepreneurs in Kazakhstan. Since its formation the Association has pursued a multidimensional program for reducing administrative barriers. According to the president of the association, Viktor Yambaev (2005), the major problem any Kazakh business faces is "uncontrolled regulatory rulemaking" that leads to the creation of "unsurpassable administrative hurdles" and corruption. The association sees the solution to these problems in the state's withdrawal from microregulation of business and the dismantling of bureaucratic hurdles, thereby creating a favorable business environment. Starting from its establishment in 1998, the association has been active in publicizing its position, submitting its proposals for new laws shaping the business climate, and organizing events making businesspersons aware of their common problems and strengths.

The majority of the association's members – small family-owned firms – complained about endless, unannounced inspections from about fifty regulating agencies that slowed down their operation by demanding side payments. These unannounced visits, "during which the former [inspectors] would often pressure the latter [entrepreneurs] into paying bribes" (Nazarov, quoted by Chebotarayov 2003), were seen as particularly destructive to small businesses. To address member complaints, the association advocated a halt on unannounced inspections. In 2002, in response to the public campaign initiated by a number of business associations and foreign-sponsored development agencies, state authorities implemented an experimental measure of suspending unannounced regulatory inspections. The Almaty Association of Entrepreneurs signed an agreement with the state agencies allowing its legal team to monitor implementation.[19]

The 2002 suspension of unannounced inspections, although positively evaluated by both the business community and high-ranked state officials, was a temporary measure that failed to become a permanent rule. Once the experiment ended, building on its experience of monitoring the legality of inspections, the association hired a small group of lawyers and accountants that its members could call on at the time of the inspection. This mobile, emergency-response legal team was available at the request of the association's members. The expert team would come to the enterprises' premises, and its presence at the time of inspection made bureaucratic abuse less likely. This service is provided to the association's members and, for an additional fee, to other interested enterprises. This is a clear example of a selective incentive in providing protection from corrupt implementation of extensive bureaucratic regulations. Relatively high institutional constraints the street-level bureaucrats have in implementing the official regulatory norms enhance this team's success (e.g., the existence of clearly defined, although numerous, regulatory procedures that the bureaucrats have to follow).

These examples of business associations providing protection from predatory bureaucratic behavior and navigating businesses through administrative barriers reveal the causal mechanism underpinning the defensive organization hypothesis. Associations offer legal advice, channel collective complaints, supply information about firms' rights and mechanisms of dealing with state regulatory regimes, initiate class-action suits, and, in some cases, take over the functions of regulatory oversight. Associational membership not only alters business behavior and patterns of interaction with state bureaucracy but also serves as a marker of better business practices. The simple fact of membership in a reputable association, in some cases, provides protection from bureaucratic

---

[19] See http://www.aaekz.com/org/five/.

What You Do Is What You Are 155

harassment and expropriation. Membership in reputable associations sends a strong signal about enterprise's compliance with rules and regulations as well as about available mechanisms of protection and influence that attest to the firms' connections to the political and economic elites. The reputational advantage, however, is usually associated with associations' public actions in defense of collective interests. Providing collective goods, however, presents more organizational challenges.

5.5 Collective Goods

Although much of the reduction in bureaucratic pressures is often achieved through selective incentives available to association members only, another way of defending firms against invasive regulatory regimes is to alter the regulatory framework affecting the entire business community. Some associations are able to organize collective actions to provide industry- or economy-wide benefits. Such a course of action creates collective benefits that assist firms participating in associations and contributing to the collective efforts as well as to those firms that free-ride on the collective efforts of others. The collective-action problem greatly impedes the provision of collective goods. Firms lack the incentive to actually participate in associations that provide free services for members and nonmembers alike. Still, some associations are able successfully to fight corrupt regulatory practices in a way that benefits both members and, perhaps unintentionally, nonmembers. Such efforts, however, are most likely to succeed when associations effectively solve the collective-action problem in the first place. Therefore, providing collective goods, in most cases, becomes an important activity for already established associations or associations emerging in small sectors in which the configuration of latent group interests makes collective action more likely.

Association of Trade Companies and Producers of Appliances and Electronics

The story of the Russian Association of Trade Companies and Producers of Appliances and Electronics (Russian acronym RATEK) illustrates that associations concentrating on the continuous provision of member benefits can often provide collective goods as a by-product of defending the interests of their members. The RATEK was created in 2000 as a professional association of the consumer electronics sector. By 2005 the association united fifty-five companies, including domestic producers, distribution and service networks, and companies trading in appliances, electronics, computer equipment, and mobile phones – companies that operate in four hundred Russian cities. In 2005 the association estimated that its members comprise about 60 percent of the Russian electronics market. The association's functions include voluntary product certification, organization of business forums, seminars on the development of new markets, joint advertising campaigns, market research (some results are published, whereas others are provided exclusively to the members), comprehensive marketing and technical databases, and lobbying sectoral interests (Onishchuk 2005; Guskov 2005). The association's members enjoy discounts on a number of services provided by the association's affiliates.[20] Since 2002 the RATEK has published a magazine, *Electronika*, and in 2003 it launched a website. The association is a member of the CCI, the RUIE, Moscow International Business Association, and other business organizations.

My interview with the vice president of the RATEK, Aleksandr Onishchuk, and the director for public relations, Anton Gus'kov, was hard to schedule despite our initial agreement. Unlike some other Russian associations that were hard to schedule interviews with, the RATEK had a convincing reason to postpone the interview. At the time of my visit to Moscow in August–September 2005, the cellular sector was in the midst of a public scandal. On August 17, 2005, at the Sheremetyevo air cargo terminal, the Ministry of Interior seized a large shipment – three hundred tons – of cellular phones and accessories (Zaharov 2005). Another shipment of fifty-five tons was seized a few weeks later. These amounted to two months' national sales of cellular phones.

The firm importing these mobile phones was charged with smuggling and tax evasion. The "gray schemes" of electronic supplies that this trading company used involved declaring such products as scrap metal or other cheap products at the customs office and paying value-added tax (VAT) on the understated value. These were later sold to retail chains and mobile-service providers – the members of the RATEK. Although the import machinations were carried out by "one-day firms" that had no ties to the industry, authorities initiated an inquiry into the legality of many retail operations (Belous and Dorohov 2005). Rumors about possible confiscations of phones and accessories already bought by retail chains from "gray" importers and charges of tax evasion affected even the largest cellular companies.

The RATEK leadership reacted quickly by formulating its position based on an analysis of the existing legislation. The association maintained that its member companies involved in retail trade had not violated the law by making purchases from the importing companies. The RATEK analyzed the sales contracts of its members and concluded that there was no evidence of fraud or tax evasion on the part of the retailers; they were buying products that were in their original manufactured packages, designated for the Russian market, and accompanied by the standard customs documentation. The RATEK leadership participated in countless meetings with state officials and investigative authorities to prevent unlawful persecution and save the public reputation of the member companies.

Even though the association's actions helped defend members' property rights, the "August cellular crisis" had a strong economic impact on the sector. The RATEK' s monitoring of cellular-market fluctuations indicated an

---

[20] See RATEK, http://www.ratek.org.

immediate increase in the average retail prices resulting from the emerging shortage. The association's members as well as other retailers faced long-term losses because of the disrupted supply chains. Although mobile-service providers and retailers have decided to start purchasing directly from manufacturers, developing new contacts requires time and expertise. An immediate task for the RATEK was to push for the release of the seized 355 tons of equipment to the market so its members could purchase the products stored at the Sheremetyevo facilities. The RATEK's members were interested in buying these products after legally clearing them through customs. To facilitate the release of the cargo, the association undertook the task of evaluating the value of different models of arrested mobile phones so that a proper VAT could be applied to the shipment. The RATEK's participation facilitated the legalization of the shipment, making it available for the retailers to purchase and quickly resolving market imbalances. This one-time response to an emergency situation foisted on the cellular phone market by the antismuggling efforts of state prosecutors provided a much-needed intermediate solution until the newly established direct contacts between foreign producers and Russian retailers could restore the normal flow of goods to the Russian consumers. Although the RATEK's actions reflected the desire to serve the interest of its members, its participation in the process of product appraisal and release was beneficial to the entire sector.

The Association of Croatian Exporters

The Association of Croatian Exporters (ACE) is one of the voluntary groups providing organizational alternatives to Croatia's official compulsory business organizations. Created in 2004 by the managers and owners of several reputable domestic enterprises (some are also well-known political figures), the ACE declared its independence from the official Chamber of Economy and emphasized voluntary membership. According to one of the members of the ACE governing board, the reason for forming this association was that the official chambers were unable to respond adequately to the needs of Croatian exporters. The Croatian Chamber of Economy did not facilitate a two-way information flow in the organization, a fact that impeded timely response to the dynamic environment (Babić 2006). Although the ACE' s statute defines its membership base as enterprises exporting or seeking to export Croatian products, membership includes many firms that cannot be classified as exporters (e.g., Croatian Airlines, Hauska & Partner International Communications, and the Institute for Business Research).

By 2006 the ACE had hired two paid, full-time staff members, utilized the services of a legal adviser, united 800 dues-paying members (with an estimated potential membership base of 1,500), and derived 90 to 95 percent of its financing from membership dues (Schaw 2006). According to the US Agency for International Development (USAID) evaluation report, the ACE is very effective in making its members' wishes known to its leadership through regular member surveys. The ACE provides informational services by publishing a newsletter and maintaining a password-protected Web site that facilitates information flow between members. Approximately half of the association's participants list their products, services, and business interests in the association's database. This procedure provides members with information on potential business partners, suppliers, and transporters. The ACE also received "good" evaluations in the public policy advocacy category, due to the political activism of its leaders, and in the impact category, indicating the effectiveness of its advocacy campaigns in addressing members' demands (Schaw 2006).

The inability of the official institutions of business representation to address the problem of corruption in customs initiated the formation of ACE. With the customs offices open on weekdays only, many owners of perishable goods were at the mercy of customs officials, who could deliberately delay the processing of goods in expectation of a side payment. After failing to attract due attention from the Croatian Chamber of Industry, a group of active business leaders organized the unaffiliated association. The ACE initiated a public campaign and demanded the extension of the working hours of the customs offices. This would minimize delays that frequently gave rise to the demands for unofficial payments to speed up customs clearance. The ACE initiative was successful. Around-the-clock operation left less room for bureaucratic abuse. This was an important victory for the ACE that created a collective good of more accessible customs for all exporters, irrespective of their membership in the ACE.

Another example of a public good achieved by the ACE' s actions is the case of the EU sugar quota. In 2004–2005, as part of the reform of the EU sugar industry, the European Council's Commission started re-evaluating the duty-free import quotas on sugar from non-EU countries. On February 28, 2005, the European Council's Commission opened negotiations with the Republic of Croatia to amend the preferential arrangements that had regulated Croatian imports since 2002. These preferential, unlimited, duty-free arrangements were established under the Stabilization and Association Agreement (SAA) between the EU member states that the Republic of Croatia signed in Luxembourg in October 2001 and under the Interim Agreement on trade and trade-related matters effective since January 2002. The proposed levels of a duty-free import quota would have resulted in a substantial increase of the price of Croatian sugar on the EU market; the resultant decreasing demand for Croatian sugar would have put Croatian sugar beet growers and the processing industry under pressure.

The ACE organized a coalition that included the National Bank, the Croatian Employers' Association, and the Chamber of Economy, to put pressure on both the Croatian government, which was negotiating the new agreement, and the members of the European Commission (Schaw 2006). It emphasized the negative impact on Croatian agriculture that could result from setting the quota at the proposed 80,000 tons per year. The ACE demanded an increase of this quota to 180,000 tons, referring to similar deals with other Balkan

What You Do Is What You Are 159

countries. On March 14, 2006, the Commission concluded the negotiations with Croatia with a new arrangement that would come into effect in January 2007 that permits Croatia to export sugar to the EU under a duty-free quota of 180,000 tons (European Commission 2006). With an estimated capacity of the Croatian industry to export 170,000 tons in the following years, the tariff quotas effectively preserved the duty-free exports, securing the Croatian sugar industry unrestricted access to the European market. Higher tariffs benefited some 2,000 family farms growing sugar beets (these small family farms account for over half of the beet cultivation area in the country and, naturally, are not members of the ACE) as well as sugar-processing plants scattered throughout the country (Agripolicy Network 2005). This exemplifies the association's capacity to reduce regulatory constraints that, in this case, were imposed not by the domestic government but by a foreign party.

Coordinating Expert Center of Business Associations of Ukraine and the Stamp Duty Case

The Coordinating Expert Center of Business Associations (CEC) was founded in 1998 by a number of Ukrainian business associations, with the purpose of coordinating associations' contacts with state authorities. The CEC concentrated on monitoring authorities' initiatives in the regulatory arena and other business-related spheres, analyzing draft legislation, and developing proposals that reflected the demands and interests of the business community. The CEC think tank was established in 1999 to:

1) Carry out complex legislative expertise of draft laws ... analyze their direct and indirect impact ... define effective mechanisms of influence and evaluate the consequences of regulation. 2) Elaborate independent recommendations and analytical materials; provide organizational support and coordination for advocacy and promotion of draft legislation. 3) ... Assess the effectiveness of implementation of regulatory norms. (Liapin 2005a, 29–30)

As seen from the program statement of the CEC, tracing changes and affecting the content of the regulatory environment has been the primary purpose for creating this umbrella group that by 2005 had united sixty member associations, including national, sector-specific, and regional organizations. The association has opened offices in five regional centers. As an umbrella group, the CEC has rejected calls to participate in activities benefiting narrow interests and advocates public benefits only. This has limited its attractiveness to member associations but significantly strengthened its political weight in conflicts over regulatory reform.[21] The CEC' s activities concentrated on coordinating member associations in their advocacy campaigns. Its analytical and coordinative

---

[21] As an umbrella group for the existing business associations, the CEC does not need to attract individual members, hence no selective incentive provision. Its existence has been predicated on the successful collective action on the part of member associations.

160 *Building Business*

functions were indispensable in coordinating efforts of several business associations to solve common problems. Some believe that this association's support has increased the efficiency of business campaigns and contributed to the successful resolution of the controversial tax stalemate that developed under President Leonid Kuchma in 1999 (Liapin 2005a).

In 1998, the Ukrainian state budget was in dire straits. An economic crisis stripped the country of needed investment. Declining production and growing unemployment occurred against the backdrop of a largely unreformed state sector and social safety net. This created demands for additional state spending while tax revenues were falling because of the stagnating economy and record-high tax evasion. In an attempt to improve tax collection, President Kuchma enacted the Decree on Stamp Duty. This expanded the tax base and improved the process of tax collection, which had been lagging due to legal loopholes, bureaucratic incompetence, and corruption. The newly introduced stamp duty was in essence a regressive sales tax collected by issuing prepaid sales stamps. Any sales contract as well as any sales invoice (in the absence of a contract) was subject to the stamp tax. The issued sales stamps were of equal value; thus, the lower the value of the contract, the larger the share to be paid in dues. The stamp duty immediately reduced enterprises' consumption, and this was particularly harsh on small firms that tended to make multiple small purchases (Liapin 2005a).[22]

One month after the decree introducing the stamp duty was signed (becoming effective in 1999), the CEC presented to Verkhovna Rada (the Parliament) an analytical note on the detrimental effects of the tax on the national economy. The arguments against the stamp duty included its regressiveness, suppression of economic activity, overwhelming burden on the small enterprise sector, incentives for underreporting economic activity, and a greater risk of entering unenforceable contract obligations. Efficient enforcement would have required expanding control functions of tax authorities to monitor the large number of small-scale operations. Verkhovna Rada failed to consider the matter, and the decree became effective in January 1999. By February 1999, businesspeople flooded business associations with appeals and complaints about the injustices of the new tax. Practically all member associations (fourteen at the time) made proposals to the CEC to organize a united campaign to stop stamp duty collection.

The campaign started in the media, with representatives of business associations demonstrating the detrimental impact of the stamp duty on small domestic firms and calling for its elimination. Business associations sent official letters to the legislators, demanding they put the issue on the parliamentary agenda. Overturning the presidential decree would require a simple majority, but by that time the stamp duty revenue had made its way into the next year's budget, and to expect full cancellation seemed unrealistic (Liapin 2006).

---

[22] In some instances the stamp duty on a sale could even exceed the value of the goods exchanged.

What You Do Is What You Are 161

The CEC leaders found allies in the parliamentary Committee on Finance and Banking Activities who had developed an alternative draft of "On Stamp Duty" that would completely redefine the nature of activities subject to such a tax. Under this alternative bill, the stamp duty was imposed on import cargo only (CEC analytical note, February 18, 1999). To put this bill on the parliamentary agenda would require the support of 150 legislators. The CEC utilized the political capital of its president, Yuri Yekhanurov, who was able to gather 150 signatures to put the bill on the floor. The bill was returned to the committee because it contradicted other legal regulations allowing for duty-free imports, but after adding provisions for a minimum value of imports subjected to the stamp duty, the bill was passed in the second reading. To speed up the second reading, CEC members exerted pressure on legislators through a massive media campaign and petitions. On May 13, 1999, the new law limiting the stamp duty's application to imported goods was passed. In the final stage of the campaign the CEC members sent an open letter to the president. The bill's supporters feared that the president would veto the law that was so dramatically different from his initial intent. Against the backdrop of heated parliamentary debates and enormous attention to the issue in the mass media, the president signed the new law on May 29, 1999. This first victory for the CEC and its members was a significant event that demonstrated its ability to defend the business community – primarily small businesses – from the pressure of increasing taxation.

The Ministry of Ice Cream: The Russian Association of Ice Cream Producers

The Russian Association of Ice Cream Producers (RAICP) was established in 2000. The list of its 11 founding organizations includes ice-cream plants, milk processors, equipment manufacturers, distribution and marketing corporations, and a research institution. As with many other Russian business associations whose development was facilitated by state agencies, the RAICP has received organizational support from the Federal Agency on Food Regulation under the Ministry of Agriculture. By 2005, the RAICP had grown from 11 to 175 members, including 5 producer associations, 67 manufacturers, 8 retail companies, 25 producers of raw materials, 35 equipment and packaging suppliers, 9 research and educational institutions, 11 publishing houses and media outlets, and 17 foreign companies (Russian Association of Ice Cream Producers 2005).

In the first years of its existence, the RAICP had to compete for membership, media attention, and reputation with another business association of ice-cream producers, but by 2005 it had virtually monopolized sectoral representation. The competing Association of Russian Producers of Ice Cream and Frozen Products was established in 2001 as an organization of thirty-eight domestic producers of ice cream, whose output amounted to over half the national production of ice cream. This association, after a couple of years of independent existence and competition with the RAICP, joined the RAICP and ended the fragmentation in sectoral representation (Elhov 2005).

The consolidation of sectoral representation was achieved due to the RAICP' s aggressive activities in the spheres of membership recruitment, information-sharing (the newspaper, monthly magazine, and annual pamphlet) and exposition services (annual international and sectoral trade shows and numerous regional events), research and training programs, promotion of sectoral cooperation, and representation in the state institutions (including an Expert Council on Food Regulation under the parliamentary committee) (*Ezhegodnik* 2005; *Morozhenshchik Rossii* 2005). Because of its elaborate organizational structure and multidirectional activities as well as the near-universal participation of the sectoral enterprises, both its members and state institutions have called the RAICP "The Ministry of Ice Cream" (Shipov 2005).

Not being a separate sector under the planned economy, the self-organization of the ice-cream industry has marked a new development in structuring business relations. According to the association leadership, at the dawn of the market economy ice-cream producers faced greater regulatory obstacles and more promising growth opportunities compared to other spheres of food processing. Greater technological sophistication and expanded opportunities associated with newly available technology, recipes, ingredients, and marketing techniques of the ice-cream industry could have led to greater benefits if changes were introduced in the regulatory environment, which at the time was still dominated by archaic standards in food processing and distribution. The state standard (GOST) regulating production processes and product quality in the industry had been developed decades ago and in many cases prevented the use of new ingredients and more sophisticated technology. Many enterprises that purchased new equipment and introduced new products later found themselves in violation of the outdated regulations.

The association vigorously lobbied for the development of the new GOST for whole-milk ice-cream products, traditionally the most popular in Russia. The RAICP has provided research facilities as well as organizational and financial support for the development of the new state standard, which the regulating authorities approved in February 2003. This milestone regulation affects all the industry participants, providing the collective benefit of a standardization scheme based on contemporary production technologies, consumer preferences, and modern ingredients. Other activities of the RAICP that have extended regulatory relief include the reduction of the VAT on ice cream from 20 to 10 percent and a campaign for lifting tariffs on imported equipment and ingredients that do not have domestic substitutes. These actions provide regulatory relief in the form of collective benefits for the entire ice-cream industry.[23]

---

[23] In addition to these collective goods the RAICP provides its members with a large array of selective benefits. For instance, it has acquired the right to certify the production facilities of its members, ending the state monopoly on certification. This serves as a selective protection from bureaucratic predation in the certification process.

What You Do Is What You Are 163

5.6 The Lost Battles

Business associations often start providing public goods once firmly established and after securing their membership base. In contrast, associations that struggle for membership and public recognition rarely excel in providing collective benefits. The following section presents cases of campaigns for collective benefits that business associations lost against state institutions or other interest groups. These cases illustrate the difficulty of organizing a collective action for the common good of large, disorganized economic interests. Still, unsuccessful attempts at providing public goods often lead to the establishment of more specialized organizations that concentrate on the provision of excludable, member-oriented services.

Kazakh Business Forum

The Kazakh Business Forum (the Forum) was created in 1992 by a group of young entrepreneurs who relied on the organizational support of the Kazakh Youth Union (formerly the communist youth organization). It was supported by the country's president, Nursultan Nazarbayev, who attended and delivered a speech at the Forum's first convention in June 1992.[24] The Forum's publicity and regular participation in high-profile meetings with the country's political leadership over the years prompted large companies, business leaders, and other associations to join the membership ranks. The Kazakh Business Forum unites ninety members and has regional offices in all provinces. The regional offices function as integral parts of the Forum. In addition, thirteen business associations joined the forum while maintaining their organizational and financial independence.

As described in Chapter 3, in the 1990s Kazakh business associations and directors of large firms were able to voice their opinions during annual meetings with the president of Kazakhstan (Libman 2008). The Forum was a regular participant in these high-profile meetings. In the early 2000s, a passive recognition replaced authorities' keen attention on the business community, and this coincided with the proliferation of sector-specific and cross-sector business associations. In the 2000s the Forum initiated a number of media campaigns and lobbied business interests using its government connections.

For instance, the Forum rallied against increasing bureaucratic burden in the highly publicized case of tobacco advertising. In 2005, the Almaty city government attempted to increase fees on tobacco advertising. In January 2005, the city government increased the fees for displaying visual advertisements and tobacco companies' logos.[25] This local regulation followed the 2003 national law banning tobacco advertising in public places. According to the legislation, the only places legally permitted to display visual tobacco advertising were retail locations.

---

[24] See http://www.businessforum.kz/.
[25] See http://www.zakon.kz.

164   *Building Business*

Although the Kazakh Business Forum did not oppose the 2003 law, it organized a vigorous campaign against the local regulation and brought the issue
to court, arguing that the city government had no right to raise fees. A number
of Almaty newspapers reacted with a fierce criticism of the Forum's initiative, citing the Law on Prevention and Limitation of Tobacco Consumption
("Uspeshnyi Predprinimatel" 2005; Shahnazarov 2005). The proponents of the
Forum's position maintained that the city government's actions had little to
do with public health concerns and claimed that the regulation gave government inspectors an additional reason to demand higher bribes. The Forum's
campaign resulted in a dubious victory: the city authorities refused to lower
the advertising fees, but they did agree to clarify local regulations on tobacco
advertising, making retailers less vulnerable to bureaucratic abuse. In essence,
the Forum was able to reduce the unofficial regulatory pressures but failed to
change the official regulatory policy.

The high sensitivity of this case demonstrates how hard it is to draw a clear
line between lobbying for particular interests and carrying out the fight against
increasing regulatory burden and extortion. In the tobacco-advertising case the
Forum advocated the common interest of the small, disorganized, retail sector.
Firms in this line of business, however, had not been organized by this or any
other business association. Only a small fraction of Almaty tobacco retailers
contributed to the Forum's campaign, and this ultimately signaled the weakness of the business community in defending its interests and allowed the city
administration to portray the Forum as encroaching on the public interest.

The 2000 Cash Registers Case and the Ukrainian National Association for the Development of Trade and Services (UNADTS)

Associations uniting large and small retail traders in Moscow and Kyiv – the
League of Trade Merchants and the National Association for the Development
of Trade and Services – are quite similar with respect to their membership
base and issues they deal with. However, unlike the Russian association, which
emerged in the early 1990s, the Ukrainian organization was established in
2003. Its development was stimulated by a failed campaign to confront the
new regulations on cash registers that were introduced in 2000, creating a
situation quite similar to the one discussed in the Russian League of Trade
Merchants case. The Moscow association's case presents a successful example
of protection from regulatory pressure and corruption in the form of selective
incentives for the association's members. The League offered legal protection
to its members but did not attempt to change the regulatory mechanism affecting a large number of enterprises nationwide. When confronted with virtually
the same problem, Ukrainian business associations fought for free-for-all collective benefits and lost the battle.

On June 1, 2000, Verkhovna Rada (the Ukrainian parliament) passed
the Law on the Use of Electronic Cash Registers (ECR) and Cash Books in
Processing Payments by Consumers in Trade, Public Catering, and Service

What You Do Is What You Are 165

Sectors. The new regulation required the installation of ECRs, and an army of inspectors threatened noncompliant firms with large fines in an expectation of bribes. After the law was passed, about 90 percent of firms inspected by public officials were found in violation of the new regulation and were fined (Blyzniuk 2006). The penalty under the new regulation was high and did not discriminate between small and large firms or the gravity of a violation. Although the law was circulated as a draft in 1998–1999, it attracted no attention on the part of the organized business community that it would directly affect. No attempts were made to contact the legislators sympathetic to the interests of small businesses. When the law was introduced to the floor, all but one legislator voted in its favor, and many later admitted that they were unaware of its content (Liapin 2005a).

The new regulation directly threatened the interests of the most disorganized sectors – small retail traders and family-owned businesses in the service sector. For these businesses, the new regulation meant additional expenses associated with not only purchasing new registers but also the increased vulnerability to corrupt bureaucrats (in a sense, the law drove up the cost of compliance that business associations would need to offset in order to make any collective action worthwhile). The law also effectively invalidated any benefits available under the simplified taxation mechanism (the flat merchant tax instead of the VAT on each transaction). A number of associations recognized these interests; however, at that time none specialized in representing the interests of small retailers. The Coordinating Expert Center of Business Associations (see the discussion of the stamp duty campaign earlier in this chapter) took over the issue and organized a public campaign to put pressure on the executive and legislative authorities.

The specialized interests that benefited from the new regulation, however, were better organized. The Association of ECR Manufacturers and Service Centers, created shortly after the start of the cash register campaign, advocated for the new regulations, citing international practices. It was not a secret that the new law created greater demand for the services of the association's members; their commercial interests were obvious to all involved parties (Liapin 2005a, Blyzniuk 2006). The CEC leaders petitioned the president and the Cabinet and raised the issue in the Business Association Council under the Cabinet of Ministers of Ukraine. The ECR Manufacturers Association was able to block the CEC's attempts to persuade the president into vetoing the law. Then, on July 6, 2000, a number of business associations called for picketing Verkhovna Rada, and about 3,000 businesspeople joined the rally, demanding that the law be put on hold until 2001 (Liapin 2005a). Although the deputy speaker and the first prime minister supported the demands, in the absence of a dedicated pressure group, no procedural steps were taken to secure deferment of enacting the law to a later date. At the same time, the association of ECR manufacturers organized a counter-campaign that emphasized the new law's benefits for consumers.

166   *Building Business*

It took another rally that gathered about 5,000 participants in front of the Parliament building on July 13 to secure the required 300-vote majority to postpone the enactment of the law until January 1, 2001. It took five more months of petitioning, press conferences, pamphlet publication, and lobbying efforts for the parliamentary Committee on Financial and Banking Affairs to propose changes exempting only street-market vendors from the new requirements. These amendments were made on December 21, 2000, and the law came into force, marking the defeat of small-business interests. In a situation in which the harsh regulatory environment directly threatened business interests, a coalition of general-purpose business associations was unsuccessful in altering regulatory requirements, a move that would have provided collective benefits for the small-business sector. Faced with opposition from concentrated industrial interests, the CEC's advocacy campaign was able to achieve only limited benefits for the small-business sector.

The unsatisfactory outcome of the cash-registers campaign made businesspeople realize the limitations of general-purpose organizations. In response, businesses in the retail sector formed the Ukrainian National Association for the Development of Trade and Services in 2003 (Blyzniuk 2006). The association has concentrated on providing informational and legal support to its members and on advocating their interests in the press and state institutions. Some of the successful actions of the new association include a 2005 campaign against new food-safety permits, which discriminated against retail trade in baked goods, and a more recent advocacy against monopolistic schemes of introducing plastic-card-processing terminals in the retail sphere (Chernyi and Fedorchenko 2006).

The cash-registers campaign, which led to the formation of a more specialized sectoral association, is indicative of a general trend toward sectoral and professional representation. The provision of public goods that the general-purpose groups struggling for membership and recognition often attempt is rarely successful in post-communist countries. Many associations that fail in this endeavor, however, shift their activities toward excludable benefits targeted to narrower constituencies. Unsuccessful attempts at providing public goods, therefore, often lead to the discovery of other ways of defending business interests, bringing us back to the selective incentives of informational and educational services, business contact facilitation, use of courts and legal assistance, and self-regulation discussed in the beginning of this chapter.

5.7 Dogs That Never Barked

In order to evaluate conditions that might account for firms' reluctance to engage in collective action, this section briefly discusses examples of sectors that failed to develop organized groups. Cases of the nonemergence of business associations are hard to study because of the difficulty in identifying the relevant set of latent interests that fail to organize. The fact that businesses

What You Do Is What You Are 167

may organize on regional, sectoral, professional, and issue-specific bases complicates the task. A national association's successful articulation of its firms' interests might offset the lack of associations in a particular region. Similarly, participating in general-purpose or issue-specific organizations might compensate for the absence of professional groups. The absence of industry-level associations, therefore, is not a definitive indication of firms' inability to pursue their collective interests; nonetheless, it does reflect the underlying structure of those interests that may or may not unite firms in the industry.

One can expect collective action in cases with clearly identifiable latent groups, such as economic sectors that consist of firms sharing the same market, labor force, technology, and institutional environment. Sectors of the economy with clearly distinguishable characteristics setting them apart from other markets are the prime candidates for investigating the issues of organizational failure. These are like dogs that do not bark: one can feel their presence and potential (for organization) but not observe their (collective) action.

One of the most visible cases of the nonformation of sectoral business associations is Russia's coal-mining sector.[26] Geographical concentration, high resource specificity, large enterprise size, and a militant labor force, as well as the threat of economic losses associated with economic restructuring, seem to be strong reasons to expect a sectoral association to emerge, uniting managers and new owners of the coal-producing enterprises.[27] Still, no association to represent the interests of the coal business has yet established itself in Russia. The argument developed in Chapter 2 provides a good explanation: if firms join associations when other means of regulatory relief are costly or ineffectual, perhaps the Russian coal sector simply has no need for such a development. Although the coal-industry companies had exercised considerable direct political influence in the 1990s, they failed to organize a representative association that would speak on behalf of the entire sector.[28] The coal-sector case shows that large firms' ability to promote their interests directly through crony relationships with state institutions jeopardizes collective action on the part of Russian industry.

Business associations attract members by offering services and activities that provide targeted regulatory relief to businesses. The absence of suitable and affordable mechanisms of direct political influence therefore facilitates the development of business associations, meaning firms join associations because they cannot offset regulatory costs through cronyism, corruption, and capture.

---

[26] For a comprehensive review of the Russian coal industry, see Crowley (1998, 2000).

[27] These factors are discussed in Chapter 4 as important potential explanatory variables in the group-formation puzzle.

[28] As Hart (2004) convincingly argued, individual companies, although they routinely pursue government-influence strategies, are not interest groups: "The government affairs function of a large corporation has very different incentives and decision-making processes than those that characterize the ideal typical voluntary association of citizens that occupies the core of most theories of interest groups" (49).

168   *Building Business*

If the direct transactions with the state are relatively "cheap," business associations will not be able to attract members by providing legitimate regulatory relief. This has been precisely the case with the Russian coal industry. The coal sector enjoyed close direct ties between enterprise management and the state officials, allowing for informal influence and protection. This made firms less likely to invest in collective action.

The flagship of Soviet industrialization, the coal-mining sector, came under strain following the arrival of cheaper energy sources in the 1970s. Despite the worldwide trend of downscaling coal production, the sector's size, output, and employment were maintained through a system of direct and indirect transfers. At the beginning of the post-communist economic transition, the coal industry presented a state monopoly that was selling coal at a fraction of the world price while simultaneously receiving subsidies amounting to 1.4 percent of the country's GDP. Naturally, in the early 1990s the sector became the target of economic restructuring programs pushed by the reformist Chubais government and the World Bank (Ashwin 1995; Kudat and Borisov 1996; Crowley 1998).[29] The political influence of the state-owned coal company Rosugol and political activism of the sector's labor force slowed down these restructuring programs. Professional solidarity and the large size of production units in the coal industry made coal workers the most potent labor group in Russia, with a history of coal strikes dating back to the late Soviet times.[30] Fearing the resistance on the part of Rosugol and the unions, the World Bank pushed for the breakup of the industrial giant, a feat accomplished in the mid-1990s.

Emerging from the profound restructuring programs at the turn of the century, the sector employed 233,000 people and had 449 enterprises territorially concentrated in the coal-producing regions of Western and Eastern Siberia (Sokolin 2004). The average firm size in the industry is about 600 employees, compared to the economy-wide average of 85 employees.[31] Due to privatization, 76 percent of coal mines and infrastructure-supporting companies were in private hands by 2003. Another 7 percent have mixed Russian-foreign ownership, which is two times higher than the mixed Russian-foreign ownership share economy-wide. Due to the nature of production and high pre-existing levels of fixed-capital investment, the industry remains one of the most resource-specific sectors in Russia. Although restructuring programs has somewhat reduced market concentration, the number of independently operated production units remains small compared to the rest of the economy. Since the early 2000s,

---

[29] In 1996, the World Bank approved the first coal-sector adjustment loan in the amount of US$500 million (Coal SECAL I). It was followed by a second loan in the amount of US$800 million (Coal SECAL II), half of which was disbursed in 1997. The disbursement of the remainder of the funds was made conditional on the sector's program performance (Haney and Artemiev 2002).

[30] In fact, the coal workers are characterized as "the most militant segment of Russia's labor force" (Crowley 2000, 130), staging strikes in 1989, 1993, and 1996.

[31] In 1990, the sector had 334 enterprises (a majority of those controlled by the giant, state-owned monopoly Rosugol) employing 484,000 people (Sokolin 2004).

What You Do Is What You Are 169

Russia regained its status of net exporter of coal, gradually shifting from the EU to East Asian destinations (Ignatov 2010). This coincided with the rise of Evraz Group and SUEK corporations as the dominant companies in the industry. Currently, 20 leading companies account for over 90 percent of Russia's coal production (Ignatov and Company Group 2010).

According to the standard collective-action arguments, the sector is a likely setting for successful collective action because of its concentration, political importance, and resource specificity. Contrary to expectations, the coal industry failed to develop nonprofit representative institutions. This outcome, however, is consistent with the defensive organization theory. Before the 1997 dismantling of Rosugol, the sector enjoyed a rather unrestricted direct access to federal regulators and politicians through Rosugol's direct lobbying. Even after the restructuring, large, politically powerful enterprises still dominated the sector (which has become somewhat less concentrated). Because of their large size and regional importance as large employers and infrastructure providers, coal companies retain their direct ties to federal and regional authorities and often find themselves in positions of significant political influence. High levels of market concentration and monopolization ensure that the single-company influence and direct contacts with public officials continue to be reliable and cost-effective strategies of regulatory relief.[32] The government's inability to restrict such influence (ineffective anticorruption measures) and the relative ease of access (cronyism) have promoted single-company influence and diminished the prospect for collective action.[33]

Another example of a sector that also has not developed an association is the Russian healthcare sector. Russia has never managed to reform its highly socialized healthcare system.[34] With the exception of dentists, plastic surgeons, and a few other medical specialists, Russian doctors and hospitals are financed primarily by the state health insurance fund, with virtually no market mechanism introduced in the selection and provision of medical services to the population. State-financed and underfunded, healthcare professionals and hospitals have enjoyed an insider status with state institutions. The regulatory mechanisms continue to be fused with the provision of medical services, allowing for easy insider access. Although reports of corruption in the health sector abound, they exclusively refer to doctor-patient bribes and compensations, with little evidence of bureaucratic predation in the sphere of state regulation. In this environment of the fusion between regulatory and service-provision functions

---

[32] Pecorino's (2001) theoretical work about the nonlinear relationship between industrial concentration and collective action supports this conclusion. According to his argument, collective action is less likely not only in highly fragmented industries but also in those dominated by a few large firms.

[33] Because of the industry's direct access to policy-formulating and policy-implementing authorities, both official and unofficial regulatory costs remain largely irrelevant in this story.

[34] For a review of the Russian health care system, see Figueras and Marshall (1998) and Tragakes and Lessof (2003).

and insider access to the state, no association of hospitals or medical practices (as opposed to the professional medical organizations) has come into existence. At the same time, a number of associations of private dentists and dentistry clinics were created in Russia in the 1990s, when independent practitioners started expanding their businesses as profit-making enterprises subject to economic regulation.

These examples are important cases for evaluating the validity of the defensive organization argument. The coal and medical sector have clearly identifiable latent interests that failed to organize on sectoral bases. They are characterized by the lack of effective deterrence against informal means of regulatory relief and convenient channels of access to the relevant state institutions. These factors ensure that enterprises in these industries obtain their regulatory relief directly from the politicians and the state bureaucracy, thus creating disincentives to engage in collective action. The absence of business associations in these sectors presents an additional support for the causal relationship suggested by the defensive organization hypothesis.

5.8 Tallying Up the Evidence

In conclusion, it is important to reiterate the central argument scrutinized in this chapter: businesses found and join associations in a search for more effective ways to deal with the regulatory environment. Case studies in this chapter attest that business associations can, in fact, reduce regulatory costs associated with running a business. The cases of business associations in Russia, Ukraine, Croatia, and Kazakhstan demonstrate different mechanisms available to business associations for providing protection from burdensome regulations and bureaucratic corruption. Contrary to the traditional arguments that link organized business to rent-seeking behavior that advances producer interest at the expense of labor or other sectors (e.g., trade protection, subsidies, and tax exemptions), the qualitative process-tracing data paint a more nuanced picture. Business associations, through their member-oriented services and general-purpose activities, are able to raise the bureaucratic costs of preying on business and normalize their regulatory environment by strengthening predictability and clarity of economic regulations. As the nature of business relations with the regulatory institutions changes, business associations adjust their services and activities to accommodate the changing needs of their constituents.

My analysis of activities undertaken by business associations unravels the causal mechanism linking the development of industry associations to regulatory pressures and bureaucratic corruption. As seen from the examples of associations' activities, business associations recognize the state regulatory pressure (official, but more frequently unofficial) as a threat to their constituents and organize actions to counteract such a threat. This, coupled with the evidence that dealing with corrupt officials is increasingly costly for businesses, provides a causal link between corruption and associational-membership levels.

What You Do Is What You Are 171

The case studies represent a wide range of functions and activities that post-communist business associations commonly perform. Some associations attempt to reduce the cost of complying with rules and regulations affecting businesses; others try to change these regulations or their enforcement practices. For businesspeople suffering from extensive bureaucratic barriers and irritated by corrupt officials, business associations that fight concrete regulations (e.g., Ukrainian Coordinating Expert Center, Kazakh Business Forum, ACE) and provide services that protect against bureaucratic abuse (e.g., Almaty Association of Entrepreneurs, Russian League of Trade Merchants, UALCE) offer valuable organizational opportunities for defending their interests. Case studies have shown that when corruption is costly and bureaucratic predation is high, associations can provide protection in the form of selective incentives or collective benefits by altering the underlying regulatory regimes and cutting bureaucratic red tape. Although the alternative outcome – a failed attempt to organize a business association or no attempt at all – is hard to investigate, the comparison between costly corruption (a net loss for small businesses) and affordable corruption (the net benefit of cronyism in the coal and health care sectors) provides additional support for this causal mechanism.

Qualitative, causal, process-tracing evidence reveals that much of the activity business associations undertake, although in many cases not fighting corruption at large, is directed at the root of corruption – extensive or arbitrarily enforced state regulation of economic activity. Although one might doubt that the source of corruption actually lies at the bottom of the bureaucratic hierarchy, those familiar with the post-communist business environment are unlikely to dispute the fact that bureaucratic barriers and corruption are linked. Thus, when confronted with high bureaucratic corruption, businesspeople become more likely to throw their support behind organized groups fighting state regulations and convoluted enforcement practices. At the same time, concluding that businesses always favor fewer regulations would be incorrect; oftentimes they advocate changes that would make bureaucratic discretion and thus predation less likely. Case studies demonstrate that many associations provide regulatory relief by forming alternatives to the state regulatory mechanisms that impose strict standards (e.g., RAICP, UCCI, PARTAD), whereas others advocate for more transparent, easily enforceable, and nondiscriminatory regulatory practices (e.g., Federation of Restaurants and Hotels, ACE). Obscure regulatory mechanisms that yield a wide range of bureaucratic interpretation (particularly within the underdeveloped or rapidly changing regulatory frameworks) have been frequent catalysts for the growth of interest groups. In some cases, businesses join associations to pool resources necessary to alter such regulatory mechanisms and sometimes to develop alternative schemes of structuring and regulating the markets.

6

Compulsory versus Voluntary Membership

> Peak associations cannot always satisfy the policy preferences of their diverse constituencies. Larger associations tend to take positions that minimize internal conflict, thus encouraging specialized interests to develop independent strategies.
> – Heinz et al. (1993)

Throughout this book I have argued that business associations arise as defensive mechanisms against regulatory pressures and as alternatives to bureaucratic corruption. This implies that businesses join associations to find legitimate ways of protecting their interests from state regulation and bureaucratic predation. Business associations, according to this theoretical argument, are attractive organizational choices only insofar as they can provide regulatory relief that goes beyond unenforceable corrupt deals with regulating bureaucrats. The previous chapters presented theoretical and empirical evidence that supports this theory by examining the formation of and business participation in voluntary associations. But how does this theory apply to the cases in which legislation mandates that businesses join official organizations? Would businesses still seek protection through associational membership? Would associations still offer services that reduce regulatory burden and curtail corruption? This chapter argues that by changing the incentive structure of business associations, compulsory membership radically changes the member–association relationship. Still, even in the compulsory-membership system businesses' desire to obtain legitimate regulatory relief often leads to the emergence of alternative (voluntary) business associations.

This chapter focuses on a particular model of business representation that relies on compulsory membership in state-created peak associations. This model characterizes several countries of the region and is frequently labeled corporatist, although closer examination reveals its profound differences from the classical democratic corporatism of Western Europe and the bureaucratic

172

Compulsory vs. Voluntary Membership 173

corporatism of the developing world. This chapter takes a close look at the compulsory business associations that governments in some post-communist countries have created.

The chapter is organized as follows. After introducing two alternative ways of structuring business representation, I extend the mathematical model of business participation developed in Chapter 2 to the analysis of compulsory-representation regimes. One implication of this extension is that compulsory-membership institutions should be less effective in channeling the interests of the business community. This happens because compulsory membership removes the incentive to attract members by providing valuable member benefits. As a result, demands for alternative means of representation should emerge in compulsory regimes. I evaluate this argument through a qualitative analysis of business representation in compulsory systems. The historical sketch of the development of systems of business representation in post-communist countries supports the model's predictions: compulsory legal frameworks that some countries adopted in the early 1990s did not preclude the development of organizational pluralism and voluntarism in subsequent years. This chapter also refers to empirical evidence from Croatia, a representative case of a compulsory-membership system. The chapter concludes with discussions on how divergent legal frameworks have affected participation in business associations.

6.1 Alternative Models of Business Representation

Corporatism and pluralism are two alternative analytical categories that have been applied in the analysis of interest representation (Schmitter 1974; Schmitter and Lehmbruch 1979; Lehmbruch 1982; Cawson 1986; Hodgson 1998). Returning to the classic definitions Schmitter (1974) provided, pluralism is characterized by the existence of multiple, competing organizations representing different social interests, whereas corporatist (neocorporatist) arrangements are associated with the existence of encompassing associations organized in a highly hierarchical manner and effectively monopolizing group representation vis-à-vis the state. Schmitterian definitions of the ideal-typical alternatives are based on several dimensions of group characteristics and their interactions with other groups and the state. These include the number and representative claims of interest organizations, their internal organizational structure, functional differentiation, fragmentation, and competition as well as their relationship to the state that may or may not create, license, and grant representational monopoly (Schmitter 1974, 93–94).

The analytical categories of corporatism and pluralism affect the way we think about different types of capitalist economies in the world, and in the 1990s these made their way into scholarly analysis of the emerging capitalist economies in post-communist Europe and Eurasia. Specifically, a number of scholars have explored the notion of corporatism as an analytical tool for making sense of post-communist business-state relations. Some have

174   *Building Business*

pointed to the seemingly corporatist features of these relations developing in a number of countries. That led to a premature characterization of some Eastern European polities as developing corporatist-style arrangements, if not for all production-related social groups, at least in the area of business representation.[1] Russia and Ukraine, for example, have been cited as developing a corporatist mode of representation due to the large associations of capital and labor dominating the interest-group scene and enjoying close relations with the state (Colton 1992; Kubicek 1996; Remington 2004). Waller (1994) argued that "pluralism with corporatist features" has been developing across Eastern Europe. Myant (1994) detected corporatist arrangements in the patterns of tripartite negotiations in the Czech Republic and Slovakia.

Discussions of post-communist "corporatism" that emphasized subtle variations distinguishing institutional, functional, and relational forms of group representation – the permanent or occasional tripartite negotiations (Waller 1994), cohesion of positions and proposals in corresponding policy areas (Myant 1994), the government's preferential treatment of loyal but not necessarily representative groups (Colton 1992; Kubicek 1996), or predominance of umbrella associations (Remington 2004) – have led many authors to somewhat stretch the notion of corporatism, extending it beyond its conventional meaning. All these analyses extended the corporatist label to systems characterized by organizational fragmentation and volatility, voluntary and cross-cutting membership, few institutionalized channels of interaction between business associations and the government, and the inability of employer organizations to enforce collective agreements.

Such analyses inevitably blur the corporatist-pluralist distinction and create the need to introduce a number of qualifiers (e.g., "pseudo," "post-communist," "mixed"). Moreover, as the detailed descriptive analysis presented in Chapter 3 suggests, the overall comparison of the distinctive elements characterizing the emerging post-communist systems of business representation is more favorable to the pluralist pattern. Table 6.1, reproduced from Schmitter (1993, 329), summarizes the defining traits of ideal-typical corporatist and pluralist systems. Based on the descriptive analysis of post-communist business representation presented in Chapter 3, I underlined the items in Table 6.1 that are found across post-communist systems of business representation.

The representation patterns taking root in Eastern Europe and in the former Soviet republics, although undeniably containing the elements of functional differentiation, hierarchy, and, in some cases, involuntary membership and explicit state recognition, nevertheless are strongly competitive and increasingly

---

[1] In the area of labor representation in the 1990s, for instance, many post-communist countries were a close fit to the corporatist model. From communist times they inherited large, hierarchically organized unions, closely integrated in the economic decision making at the enterprise and state levels and performing extensive social, educational, and welfare functions (Crowley and Ost 2001; Kubicek 2004; Clarke 2006).

Compulsory vs. Voluntary Membership 175

TABLE 6.1. *Pluralist and Corporatist Models of Intermediation*

	Pluralist	Corporatist
Representation		
In relation to members	Multiple units	Monopolistic units
	Overlapping claims	Differentiated domains
	Autonomous interaction	Hierarchical coordination
	Voluntary adherence	Involuntary contribution
In relation to interlocutors	Mutual tolerance	Explicit recognition
	Opportunistic access	Structured incorporation
	Consultative access	"Negotiative" role
	Shifting alliances (log-rolling)	Stable compromises (package-dealing)
Control		
In relation to members	Persuasive conviction	Interest indoctrination
	Leader prestige	Organizational authority
	Discriminate treatment	Coercive sanctions
	Selective goods	Monopolistic goods
In relation to interlocutors	Provision of information	Organization of compliance
	Irresponsibility for decisions	Co-responsibility for decisions
	Autonomous monitoring	Devolved implementation
	Mobilization of pressure	Withdrawal from concentration

Note: This table has been reproduced from P. C. Schmitter, "Corporatism as Organizational Practice and Political Theory," figure 1, p. 329, in *International Handbook of Participation in Organizations*, edited by Eliezer Rosenstein and William M. Lafferty, 327–43 (Oxford: Oxford University Press, 1993), by permission of Oxford University Press.

voluntary, and they exhibit consultative and opportunistic patterns of access. In terms of member and policy control, post-communist business representation gravitates even more toward the pluralist ideal type, with little evidence of organizational capacity for coercive sanctions, binding decisions, and effective enforcement. Without a doubt, post-communist cases do not provide the perfect fit for the ideal types of corporatist and pluralist interest representation because they are still in the process of forming.[2] The compulsory-membership requirement, however, stands out as the most important institutional element separating Eastern European systems of business representation into two different groups.

---

[2] For the sake of conceptual clarity in the subsequent discussions I refrain from using the corporatist-pluralist distinction to qualify a developing system of interest representation and, thus, avoid stretching the terms to accommodate idiosyncratic features. Instead, I use clearly demarcated categories based on identifiable and uncontroversial voluntary- and compulsory-membership requirements. I use specific and easily measured criteria to distinguish between two distinct types of business representation: primarily, the existence of a *compulsory*-membership requirement in organizations officially recognized by the state as exclusive channels of business representation, and also self-regulation. It should be kept in mind that this research is concerned with the patterns of business representation, which might or might not be paralleled by structures of representation of other social interests. Thus, when discussing the compulsory-membership model, I refer specifically to business organizations.

Compulsory- and voluntary-membership organizations have different implications for collective action. The major problem encountered in organizing a group of actors to pursue their common interest is free-riding, or underprovision of individual contributions toward collective activity (Olson 1965). The corporatist-type compulsory institutions in which the state punishes free-riders provide a definitive solution to the collective-action problem. An outside authority, however, is not implicated in the formation of voluntary associations; therefore, voluntary collective action presents greater difficulties. By solving the endemic free-rider problem, compulsory organizations should have more resources, produce coherent collective action, and, ultimately, better represent the interests of their members. Membership in a compulsory organization, with all other things being equal, should entail fewer risks associated with free-riding and greater benefits resulting from guaranteed contributions.

The formation of voluntary associations seems to be even more problematic where compulsory-membership groups already exist. Why would such indisputably rational and money-maximizing actors as firms and businesspeople participate in forming voluntary organizations subject to the classic free-rider problem, especially when they are already paying members of a compulsory group not subject to free-riding? Although at first glance, participation in voluntary associations seems to be unnecessary for already-organized business interests, the following theoretical discussion demonstrates that the compulsory-membership system leaves ample reason for businesses to form organizational alternatives to the official associations.

In the following section I extend the model developed in Chapter 2 to compulsory-membership settings. The base model, as presented earlier, applies specifically to voluntary-association formation. Still, it can easily be extended to and has important implications for the behavior of associations and firms in compulsory regimes. The compulsory-membership environment alters the organizational goals of business associations, making the latter less attentive to the needs and demands of their constituents. Based on the formal model of business participation in associations, the remainder of this chapter advances an argument suggesting that compulsory, encompassing associations lack the motivation to provide services that firms in post-communist settings seek most. From the perspective of the firm such organizations are inferior to well-motivated voluntary organizational alternatives; thus, they do not preclude self-organization of the business community.

6.2 Modeling Voluntarism in Compulsory Systems

Chapter 2 proposed a model of business participation in voluntary associations that took into account businesses' desire to minimize the cost of compliance with state-enforced rules and regulations governing economic activities. The model assumed that membership in an association entails both costs and benefits. To attract members, a business association offers the particularistic

Compulsory vs. Voluntary Membership

benefits, or selective incentives, of legal and professional help in complying with rules and regulations. The association also charges membership dues. Under voluntary membership, a firm joins the association when the benefits of joining (net of membership dues) exceed the benefits of not joining and confronting regulatory costs or engaging in corrupt behavior. In this formulation, particularistic goods along with the collective goods provided by the associations become the important factors affecting participation in associations.[3]

To extend this model of business participation to the analysis of compulsory-membership organizations, consider the original set-up. The players are a firm (F), a bureaucrat (B), and an organization (O). All are assumed to be rational utility maximizers. They maximize income, which, for the firm, involves considerations of revenue (r), cost of production (c_p), and regulatory cost (c_r). The bureaucrat's income is derived from his/her salary (s) and a bribe (b). The organization's income consists of the difference between dues (d) and the cost of providing particularistic goods (αg). The particularistic goods, or selective incentives, are in the form of legal and professional help in complying with rules and regulations (selective reduction of regulatory burden). In voluntary-organization settings, the firm chooses among three strategies: *comply* with the existing regulation at a cost of c_r, *bribe* the bureaucrat, or *join* the organization and receive assistance in complying with the existing regulations. The bureaucrat's strategies include *honesty* or *corruption*; the organization chooses the combination of dues, d, and particularistic goods, g.

Consider what happens when compulsory membership is introduced. Because now the organization receives dues (d) with certainty and the firm joins irrespective of the amount of collective good (g) supplied,[4] d becomes absorbed in the firm's cost function. Compulsory membership reduces the firm's choice set to *join and comply* and *join and bribe*, with the payoffs as follows:

$$I_F \, (join + comply) = r - c_p - c_r - d + g,$$
$$I_F \, (join + bribe) = r - c_p - d - b + pf$$

Because g is defined in terms of reduction in compliance cost c_r, when a firm selects *join and bribe*, effectively avoiding c_r, it also cannot receive the benefit of g.

The bureaucrat maximizes income I_B, where s is salary:

$$I_B(honest) = s,$$
$$I_B(corrupt) = s + b.$$

---

[3] The model does not specify a firm's ability to influence the association's policy and functions. The assumption that members do not have a decisive voice in organizational governance is retained in the theoretical extension presented here. This is justified on two grounds. First, the descriptive analysis presented here and in Chapter 3 reveals the weak mechanisms of internal accountability in compulsory- and voluntary-membership groups. Second, theories of social choice suggest that member influence over an organization's governance should fall proportionally to the number of interests the organization encompasses.

[4] Note that now g is a collective, but not a club, good due to the universalistic nature of organizational membership.

178   *Building Business*

The bureaucrat is corrupt whenever $I_B(corrupt) > I_B(honest)$, or

$$b > 0 \tag{5}$$

The organization maximizes its utility $I_O(F) = d - \alpha g$ under the constant contribution d by minimizing the cost α or the member benefits g.[5] Assuming that organizational mission permits any non-negative level of member benefits provision, $I_O(compulsory) = d - \alpha g$ is maximized at $g = 0$.[6] The bureaucrat proposes a bribe b such that (1) holds; otherwise, B is *honest*. The firm chooses *join and comply* over *join and bribe* if and only if $I_F(join + comply) \geq I_F(join + bribe)$ or when $c_r - g \leq b + pf$. When $g = 0$, this reduces to $c_r < b + pf$. To entice the firm into corrupt behavior, the bureaucrat must offer a bribe such that $I_F(join + bribe) > I_F(join + comply)$, or

$$b \leq c_r - pf \tag{6}$$

Whenever $c_r > pf$, B's best strategy is to offer $b = c_r - pf$, and F's best strategy is to *bribe* rather than *comply*. When $c_r \leq pf$, the equilibrium outcomes are B: *honest*, F: *comply*, and O: $g = 0$.

Under compulsory membership the firm's choice has been effectively reduced to *comply* versus *bribe*, with the compulsory organization becoming an irrelevant actor in the firm-bureaucrat interaction. It follows that the compulsory organization in the equilibrium creates no benefits that would reduce the cost of regulatory compliance to the member firm, leaving this niche of activities open to other (voluntary) organizations. This brings us back to the voluntary-organization game, with the only difference being that compulsory-membership fees is now incorporated as an obligatory payment in the firm's regulatory cost $c_r' = c_r + d_{comp}$.

The major implications are as follows. First, compulsory organizations do not deter corruption. (Instead, corruption is reduced by effective anticorruption measures and liberal regulations.) Second, participation in compulsory business associations does not substitute for participation in voluntary associations. Third, because compulsory-membership dues effectively become part of the regulatory cost, particularistic benefits sought by voluntary associations might include measures directed against the compulsory-membership systems.[7] The

---

[5] The model assumes constant contributions d specified by law in a compulsory system and allows the organization to choose the level of collective good g. An alternative conceptualization would involve a set level of collective goods g mandated by the law and organizational choice over the amount of contribution d. Clearly, organizations would set d such that $(d - ag) > 0$, and the model predictions would hold.

[6] At the same time, the association might provide other benefits that do not involve regulatory relief and, hence, are not a substitute for bribery. Those benefits, however, are irrelevant to the firm's decision to engage in bribery.

[7] There is another important implication not directly relevant to the focus of this chapter but highly suggestive for the study of business associations' development and bureaucratic corruption: assuming that under voluntary participation $(g - d) > 0$, ceteris paribus b (2) $< b$ (5). This

model suggests that, irrespective of the existence of compulsory organizations, voluntary business associations should provide an attractive alternative to the corrupt ways of "getting things done." Because compulsory organizations do not have to lure businesses in by offering valuable services that decrease firms' cost of doing business, voluntary associations offering such services will rise and attract new members. In effect, compulsory organizations' lack of incentive to provide regulatory relief as a means of increasing membership opens the way to organizational pluralism.

Yet another implication of the model is that under compulsory-membership arrangements, membership dues, in fact, become an element of regulatory burden. This predicts the eventual opposition to compulsory-membership systems on the part of businesses striving to reduce regulatory costs. Note that for such a prediction to hold, compulsory membership does not necessarily have to be associated with net losses, such that $d - g < 0$; it just has to be *perceived* as such. Even if compulsory organizations might be providing valuable services to the firms, by the nature of the system such goods are common to all firms in the economy and, thus, are unlikely to be seen as a direct result of compulsory-organizational arrangements. Firms are likely to take the provision of such goods and services for granted, without giving credit to the compulsory association and the legal framework mandating universal participation and contributions. Thus, firms will tend to underestimate the benefits and overestimate the costs of compulsory membership and favor its abandonment. Voluntary associations could start campaigning against such obligatory contributions to reduce the cost of compliance for their members. This creates an organized opposition to the compulsory-membership system, increasing the chances of reforming the institutional underpinnings of compulsory business representation.

Do the model predictions with regard to the associational functions, enterprise demands, and bureaucratic position correspond to reality? The next section analyzes the development of compulsory-membership business representation across Eastern European countries. The post-communist cases offer an opportunity for testing model's implications in a natural, nearly experimental setting. At the time of their inception post-communist systems of business representation have taken different routes, following what at the time seemed to be distinct models of state-society relations. This has separated the post-communist countries into a test group experimenting with compulsory-membership associations and a control group that lacked compulsory requirements. A historical analysis of the development of two alternative models of business representation offers a "clean" test of the model implications for the following reasons. First, the existence of a "control" group of voluntary-based systems that share similar regulatory, political, and economic challenges ensures that developmental patterns

means that in the absence of voluntary organizations, corrupt bureaucrats can charge higher bribes in exchange for overlooking noncompliance.

180   *Building Business*

in the compulsory-membership systems are not due to the idiosyncratic country characteristics. Second, as "new" institutions, these are less likely to reflect the past actors' choices and preferences, which often account for the lingering institutional forms in other parts of the world.[8]

6.3 From Difference to Convergence

In the early stages of post-communist transition new legislation laid out formal foundations of business representation. The emerging systems of representation generally fell into two patterns: some countries opted for the so-called continental chamber system that emphasized *compulsory* membership and exclusive claims for representation on the part of the chambers of commerce (for the Hungarian case, see Ingleby 1996). But the legal framework in the majority of the post-communist states provided for *voluntary* membership in chambers of commerce and other business and employer associations and created conditions for the emergence of organizational pluralism in the sphere of business representation and self-coordination (see Fortescue 1997, for the Russian case). With the exception of Moldova,[9] East-Central Europe and the former republics of the USSR adopted voluntary arrangements; in the Balkans, Hungary, and Slovakia, compulsory institutions have taken hold.

Chambers of commerce and industry are pivotal for understanding the differential organizational forms and participatory dynamics across these different systems of representation. Although at the beginning of economic transition the post-communist countries lacked a developed business community,

---

[8] Such historical legacies and idiosyncratic features are often found to be responsible for the continuing existence of compulsory systems in a number of Western European countries. Although the result postulating the superiority of voluntary organizations in addressing the demands of their constituents is applicable to Western Europe as well, corporatist institutions are able to survive in a number of European and Latin American nations for decades due to a number of historical factors. The presence of oppressive political regimes that suppress voluntary organizations (as in Latin America and 1930s Italy and Germany) is one of these factors. Additionally, the survival of compulsory systems in democratic settings (democratic corporatism) can be predicated on strong labor organizations and the conciliatory rather than competitive political leadership of the post–World War II era. Even where compulsory-membership representation seems to have taken deep roots, more recent developments attest to the failure of corporatist-style institutions to accommodate the demands of their constituents (Hassel 1999; Beyer and Hopner 2003; Kinderman 2005; Martin and Thelen 2007).

[9] Moldova presents a hard-to-classify case. The 1999 Law on Chambers of Commerce and Industry created a compulsory-membership system but did not provide for automatic membership. Small and agricultural enterprises may join the chambers on a voluntary basis, and the chambers are responsible for reviewing member applications and collecting membership dues. By 2005 the Moldovan National Chambers of Commerce reported that small businesses constituted 70 percent of their members, and nearly 100 percent of their operating revenue derived from the sale of their services to members and nonmembers. Based on its membership and activities, it appears that the Moldovan Chamber evolved into a service-providing institution engaged in active efforts to expand its membership on a voluntary basis.

Compulsory vs. Voluntary Membership

organizations uniting employers and managerial elites preceded the capitalist transition and the emergence of genuine business elites (Waller 1994; Kubicek 1996; Fortescue 1997; Remington 2004). In this respect the post-communist organizational landscape in the early 1990s was not the tabula rasa of many early accounts (Jowitt 1992b; Schopflin 1994; Geddes 1995; see also McMenamin 2002 evaluating the "flattened landscape" argument). Under communist rule all the countries of Eastern Europe and the Soviet Republics had quasi-state chambers of commerce and industry that coordinated inter-state trade and economic cooperation, mediated cross-enterprise disputes, and enforced technical standards. Following the political transitions, such organizations were reorganized as public entities independent of the state.

Special pieces of legislation created national chambers of commerce and industry in all post-communist countries. Many countries passed additional laws regulating the formation of other institutions of business representation. In line with the continental chamber model of representation, the successor states to the former Yugoslavia, Albania, Hungary, and Slovakia (Ingleby 1996; Luksic 2003) as well as Moldova starting in 1999 have created compulsory business organizations with guaranteed access to political decision making and exclusive participation in the mechanisms of tripartite negotiations. They were also given a number of state-prescribed functions in the sphere of economic regulation. Such institutional arrangements – hierarchical, territorial, and sectoral structures; regulatory functions formerly performed by the auxiliary state institutions; and compulsory membership[10] – have been explicitly modeled after the Austrian and Italian chambers of commerce.

There has been some variation in this group of countries to the extent of organizational fragmentation of compulsory representation. Some countries (e.g., Albania and Slovenia) established centralized organizational structures uniting the entire business sector (Luksic 2003; Fink-Hafner and Krasovec 2005). Others, such as Croatia and Hungary, created several compulsory hierarchical organizations that split the responsibility for organizing small artisan-type producers, industrial enterprises, and the agricultural sector. Despite these differences in the number of the hierarchically organized compulsory groups, their functions, internal structures, and patterns of interaction with the state have exhibited strong similarities within the corporatist-type category while also drastically differing from those organizations developed in the compulsory-membership context.

Other countries in the region, including Poland, Czech Republic, Bulgaria, Romania, the Baltic countries, CIS, and Mongolia, have reorganized their communist-era chambers of commerce along the lines of voluntary membership, removing virtually all state backing of the chambers and creating legislative frameworks for the formation of alternative organizations for business

---

[10] In most cases compulsory membership is automatic for all enterprises filing their incorporation documents with the state authorities.

182   *Building Business*

TABLE 6.2. *National Chambers of Commerce: Type of Membership*

Compulsory Membership[a]	Transitioned from Compulsory to Voluntary	Voluntary Membership[b]
Albania (8,000)	Hungary 2000 (45,000)	Bulgaria (43,000)
Bosnia-Herzegovina (40,000)	Slovakia 1996 (7,512)	Czech Republic (13,000)
Croatia (68,683)	Slovenia 2006 (61,000)	Estonia (3,324)
Serbia (130,000)	Macedonia 2004 (149,386)	Latvia (1,030)
Montenegro (10,800)		Lithuania (16,000)
Moldova (1,326)		Poland (300,000)
		Romania (8,104)
		Armenia (2,180)
		Azerbaijan (305)
		Belarus (1,600)
		Georgia (3,000)
		Kazakhstan (670)
		Kyrgyz Republic
		Russia (25,000)
		Mongolia
		Tajikistan (170)
		Ukraine (5,000)
		Uzbekistan

[a] Categories of enterprises required to join chambers of commerce differ across countries. Albania, for instance, excludes agricultural enterprises, whereas Croatia has additional compulsory associations for cooperatives (mostly agricultural) and artisans. Serbia effectively excludes microbusiness from the compulsory-membership clause.

[b] This refers to member enterprises. Some countries require local employer organizations to join the corresponding national organizations. Ukrainian legislation, for example, mandates that all provincial and local organizations that use the name "Chamber of Commerce" be a part of the national Chambers of Commerce system.

Note: Official membership figures, where available, are reported in parentheses.

Source: The Chambers of Commerce and Industry: Summary, Central European Initiative, Euro Chamber, http://academy.eurochambres.eu, http://www.unioncamere.net/cei/whoswho.htm, 2005.

representation, coordination, and self-governance. Table 6.2 groups the post-communist countries according to the basis of membership in chambers of commerce and provides the 2005 membership figures.

The adoption of such different institutional structures of business representation can be explained through path dependencies and the institutional continuity of the chambers' structures. Chambers of commerce (or chambers of economy) trace their history to nineteenth-century organizations established throughout Eastern Europe under the influence of the Western European tradition and to those that grew out of the indigenous medieval merchant associations. For example, in the Austro-Hungarian partition of Poland the first chambers were created in 1850 (Wykrętowicz 2004). The Croatian Chamber

Compulsory vs. Voluntary Membership 183

of Economy in Zagreb was established in 1852, although the Chamber of Economy of the city of Dubrovnik, which traditionally engaged in European maritime trade, was created much earlier, in 1808.[11] The history of voluntary merchant associations in the Russian empire dates back to the Moscow Merchant Society established in 1813.[12] Compulsory merchant organizations were established in Russia in 1909 under the name of chambers of commerce; however, they did not survive the 1917 revolution.

Two competing traditions of business representation and self-regulation have influenced Eastern Europe. In the areas that in the nineteenth century were ruled by Austro-Hungary, a compulsory-membership chamber system has taken root. This compulsory, encompassing system was historically a French creation, first established by Napoleon Bonaparte in 1802 and later introduced to the rest of Europe in the course of the Napoleonic conquest. Where such influence has not been profound, traditions of voluntary business associations have developed. The Baltic States in the interwar era, for instance, established chambers of commerce and crafts based on voluntary membership.[13]

Under communist rule both the compulsory, state-affiliated chambers of commerce and voluntary organizations of capital were first liquidated and later revived as auxiliary state organizations serving coordinating, intermediating, and standard-setting functions, predominantly in foreign trade. They were designed to parallel some functions of Western business associations (third-party arbitrage, certification, and facilitation of economic contacts) and largely served as institutional façade for state-planned economies in the international economic arena. Such organizations, however, were not genuine associations of businesses, because they (1) did not rely on membership for their survival; (2) were financed, staffed, and directed by the state; and (3) lacked any representative functions vis-à-vis the state. Membership in these organizations was either nonexistent or nominal. As a result, despite institutional continuity of the chambers throughout the communist era, these organizations lost their substantive significance and were reduced to mere institutional shells operating as extensions of the state bureaucracy.

The redefinition of chambers of commerce that followed the postcommunist transitions has, for the most part, been a rediscovery of precommunist patterns of business organization. It is of little surprise, therefore, that the majority of countries with precommunist legacies that were associated with the Austro-Hungarian empire – Hungary, Croatia, Slovenia, Slovakia, Bosnia-Herzegovina – have recreated the compulsory-chamber system, whereas

---

[11] See Croatian Chamber of Economy, www.hgk.hr.
[12] See Chamber of Commerce and Industry of the Russian Federation, http://www.tpprf.ru/en/.
[13] With French capital and commerce playing an important role in the economic development of Eastern Europe in the nineteenth and early twentieth centuries, the compulsory-chamber tradition has influenced all of Eastern Europe – hence, the Russian compulsory experiment of 1909 and Polish all-encompassing chambers of the interwar period.

184   *Building Business*

countries ruled by the Russian empire as well as Bulgaria and Romania have adopted voluntary pluralist arrangements.[14] In the countries that adopted the compulsory-membership system, explicit references were made to Austrian, Italian, and German compulsory institutions that seemed to be a good fit for the post-communist societies, characterized by the lack of pre-existing articulated interests, distrust in formal institutions, and low levels of civic engagement.[15]

Following the creation of the formal institutional foundations that put Eastern European countries on the diverging paths of business representation, interesting developments were under way in a number of countries. The compulsory system, for the most part, did not live up to the high expectations of either business community or government. Although representative and regulating functions of the compulsory chambers were expected to generate close integration of the business community into the political processes and a gradual development of beneficial self-regulation, businesses in different countries started voicing their dissatisfaction with the compulsory nature of the system and the chambers' inability to reflect their demands and protect their interests adequately. In particular, the compulsory chambers were criticized for giving little recognition – and virtually no representation – to the small-business sector and emerging industries.[16] The official responses to this criticism ranged from legislation mandating the creation of a specialized compulsory organization for representing underrepresented sectors (Croatia in 1993), reforms of the internal organizational and governance structures of the chamber (Serbia in 2001 and 2003, Croatia in 1994), and the abandonment of the compulsory-membership clause altogether (Slovakia in 1996, Hungary in 2000, Macedonia in 2004, and Slovenia in 2006).

Alternative Business Organizations and the Decline of Compulsory Institutions

The business community's growing dissatisfaction with the work of the compulsory chambers of commerce/economy has produced the spontaneous self-organization of rival business associations. A number of sector-specific and cross-sector organizations emerged to represent businesses who felt that state-created compulsory chambers ignored their interests and vision. Such

---

[14] More interesting in this respect are the cases of Poland and Czech Republic, both of which followed the pluralist model. Their deviation from the nineteenth-century and interwar institutional patterns may be traced to the indigenous traditions of the medieval merchant institutions preceding foreign-imposed chambers of commerce and to the desire to stimulate the development of societal voluntarism and pluralist competition deemed essential for the survival of their new democracies.

[15] Italian practices clearly influenced the 1999 law that created a compulsory-membership system in Moldova.

[16] Table 3.9 in Chapter 3 attests to these claims. On average, business satisfaction with associations in voluntary-membership systems is 30 percent higher than in compulsory-membership regimes.

Compulsory vs. Voluntary Membership

alternatives to the official chambers of commerce included organizations of small businesses and leading industrial enterprises, banks, and trade corporations. Perhaps the largest and most influential of such voluntary associations are the national employer associations that by the late 1990s had organized predominantly large businesses in different countries of the region. In such countries as Croatia and Macedonia, the employer associations have successfully demanded an exclusive role in the tripartite negotiations, becoming the official organizations representing countries' businesses in general agreements in the sphere of industrial and labor relations. In Slovenia the Association of Employers unites more than 1,200 enterprises that jointly constitute about half of the entire private sector.

In Albania the first voluntary business association providing an organizational alternative to the official chambers of commerce – Union of Democratic Businessmen – was created as early as 1993. Currently, the two largest voluntary umbrella business associations are the Albanian Council of Employer Organizations and the Union of Organizations of Albanian Businesses. Similarly, two major voluntary associations competed for membership in Serbia and Montenegro: the Employers' Association and the Association of Industrialists and Entrepreneurs of Serbia and Montenegro. There has been a steady increase in the number of sector- and issue-specific voluntary associations throughout the region, in both pluralist- and corporatist-type systems. Examples of successful voluntary associations that developed alongside the compulsory-chamber systems include the National Real Estate Association and the Professional and Business Women Association in Albania, the Association of Serbian Banks, the "Krov" Association of Real Estate Agencies of Serbia and Montenegro, the Croatian Association of Travel Agencies, the ACE, and many others.

As the above examples demonstrate, the existence of the compulsory-membership requirement did not prevent firms from seeking membership in alternative voluntary-membership organizations. Paradoxically, the compulsory-representation system, despite providing a strong resource base, solid legal foundation for the business's role in political decision making, and, most importantly, solving the problem of collective action involved in the initial organizational development, could not prevent the development of voluntary associations. Although participation in and contributions to voluntary associations do not replace the requirement to pay compulsory-membership dues, businesses in compulsory systems have formed and actively participate in alternative voluntary associations. Some associations not only attained considerable membership, expanded their functions and activities, and actively participated in the political process; they also attained an officially recognized status in representing the business community. Finally, four countries – Slovakia, Hungary, Macedonia, and Slovenia – have replaced compulsory institutions with pluralist systems.

The dismantling of compulsory-membership chambers in Slovakia, Hungary, Macedonia, and Slovenia was a result of deliberate government efforts backed by the business community and was precipitated by the competitive pressures emanating from the emerging voluntary organizations. In Slovakia the elimination of automatic membership established under the 1992 law was proposed as a means to enhance competition and reduce undue corporate influence. The move was part of a broader political agenda that resulted in the reorganization of fifteen professional chambers into voluntary civic associations (Malová and Rybář 2003). The business community embraced this reorganization at least in part because of the growing influence and active political role of a voluntary peak organization – Federation of Employers' Associations (AZZZ), which at the time became the primary force in the emerging institutions of social dialogue (Malová, n.d.).

Similarly, the abandonment of the compulsory-membership requirement in Hungary (Chamber Act of 1999) came as a government initiative directed against the amalgamation of the certifications, quality control, and licensing functions under the self-governing and largely autonomous Hungarian Chamber of Commerce (Pola 2007). In the 2000s Hungary also abolished compulsory-membership requirements in a number of professional associations and transferred their regulatory functions to state institutions. The law that stripped the Chamber of Commerce of automatic member contributions and regulatory functions was backed by the business community, which repeatedly raised concerns about the chamber's disincentives to expand its member-oriented services, its ineffectiveness in carrying regulatory functions, and its inability to represent economic interests in politics effectively. The program statement of the reformed voluntary chamber states, "It is obvious that enterprises will be keen to join the Chamber if they are offered something in return." It declares that the Chamber's major objectives include "safeguarding the interests of Hungarian entrepreneurs, and ensuring that the Chamber becomes service-oriented."[17]

Member dissatisfaction with the compulsory system and the growing competitive pressures from the politically active voluntary-membership associations are also responsible for the passage of the 2004 Macedonian Law on the Economic Chamber and the 2006 Slovenian Law on Chambers of Commerce and Industry, both of which annulled the compulsory-membership status of the Macedonian Chamber of Economy and Slovenian Chambers of Commerce, Industry, Craft, and Small Businesses. According to Eurochambers, following these changes, Macedonia and Slovenia experienced a decline in membership from 149,386 and 64,818 companies in 2004 to 15,000 and 13,093 members in 2009, respectively.[18]

In Slovenia the passage of the 2006 law was linked to another important legislative change: the 2006 Law on Collective Agreements stipulated that starting in 2009, no compulsory-membership employer association could enter

---

[17] See http://www.mkik.hu.
[18] See Eurochambres, http://www.eurochambres.be.

into binding collective agreements (Sledar 2010). According to the European Industrial Relations Observatory, the move away from compulsory-membership chambers had little effect on the nature of collective bargaining because prior to 2006 a number of voluntary-membership groups were participants to tripartite negotiations.

These developments point to a de facto erosion of corporatist-style systems of business representation in Eastern Europe and their evolution toward greater pluralism. Despite the clear advantages of compulsory associations in solving the collective-action problem of organization and contributions, the compulsory-chamber systems seem to have failed to satisfy the needs of at least a part of the business community, leading to calls for compulsory-membership arrangements to be dismantled. Discussed empirical developments are consistent with the prior theoretical expectations derived from the formal analysis of participation in compulsory groups.

In Chapter 3 I presented a detailed description of the formation of the compulsory system of interest representation in Croatia and its evolution toward greater pluralism. With nearly universal business participation, Croatian peak associations were developing nonstate mechanisms of carrying out economic policies and monitoring economic regulations. The compulsory institutions have promised greater participation, cohesion, and representativeness that would translate into a stronger position of the business community vis-à-vis the state. The compulsory-membership organizations, however, did not create effective mechanisms for defending the interests of business and regulating intra-industry relations. The lack of strong ties between the compulsory chamber and its diverse members and low incentives to provide them with valuable member benefits led to the development of alternative voluntary associations that took on the roles forsaken or inadequately fulfilled by official peak organizations. Self-organization of rival associations and the proliferation of officially recognized associations have annulled the CCE monopoly on business representation and introduced principles of voluntarism and competition. In Croatia the developments in the sphere of business representation strongly support the defensive organization hypothesis. As the examples of ACE (Chapter 5), CEA, and Croatian Association of Travel Agencies (Chapter 3) clearly demonstrate, the inability of the compulsory-membership CCE to effectively address specific issues plaguing parts of the business community was the primary motivation for organizing these as well as many other voluntary-membership business associations. The Croatian case shows that when compulsory business associations fail to provide selective incentives of regulatory relief, businesses form alternative organizational channels of protection, even if these involve additional organizational costs.

Despite the clear advantages of compulsory associations in solving the collective-action problem through the prevention of free-riding and certainty of contributions, the compulsory-chamber systems have failed, on many occasions, to satisfy the needs of at least a part of the business community. Naturally,

188   *Building Business*

some dissatisfaction with the compulsory-chamber systems stems from the fact that businesspeople perceive organizational dues as a universal tax that does not provide any benefits to the firms. Still, this does not explain why businesses throughout the compulsory-membership systems were eager to join alternative voluntary associations – a decision involving additional contributions of time and money.

Membership Costs

In part, the theoretical model of organizational formation in compulsory and voluntary settings rests on the assumption that organizational membership entails costs. A potential counterargument in explaining the genesis of voluntary organizations might suggest costless participation. According to such an alternative explanation, the proliferation of voluntary organizations of business could happen because of the low cost of membership. To rule out this alternative explanation it is important to demonstrate that participation in industry associations is in fact costly.

Although it varies from country to country and sector to sector as well as between national and local associations, the cost of membership is far from trivial, especially for small and medium-size firms. For example, in 2003 membership fees in the Russian Chamber of Trade and Industry were 60,000 rubles, or about US$2,330, whereas annual fees in the Russian Union of Industrialists and Entrepreneurs were 150,000 rubles, or US$5,820 (Union of Industrialists and Entrepreneurs 2003).[19] At the same time, the average annual wage in the Russian economy in 2003 was estimated at 65,982 rubles (Sokolin 2004). Thus, the annual cost of membership in a voluntary organization was equivalent to or greater than the cost of hiring an additional worker. Notice that in these examples the membership fee schedules do not discriminate between large and small enterprises, increasing the relative cost of participation as the enterprise size decreases. Other associations, however, have flexible fee schedules, tagging contributions to the enterprise size, assets, and profits. For instance, the compulsory-membership Croatian Chamber of Economy distinguishes between three categories of member enterprises. Depending on the number of employees and a firm's assets and profits, monthly membership fees range from 55 Croatian kuna (US$10) to 5,500 kuna (US$1,015). This amounts to 660 kuna to 66,000 kuna annually.[20] Compare this to the membership fees in the voluntary Croatian Employers' Association, ranging from 150,000 kuna to 500,000 kuna (roughly US$27,700 to US$92,340) annually, plus .05 percent of a firm's profit (Croatian Employers' Association 2004). These numbers do not include membership fees in sectoral groups organized within these associations. Within the Croatian Employers' Association these annual fees range

---

[19] Dollar equivalents are calculated using the corresponding year's exchange rates. Also, see www.rspp.ru.

[20] See Croatian Chamber of Economy, http://www.hgk.hr.

Compulsory vs. Voluntary Membership 189

from US$350 for membership in the textiles association to US$1,108 for membership in the financial-sector association. To put these figures in perspective, in 2003 the average annual wage in Croatia was 47,064 kuna.

These examples suggest that the monetary costs of participation in associations, although generally not prohibitive, nevertheless cannot be regarded as negligible. Added to these are the nonmonetary costs of managerial time, paperwork, and other organizational activities associated with membership in one or several associations. Neither enterprise managers nor analysts of the collective-action dilemma can ignore such costs. Thus, costless membership should be ruled out as a possible explanation for the development of multiple organizations representing business.

The erosion of compulsory-membership regimes, manifested in the development of multiple voluntary business associations, loss of monopoly on representation, and, in some cases, formal abandonment of the compulsory institutional forms, is consistent with the implications of the formal model of defensive organization. Neither the emergence of nor growing participation in voluntary business associations nor still the reforms of compulsory systems toward greater pluralism are unexpected in the light of the formal argument advanced earlier. According to the logic of defensive organization, under compulsory membership official associations should have less motivation for developing member-oriented services. Compulsory organizations of the business community, therefore, do not preclude the formation of voluntary associations. The development of organizational pluralism and voluntarism in the post-communist countries that initially adopted the compulsory-membership organizations provides empirical evidence in support of these arguments.

6.4 Membership Rates

As the preceding discussion demonstrates, the existence of the compulsory-membership requirement does not prevent firms from seeking membership in alternative voluntary organizations. Theoretical predictions and empirical evidence suggest an increasing similarity between systems of representation that were originally based on compulsory and voluntary membership. Empirical analysis presented in the previous chapters shows that although the repertoire of associational activities might differ depending on sectoral and country-specific conditions, in both systems the business associations perform analogous functions. But how does the compulsory- versus voluntary-membership distinction influence the overall levels of participation in associations?

This question goes back to the quantitative cross-national analysis presented in Chapter 4, in which business survey data were analyzed to assess a number of competing hypotheses about determinants of associational membership. Does the existence of compulsory-membership regimes invalidate the results of

190   *Building Business*

TABLE 6.3. *Share of Participatory Firms in Compulsory- and Voluntary-Membership Systems*

	1999		2002		2005	
	Compulsory	Voluntary	Compulsory	Voluntary	Compulsory	Voluntary
Current regime	.43	.19	.66	.38	.60	.36
Initial institutional design	.39	.19	.62	.37	.61	.34

Source: World Bank and BEEPS 2000–2005.

this analysis? Here I argue that the compulsory-membership requirement does not invalidate the conclusions based on my comparative analysis of business survey data.

A brief glance at the mean levels of membership across the compulsory- and voluntary-membership regimes should rule out any suspicion that compulsory membership translates into universal participation. Still, compulsory-membership arrangements result in significantly higher levels of participation. Table 6.3 presents average shares of firms reporting participation in business associations in compulsory- and voluntary-membership regimes, according to the 1999, 2002, and 2005 BEEPS data. Group averages are based on two different classifications. The "current regime" category groups countries according to the legal arrangement in place at the time of the survey. The "initial institutional design" category reflects the original post-transition representation system, with Hungary, Slovakia, and Macedonia included in the compulsory membership and Moldova in the voluntary-membership groups.

As shown in the table, the difference between participation levels in compulsory- and voluntary-membership associations has gradually diminished over time. In the voluntary-membership category, participation almost doubled between the 1999 and 2002 surveys, jumping from 19 percent to almost 40 percent.[21] The share of participatory firms in compulsory-membership systems stabilized at about 60 percent in the mid-2000s. The 60–66 percent

---

[21] The means are computed using base sample weights. Because of the unavailability of sampling frames for some participating countries, no adjustments were made for firm size and ownership. Although the survey was designed as self-weighted, imposing ownership and size quotas resulted in overrepresentation of larger and foreign-owned companies in the smaller countries of the region. Taking into account the fact that firm size and foreign ownership positively correlate with associational membership, these figures somewhat inflate the extent of organizational participation in the compulsory-membership category.

Compulsory vs. Voluntary Membership 191

membership, however, is much lower than the universal membership that the compulsory-membership legislation prescribes.[22]

It should be taken into account that the compulsory-category figures include participation in both voluntary and compulsory associations and do not discriminate between compulsory and voluntary membership. The recent growth in the number of and membership in voluntary groups throughout compulsory-membership countries, documented in this chapter, suggests that these membership figures, at least in part, capture membership in voluntary groups. Formal analysis outlining the motivation for joining voluntary organizations in the compulsory-membership settings provides a strong theoretical rationale for expecting growing participation in voluntary groups. In addition, although there is a positive correlation between membership levels and the compulsory-membership requirement, compulsory membership by itself does not explain within-country variation with respect to business organization.

Given the ongoing evolution of compulsory-membership systems toward greater voluntarism, the existence of differential systems of representation does not present a problem for the quantitative analysis that pools together compulsory- and voluntary-membership systems. Evidence presented throughout this book suggests that business associations across compulsory and voluntary regimes, although with differential degrees of effectiveness and member satisfaction, perform very similar functions that help protect their members from regulatory pressures. Regression analysis conducted in Chapter 4 demonstrates that the differences in the level of participation in associations are not overdetermined by the compulsory nature of business representation. If anything, the country-specific effects incorporated in the analysis of the cross-national survey data ensure the accuracy of the qualitative data analysis. Although the compulsory-membership requirement has some effects on the levels of participation, such effects were modeled and accounted for in a cross-national research design. The empirical results of quantitative analysis performed earlier in this book, therefore, is valid for both the compulsory- and voluntary-membership systems. Most importantly, as the qualitative evidence clearly demonstrates, business associations in fact are quite similar institutions in all post-communist countries.

6.5 Labor Relations and Business Organizations

This chapter explained the tendency of compulsory systems to incorporate pluralistic features by referring to the poor incentive structure of compulsory organizations. By linking businesses' participation in interest groups to the provision of selective incentives rather than collective goods, this argument

---

[22] As discussed in Chapter 3, in the case of Croatia I interpret the survey-based rates of membership as capturing the "awareness" of membership and as actual _active_ participation rather than as an indicator of nominal and automatic membership.

implies that when associations no longer need to vie for members' support, they become ineffectual as means of representation. Many areas of business interest, however, demand collective solutions that cannot be effectively addressed through selective services.[23] Labor relations are perhaps one of the most universally important reasons for businesses' collective action. Collective-bargaining rights force businesses to coordinate their strategy and speak with a unified voice against the demands of labor. In post-communist settings, official and independent trade unions presented an immense social force supported by vast and politically mobilized membership, enormous organizational and material resources, and strong legal rights.[24] In comparison to fledgling business organizations, unions were a colossal force in post-communist social and industrial relations (Allio 1997). Business–labor relations, however, played a rather marginal role in the organizational dynamics of the post-communist business community. The reasons are both political and institutional.

On the political side, labor relations generally posed little threat to post-communist business interests. This absence of the labor threat stems from the lack of what Kubicek calls the "labor agenda" (2004). Although in the aftermath of regime transitions official and independent labor unions emerged as the most significant post-communist social force, their political capital was spent on the battle against the state and the reconstruction of their own identity as representatives of employees' interests. In the early years of post-communist transition the state continued to be the primary employer, so labor demands against layoffs, privatization, and declining real wages were directed at the state rather than at private-sector employers (Allio 1997; Clarke 2006). As market reforms accelerated, labor found itself in a rather peculiar position. Unions' strong position at the enterprise level – unions' roles in management and distribution of social welfare mostly remained in place until the late 1990s – often allied them with management (Crowley and Ost 2001).

During the most turbulent years of economic transition, post-communist governments sought support for their reform policies through social-dialogue institutions that took the form of tripartite negotiations among labor, capital, and the state. Clarke (2006) offers a detailed analysis of Russian tripartite negotiations that highlights themes common to many post-communist cases. He writes, "The primary object of tripartism in practice has not been for the unions to extract concessions from the employers, with the state serving as

---

[23] Compulsory-membership organizations (as in the case of Austrian WKÖ, for example) can significantly enhance employers' position in negotiating collective agreements, making them indispensable in advancing business interests in the sphere of labor relations.

[24] In fact, in the 1990s many post-communist countries strengthened the labor code in favor of labor interests (Allio 1997). At the same time, peak union organizations have progressively lost their redistributive and social functions to the state institutions. Only in mid-2000s, after organized labor was effectively neutralized through the declining membership rates, diminishing resources, and reduced functions, did the state engage in the reform of labor codes that legislatively acknowledged diminished labor standards and collective rights (Fulton 2011).

Compulsory vs. Voluntary Membership 193

mediator and guarantor of the agreement, but for the unions and the employers to extract concessions from the state" (75). Clarke goes on to explain: "The primary organizations of the trade unions expressed the dependence of the employees on their employers and so were in no position to articulate any conflict that could be expected to arise as employers chose or were forced by market pressures to cut costs by intensifying labor, cutting wages, and reducing employment."

The reasons for such an unconventional relationship between employers and the unions include such things as the preoccupation of labor organizations with traditional welfare-distribution factions that directed their demands against the state rather than against the employers, the co-opting of labor organizations by the management at the enterprise level, and also a limited capacity of employer associations to enforce tripartite agreements. Institutionally, a relatively weak organizational structure of post-communist employer organizations has proven to be their asset rather than their peril. Associations' inability to enforce collective agreements meant low levels of employers' responsibility vis-à-vis the labor, greater flexibility within existing labor regulations, and deflection of the labor force's attention from the employers to the state institutions that remained the sole guarantors of collective agreements.

Such strategic self-limitation on the part of the business community was achieved through two routes. The first mechanism was through the proliferation and fragmentation of employers' representation. Multiple organizations made it virtually impossible to rely on business self-governance as a means of securing employers' commitment in the sphere of social policy. For example, in Romania thirteen national peak associations directly participate in the national social dialogue, whereas Slovenia, with its meager population of two million, has five such associations.

Organizational fragmentation as a means of self-limitation of business representation in the sphere of labor relations was clearly unavailable in compulsory-membership systems. There, the second strategy became a predominant form of self-limiting employers' role in labor relations. It took the form of specialized peak organizations in the sphere of social relations that could maintain ambitious representativeness claims without effectively controlling their members. The creation of voluntary-membership Albanian, Croatian, and Serbian national Employers' Associations, all of which became the designated partners of social dialogue, provides examples of this mechanism.

The strategy of functional differentiation, however, was not limited to the compulsory-membership systems. Until 2004, Slovakian AZZZ was the designated partner in the social dialogue. It was created as national peak association specializing in business representation in the institutions of social dialogue. Yet other cases combine two mechanisms. Russian CCEO, for instance, not only is organizationally independent from the most significant national groups (RUIE and CCI) but also is a loose institutional umbrella for organizationally independent national, regional, sectoral, and professional associations. Similarly, the Lithuanian Confederation of Industrialists is an umbrella institution that has little control and no binding power over its member associations.

Although the political, legal, and organizational strengths of unions in the early years of the post-communist transition seemed to indicate the demand for unified (and perhaps compulsory) organizations of capital, clashes between capital and labor have not been characteristic of the transitional politics. The relative weakness of representative employer organizations and the organizational fragmentation of business representation in general helped maintain the low levels of business–labor conflict.[25] This, for the most part, explains the virtual absence of labor relations from the analysis of the formation of post-communist business associations presented in this book.

6.6 Beyond Corporatism

Summing up, this chapter has traced interesting patterns in the institutional development of business representation across post-communist Eastern Europe. In the early 1990s governments in Eastern Europe created legislation on interest representation that varied dramatically across countries. Some countries chose voluntary forms of membership, whereas others chose compulsory-membership models of business representation. Subsequently, however, these models have begun to converge. Some countries abandoned compulsory-membership models and others evolved toward greater pluralism and voluntarism. In explaining these developments, I argued that compulsory institutions have been ineffective in channeling the interests of the business community, giving rise to voluntary associations that compete with officially designated groups to provide business representation and business "protection."

The existence of drastically different models of business participation based on the compulsory and voluntary membership has presented additional problems in studying the logic of organizational formation. The analytical model developed to account for strategic interaction between the bureaucrats, firms, and business associations can easily be extended to the analysis of compulsory regimes. The model predicts that compulsory business associations should not alter the calculus of firms' interactions with regulatory agencies. In fact, the cost of participating in a compulsory-membership group is likely to be perceived as a part of the regulatory burden. The defensive organization theory argues that the forces shaping the interaction between voluntary organizations, businesses, and bureaucrats under the compulsory-membership requirements are the same as in voluntary systems.

---

[25] The intensity of this conflict varied across time, countries, and industries. In some instances the interest of the employers converged with those of labor. In other cases they aligned with the state against labor interests. Moreover, the interests of labor and employers on social issues often diverged from the strategic positions their representative associations occupied. Post-communist labor relations are a fascinating and complex subject in their own right and deserve a separate study.

Compulsory vs. Voluntary Membership   195

In analyzing voluntary organizations that developed in the compulsory-membership countries, I paid special attention to the calculus of voluntary group formation, which has to take place in the corporatist system for pluralism to take root. By returning to the model of strategic interaction between post-communist firms, business associations, and the state bureaucracy, I arrived at the conclusion that despite certain advantages associated with the prior solution of the collective-action problem, compulsory associations have fewer incentives to satisfy business demands. This opens up opportunities for voluntary groups to develop.

Voluntary business associations formed in all post-communist countries that initially endorsed the principles of compulsory membership. After the abandonment of compulsory-chamber systems in four out of nine compulsory-membership regimes, and with respect to the growing number of independent voluntary groups in others, it became apparent that organizational pluralism and voluntarism are becoming points of convergence. This finding runs contrary to the plethora of scholarly accounts of the growing dissimilarities between post-communist countries in the political, economic, and social spheres (Ericson 1992; Crawford 1995; Stark 1995; Holmes 1996; Stark and Bruszt 1998; King 2000; Fish 2001). The analysis presented in this chapter suggests that business representation exemplifies one of the few areas of increasing institutional convergence across post-communist countries since the early 1990s. This finding is particularly surprising because of the post-communist adoption of drastically different institutional arrangements that seemed to mark the "branching point" in the area of business representation.[26]

One can detect parallels between the erosion of the post-communist compulsory peak associations and those in the developed capitalist world. Centralized peak associations' monopolization of interest representation no longer characterizes many long-term corporatist systems (Lash and Urry 1987). Although the *varieties of capitalism* literature has argued for increasing divergence among and bifurcated convergence within different types of capitalist economies (Soskice 1990; Iversen and Pontusson 2000), a growing number of analysts have documented the erosion of Western European institutions of economic coordination, including employer associations (Hassel 1999; Beyer and Hopner 2003; Kinderman 2005; Martin and Thelen 2007). Although there is no consensus on what factors instigate this institutional disintegration, scholars acknowledge "the failure of traditional institutions ... to satisfy employer needs" (Kinderman 2005) and the inability of industry-level coordination to address globalization and the shift to the service economy (Martin and Thelen 2007). Although this indicates the applicability of the logic of defensive organization in Western Europe, more research is needed to establish the validity of these propositions in the cross-regional (Eastern and Western European) context.

---

[26] On the notion of "branching points," see Gourevitch 1986 and Collier and Collier 1991.

7

Conclusions

> If they think that by joining they can solve the problems of THEIR business, I have to disappoint them. By joining our and many other associations, they help solve the problems of OUR businesses – the problems that all of us have in common.
>
> – A. D. Ioffe, president of ADSMB

This book opened up with a puzzle: why do post-communist firms organize in industry associations despite all rational arguments against collective action and the abundance of practical impediments to the formation of organized groups? After summarizing the central findings of this study, this chapter looks beyond the puzzle of the formation of business associations to discuss the place of business associations in post-communist economies, politics, and societies. I bring together different aspects of group activities that I analyzed throughout the book in order to advance a more comprehensive understanding of business associations' role in shaping the nature of industrial relations, markets, and states. I also speculate about implications of the results and briefly outline promising directions for future research on this subject.

7.1 Summary of Arguments and Findings

This book explored the formation and evolution of one of the most important and highly developed institutions of post-communist civil society – business and employer associations. Despite having many commonalities at the start of the transition, firms across states and sectors formed associations at wildly different rates. Moreover, many standard accounts of collective action fail to capture this variation. Chapter 2 advanced a theoretical argument emphasizing the defensive functions of business associations as the major driving force behind growing membership. The central argument emerging from the theoretical and empirical exploration of this topic is that businesses join associations

196

Conclusions 197

in response to regulatory regimes imposed by state bureaucracy. In the face of insecure property rights, tenuous rule of law, unpredictable regulation, and predatory bureaucrats, business associations pool firms' resources to stabilize the business environment. The analysis revealed that economic sectors and countries where business associations are able to find cost-effective ways of protecting member interests against regulatory uncertainty and the adverse effects of bureaucratic predation enjoy greater participation than do economic sectors and countries that lack this capability.

The post-communist empirical diversity has presented a wonderful testing ground for investigating conditions that facilitate collective action on the part of unorganized economic interests. Throughout the book, I reviewed a host of theories providing explanations for why interests organize and tested them against empirical data. Through a multilevel, nested-design empirical analysis, I found support for some factors advocated in the literature. For instance, smaller group size (the number of firms per sector), ownership structure (foreign and private ownership, in particular), and the relatively large size of enterprises increase the likelihood of association formation. At the same time, the existence of large business and employer associations that transcend sector and regional divisions attests to the fact that diversity of interests and the multitude of group members do not preclude the establishment of voluntary groups. In fact, cross-industry associations were among the first ones to form in Eastern Europe, well before the formation of industry-specific groups (Fortescue 1997; Pyle 2006).

Other theoretical explanations were proven to have only limited relevance to the post-communist context. Although cross-national variation in the levels of membership in business associations seems to be related to overall levels of economic development and the success of market reforms, hypotheses derived from the economic development theory, on closer consideration, find weak support in post-communist countries. Rather than economic development and macroeconomic transformation per se, more institutionally based factors, such as the bureaucratic and regulatory environment, appear to be directly responsible for the observed cross-national differences in the development of business associations.

This book finds that although resource specificity appears to be related to interest aggregation, other industry-specific factors produce much of the cross-sectoral variation in membership rates. Specifically, rules and regulations structuring industrial relations, production processes, and business practices have played an important role in stimulating organizational responses from post-communist firms. As these rules and regulations vary not only across national borders but also across different industries and spheres of economic activity, varying levels of organizational formation can be observed in different sectors within a given country.

Contrary to standard approaches to analyzing organized interests and their relationship with state regulatory intervention, this study found that invasive regulatory regimes on their own discourage rather than encourage collective action. This empirical finding is at odds with existing approaches to interest groups and regulation. The theory of defensive organization advocated in this book offers a powerful explanation: because collective action is predicated on successfully providing selective regulatory relief, business associations are better able to operate in a relatively nonrestrictive regulatory environment. To attract members, business associations have to provide particularistic benefits that correspond to the extent of regulatory burden. When regulations are extensive, organizational entrepreneurs have to find more effective opportunities to lower regulatory pressures. Therefore, fewer business associations can successfully overcome the problem of collective action when regulatory pressures are particularly high.

The comparative analysis of functions and activities business associations perform in response to regulatory pressures their constituents face points to the importance of particularistic benefits that associations offer exclusively (or cost-effectively) to member firms. Member benefits appear to be the most potent rational incentive for joining industry associations. This situation provides an effective solution to the collective-action problem. Once the problem of organization is solved, associations become important agents for providing collective goods.[1]

Another finding reflects the effects of bureaucratic probity on business-interest organization. Lobbying is frequently seen as instrumental to state capture and pervasive corruption. This book finds that high levels of bureaucratic corruption, in fact, stimulate participation in business associations. Contrary to the widespread belief that corruption and business interests go hand in hand, I find that business associations, rather than using corruption to advance their causes, provide an organizational alternative to corrupt practices. When corruption is pervasive, bribing the bureaucrats responsible for enforcing state regulatory practices becomes much less cost-effective than seeking regulatory assistance from a legitimate organization. In these settings, business associations, through their targeted member benefits and collective actions directed at reducing the cost of regulatory compliance, become an attractive substitute for corrupt behavior. Firms, therefore, join associations as an alternative to a corruption strategy of dealing with state regulatory agents. Of course, this does not mean that individual firms that are members of business associations never pay bribes to bureaucrats. It does, however, indicate that expensive bribery in heavily regulated sectors increases the incentive to form business associations to protect business interests.

I also find that the rule of law stimulates the collective action, whereas the bureaucrats' ability to interpret the regulations freely and apply them in a haphazard manner makes the official regulatory policy rather irrelevant in defining the post-communist business environment. Costly regulatory regimes,

---

[1] See also Pyle (2006) on this issue.

Conclusions

therefore, tend to suppress organizational membership only if bureaucrats consistently enforce them. This finding highlights the importance of distinguishing between the content of state intervention and its enforcement capacity, which are often conflated.

Yet another important finding involves the effects of legal foundations laid out for the development of business representation at the outset of transition. Although in the early 1990s two distinct systems of business representation were adopted in Eastern Europe – one based on voluntary membership and the other on compulsory membership in state-created associations – subsequent developments brought these systems closer together. Voluntary business associations have become the most common form of business representation throughout the region. The central argument of this book, postulating that post-communist businesses participate in associations as a way of protecting their economic interests against regulatory pressure emanating from cumbersome and inconsistently enforced regulations, has a broader applicability throughout the region, regardless of the legal foundation for organizational development.

Among these findings a particularly interesting image of post-communist business associations has emerged. Rather than being primarily instruments of influence, business associations are clearly important in fostering club goods for their members, and often they provide public goods as well. They function as substitutes for state and private mechanisms of lowering transaction costs, protecting property rights, and enforcing contracts. They challenge corrupt bureaucracy and contribute to the establishment of effective and predictable regulatory regimes. Moreover, in many cases they build centers of political power that are not directly linked to the state institutions and have the potential to challenge the existing political arrangements.

7.2 Political and Socioeconomic Roles of Business Associations

Business Associations and Rent-Seeking

Although the majority of research in political science sees business associations as rent-seekers that lobby the government for preferential treatment and privilege, this book offers a different perspective. This research has demonstrated that rather than primarily seeking benefits from the government, business associations provide important services and benefits that compensate for the lack of established market mechanisms of coordination, information transfer, and reputation-building as well as for the state's failure to supply public goods, secure property rights, implement fair and unbiased regulation, and create long-term stability.

Because of the number of constraints they face in the political and institutional environment and, more importantly, the strong advantages individual firms have in the sphere of lobbying, influence, and corrupt transactions, post-communist industry and employer associations are rather ineffective

200   *Building Business*

TABLE 7.1. *Assessment of Relative Political Influence of Business Associations*

How Much Influence Do You Think the Following Groups Actually Had on Recently Enacted National Laws and Regulations that Have a Substantial Impact on Your Business?*	Mean Assessment of Influence (0 = No Influence; 4 = Considerable Influence)
Your firm	.39
Labor unions	.77
Your business association	.79
Other domestic firms	.86
Other business associations	.86
Organized crime	.88
Those with ties to politicians	1.52
Dominant firms/ conglomerates in key sectors	1.64

Source: BEEPS 2002.

mechanisms of rent-seeking. As evident in Table 7.1, businesspeople rank business associations rather low with respect to their ability to influence government policies. Business associations are ranked below well-connected individual firms, organized crime, and industrial conglomerates on the level of their influence. However, their political weight is ranked higher than that of labor unions and average firms. This situation reinforces the overall picture of business associations as rather marginal agents of lobbying and political influence, putting more emphasis on their market-enhancing and regulatory functions (Table 7.1).

Business Associations and Cartels
Cartels are a form of collusion among firms that attempt to increase profits by reducing the industry output, fixing product prices, establishing common sales or purchase agencies, or otherwise limiting competition. Such behavior undermines or bypasses market mechanisms and thus may have very destructive consequences, including severe inefficiencies, high costs to consumers, and exploitation of the contiguous industries. In most modern societies, such agreements are illegal and are subject to antimonopoly legislation. As firms are likely to hide their cartel agreements, they may use smilingly benign organizational forms to disguise forbidden practices. Researchers studying industry organizations in different capitalist countries have documented such arrangements.[2] If post-communist business associations provide venues for cartelization, the positive assessment of business associations emerging from this study would be significantly damaged.

---

[2] For instance, Schaede (2000) presents a thorough account of trade associations being instrumental in enforcing cartel agreements between Japanese producers. He finds that Japanese

Conclusions 201

On the contrary, this study has provided much evidence that most of the associations uniting businesses in the post-communist countries are not a form of collusion. Three types of evidence support this notion. First of all, for cartel arrangements to produce benefits, they have to restrict membership to a specific set of firms (when the cartel discriminates against the competitors) or to a given sector (when the cartel takes advantage of the downstream producers/ consumers). Unlike many interest groups that exist in other parts of the world, most post-communist business associations have open membership. This means that any corporate entity (or individual) has the right to join. Even professional and sectoral groups rarely discriminate against firms or public entities lacking corresponding professional or industry credentials. The descriptions of membership in Chapters 3 and 5 provide ample examples of educational institutions, research labs, newspapers, other business groups, and firms from different sectors participating in sectoral associations.

Second, to be successful, cartel agreements have to be made in oligopolistic settings or in industries characterized by the existence of only a few firms that dominate the market. The empirical investigation has found no evidence that firms with larger market shares are more likely to join associations than are firms with smaller market shares. In fact, there is a negative correlation between resource concentration and the probability of membership. Firms with larger market share are less likely to participate in associations.[3] Even if one is willing to entertain the idea of collusion between firms with small market shares, multiple associational membership and competing organizations make enforcing any cartel agreement practically impossible.

In addition, small and microfirms constitute the largest share (in absolute terms) of associations' membership. Small firms in dynamically developing industries are antithetical to oligopolistic arrangements. Further evidence against cartelization is the fact that a large number of associations are organized on a cross-industry basis. Such associations unite firms that share other

---

associations self-regulate in two broad terms: administratively and protectively. The first category refers to "the activities that aim to structure the rules and regulations of the industry, with the primary motive to facilitate or enhance trade," whereas the latter describes "all activities aimed to shield the industry from competition by creating defensive boundaries to trade" (7–8). Unlike in the Japanese case, post-communist business associations have little incentive or power to erect trade boundaries. The shrinking state sector and falling incomes in the earlier years of the post-communist transition have diminished the attractiveness of domestic markets. Shielded from global trade for decades, post-communist industries had much to gain from open trade and open finance. Later on, the most active parts of the business community were foreign-trade oriented rather than inward-looking. Using Schaede's terminology, post-communist self-regulation is predominantly "administrative." The term "defensive organization" is used in this study to suggest industry defense against state intervention and extortion. This should not be confused with the protectionist defense that Schaede's definitions captured.

[3] The bivariate correlation between associational membership and firm's market share is -.3. The effect disappears when other controls are introduced and is not included in the final model estimation.

202   *Building Business*

characteristics, such as geographical location, size, or vulnerability to bureau-cratic controls. Representing different industries and operating on different markets, such firms have little basis for cartel-like behavior.

Business Associations and Economic Regulations

Effective regulatory regimes are essential in providing a stable and secure environment for market players. But what is the role of market participants in shaping their own regulatory environment? A vast body of literature on interest-group theories of regulation (Stigler 1971; Peltzman 1976, 1989; Keeler 1984) and deregulation (Weingast 1981; Noll and Owen 1983) links the emergence of regulation to demands of special interest groups (produc-ers) who pressure politicians to enact regulations advancing their interests at the expense of public interest (consumers). Similarly, according to this litera-ture, deregulation occurs when existing regulations no longer serve producers' interests, prompting them to pressure the politicians for the state's withdrawal. Theories of rent-seeking stress that private interests support regulatory inter-vention because it creates opportunities for rents. At the same time, politicians and bureaucrats enjoy rent-creation because of the resources it brings in the form of campaign contributions and bribes.

This vast body of literature offers limited guidance in accounting for vari-ation among the reforms of regulatory regimes in post-communist economies. Previous research that examined deregulatory movements in established cap-italist economies did not have to deal with many issues that are central to transitional economies; thus, its conclusions have somewhat limited relevance to the drastically different post-communist socioeconomic context. Theoretical implications of the interest-group theory of regulation oftentimes contradict empirical developments in post-communist countries. Specifically, interest-group theory does not explain producers' desire to self-regulate at a cost and does not specify the content and form of "best" regulatory practices.

The empirical work on business-state relations in Eastern Europe points to an unorthodox preference structure of the state and industry actors as well as to the uneven record of regulatory initiative on the part of the state and industry. On one hand, the state bureaucracy was responsible for initiating deregulatory measures (Locatelli 2003).[4] On the other hand, state bureaucra-cies were noted for their fierce resistance to any reduction in state involve-ment in the economy (Yakovlev and Zhuravskaya 2007). As this volume has demonstrated, in addition to the classic deregulation stand, some industrial interests consistently favor stricter regulatory oversight. This comes as an even greater surprise given that oftentimes the regulations that firms advocate cre-ate greater hurdles for the same firms that push for them in the first place. Moreover, the examples of self-imposed and self-enforced regulatory norms practiced by firms in the service sector, trade, finance, and industry present

---

[4] Vogel (1998) makes an important point that liberalization does not equal deregulation.

Conclusions 203

additional problems to the analytical approach that sees regulations as the focal point of rent-seeking.

The theory of defensive organization developed in this book suggests re-examining the issue of regulation/deregulation in the light of the record of deregulatory and new regulatory initiatives of post-communist business associations. The empirical analysis demonstrates an important role of industry associations in promoting both a regulatory and deregulatory agenda. Although the rent-seeking theories of regulation are too often inconsistent with results from the cases at hand, the defensive organization argument opens a new perspective to account for differential combinations of preference for regulation on the part of the state, regulatory agencies, and the industry. The evidence from post-communist countries suggests that business interests in fact favor regulations that are predictable and well-enforced. The "good" regulation that industry participants prefer is not always the least regulation (as the neoliberal perspective would suggest). Neither are the preferences for regulatory regimes solely driven by rent-seeking or protectionist demands. Post-communist business associations have consistently pushed for the kinds of regulatory regimes that guarantee less bureaucratic discretion, better enforcement, and fewer opportunities for misinterpretation and bureaucratic abuse. Organized business groups, therefore, rather than exhorting a malignant influence, tend to play a stabilizing role by limiting the opportunities for rent-seeking on the part of state bureaucracy.

Business Associations and Economic Growth

Mancur Olson, in his seminal work, *The Rise and Decline of Nations: The Political Economy of Economic Growth* (1982), developed an appealing argument about the detrimental effects of special interests on domestic political institutions responsible for facilitating growth and efficiency. Olson identified two sources of economic growth that interest-group activity might potentially affect – capital accumulation and technological advance. He argued that political systems characterized by proliferation and entrenchment of interest groups would suffer from redistributive and protectionist pressures emanating from special interests. These "sclerotic" effects of organized interests suppress economic growth.[5]

---

[5] This argument received rigorous empirical scrutiny (Choi 1983; Bernholz 1986; Gray and Lowery 1988; Tang and Hedley 1998; Crain and Lee 1999; Heckelman 2000; Coates and Heckelman 2003; Knack 2003; Coates and Wilson 2007). Although the empirical results remain mixed, the majority of these studies find a negative relationship between group development and economic growth, and this generally supports the Olsonian argument. The biggest challenges facing this literature, however, are the validity of its instruments and the endogeneity of groups to growth. Many studies have used the number of organized groups and indicators of socioeconomic and political stability as proxies for groups' influence. This offers a rather indirect and tentative test of the Olsonian theory. An additional problem is that the poorest countries that tend to grow faster also have fewer formally organized groups; thus, correlation might be spurious.

Contrary to the "sclerotic effect" argument, this research shows that many producer groups in the dynamically changing new capitalist economies are in fact reducing transaction costs, freeing up managerial resources, solving coordination and information-sharing problems, and providing other services that promote efficiency and remove impediments to growth. In this respect, the findings of this book are similar to those suggested by Pyle (2006), Tucker (2008), and Doner and Schneider (2000), who argue that interest groups act as industry reputation agents and promote efficiency. The development of the post-communist producer and employer associations testifies against the logic of economic policy "sclerosis" and growth-retarding influence of organized interest.

The defensive organization argument advanced in this manuscript provides a theoretical alternative to the Olsonian thesis. Unlike the "sclerotic" development argument that sees business interests as venues of rent-seeking and as having negative consequences on economic performance, accountability, fairness, and efficiency, the defensive organization argument paints an optimistic picture. By joining associations, businesses enter the field of legitimate rather than corruption-prone interactions with the state regulatory institutions, with many positive consequences that involve institution building, improved business climate, and efficiency. This research demonstrates that formation of business-interest groups often results in improvements in public institutions, promotes better governance practices, and, as a result, facilitates efficiency and growth.

Business Associations, Civil Society, and Democratic Development

Although business associations are formed in democratic as well as authoritarian polities, political freedoms and democratic political institutions influence the mechanisms that business associations use to protect the interests of their members and the levels of their success. Business associations enjoy more prominent public positions in democracies, which are usually associated with greater institutionalization of political parties, cleaner electoral practices, and less personalized political power. Democratization of the political sphere, as the recent Ukrainian examples suggest, gives business associations more opportunities to use the public space in the interests of their members, appeal to higher political authorities, and influence public opinion. At the same time, this study has shown that business associations are perfectly functional in nondemocratic contexts; they use the legal system and strictly economic self-organized actions and attain leverage in relation to bureaucrats and political authorities based on the specialized knowledge and information they possess.

This, however, does not mean that business associations are largely inconsequential to the countries' political development. Transitions to democracy and the survival of democratic regimes have been linked to entrenched civil traditions (Tocqueville 1835; Lerner 1958; Almond and Verba 1963; Putnam 1993). Civil organizations that go hand in hand with strong civic engagement,

Conclusions 205

interpersonal trust, and participatory political culture, however, are largely lacking in the post-communist context. The underdevelopment of civic organizations that could counterbalance the power of the state and become the foundation of a democratic participatory culture is frequently named as the major impediment to the progress of democratization in Eastern Europe and the former Soviet republics.

This research shows that business associations have emerged as organizationally stable and self-sustaining institutions of civil society in the post-communist context. Even in countries where the state has taken an active part in organizing business interests under state-created official chamber systems, voluntary business associations have organized outside the state authority. In such regimes, despite the state's attempts to control business representation through officially designated associations, nonstate voluntary organizations based on complete organizational and financial independence have taken root.

By creating an alternative to state centers of power, business associations are becoming the organizational platforms for criticism: they often challenge the governments and someday may assume democratizing functions. The example of Ukrainian business associations that have played an active role in the Orange Revolution by organizing street protests and media campaigns is particularly telling. It was also symbolic that the only interest organizations in Russia that openly condemned the arrest and imprisonment of Russian millionaire and head of the Yukos oil company, Mikhail Khodorkovsky, were business associations (Sikamova et al. 2003; Gevorkian and Smirnov 2003).[6] If the property-owning classes are going to be as important in bringing about and supporting the entrenchment of state-limiting institutions in the post-communist world as they historically have been in the West, following Barrington Moore's (1966) "no bourgeoisie, no democracy" formula, students of democratic change in the region should take seriously organizations that unite the interests of the property-owning class.

This does not mean, however, that business associations will necessarily play a positive role in promoting democracy.[7] Democratic politics offer collective benefits to organized groups. As a consequence, democratic reforms may fall victim to the collective-action problem that numerous organizations face. When presented with strategic opportunities to advance their agenda, some voluntary organizations representing economic interests may ally with authoritarian governments. Such alliances, nevertheless, will necessarily require concessions from the government and, hence, will limit rather than strengthen the power of the state.

---

[6] Business associations were joined only by the human rights groups and the marginalized opposition parties, whose interests in the Khodorkovsky case were purely professional and political.

[7] In Ukraine, for instance, a number of business associations representing the interest of East Ukrainian industries have backed Yanukovich's rollback against democratic reforms.

7.3 Broader Implications and Directions for Future Research

The theoretical arguments and empirical findings of this book have implications stretching beyond industrial relations, business-state relations, and interest-group politics; they have theoretical importance for much broader socioeconomic and political theory. This study contributes to the ongoing exploration of the foundational principles of capitalism, broadly conceived issues of governance, and institutional (organizational) development. It also opens new perspectives in the study of labor relations and class politics.

Economic Transitions and the Development of Capitalism

The best way to conceptualize business associations is to think of them as institutions distinct from states and the markets, having the potential to promote economic coordination, link economic and political systems, and shape patterns of distribution and allocation of economic and political resources. This book, by focusing on business and employer associations as intermediary institutions filling a gap between the state and the market, calls into question some of the underlying assumptions in scholarly accounts of post-communist transitions.

With the collapse of communism, the liberal market economy came to be seen as the ultimate alternative to the centrally planned economic system (Hardt and Kaufman 1995; Crawford 1995; Sachs 1993; Crawford and Lijphart 1997). Such a notion goes back to Hayek's (1945) analysis of planned and market economies as two mutually exclusive alternatives. The free market is often treated as the single-most crucial element of capitalism, and any attempt at circumventing market forces is perceived as a step toward socialist planning. Influenced by this approach, many studies of the post-communist transition naturally focused on the processes of establishing free-market, private property, and stable macroeconomic policies.

The calls to put more emphasis on local knowledge and institutional experimentation have challenged this neoliberal paradigm (Ickes and Ryterman 1995; Shleifer and Treisman 2000; Johnson, McMillan, and Woodruff 2000; Hellman et al. 2000). In contrast to the neoliberal approach, the evolutionary-institutionalist perspective (see Roland [2000] for the definition) has emphasized institutional diversity (Murrell 1992a) and the importance of local knowledge (Stark 1995) in devising the most appropriate strategies and methods of achieving better economic and social outcomes. Corporate governance structures, the development of financial institutions and capital markets, and state structures facilitating information exchanges and securing property rights are examples of institutional mechanisms reinforcing competitive markets. Prior research has shown that these nonmarket institutions have to a large extent shaped the outlook of capitalist societies by affecting the patterns of distribution, macroeconomic stability, and developmental paths available to different capitalist countries (Murrell 1992b; Hall and Soskice 2001; Hiscox and Rickard 2002).

Conclusions 207

By properly placing the institutions of business representation in the context of industrial relations, this research has contributed to the evolutionary-institutionalist perspective in the study of capitalism. By documenting the mechanisms by which business associations promote economic coordination, skill acquisition, improved business practices, and more effective methods of economic regulation, it further advances understanding of the type of capitalism that has emerged in Eastern Europe and the former Soviet republics.

This book demonstrates that business and employer associations are becoming entrenched in the post-communist countries as important nonmarket and nonstate institutions of information transfer, standard setting, economic coordination, and public-policy setting. As such, business associations help to define the nature of emerging capitalism. Their patterns of organization and influence have an effect on the developing norms and practices of state economic intervention and regulation as well as private-sector behavior. All of these reinforce the notion that the study of capitalism cannot be reduced to the analysis of markets and the states but should also look at the broader institutional foundations that connect the markets and the states.

Regulatory Failure, Nonstate Solutions, and Good Governance

By analyzing the interaction between state institutions and organized economic interests, this book underscores the importance of state bureaucracy and contributes to the ongoing debate about causes and effects of good governance (Holmes 1996; Whitley and Kristensen 1997; Hellman et al. 2000; Kaufmann, Kraay, and Zoido-Lobaton 1999; Kurtz and Schrank 2007). As the statistical analysis of the cross-national survey data suggests, bureaucratic corruption that in recent years has become a notorious characteristic of many post-communist states is an interesting and novel explanatory variable for group-formation dynamics. The implication of the defensive organization argument is that the effects of bad public governance (e.g., bureaucratic predation) should include not only impediments to economic growth but also stimuli for bottom-up institutional development, mitigating its negative effects on economic actors.

This book has linked participation in industry and employer associations to the pre-existing state's failure to provide essential public goods (e.g., fair regulatory environment, effective enforcement, and secure property rights). State regulation of industry is a clear example of collective goods that are subject to the collective-action problem. When regulation is well designed (e.g., ensures the transfer of information, structures volatile markets, provides for reputation-building, and lowers transaction cost through other means) and is applied universally across all market participants (as the principle of the rule of law would require), it constitutes an important collective benefit. Corruption that makes noncompliance possible undermines the benefits of regulatory regimes and diminishes the value of collective goods. When bribery is an available strategy, it becomes irrational for firms (in individual terms) to comply with regulatory restrictions, even if the benefits of universal compliance outweigh the benefits of single defection. This is because firms cannot trust their competitors to be honest and comply with collectively beneficial and individually costly regulatory requirements. This becomes the classic prisoners' dilemma and results in a socially suboptimal output in terms of the provision of public goods.

This work suggested that business associations are solving this dilemma by providing club alternatives to purely collective goods. Their activities are directed at providing precisely the same benefits that would be available under a well-designed and strictly-enforced regulatory regime: secure property rights, cost-effective information-sharing, a predictable business climate, and effective contract enforcement. These, however, are achieved somewhat differently from the customary state-enforced mechanisms of economic governance, instead relying on voluntary compliance, expanded time horizon, and networking.

Theory of Social Organizations

This study has documented the development of organizations that aspire to provide collective benefits to their constituent members, simultaneously dedicating themselves to providing a wide range of targeted selective benefits. As other works have argued before, organization to produce collective goods is costly and hard to attain. This book, however, went beyond the confines of the collective-action paradigm in searching for tools and strategies that foster organizational development. It presented an account of multipurpose, adaptive, and opportunistic organizations that build their membership base by selective incentives and seek innovative ways of attaining their goals.

This account of multipurpose organizations that constantly re-equip themselves with various tools and methods of working with their members should be of interest to anyone concerned with the developments of complex civil organizations, such as unions, churches, consumer groups, and political parties. The primary function of political parties, for instance, often is supplemented by community service and other instrumental activities that keep organizations active in off-election years. Researchers interested in the primary purpose and the most visible activity of a given organization often ignore this property of organizations to rely on the performance of multiple functions and supplementary mechanisms of working with their members.

This research has shown that disregarding these "supplementary" and "instrumental" activities of complex social organizations might lead to misunderstanding their broader sociopolitical roles and capabilities. The continuing provision of these supplementary functions, however, is often a crucial condition of membership growth and organizational stability. In the case of post-communist business associations, ignoring their member-oriented selective incentives would have led to understating their true socioeconomic impact. Similarly, ignoring the social, networking, self-help, and informational functions of political parties and religious organizations unduly limits theoretical

Conclusions 209

and empirical research. This work demonstrates the importance of studying how organizations bundle different functions so as to overcome the problem of collective action, expand their membership, and survive crises.

Another contribution of this study to the theory of social organizations is the idea of compensatory organizational development. The single-most important characteristic of the post-communist business organizations that distinguishes them from their counterparts in established capitalist economies is that they had to organize in an environment of underdeveloped property rights, lax regulatory enforcement, and general scarcity of impartial, reliable, and affordable justice. To compensate for this lack of secure property rights and impartial mechanisms of conflict resolution that are usually provided by the state, post-communist industry groups have adopted alternative mechanisms of achieving comparable outcomes. They have created arbitration courts, informed their members about their rights, and represented them in courts. Compensatory behavior might have comparable dynamics in other types of organizations; for instance, in the absence of the established party organizations, other institutions (e.g., unions, churches, civil-rights organizations, or paramilitary groups) may take on the role of political parties. Such compensatory behavior of different kinds of social organizations deserves further scholarly attention.

Factoring in Labor Organizations

Some scholars studying the developed world believe that the organizational and political strength of labor groups conditions the extent of organizational concentration as well as the nature of issues that business organizations undertake. Streeck and Schmitter (1992), for instance, assert that "neo-corporatism has always been conditional on a measure of political strength of organized labor." (216). The absence of strong labor organizations, therefore, precludes the emergence of "significant factions with an active interest in centralized negotiations with labor" on the part of business (206).[8]

An examination of the organizational patterns and political strength of labor interests, however, remained mostly outside the scope of this project. As was discussed in Chapter 6, post-communist business groups have not become major players in labor conflicts. I speculated that organizational fragmentation (perhaps strategic) on the part of the business community can provide some explanation for the virtual absence of labor as a conditioning factor in business organization. Any satisfactory investigation of the unconventional patterns of post-communist business-labor relations, however, requires a comprehensive analysis of the socioeconomic conditions that have led to labor organizations' near-universal weakness throughout the post-communist space.

Lacking an available comprehensive analysis of distinctive models of labor representation across the post-communist cases, this study was unable to make

---

[8] There have been other accounts linking specific configurations of business interests to the patterns of labor organization. See, for example, Salisbury (1979).

a valid comparative assessment of the effects of labor politics on the formation and development of business organizations. Exploration of business representation in the complex system of class and functional interest representation that has developed in post-communist countries presents a promising venue for future research. Research along these lines would help put business representation into the larger perspective of social-interest organization and class politics and is an attractive topic for future studies.

Long-Term Effects

One of the most imposing limitations of this analysis has been the fact that not enough time has passed for the long-term developmental patterns and consequences of the organizational dynamics of the business community to be realized. The available data did not allow for exploring the long-term consequences of the development of industry associations. The long-term extensions, however, are not only an important source for building a falsifiable theory but also are of primary theoretical importance in their own right. As more data are becoming available, the effects of interest-group politics on the trajectories of the economic and political development of post-communist countries will become not only attractive theoretical topics but will also be easier to research. The long-term effects of business organizations are likely to have important implications for the developmental strategies of post-communist states. In this respect, this research is an important first step in the ongoing exploration of the evolution of business-state relations, industry self-regulation, and the building of organizational capacity of the property-owning classes in the post-communist countries of Eastern Europe and the former Soviet republics.

7.4 Associations and Their Power

On a parting note, I will return to the epigraph to this chapter. On one of my first interviews I asked the questions I subsequently asked all my respondents: "Why do you think businesses (businesspeople) join business (employer) associations? What benefits does the membership in associations provide?" I anticipated that my respondent, a long-time leader of one of the oldest and most well-established Russian business associations, would talk about how influential his organization was and how much a firm can gain by joining; instead, the answer was rather self-effacing. He told me that the organization could only address the problems most commonly encountered by the majority of small firms. Even if it had unlimited resources (which was clearly not the case), the association could not attempt to serve members' interests on a case-by-case basis. In many instances, such particularistic interests conflict with other members' interests, so by helping some of its members, the association would alienate others. But more importantly, the association's reputation and public recognition have rested on its balanced and mediated position that the association leaders claimed to represent the entire small-business community in the country.

Conclusions 211

This seemed to indicate that ADSMB provided only collective goods that served the interests of all small businesses; however, a closer look at the services and activities of this business association revealed that virtually all its benefits in the sphere of market information, legal consulting, clerical support on regulatory issues, and professional training (in accounting, tax preparation, and property registration) were available only to its members. Although the association's services were directed at solving problems common to all small businesses, these services were provided only to those who paid the membership dues, thus indicating selective rather than collective regulatory relief. Although ADSMB was helping only its members, the types of services it offered had to appeal to broad segments of the small-business community to ensure its attractiveness to new members.

Later, I discovered that many association leaders had a rather reserved assessment of industry organizations' role and capabilities. Some were more optimistic, others more cynical. This, however, did not preclude me from discovering a multitude of ways in which business associations in fact made the operation of member businesses smoother and less vulnerable to predation and uncertainty. Some associations provided services that reduced the transaction costs associated with unstructured markets, others protected members' property from bureaucratic expropriation, and still some others extended a self-regulation framework that ensured greater stability and predictability. The element that united virtually all industry associations is that all of them in one form or another have offered protection against problems faced by an average firm in their respective sectors/countries/regions. Business associations do not focus on the least reputable firms that engage in tax evasion and other illegal activities; neither do they focus specifically on the large and well-connected corporations that are capable of advancing their private agenda without any organizational assistance. The power of business associations rests on their ability to serve vulnerable businesses disadvantaged by insecure property rights, unpredictable regulations, lax enforcement, bureaucratic graft, and high transaction costs. Throughout the book I have argued that business associations arise as a legitimate alternative to the corrupt ways of doing business in post-communist countries. Through their member services and public campaigns, business associations help remedy these insecurities. They empower post-communist firms in the everyday tasks of running business.

Appendix A

Research Note on Qualitative Data Collection

During my two research visits to Russia in 2005 I conducted twenty-eight interviews, which yielded qualitative data on the development of twenty-one business associations, nineteen of which were in Moscow and two of which were regional associations in the provincial centers of Kaliningrad and Perm oblasts. I also sent written questions to representatives of three other associations, who provided extensive written answers. Five of my respondents did not represent business associations but rather were state officials in frequent contact with parliamentarians, a high-ranking official in the ministry of Economy and International Trade, and two provincial officials (one retired).

My research visit to Ukraine in March–April 2006 resulted in personal interviews with nineteen state officials and leaders of business associations, providing qualitative data on sixteen regional and national business associations. I also conducted interviews at the Ukrainian State Committee for Regulatory Policy and Entrepreneurship, the National Committee for Tripartite Negotiations, and independent research centers working on economic transition and civil-society development. These interviews contributed more balanced information on the development of business representation in Ukraine.

In July–August 2006 I interviewed representatives of five Croatian business associations, former members of the Croatian cabinet, and the staff of the Croatian Ministry of Economy. Although I did not conduct field research in Kazakhstan, I obtained qualitative data on the development of Kazakh business associations through Internet sources, newspapers, and personal connections in Kazakhstan. Appendix C contains the names and classifications of business associations that I identified as currently functioning in Kazakhstan. From published materials, I closely traced the development and activities of a number of these associations. Overall, during my field trips and through my review of print and Internet sources, I collected detailed qualitative data on the development of fifty business associations in Russia, Ukraine, Croatia, and Kazakhstan. These are listed in Table A.1.

214 Research Note on Qualitative Data Collection

TABLE A.1. *Business Associations Investigated Through Qualitative Research*

Russia	Ukraine
Union of Industrialists and Entrepreneurs (Employers) of Kaliningrad Oblast	Association "New Formation"
Russian Union of Industrialists and Entrepreneurs	National Association for the Development of Trade and Services
Union of Producers of Alcoholic Beverages	European Business Association
All-Russian Social Organization of Small and Medium-Size Business "Opora"	Ukrainian Association of Business Incubators and Innovation Centers
Russian Association for the Development of Small and Medium-Size Business	Ukrainian Franchising Association
Chamber of Commerce and Industry of the Russian Federation	Ukrainian Union of Leasing Companies
Coordinating Council of Employer's Organizations, Russia	Civic Organization "Board of Entrepreneurs"
Russian Banking Association	Association of Ukrainian Banks
Moscow Chamber of Commerce and Industry	Ukrainian Union of Small, Medium, and Privatized Enterprises (USMPE)
Moscow International Business Association	
Russian Franchising Association	
Russian Association of Ice Cream Producers	Ukrainian Employers' Federation
Business Association of the Confectionary Industry	Ukrainian League of Industrialists and Entrepreneurs
Union of Manufacturers and Consumers of Packaging Products	League of Entrepreneurs of Small and Medium Business "Left Bank"
Russian Construction Union	Tenders Chamber
Federation of Restaurants and Hotels	Ukrainian Chamber of Commerce and Industry
Moscow Contractor's Club	
Noncommercial Partnership "League of Trade Merchants"	Construction Industry Union
Association of Trade Companies and Producers of Appliances and Electronics	Association of Tobacco Companies
Russian Association of Owners of Trademarks	
Guild for the Development of Audio-Video Trade	
Russian Associations of Regional Banks	
Perm Chamber of Commerce and Industry	
Association of Farmers and Agricultural Cooperatives	

Croatia	Kazakhstan
Association of Travel Agencies	Kazakh Business Forum
Union of Entrepreneurs	Chamber of Commerce and Industry of the Republic of Kazakhstan
Croatian Union of Cooperatives	Almaty Association of Entrepreneurs
Association of Croatian Exporters	Kazakh Association of Casinos
Croatian Chamber of Economy	Kazakh Energy Association

Appendix B

Qualitative Research Instruments

Interview Questionnaire (Business Associations)

1. Please describe the goals and functions of your association. Have they changed since the association was first formed? If so, what influenced this?
2. In your opinion, why do businesses (businesspeople) join industry/employer associations? Are there any benefits associated with membership in business associations?
3. What kinds of businesses join your association? Why do you think they join your association but not other associations? Do you track the growth of membership in your organization?
4. What is the role of your association in promoting the interests of its members?
5. Are there conflicts of interest among members of your association? How are those conflicts usually resolved?
6. What is the nature of the relationship between your association and other interest groups? Would you describe your interactions with other interest groups as discordant or harmonious?
7. Do business associations in general and your association in particular combine their efforts with other associations in solving any specific issues? What are those issues? What specific associations does your organization interact with?
8. In your opinion, how representative are business associations of the business community in your country/region/city/sector?
9. How active are business associations in your country (region/sector) in lobbying for the interests of their members? How would you assess the level of political influence of business associations?

216   *Qualitative Research Instruments*

10. Does your association lobby the government? Can you give any specific examples?
11. Does your organization have any contacts with the state agencies? Through what channels do you usually interact with politicians and state bureaucrats? Has the relationship between your organization and state agencies changed over time?

Interview Questionnaire (State Institutions)

1. Does your agency (ministry, committee, etc.) have contacts with the business community? How are these contacts usually conducted? What roles do business associations play in shaping these contacts?
2. What businesses contact your organization (ministry, committee, etc.), and what issues do they usually raise? Would you say these issues are usually related to the functions of your agency?
3. In your opinion, how often do the interests of business (industrial) circles disagree with the goals and objectives of your agency (ministry, committee, etc.)? When the conflicts of interests arise, do they usually increase or decrease the intensity of contacts between the business community and your agency?
4. In your current capacity, have you directly interacted with business associations? Please describe the nature of such interaction. Have business associations lobbied your office? Did they provide support, organize protests, or offer expert assistance?
5. What is the nature of the relationship between your organization and business associations? Does your organization benefit in any way from these contacts? Is it impaired by the activities of business associations?
6. Does your organization have any policies with respect to business associations? Does it encourage the development of business associations?
7. How would you evaluate the political importance of business associations in your country? Are there specific associations you would single out as the most influential? What are the sources of this influence?
8. In the past have there been any changes in the political roles and significance of business associations in representing business interests?
9. Over the years the number of business/employer associations has been increasing in your country. In your opinion, does this development have any consequences for your agency?
10. Do you agree with the opinion that interactions between state institutions and business associations can solve many problems? Or would you say that activities of business associations create more problems than they solve?

Appendix C

Regional and Municipal Business Associations in Ukraine

TABLE C.1. *Number of Registered Ukrainian Business Associations by Administrative Unit (According to the Ukrainian State Administration)*

Region	Regional Associations	Municipal Associations	Total
Autonomous Republic Krym	14	no data	14
Vinnyts'ka oblast	13	12	25
Volyns'ka oblast	21	10	31
Dnipropetrovs'ka oblast	35	7	42
Donets'ka oblast	20	8	28
Zhytomyrs'ka oblast	11	11	22
Zakarpats'ka oblast	8	15	23
Zaporiz'ka oblast	27	35	62
Ivano-Frankivs'ka oblast	10	14	24
Kyivs'ka oblast	4	7	11
Kirovohradc'ka oblast	20	67	87
Luhans'ka oblast	45	22	67
L'vivs'ka oblast	15	no data	15
Mykolaivs'ka oblast	8	5	13
Odes'ka oblast	23	no data	23
Poltavs'ka oblast	26	30	56
Rivnens'ka oblast	14	11	25
Sums'ka oblast	8	1	9
Ternopil's'ka oblast	9	no data	9
Kharkivs'ka oblast	17	no data	17
Khersons'ka oblast	38	38	76
Khmel'nyts'ka oblast	20	26	46
Cherkas'ka oblast	8	13	21
Chernivets'ka oblast	7	2	9
Chernigivs'ka oblast	5	no data	5
Kyiv city	34	59	93
Sevastopol' city	5	no data	5
Total	465	393	858

Note: The Autonomous Republic of Krym has a special status within Ukrainian unitary arrangements. In the Ukrainian official documents its administrative and civic institutions are referred to as "republican" rather than provincial. For the purpose of simplification, instead of "provincial and republican," I use more generic "regional" in reference to Ukrainian subnational political and social institutions and organizations.

Appendix D

Kazakh Business Associations

TABLE D.1. *Kazakh Business Associations Active by the End of 2006 (Data Gathered with the Assistance of the Kazakh Chamber of Trade and Industry)*

	Association, Establishment Date	Sectoral	Scope	Member of an Umbrella Group	Membership Size
1	Kazakh Business Forum, 1992	No	National	Yes	82
2	Confederation of Employers of the Republic of Kazakhstan, 1999	No	National	No	90
3	Chamber of Trade and Industry of the Republic of Kazakhstan, 1959	No	National	No	
4	Chamber of Trade and Industry, Astana, 1994	No	Regional	Yes	
5	The Eurasian Industrial Association, 2001	Yes	National	Yes	
6	The National Union of Entrepreneurs and Employers "Atameken," 2005	No	National	No	
7	Association of Retirement Funds	Yes	National	Yes	8
8	Association of Enterprises of Light Industry (Manufacturing)	Yes	National	Yes	28

Kazakh Business Associations 219

	Association, Establishment Date	Sectoral	Scope	Member of an Umbrella Group	Membership Size
9	"Quality" Association	No	Regional	Yes	20
10	Banking Association of the RK	Yes	National	Yes	6
11	Better Business Bureau (Association)	No		Yes	48
12	Association "Medfarm" Kazakhstan	Yes	National	Yes	23
13	Association of Independent Media of Central Asia	Yes	International	Yes	30
14	Kazakh Brewers' Association	Yes	National	Yes	17
15	Association of Autotransport Complex	Yes	National	Yes	142
16	Association of Commodity Producers	No	Regional	Yes	7
17	Association for the Development of the Pharmaceutical Industry, Shymkent	Yes	Regional	Yes	
18	Association for the Support and Development of the Pharmaceutical Industry	Yes	National	No	
19	Association of Pharmaceutical Importers	Yes	National	No	
20	Guild of Pharmacists of Astana	Yes	Regional	Yes	
21	Northern Kazakhstan Association of Pharmaceutical Organizations	Yes	Regional	No	
22	Association of Medical Entrepreneurs	Yes	Regional	Yes	23
23	Stock Exchange Union	Yes	National	Yes	11
24	Petroleum Union of Kazakhstan	Yes	National	Yes	11
25	Almaty Association of Entrepreneurs	No	Regional	Yes	

(continued)

TABLE D.I. (*continued*)

	Association, Establishment Date	Sectoral	Scope	Member of an Umbrella Group	Membership Size
26	Union of Construction Firms of Kazakhstan	Yes	National	Yes	
27	Union of Food Producers	Yes	National	Yes	31
28	Yugur Association of Industrialists, Entrepreneurs, and Agrarians	No	National	Yes	95
29	Association "Pavlodar Business Forum"	No	Regional	Yes	27
30	Union of Industrialists and Employers of South Kazakhstan	No	Regional	Yes	
31	Association of the Producers of Mining Equipment	Yes	National	Yes	25
32	Union of Employers of Akmola	No	Regional	Yes	8
33	Confederation of Employers (entrepreneurs), Astana	No	Regional	Yes	34
34	Business Association of Central Kazakhstan, Karaganda	No	Regional	Yes	
35	Union of Industrialists and Employers of Almaty	No	Regional	Yes	17
36	Atyrau Chapter of the Union of Industrialists and Entrepreneurs	No	Regional	Yes	22
37	Aktiubinsk Regional Union of Industrialists and Employers	No	Regional	Yes	
38	Confederation of Civic Organizations and Employers of East Kazakhstan	No	Regional	Yes	
39	Kazakh Association of Customs Brokers	Yes	National	Yes	
40	Association of the Printing Industry	Yes	National	Yes	

Kazakh Business Associations 221

	Association, Establishment Date	Sectoral	Scope	Member of an Umbrella Group	Membership Size
41	Association of TV and Radio Broadcasters of Kazakhstan	Yes	National	Yes	
42	Kazakh Association of Independent Consultants and Appraisers	Yes	Regional	Yes	
43	Kazakh Association of Gaming Business	Yes	National	Yes	11
44	Association of National Freight Forwarders	Yes	National	Yes	
45	National Association of Freight Forwarders	Yes	National	Yes	
46	Union of Entrepreneurs and Employers of Atyrau Region	No	Regional	Yes	83
47	Association for Support of Entrepreneurship, Kostanai	No	Regional	Yes	18
48	Kazakh Association of Business Women	No	National	Yes	
49	Alamaty Chamber of Trade and Industry	No	Regional	Yes	
50	Association of Lumber Processing and Furniture Producing Enterprises	Yes	National	Yes	
51	Kazakh Franchising Association	Yes	National	Yes	
52	Association of Milk and Dairy Producers	Yes	Regional	Yes	
53	Kazakh Association of Producers of Office Supplies	Yes	National	Yes	
54	National Energy Association	Yes	National	Yes	
55	Sectoral Association of Recycling Metallurgy	Yes	National	Yes	
56	Kazakh Tourist Association (Association of Hotel Industry)	Yes	National	Yes	

(continued)

222 Kazakh Business Associations

TABLE D.I. (*continued*)

	Association, Establishment Date	Sectoral	Scope	Member of an Umbrella Group	Membership Size
57	Union of International Auto Transporters	Yes	National	Yes	
58	Association of Producers of Milk and Dairy Products	Yes	National	Yes	
59	Kazakh Association for the Protection of Copyrights	No	National	Yes	
60	Independent Professional Union for Protecting Small and Medium Business	No	Regional	Yes	
61	Professional Union of Small and Medium Businessmen	No	Regional	Yes	
62	Chamber of Auditors of Kazakhstan	Yes	National	Yes	
63	Public Foundation "Business and Development"	No	Regional	Yes	
64	Association "Business," Pavlodar	No	Regional	Yes	
65	Professional Union for Small and Medium Businesses, Ust'-Kamenogorsk	No	Regional	Yes	
66	Association for Protecting the Rights on Entrepreneurs, Petropavlovsk	No	Regional	Yes	
67	Association of Kyzylorda Entrepreneurs	No	Regional	Yes	
68	"Asem" League of Entrepreneurs	No	Regional	Yes	

Appendix E

Relaxing Two Simplifying Assumptions

Here I extend the theoretical argument to situations in which (1) the bureaucrat bears the cost of corruption and (2) the organization provides selective incentives other than regulatory relief. I will show that the model predictions generally hold under these conditions.

First, suppose that when the firm and the bureaucrat engage in corrupt behavior, both risk being prosecuted with probability (p) and paying a fine (f). This does not alter the payoff structure for the firm and the organization, but the bureaucrat now maximizes income (I_B) as defined below:

$$I_B \ (honest) = s$$
$$I_B \ (corrupt) = s + b - pf$$

This means that now the bureaucrat resorts to corruption only if he or she can charge $b > pf$. In general, the bureaucrat's reservation value for bribery increases when he or she faces a positive level of punishment for corruption. In this example, the bribe has to satisfy $b < c_r + d - g - 2pf$. In equilibrium, the organization provides the benefits $g = d = c_r$ for all $c_r \leq 2pf$, sets $g = c_r$, $d = 2pf$ for $ac_r < 2pf < c_r$, and does not form when $ac_r > 2pf$, so the bureaucrat captures all corruption rents. Comparing these to the outcomes of the original model, we see that imposing corruption-related costs on the bureaucrat makes it easier for the organization to provide membership-enticing regulatory relief.

Second, consider an association that provides excludable member benefits other than regulatory relief. Additionally, assume that the firm may simultaneously pursue bribery and membership. The firm may join the organization for member benefits unrelated to regulatory relief and still receive regulatory relief from bureaucratic corruption. Let h denote member benefits in addition to the regulatory relief, d, whereas j will capture the associated membership dues. Now the firm faces the following payoffs:

$$I_F(comply) = - c_r$$
$$I_F(bribe) = - (b + pf)$$
$$I_F(join) = -c_r + (g - d) + (h - j)$$
$$I_F(join + bribe) = - (b + pf) + (h - j)$$

Note that $g - d$ is not part of the firm's utility under the (*join* + *bribe*) strategy because when the firm does not pay c_r, it forgoes any benefits of regulatory relief. Let $I_O(F) = d - \alpha g + j - \gamma h$ be the organization's utility function, where γ is the cost of providing member benefits h. The organization provides g, h for any $\alpha g > d$, $\gamma h > j$.

For any $h - j > 0$, $I_F(join + bribe) > I_F(bribe)$, so the firm joins irrespective of the regulatory relief opportunities. The firm, however, prefers organizational membership without corruption over membership with corruption when $I_F(join) > I_F(join + bribe)$, or $- c_r + (g - d) + (h - j) > - (b + pf) + (h - j)$. Subtracting $(h - j)$ from both sides gives us condition (1) from Chapter 2. For $c_r \leq pf$ and $ac_r < pf < c_r$ the resulting equilibrium outcomes are the same as in the original model. The organization provides the regulatory relief, the bureaucrat remains honest, and the firm joins. For $ac_r > pf$ the organization does not provide the regulatory relief, $g = d = 0$, the bureaucrat bribes $b = ac_r - pf$, and the firm joins and bribes for $h - j > 0$ and bribes for $h - j \leq 0$.

In essence, when the organization provides selective benefits that go beyond regulatory relief, the firm faces the choice between membership with corruption or without corruption. Similarly to the original model, the corruption-free membership (when the organization rather than the bureaucrat provides regulatory relief) becomes more likely under lower values of c_r and higher values of pf. Hence, the comparative-statics results derived in Chapter 2 extend to the settings in which membership and corruption are not mutually exclusive strategies. The most interesting result, however, is that for any positive $(b - d)$ provided under $c_r \leq pf$ or $ac_r < pf < c_r$, the firm prefers organization-provided regulatory relief over the corrupt transactions.

Appendix F

Estimating the EU and Non-EU Samples

TABLE F.I. *Estimating the EU and Non-EU Samples*

Equation 1: Member	Mixed Effects 2-Stage Least Squares				Instrumental Variable Probit			
	Non-EU		EU		Non-EU		EU	
	Coefficient	Standard Error	Coefficient	Standard Error	Coefficient	Standard Error	Coefficient	Standard Error
Bribe (% sales)	.053	.007	.036	.014	.102	.016	.069	.028
Entry procedures	−.01	.005	−.022	.006	...	...	...	...
Transition index	...	...	...	...	.563	.208	1.912	.552
Voice and accountability	...	...	...	...	−.44	.327	−1.251	.479
Polity IV	.01	.005	.032	.026	.018	.016	−.007	.050
Private sector GDP	.009	.003	.008	.005	−.006	.007	.019	.020
Log (GPD/ capita)	.097	.083	−.247	.176	.078	.060	−.802	.493
Compulsory	...	...	.411	.078	1.044	.283	2.765	.706
Rule of law	.023	.005	.017	.005	.082	.012	.046	.008
Employees (100)	.006	.001	.006	.001	.015	.001	.023	.005
Foreign-owned	.163	.016	.137	.019	.412	.085	.403	.105
State-owned	−.031	.019	−.046	.025	−.12	.073	−.214	.090
Longevity	−.003	.001	−.003	.001	−.007	.001	−.007	.001
Privately created	−.064	.014	−.13	.018	−.191	.041	−.385	.083
Specificity	.013	.003	.012	.004	.018	.019	.04	.027
Intercept	3.501	.985	6.854	1.747	9.668	2.212	13.968	3.915
Equation 2:								
Bribe (% Sales)								
Entry procedures	−.13	.044	.062	.035	...	...	...	...
Transition index	...	...	...	...	−.482	.732	−3.339	.932
Voice and accountability	...	...	...	...	2.944	.888	2.11	.670

(*continued*)

226 · *Estimating the Eu and Non-Eu Samples*

TABLE F.I. *(continued)*

	Mixed Effects 2-Stage Least Squares				Instrumental Variable Probit			
	Non-EU		EU		Non-EU		EU	
	Coefficient	Standard Error	Coefficient	Standard Error	Coefficient	Standard Error	Coefficient	Standard Error
Polity IV	.156	.043	−.169	.156	−.18	.049	−.129	.110
Private sector GDP	−.002	.025	.023	.031	−.002	.022	.086	.031
Log (GPD/ capita)	−.397	.671	.492	1.054	−1.245	.228	−1.537	.586
Compulsory	...	...	−.173	.470	−1.333	.635	.548	.691
Rule of law	−.23	.034	−.173	.029	−.393	.055	−.176	.036
Employees (100)	−.008	.006	−.012	.005	−.013	.006	−.014	.003
Foreign-owned	−.464	.130	−.178	.110	−.522	.164	−.159	.084
State-owned	−.648	.151	−.53	.144	−.51	.164	−.492	.114
Longevity	.007	.003	.003	.002	.012	.004	.003	.003
Privately created	.326	.115	.211	.106	.493	.151	.256	.125
Specificity	.009	.026	.019	.022	.075	.040	.029	.023
Regulatory time	.053	.004	.046	.004	.074	.007	.048	.010
Clear rules	−.114	.057	−.036	.026	−.114	.057	−.028	.021
Intercept	−1.722	8.014	−6.483	10.441	−5.827	7.522	15.371	6.941
Sargan statistic	3.569	.060	.722	.396	...	...	...	...
Amemiya-Lee-Newey	...	...	...	...	3.35	.067	.157	.692
N	7586		5718		8172		5772	

Bibliography

Agripolicy Network. 2005. *Assessment and Outlook in the Sugar Sector: Agroeconomic Policy Analysis of the New Member States, the Candidate States, and the Countries of the Western Balkans.* Report. http://www.euroqualityfiles.net/cecap/Report%201/CEECAP%20report%201%20section%201%20sugar%20report.pdf.

Allio, L. 1997. "Institutional Structures, Labor Interests, and Evolving Privatization Bargains in Poland." In *The Political Economy of Property Rights: Institutional Change and Credibility in the Reform of Centrally Planned Economies,* edited by D. L. Weimer, 208–31. Cambridge: Cambridge University Press.

Almond, G. A., and S. Verba. 1963. *The Civic Culture: Political Attitudes and Democracy in Five Nations.* Princeton, NJ: Princeton University Press.

Anderson, R. D., M. S. Fish, S. E. Hanson, and P. G. Roeder, eds. 2001. *Postcommunism and the Theory of Democracy.* Princeton, NJ: Princeton University Press.

Appelbaum, E., and R. Schettkat. 1998. "Institutions and Employment Performance in Different Growth Regimes." In *Employment, Technology and Economic Needs: Theory, Evidence, and Public Policy,* edited by J. Michie and A. Reati, 91–114. Cheltenham, UK: Edward Elgar.

Ashwin, S. 1995. "'There's No Joy Any More': The Experience of Reform in a Kuzbass Mining Settlement." *Europe-Asia Studies* 47 (8): 1367–81.

Axelrod, R. 1981. "The Emergence of Cooperation among Egoists." *American Political Science Review* 75 (2): 306–18.

Babić, A. 2006, July. Personal interview with author. Zagreb, Croatia.

Bartolić, B. 2006, June. Personal interview with author. Zagreb, Croatia.

Batalov, R. 2005. *Report.* Congress of the Kazakh Business Forum. http://www.businessforum.kz.

Bates, R. H. 1981. *Markets and States in Tropical Africa: The Political Basis of Agricultural Policies.* Berkeley and Los Angeles, CA: University of California Press.

BBC. 2005. "Timeline: The Rise and Fall of Yukos." *BBC News Online.* May 31.

Becker, G. S. 1983. "A Theory of Competition among Pressure Groups for Political Influence." *Quarterly Journal of Economics* 98 (3): 371–400.

Belous, Iu., and R. Dorohov. 2005. "Mobil'niki pod Arestom." *Vedomosti* **151** (1432). August 17. http://www.vedomosti.ru/.

Bernholz, P. 1986. "Growth of Government, Economic Growth and Individual Freedom." *Journal of Institutional and Theoretical Economics* **142** (4): 661–83.

Bertelli, A. M., and A. B. Whitford. 2009. "Perceiving Credible Commitments: How Independent Regulators Shape Elite Perceptions of Regulatory Quality." *British Journal of Political Science* **39** (3): 517–37.

Beyer, J., and M. Hopner. 2003. "The Disorganization of Organized Capitalism: German Corporate Governance in the 1990s." *West European Politics* **26** (4): 179–98.

Bilych, V., V. Bykovets, N. Boiko, O. Mihailishyna, O. Svirus, T. Svirus, eds. 2005. *Shcho Neobhidno Znaty Pidpryiemtsiam pro Biznes-Asotsiatsii*. Kyiv, Ukraine.

Bischoff, I. 2003. "Determinants of the Increase in the Number of Interest Groups in Western Democracies: Theoretical Considerations and Evidence from 21 OECD Countries." *Public Choice* **114** (1–2): 197–218.

Blyzniuk, A. (director general, UNADTS). 2006, March. Personal interview with author. Kyiv, Ukraine.

Borjas, G. J., and G. T. Sueyoshi. 1994. "A Two-Stage Estimator for Probit Models with Structural Group Effects." *Journal of Econometrics* **64** (1/2): 165–82.

Boycko, M., A. Shleifer, and R. Vishny. 1995. *Privatizing Russia*. Cambridge, MA: MIT Press.

Brunetti, A., G. Kisunko, and B. Weder. 1997. "Institutional Obstacles to Doing Business: Region-by-Region Results from a Worldwide Survey of the Private Sector." World Bank Working Paper #1759.

Bunce, V. 1999. *Subversive Institutions: The Design and the Destruction of Socialism and the State*. Cambridge: Cambridge University Press.

Campos, N. F., and F. Giovannoni. 2005. "Lobbying, Corruption and Political Influence in Transition Countries." Unpublished Paper.

Cawson, A. 1985. "Varieties of Corporatism: The Importance of the Meso-Level of Interest Intermediation." In *Organized Interests and the State: Studies in Meso-Corporatism*, edited by A. Cawson, 1–21. London: Sage Publications.

    1986. *Corporatism and Political Theory*. New York: Blackwell.

Chaisty, P. 2006. *Legislative Politics and Economic Power in Russia*. Basingstoke: Palgrave.

Chebotarayov, A. 2003. "Kazakhstan: Corruption Boosts Economy." Institute for War and Peace Reporting, Report #227. IWPR, http://www.iwpr.net.

Chernyi, R., and T. Fedorchenko. 2006. "NBU Vytiagivaet Nuzhnye Karty." *Kommersant Ukraina* **95**, June 8. http://www.kommersant.ua/.

Choi, K. 1983. "Statistical Test of Olson's Model." In *The Political Economy of Growth*, edited by D. Mueller, 57–78. New Haven, CT: Yale University Press.

Clarke, S. 2006. "Social Partnership, Civil Society and the State in Russia." In *Perspectives on the Russian State in Transition*, edited by Wolfgang Danspeckgruber, 66–97. Princeton, NJ: Princeton University Press.

CNews.ru. 2003. *MVD – Luchshii drug bortsov s piratami?*, September 17.

Coase, R. H. 1960. "The Problem of Social Cost." *Journal of Law and Economics* **3**: 1–44.

Coates, D., and J. C. Heckelman. 2003. "Interest Groups and Investment: A Further Test of the Olson Hypothesis." *Public Choice* **117** (3): 333–40.

Coates, D., J. C. Heckelman, and B. Wilson. 2007. "Determinants of Interest Group Formation." *Public Choice* **133** (3–4): 377–91.

    2010. "The Political Economy of Investment: Sclerotic Effects from Interest Groups." *European Journal of Political Economy* **26** (2): 208–21.

Bibliography

Coates, D., and B. Wilson. 2007. "Interest Group Activity and Long-Run Stock Market Performance." *Public Choice* **133** (3–4): 343–58.

Collier, D., and R. Collier. 1991. *Shaping the Political Arena: Critical Junctures, the Labor Movement and Regime Dynamics in Latin America*. Princeton, NJ: Princeton University Press.

Colton, T. J. 1992. "Politics." In *After the Soviet Union: From Empire to Nations*, edited by T. J. Colton and R. Legvold, 17–49. New York: W. W. Norton and Company.

Crain, M. W., and K. J. Lee. 1999. "Economic Growth Regressions for the American States: A Sensitivity Analysis." *Economic Inquiry* **37** (2): 242–57.

Crawford, B. 1995. "Post-Communist Political Economy: A Framework for the Analysis of Reform." In *Markets, States, and Democracy: The Political Economy of Post-Communist Transformation*, edited by B. Crawford, 3–42. Boulder, CO: Westview Press.

Crawford, B., and A. Lijphart, eds. 1997. *Liberalization and Leninist Legacies: Comparative Perspectives on Democratic Transition*. Berkeley, CA: International and Area Studies.

Croatian Chamber of Economy. 2006. *Podrucja Posebne Drzavne Skrbi*. Zagreb, Croatia: Croatian Chamber of Economy.

Croatian Employer's Association. 2004. *Pravilnik o Obracunavanju i Placanju Clanarine*. Zagreb, Croatia: Croatian Employer's Association.

Crowley, S. 1998. "The Kuzbass: Liberals, Populists, and Labor." In *Growing Pains: Russian Democracy and the Election of 1993*, edited by T. Colton and J. Hough, 533–66. Washington, DC: Brookings Institution Press.

———. 2000. "Between a Rock and a Hard Place: Russia's Troubled Coal Industry." In *Business and State in Contemporary Russia*, edited by P. Rutland, 129–50. Boulder, CO: Westview Press.

Crowley, S., and D. Ost, eds. 2001. *Workers after Workers' States: Labor and Politics in Post-Communist Eastern Europe*. Lanham, MD: Rowman and Littlefield.

Djankov, S., R. La Porta, F. Lopez-De-Silanes, and A. Shleifer. 2002. "The Regulation of Entry." *The Quarterly Journal of Economics* **117** (1): 1–37.

Doner, R., and B. R. Schneider. 2000. "Business Associations and Economic Development: Why Some Associations Contribute More than Others." *Business and Politics* **2** (3): 261–88.

Dorohov, R., and G. Krampets. 2003. "Piratskii Peterburg." *Vedomosti* **133** (933), July 30.

Duvanova, D. 2011. "Firm Lobbying vs. Sectoral Organization: The Analysis of Business-State Relations in Post-Communist Russia." *Post-Soviet Affairs* **27** (4): 387–409.

———. 2012. "Bureaucratic Discretion and Regulatory Burden: Business Environment under Alternative Regulatory Regimes." *British Journal of Political Science* **42** (3): 573–596.

Economist Intelligence Unit. 2003. "Nazarbayev Cornered." *Views Wire*, no. **301**.

Elhov, V. (executive director, RAICP). 2005, August 22. Personal interview with author. Moscow, Russia.

Enterprise Surveys. 2002–2006. The World Bank. http://www.enterprisesurveys.org.

Ericson, R. E. 1992. "Economics." In *After the Soviet Union: From Empire to Nations*, edited by T. J. Colton and R. Legvold, 49–83. New York: W. W. Norton and Company.

European Bank for Reconstruction and Development. 1999. *Transition Report*. London: EBRD.

European Bank for Reconstruction and Development (EBRD) and World Bank. 1999–2005. *The Business Environment and Enterprise Performance Survey (BEEPS)*. http://beeps.prognoz.com/beeps/Home.ashx.

European Commission. 2006. COM 377 *Final Resolution* #0123. Brussels.

Evans, P. 1995. *Embedded Autonomy: States and Industrial Transformation*. Princeton, NJ: Princeton University Press.

Federation of Restaurants and Hotels. 2003. *Charter*. Moscow, Russia: Federation of Restaurants and Hotels.

Fidler, S., and J. Chung. 2006. "US Case Clouds LSE visit by Nazarbayev." *Financial Times*, November 18.

Figueras, J., and Marshall, T. 1998. *Health Care Systems in Transition: Russia*. Report by European Observatory on Health Care Systems. Copenhagen, Denmark: World Health Organization.

Fink-Hafner, D., and A. Krasovec. 2005. "Is Consultation Everything? The Influence of Interest Groups on Parliamentary Working Bodies in Slovenia." *Czech Sociological Review* 41 (3): 401–21.

Fish, M. S. 2001. "The Dynamics of Democratic Erosion." In *Postcommunism and the Theory of Democracy*, edited by R. D. Anderson, M. S. Fish, S. E. Hanson, and P. G. Roeder, 54–95. Princeton, NJ: Princeton University Press.

Fortescue, S. 1997. *Policy-Making for Russian Industry*. London and Basingstoke, UK: Macmillan Press.

Frieden, J. A. 1992. *Debt, Development, and Democracy: Modern Political Economy and Latin America, 1965–1985*. Princeton, NJ: Princeton University Press.

Frye, T. 1998. "Corruption: The Polish and Russian Experiences." USIA Electronic Journal, *Economic Perspectives* 3 (5): 34–35.

2000. *Brokers and Bureaucrats: Building Market Institutions in Russia*. Ann Arbor: University of Michigan Press.

2002a. "Capture or Exchange? Business Lobbying in Russia." *Europe-Asia Studies* 54 (7): 1017–36.

2002b. "The Perils of Polarization: Economic Performance in the Post-Communist World." *World Politics* 54 (3): 308–37.

2004. "Credible Commitment and Property Rights: Evidence from Russia." *American Political Science Review* 98 (3): 453–66.

2010. *Building States and Markets after Communism*. Cambridge: Cambridge University Press.

Fulton, L. 2011. *Worker Representation in Europe*. Labour Research Department and European Trade Union Institute (online publication). European Trade Union Institute, http://www.etui.org/.

Gaddy, C., and B. W. Ickes. 1999. "An Accounting Model of the Virtual Economy in Russia." *Post-Soviet Geography and Economics* 40 (2): 79–97.

Ganev, V. 2001. "Dorian Gray Effect: Winners as State-Breakers in Post-Communism." *Communist and Post-Communist Studies* 34 (1): 1–25.

Geddes, B. 1995. "A Comparative Perspective on the Leninist Legacy in Eastern Europe." *Comparative Political Studies* 28 (2): 239–74.

Gehlbach, S. 2008. *Representation through Taxation: Revenue, Politics, and Development in Postcommunist States*. Cambridge: Cambridge University Press.

Gehlbach, S., K. Sonin, and E. Zhuravskaya. 2010. "Businessman Candidates." *American Journal of Political Science* 54 (3): 718–36.

Bibliography

Gevorkian, N., and K. Smirnov. 2003. "Kak Otpisalis' Oligarkhi: Kommentarii k Zaiavleniiu RSPP." *Kommersant* 196 (2799), October 27, http://www.kommersant.ru.

Global Integrity. 2006. "Global Integrity Indicators." (Online Database). http://www.globalintegrity.org/.

Golikova, V. 2009. "Business Associations: Incentives and Benefits from the Viewpoint of Corporate Governance." in *Organization and Development of Russian Business: A Firm-level Analysis*, edited by T. Dolgopyatova, I. Iwasaki, A. Yakovlev, 258–83. Basingstoke, UK: Palgrave Macmillan.

Golloher, J. 2010. "McDonald's Still Thriving in Russia after 20 Years." *Voice of America*, February 1, http://www.voanews.com/english/news/McDonalds-Still-Th riving-in-Russia-After-20-Years-83327327.html.

Gordon, S. C., and C. Hafer. 2005. "Flexing Muscle: Corporate Political Expenditures as Signals to the Bureaucracy." *American Political Science Review* **99** (2): 245–61.

Gourevitch, P. A. 1986. *Politics in Hard Times: Comparative Responses to International Economic Crises*. Ithaca, NY: Cornell University Press.

Gray, V., and D. Lowery. 1988. "Interest Group Politics and Economic Growth in the U.S. States." *American Political Science Review* **82** (1): 109–31.

Groseclose, T., and J. M. J. Snyder. 1996. "Buying Supermajorities." *American Political Science Review* **90** (2): 303–15.

Grossman, G. M., and E. Helpman. 1994. "Protection for Sale." *American Economic Review* **84** (4): 833–50.

2001. *Special Interest Politics*. Cambridge: The MIT Press.

Gryschenko, V. 2006, March. Personal interview with author. Kyiv, Ukraine.

Grzymala-Busse, A. 2007. *Rebuilding Leviathan: Party Competition and State Exploitation in Post-Communist Democracies*. Cambridge: Cambridge University Press.

Guriev, S. 2003. "Red Tape and Corruption." Unpublished Paper. Moscow: New Economic School.

Guskov, A. 2005, September. Personal interview with author. Moscow, Russia.

Hall, P. A., and D. Soskice, 2001. *Varieties of Capitalism: The Institutional Foundations of Comparative Advantage*. Oxford: Oxford University Press.

2004. "Varieties of Capitalism and Institutional Complementarities." In *Institutional Conflicts and Complementarities: Monetary Policy and Wage Bargaining in EMU*, edited by R. Franzese, P. Mooslechner and M. Schurz, 43–76. Dordrecht, Boston, London: Kluwer Academic Publisher.

Haney, M., and I. Artemiev. 2002. "The Privatization of the Russian Coal Industry: Policies and Processes in the Transformation of a Major Industry." World Bank Policy Research Working Paper #2820. April 11. SSRN, http://ssrn.com/abstract=636147.

Hanson, P., and E. Teague. 1992. "The Industrialists and Russian Economic Reform." *RFE/RL Research Report* **1** (19, May): 1–7.

2005. "Big Business and the State in Russia." *Europe-Asia Studies* **57** (5): 657–80.

Hardt, J. P., and R. F. Kaufman, eds. 1995. *East-Central European Economies in Transition*. Armonk, New York: M. E. Sharpe.

Harstad, B., and J. Svensson. 2005. "Bribe or Lobby? (It's a Matter of Development)." Mimeo, Northwestern University. Unpublished paper, available online at: http://www.eea-esem.com/papers/EEA/2005/1885/BL.pdf

Hart, D. M. 2004. "'Business' Is Not an Interest Group: On the Study of Companies in American National Politics." *Annual Review of Political Science* **7**: 47–69.

Hassel, A. 1999. "The Erosion of German System of Industrial Relations." *British Journal of Industrial Relations* **37** (3): 483–505.

Hayek, F. 1945. "The Use of Knowledge in Society." *American Economic Review* **35** (4): 519–30.

Heckelman, J. C. 2000. "Consistent Estimates of the Impact of Special Interest Groups on Economic Growth." *Public Choice* **104** (3–4): 319–27.

Heinz, J. P., E. O. Laumann, R. L. Nelson, and R. H Salisbury. 1993. *The Hollow Core: Private Interests in National Policy Making*. Cambridge, MA: Harvard University Press.

Hellman, J. S. 1998. "Winners Take All: The Politics of Partial Reform in Postcommunist Transitions." *World Politics* **50** (2): 203–34.

Hellman, J. S., G. Jones, and D. Kaufmann. 2000. "Seize the State, Seize the Day: State Capture, Corruption, and Influence in Transition." World Bank Policy Research Working Paper #2444.

Hellman, J. S., G. Jones, D. Kaufmann, and M. Schankerman, 2000. "Measuring Governance, Corruption, and State Capture: How Firms and Bureaucrats Shape the Business Environment in Transition Economies." World Bank Policy Research Working Paper #2312.

Henderson, K. E. 2000. "Halfway Home and a Long Way to Go: Russian and Kazakh Roads to Sectoral and Political Corruption." *Democratizatsiya: The Journal of Post-Soviet Democratization* **8** (4): 481–514.

Hiscox, M. J. 2001. "Class vs. Industry Cleavages: Inter-Industry Factor Mobility and the Politics of Trade." *International Organization* **55** (1): 1–46.

Hiscox, M. J., and S. J. Rickard. 2002. "Birds of a Different Feather? Varieties of Capitalism, Factor Specificity, and Interindustry Labor Movements." Paper Presented at the Annual Meeting of the American Political Science Association. San Francisco, CA.

Hodgson, G. M. 1998. "Varieties of Capitalism and Varieties of Economic Theory." In *Institutions and Economic Change: New Perspectives on Markets, Firms and Technology*, edited by K. Nielsen and B. Johnson, 215–42. Cheltenham: Edward Elgar.

Holmes, S. 1996. "Cultural Legacies or State Collapse? Probing the Postcommunist Dilemma." In *Postcommunism: Four Perspectives*, edited by M. Mandelbaum, 22–76. New York: Council on Foreign Relations.

Huber, J. D., and C. R. Shipan. 2002. *Deliberate Discretion: The Institutional Foundations of Bureaucratic Autonomy*. New York: Cambridge University Press.

Huber, P., and A. Worgotter. 1998. "Observations on Russian Business Networks." *Post-Soviet Affairs* **14** (1): 81–91.

Huntington, S. P. 1968. *Political Order in Changing Societies*. New Haven, CT: Yale University Press.

Ickes, B., and R. Ryterman. 1995. "The Organization of Markets and Its Role in Macroeconomic Stabilization during Transition." Background Paper for the World Development Report 1996. http://EconPapers.repec.org/RePEc:fth:pensta:11–95–8.

Ignatov, A. 2010. "The Bear Looks East." *World Coal*, March.

Ignatov and Company Group. 2010. *Russian Coal Market 2009–2010 (Brief Analysis)*. Moscow: Ignatov & Company.

Bibliography

Ingleby, S. 1996. "The Role of Indigenous Institutions in the Economic Transformation of Eastern Europe: The Hungarian Chamber System – One Step Forward or Two Steps Back?" *Journal of European Public Policy* 3 (1): 102–21.

International Intellectual Property Alliance. 1996. *1996 Special 301: Russian Federation.* Report. http://www.iipa.com/countryreports.html.

2002. *2002 Special 301: Russian Federation.* Report. http://www.iipa.com/countryreports.html.

Iversen, T., and J. Pontusson. 2000. "Comparative Political Economy." In *Unions, Employers, and Central Banks: Macroeconomic Coordination and Institutional Change in Social Market Economies*, edited by T. Iversen, J. Pontusson, and D. Soskice, 1–37. Cambridge: Cambridge University Press.

Johnson, C. 1982. *MITI and the Japanese Miracle: The Growth of Industrial Policy, 1925–1975.* Stanford, CA: Stanford University Press.

Johnson, J. 2000. *A Fistful of Rubles: The Rise and Fall of the Russian Banking System.* Ithaca, NY: Cornell University Press.

Johnson, S., J. McMillan, and C. Woodruff. 1999. "Contract Enforcement in Transition." CEPR Discussion Papers 2081, C.E.P.R. Discussion Papers. http://ideas.repec.org/s/cpr/ceprdp.html.

2000 "Entrepreneurs and the Ordering of Institutional Reform: Poland, Slovakia, Romania, Russia and Ukraine Compared." *The Economics of Transition* 8 (1): 1–36.

Jowitt, K. 1992a. "The Leninist Legacy." In *Eastern Europe in Revolution*, edited by I. Banac, 207–24. Ithaca, NY: Cornell University Press.

1992b. *New World Disorder: The Leninist Extinction.* Berkeley: University of California Press.

Kaganov V. Sh., and I. B. Rutkovskaia. 2001. *Possiiskie Ob'edineniia Predprinimatelei [Russian Employer Associations].* Moscow: Russian Institute for Entrepreneurship and Investment.

Kaser, M. 2003. "The Economic and Social Impact of Systemic Transition in Central Asia and Azerbaijan." *Perspectives on Global Development and Technology* 2 (3–4): 459–73.

Kaufmann, D., A. Kraay, and P. Zoido-Lobaton. 1999. "Governance Matters." World Bank Working Paper #2196.

Keeler, T. 1984. "Theories of Regulation and the Deregulation Movement." *Public Choice* 44 (1): 103–45.

Kindeev, A. 2005, August. Personal interview with author. Moscow, Russia.

Kinderman, D. 2005. "Pressure from Without, Subversion from Within: The Two-Pronged German Employer Offensive." *Comparative European Politics* 3 (4): 432–63.

King, C. 2000. "Post-Postcommunism: Transition, Comparison, and the End of 'Eastern Europe'." *World Politics* 53 (1): 143–72.

Kitschelt, H. 1999. "Accounting for Outcomes of Post-Communist Regime Change: Causal Depth or Shallowness in Rival Explanations." Paper presented at the Annual Meeting of the American Political Science Association, Atlanta, GA.

Knack, S. 2003. "Groups, Growth, and Trust: Cross-Country Evidence on the Olson and Putnam Hypotheses." *Public Choice* 117 (3–4): 341–55.

Knight, J. 1992. *Institutions and Social Conflict.* Cambridge: Cambridge University Press.

Kubicek, P. 1996. "Variations on Corporatist Theme: Interest Associations in Post-Soviet Ukraine and Russia." *Europe-Asia Studies* **48** (1): 27–46.

2004. *Organized Labor in Postcommunist States: From Solidarity to Infirmity.* Pittsburgh, PA: University of Pittsburgh Press.

Kudat, A., and Borisov, V. 1996. "Russian Coal Sector Restructuring: Social Assessment." Mimeo, World Bank.

Kurtz, M., and A. Schrank. 2007. "Growth and Governance: Models, Measures, and Mechanisms." *Journal of Politics* **69** (2): 538–54.

Lane, D. 2001. "The Political Economy of Russian Oil." In *Business and the State in Contemporary Russia*, edited by P. Rutland, 101–28. Oxford and Boulder, CO: Westview Press.

Lash, S., and Urry, J. 1987. *The End of Organized Capitalism.* Madison, WI: University of Wisconsin Press.

Leff, N. H. 1964. "Economic Development through Bureaucratic Corruption." *American Behavioral Scientist* **8** (3): 8–14.

Lehmbruch, B. 2003. "Collective Action and Its Limits: Business Associations, State Fragmentation, and the Politics of Multiple Membership in Russia." Paper presented at the American Political Science Association Annual Meeting, Philadelphia, PA.

Lehmbruch, G. 1982. "Introduction: Neo-corporatism in Comparative Perspective." In *Patterns of Corporatist Policy Making*, edited by G. Lehmbruch and P. C. Schmitter, 1–28. London: Sage.

Lerner, D. 1958. *The Passing of Traditional Society: Modernizing the Middle East.* Glencoe, Ill: The Free Press.

Levi, M. 1990. "A Logic of Institutional Change." In *The Limits of Rationality*, edited by K. Schweers Cook and M. Levi, 402–18. Chicago: University of Chicago Press.

Liapin, D. V. 2005a. *Biznes-Asotsiatsii Ukrainy Ta Ikh Vpliv Na Derzhavnu Polityku.* Kyiv: Instytut Konkurentnoho Suspil'stva.

2005b. *Biznes-Asotsiatsii v Ukraini: Otsinka Spomozhnosti i Perspektyvy Rozvytku.* Kyiv: Instytut Konkurentnoho Suspil'stva.

2006, March. Personal interview with author. Kyiv, Ukraine.

Libman, A. 2008. "Government-Business Relations in Post-Soviet Space: The Case of Central Asia." Unpublished Paper.

Lieberman, E. S. 2005. "Nested Analysis as a Mixed-Method Strategy for Comparative Research." *American Political Science Review* **99** (3): 435–52.

Lim, L. 1983. "Singapore's Success: The Myth of the Free Market Economy," *Asian Survey* **23** (6): 752–764.

Liubavina, E., and I. Nagibin. 2003. "Kompakt-diski Priravniali k Vodke." *Kommersant* 123 (2726), July 16.

Locatelli, C. 2003. "The Viability of Deregulation in the Russian Gas Industry." *Journal of Energy and Development* **28** (2): 221–38.

Lohr, E. 1993. "Arkady Volsky's Political Base." *Europe-Asia Studies* **45** (5): 811–29.

Luke, D. 2004. *Multilevel Modeling.* Thousand Oaks, CA: Sage Publications.

Luksic, I. 2003. "Corporatism Packaged in Pluralist Ideology: The Case of Slovenia." *Communist and Post-Communist Studies* **36** (4): 509–25.

Malová, D. n.d. "Limited Europeanization of Interest Groups in Slovakia." Unpublished Paper.

Bibliography

Malová, D., and M. Rybář. 2003. "EU Policies Towards Slovakia: Carrots and Sticks of Political Conditionality." In *The Road to European Union*, vol I: *The Czech and Slovak Republics*, edited by J. Rupnik and J. Zielonka, 98–112. Manchester: Manchester University Press.

Markus, S. 2007. "Capitalists of All Russia, Unite! Business Mobilization under Debilitated Dirigisme." *Polity* **39** (3): 277–304.

2009. "Firms, Stakeholders, Predators in Weak States." Paper presented at 13th ISNIE Conference, Berkeley, CA.

Martin, C. J., and K. Thelen. 2007. "The State and Coordinated Capitalism: Contributions of the Public Sector to Social Solidarity in Post-Industrial." *World Politics* **60** (1): 1–36.

McChesney, F. S. 1997. *Money for Nothing: Politicians, Rent Extraction, and Political Extortion*. Cambridge, MA: Harvard University Press.

McFaul, M. 1995. "State Power, Institutional Change, and the Politics of Privatization in Russia." *World Politics* **47** (2): 210–43.

McMenamin, I. 2002. "Polish Business Associations: Flattened Civil Society or Super Lobbies?" *Business and Politics* **4** (3): 301–17.

Mikhailova, K. 2006. "Chernaia Igra." *Megapolis* **15** (279), April 17: 1.

Miller, W. L., A. B. Grodeland, and T. Y. Koshechkina. 1999. "A Focus Group Study of Bribery and Other Ways of Coping with Officialdom in Postcommunist Eastern Europe." Paper presented at the Coalition 2000 Conference, Varna, Bulgaria.

2002. "Bribery and Other Ways of Coping with Officialdom in Post-Communist Eastern Europe." In *Political Corruption: Concepts and Contexts*, edited by A. Heidenheimer and M. Johnston, 559–81. New Brunswick, NJ: Transaction.

Moore, B. 1993 [1966]. *Social Origins of Dictatorship and Democracy: Lord and Peasant in the Making of the Modern World*. Boston: Beacon Press.

Morley, J. M. 1999. *Driven by Growth: Political Change in the Asia-Pacific Region*. Armonk, NY: M. E. Sharpe.

Morozhenshchik Rossii [Russian Icecreamer]. 2005. Multiple Issues. Moscow.

Mueller, D. C., and P. Murrell. 1986. "Interest Groups and the Size of Government." *Public Choice* **48** (2): 125–45.

Murray, M. 1999. *Small Business: A Response to Corruption in Russia*. US House of Representatives, Committee on International Relations, Testimony, October 7.

Murrell, P. 1984. "An Examination of the Factors Affecting the Formation of Interest Groups in OECD Countries." *Public Choice* **43** (2): 151–71.

1992a. "Conservative Political Philosophy and the Strategy of Economic Transition." *East European Politics and Societies* **6** (1): 3–16.

1992b. "Privatization Complicates the Fresh Start: Putting Entrepreneurs First in Eastern Bloc." *Orbis*, **36** (3): 323–33.

Myant, M. 1994 "Czech and Slovak Trade Unions." In *Parties, Trade Unions, and Societies in East-Central Europe*, edited by M. Waller and M. Myant, 59–84. Ilford, UK: Frank Cass.

Netreba, P. 2004. "The Oligarchs Didn't Meet the President." Editorial. *Kommersant*. **106** (2945, June 16): 1.

Nichols, P. 2001. "The Fit between Changes to the International Corruption Regime and Indigenous Perceptions of Corruption in Kazakhstan." *University of Pennsylvania Journal of International Economic Law* **22** (4): 863–973.

Noll, R. G., and B. M. Owen. 1983. *The Political Economy of Deregulation: Interest Groups in the Regulatory Process*. Washington, DC: American Enterprise Institute for Public Policy Research.

Olson, M. 1965. *The Logic of Collective Action: Public Goods and Theory of Groups*. Cambridge, MA: Harvard University Press.

1982. *The Rise and Decline of Nations: Economic Growth, Stagnation, and Social Rigidities*. New Haven, CT: Yale University Press.

Onishchuk, A, 2005, September. Personal interview with author. Moscow, Russia.

Pecorino, P. 2001. "Market Structure, Tariff Lobbying, and the Free Rider Problem." *Public Choice* **106** (3–4): 203–20.

Peltzman, S. 1976. "Toward a More General Theory of Regulation." *Journal of Law and Economics* **19** (2): 211–40.

1989. "The Economic Theory of Regulation after a Decade of Deregulation." In *Brooking Papers of Economic Activity: Micro Economics*, 1–41. Washington, DC: Brooking Institution.

1998. *Political Participation and Government Regulation*. Chicago, IL: The University of Chicago Press.

Peregudov, S., and I. Semenenko. 1996. "Lobbying Business Interests in Russia." *Democratization* **3** (2): 115–39.

Pickles J., and R. M. Jenkins. eds. 2008. *State and Society in Post-Socialist Economies*. New York: Palgrave Macmillan.

Pleshanova, O. 2008. "Litsenzionnyi Vid Bezdeiatel'nosti." *Kommersant* **96** (3913). May 6.

Pola, P. 2007. "The Economic Chambers and the Enforcement of Local Economic Interests." Discussion Paper #60 Centre for Regional Studies of Hungarian Academy of Sciences, Pécs, Hungary.

Polanyi, K. [1944] 1957. *The Great Transformation: The Political and Economic Origins of Our Time*. Boston, MA: Beacon Press.

Primakov, E. 2002. *Doklad Presidenta Torgovo-Promyshlennoi Palaty Rossiiskoi Federatsii na 4 S'ezde TPP RF*. Presidential Address to the 4th congress of the Chamber of Trade and Industry of Russian Federation.

Putnam, R. D. 1993. *Making Democracy Work: Civic Tradition in Modern Italy*. Princeton, NJ: Princeton University Press.

Pyle, W. 2006. "Collective Action and Post-Communist Enterprise: The Economic Logic of Russian Business Associations." *Europe-Asia Studies*, **58** (4): 491–521.

2011. "Organized Business, Political Competition, and Property Rights: Evidence from the Russian Federation." *Journal of Law, Economics and Organization* **27** (1): 2–31.

Rabotodavets' [Employer]. 2004–2005. Multiple issues. Kyiv, Ukraine.

Raudenbush, S. W., and A. S. Bryk. 2002. *Hierarchical Liner Models: Application and Data Analysis Methods*, 2nd ed. Thousand Oaks, CA: Sage Publications.

Recanatini, F., and R. Ryterman. 2001. "Disorganization or Self-Organization? The Emergence of Business Associations in a Transition Economy." World Bank Policy Research Working Paper #2539.

Remington, T. F. 2004. *Politics in Russia* (third edition). New York: Pearson Longman.

Roland, G. 2000. *Transition and Economics: Politics, Markets, and Firms*. Cambridge, MA: MIT Press.

Rose-Ackerman, S. 1999. *Corruption and Government: Causes, Consequences, and Reform*. Cambridge, UK: Cambridge University Press.

Bibliography

RUIE, Delovaya Rossiya, and Opora Rossii. 2003. "Public Statement by RUIE, Delovaya Rossia, and Opora Rossii." *Rossiiskaia Gazeta*. 3330, October 27: 4.

Russian Association of Ice Cream Producers (RAICP). 2005. *Ezhegodnik* [Yearbook]. Moscow, Russia: Russian Association of Ice Cream Producers.

Rutland, P., ed. 2001. *Business and the State in Contemporary Russia*. Boulder, CO: Westview Press.

Salisbury, R. H. 1979. "Why No Corporatism in America?" In *Trends Towards Corporatist Intermediation*, edited by P.C. Schmitter and G. Lembruch, 213–30. Beverly Hills, CA: Sage.

1991. "Putting Interests Back into Interest Groups." In *Interest Group Politics*, edited by A. J. Cigler and B. Loomis, 382–83. Washington, DC: CQ Press.

1994. "Interest Structures and Policy Domains: A Focus for Research." In *Representing Interests and Interest Group Representation*, edited by W. Crotty, M. A. Schwartz, and J. C. Green, 12–20. Lanham, MD and London: University Press of America.

Sachs, J. 1993. *Poland's Jump to the Market Economy*. Cambridge, MA: MIT Press.

Saur, G. K. 2003. *World Guide to Trade Associations*, 6th ed. Munich: K. G. Saur.

Schaede, U. 2000. *Cooperative Capitalism: Self-Regulation, Trade Associations and the Antimonopoly Law in Japan*. Oxford, UK and New York: Oxford University Press.

Schaw, W. A. 2006. *Croatian Exporters Association*. USAID Evaluation Report.

Schmitter, P. C. 1974. "Still the Century of Corporatism?" *Review of Politics* **36** (1): 85–131.

1993. "Corporatism as Organizational Practice and Political Theory." In *International Handbook of Participation in Organizations: The Challenges of New Technology and Macro-Political Change*, edited by W. M. Lafferty and E. Rosenstein, 327–43. Oxford, UK: Oxford University Press.

Schmitter, P. C., and G. Lehmbruch. 1979. *Trends towards Corporatist Intermediation*. Beverly Hills, CA: Sage Publishers.

Schopflin, G. 1994. "Postcommunism: The Problems of Democratic Construction." *Daedalus* **123** (3): 127–41.

Schwab, K., ed. 2010. *Global Competitiveness Report 2010–11*. Geneva, Switzerland: World Economic Forum.

Shahnazarov, A. 2005. "Koshelek ili zhizn." *Argumenty i Fakty Kazakhstan*.

Shipov, V. (deputy minister, Ministry of Economic Development and Trade). 2005, August. Personal interview with author. Moscow, Russia.

Shleifer, A., and D. Treisman. 2000. *Without a Map: Political Tactics and Economic Reform in Russia*. Cambridge, MA: MIT Press.

Shleifer, A., and R. Vishny. 1993. "Corruption." *Quarterly Journal of Economics* **108** (3): 599–617.

Sikamova, A., O. Tropkina, E. Mazin, and P. Orehin. 2003. "Oligarhi na pereput'ie" [Oligarchs at a crossroads]. *Nezavisimaia Gazeta*. October 28.

Sixsmith, M. 2010. *Putin's Oil: The Yukos Affair and the Struggle for Russia*. London, UK: Continuum.

Sledar, S. 2010. "Slovenia: Developments in Social Partner Organizations." European Industrial Relations Observatory and Slovenian Institute of Macroeconomic Analysis and Development. http://www.eurofound.europa.eu/eiro/studies/tn0910049s/si0910049q.htm.

Smith, A. 1909 [1776]. *An Inquiry into the Nature and Causes of the Wealth of Nations*. New York: P. F. Collier and Son.

Sokolin, V. L., ed. 2001, 2004, 2006. *Rossiiskii Statisticheskii Ezhegodnik* [*Russian Statistical Yearbook*]. Moscow: Rosstat.

Sorokin, Iu. 2005, September. Personal interview with author. Moscow, Russia.

Soskice, D. 1990. "Wage Determination: The Changing Role of Institutions in Advanced Industrialized Countries." *Oxford Review of Economic Policy* **6** (4): 36–61.

Soyuz Morozhenshchikov Rossii. 2004, 2005. *Ezhegodnik.* Moscow, Russia: Soyuz Morozhenshchikov Rossii.

Stanić, M. 2006, June. Personal interview with author. Zagreb, Croatia.

Stark, D. 1995. "Not by Design: The Myth of Designer Capitalism in Eastern Europe." In *Strategic Choice and Path-Dependency in Post-Socialism: Institutional Dynamics in the Transformation Process*, edited by J. Hausner, B. Jessop, and K. Nielsen, 67–82. Cheltenham and Aldershot, UK: Edward Edgar.

Stark, D., and L. Bruszt. 1998. *Postsocialist Pathways: Transforming Politics and Property in East Central Europe.* Cambridge, UK: Cambridge University Press.

Stigler, G. 1971. "The Theory of Economic Regulation." *The Bell Journal of Economics and Management Science* **2** (1): 3–21.

———. 1974. "Free Riders and Collective Action: An Appendix to Theories of Economic Regulation." *The Bell Journal of Economics and Management Science* **5** (2): 359–65.

Stodghill, R. 2006. "Oil, Cash, and Corruption." *New York Times.* November 5. http://www.nytimes.com/2006/11/05/business/yourmoney/05giffen.html?page wanted=all

Streeck, W., and P. Schmitter. 1992. "From National Corporatism to Transnational Pluralism: Organized interests in the Single European Market." In *Social Institutions and Economic Performance: Studies of Industrial Relations in Advanced Capitalist Economies*, edited by W. Streeck, 197–231. London, UK: Sage Publications.

Tang, E., and R. Hedley. 1998. "Distributional Coalitions, State Strength, and Economic Growth: Toward a Comprehensive Theory of Economic Development." *Public Choice* **96** (3/4): 295–323.

Taylor, M. 1990. "Cooperation and Rationality: Notes on the Collective Action Problem and Its Solutions." In *The Limits of Rationality*, edited by K. Schweers Cook and M. Levi, 222–49. Chicago, IL: University of Chicago Press.

"The Khodorkovsky Case: A New Moscow Show Trial." 2009. *The Economist.* April 2. http://www.economist.com/node/13415161.

Tocqueville, A. D. 1963 [1835]. *Democracy in America.* New York: Knopf.

Tompson, W. 2005. "Putting Yukos in Perspective." *Post-Soviet Affairs* **21** (2): 159–81.

Tragakes, E., and S. Lessof. 2003. "Health Care Systems in Transition: Russia." World Health Organization Report. Copenhagen, Denmark: European Observatory on Health Care Systems.

Transparency International. 2002. *The Impact of Corruption on Small Business.* Chişinău, Moldova: Transparency International Moldova.

Treisman, D. 1998. "Russia's Taxing Problem." *Foreign Policy* **112**: 55–66.

Truman, D. 1951. *The Governmental Process: Political Interests and Public Opinion.* New York: Knopf.

Tucker, A. 2008. "Trade Associations as Industry Reputation Agents: A Model of Reputational Trust." *Business and Politics* **10** (1): art. 4.

Union of Industrialists and Entrepreneurs of Russian Federation. 2003. *Polozhenie o Poriadke Vneseniia Chlenskih Vznosov* [Provision for membership fees payments].

Bibliography

Union of Industrialists and Entrepreneurs of Russian Federation. Internal document.

"Uspeshnyi Predprinimatel." 2005. Editorial. *Nachnem s Ponedel'nika.* **36** (596): 1.

Vandenko, I. 2003. "Tsena Zaprosa. Spikery Parlamentskih Palat ne Dogovorilis' o Lobbizme." *Novye Izvestiia.* July 28.

Vogel, S. K. 1998. *Freer Markets, More Rules: Regulatory Reforms in Advanced Industrial Countries.* Ithaca, NY: Cornell University Press.

Volkov, V. (assistant director of the Russian Association for the Development of Small and Medium-Size Enterprises). 2005, August. Personal interview with author. Moscow, Russia.

Volsky, A. 2005. "1990–2005: Itogi Piatnadtsatiletiia RSPP." Message from the president to the RUIE members, delivered at the 2005 congress of RUIE. Moscow, Russia.

Vorontsov, K. 2003. "Piraty Perepechatali Minpechati." *Kommersant* 133 (2736), July 30.

Wade, R. 1990. *Governing the Market: Economic Theory and the Role of Government in East Asian Industrialization.* Princeton, NJ: Princeton University Press.

Walker, J. 1983. "The Origins and Maintenance of Interest Groups in America." *American Political Science Review* 77 (2): 390–406.

Waller, M. 1994. "Political Actors and Political Roles in East-Central Europe." In *Parties, Trade Unions and Society in East Central Europe*, edited by M. Waller and M. Myant, 21–36. London, UK: Frank Cass.

Waller, M., and M. Myant. 1994. *Parties, Trade Unions, and Societies in East-Central Europe.* London, UK: Frank Cass.

Webster, R. 2002. "Corruption and the Private Sector." In *Sectoral Perspectives on Corruption.* Washington, DC: USAID. http://www.usaid.gov.

Weingast, B. 1981. "Regulation, Reregulation, and Deregulation: The Political Foundations of Agency-Clientele Relationships." *Law and Contemporary Problems* **44** (1): 147–77.

Werner, C. 2000. "Gifts, Bribes, and Development in Post-Soviet Kazakhstan." *Human Organization* **59** (1): 11–22.

Whitley, R., and P. H. Kristensen. 1997. *Governance at Work: The Social Regulation of Economic Relations in Europe.* Oxford, New York: Oxford University Press.

World Bank. 2004–2010. *Doing Business.* Washington, DC: World Bank Publications.

1996–2010. *Worldwide Governance Indicators.* http://info.worldbank.org/governance/wgi/index.asp.

Wykrętowicz S., ed. 2004. *Samorząd w Polsce: Istota, Formy, Zadania.* Poznań, Poland: WSB Publishing House.

Yakovlev, A., and A. Govorun. 2011. "Business Associations as a Business-Government Liaison: An Empirical Analysis." *Journal of the New Economic Association* **9**: 98–127.

Yakovlev, E., and E. V. Zhuravskaya. 2007. "Deregulation of Business." CEPR Discussion Paper #DP6610.

Yambaev, V. 2005. *Address to the Congress of Kazakh Business Forum.* Almaty, Kazakhstan: Almaty Association of Entrepreneurs. http://www.aaekz.com/info/aae/.

Yanovsky, V. (first vice president, secretary general of the UCCI). 2006, March. Personal interview with author. Kyiv, Ukraine.

Zaharov, D. 2005. "Sbyt Zael." *Kommersant* **158** (3242). August 25.

Zils, M. 1980. *World Guide to Trade Associations.* Munich: K. G. Saur.

1999. *World Guide to Trade Associations.* Munich: K. G. Saur Verlag Gmbh & Co.

Index

accountability, 9, 32, 83, 103, 107t, 118, 177n3, 204, 225t
accounting standards, 22, 133
activism, 4, 73, 106, 158, 168
Adriatic-Ionian Cooperative Initiative, 87
Agreement on Trade in Textiles (Croatia), 87, 158
Aktiubinsk Regional Union of Industrialists and Employers (Kazakhstan), 220t
Alamaty Chamber of Trade and Industry (Kazakhstan), 221t
Albania, 42, 43, 52t, 84, 85, 96n1, 106, 181, 182t, 185
  Albanian Council of Employer Organizations, 185
  National Real Estate Association, 185
  Professional and Business Women Association, 185
  Union of Democratic Businessmen, 185
  Union of Organizations of Albanian Businesses, 185
Algeria, 48n7
allocation, 17, 19, 206
  resource allocation, 16, 19
Almaty Association of Entrepreneurs (Kazakhstan), 84, 153, 154, 171, 214t, 219t
  Yambaev, Viktor, 17n1, 83, 153
anticommunist revolutions, 4
anticorruption, *See* deterrence
anticorruption measures, 23, 27, 28, 29, 33, 34, 36, 64, 73, 94, 97t, 102, 116, 117n18, 120, 138, 147, 148, 169, 178

Armenia, 52t, 96n1, 182t
Asem League of Entrepreneurs (Kazakhstan), 222t
asset specificity, 105, *See also* resource specificity
Association for Protecting the Rights of Entrepreneurs, Petropavlovsk (Kazakhstan), 222t
Association for the Development of International Business (Ukraine), 79
Association for the Development of Pharmaceutical Industry, Shymkent (Kazakhstan), 219t
Association for the Development of Small and Medium Business (ADSMB) (Russia), 57, 60, 62, 63t, 67, 82, 152, 196, 211
  Ioffe, Aleksandr, 67, 196
Association for Support of Entrepreneurship, Kostanai (Kazakhstan), 221t
Association for the Support and Development of the Pharmaceutical Industry (Kazakhstan), 219t
Association New Formation, 214t
Association of the Autotransport Complex (Kazakhstan), 219t
Association of Commodity Producers (Kazakhstan), 219t
Association of Confectioners (Russia), 63t
Association of the Construction Industry (Kazakhstan), 82
Association of Croatian Exporters (ACE) (Croatia), 87, 157, 158, 159, 171, 185, 187, 214t

241

242   *Index*

Association of ECR Manufacturers and Service Centers (Ukraine), 165
Association of Employers (Slovenia), 185
Association of Employers' Unions and Federations (AZZZ) (Slovakia), 193
Association of Enterprises of Light Industry (Kazakhstan), 218t
Association of Ice Cream Producers (Russia), 62, 68, 161, 162, 162n23, 171, 214t
Association of Independent Media of Central Asia (Kazakhstan), 219t
Association of Industrialists and Entrepreneurs of Serbia and Montenegro, 185
Association of Kyzylorda Entrepreneurs (Kazakhstan), 222t
Association of Lumber Processing and Furniture Producing Enterprises (Kazakhstan), 221t
Association of Manufacturers and Consumers of Packaging Products (Ukraine), 73n37
Association of Medical Entrepreneurs (Kazakhstan), 219t
Association of Milk and Dairy Producers (Kazakhstan), 82, 221t
Association of National Freight Forwarders (Kazakhstan), 221t
Association of Pharmaceutical Importers (Kazakhstan), 219t
Association of the Printing Industry (Kazakhstan), 220t
Association of Producers of Milk and Dairy Products (Kazakhstan), 222t
Association of Retirement Funds (Kazakhstan), 218t
Association of Russian Banks (ARB), 61, 63t, 68, 133n2, 152
Association of Russian Producers of Ice Cream and Frozen Products, 161
Association of Serbian Banks, 185
Association of the Producers of Mining Equipment (Kazakhstan), 220t
Association of Tobacco Companies (Ukraine), 214t
Association of Trade Companies and Producers of Consumer Electronics and Computers (RATEK) (Russia), 61, 63t, 155, 156, 156n20, 155, 157, 214t
Association of Trademark Holders (Russia), 62
Association of Travel Agencies (Croatia), 214t
Stanić, Maja, 90
Association of TV and Radio Broadcasters of Kazakhstan, 221t
Association of Ukrainian Banks, 214t

associations
  associational coverage, 82n46
  local associations, 10, 17, 18, 19, 38, 39, 57, 57n14, 58, 58n16, 59, 65, 68, 72, 74, 76, 78n43, 79, 82, 83, 84, 86, 88, 88n50, 92, 104, 125, 147n14, 163, 164, 182nb, 188, 206
  national associations, 74, 91n53, 180n9, 182nb
  provincial associations, 57, 75, 79, 88, 133n2, 182nb, 213, 217
  regional associations, 39, 57, 58, 60, 74, 82, 143, 213
Atyrau Chapter of the Union of Industrialists and Entrepreneurs (Kazakhstan), 220t
audio-video trade, 68, 138, 214t
authoritarianism, 54, 55, 56, 80, 84, 106, 204, 205
Azerbaijan, 43, 52t, 96n1, 182t

Babić, Ante, 157
Baltic States, 183, *See also* Estonia; Latvia; Lithuania
Bangladesh, 48n7
Banking Association of the Republic of Kazakhstan, 219t
banking regulations, 22, 130
Belarus, 43, 52t, 96n1, 182t
Blinders fees, 24
Blyzniuk, Andriy, 165, 166
Board of Entrepreneurs civic organization (Ukraine), 214t
Bonaparte, Napoleon, 183
Bosnia, 52t, 96n1, 107, 182t, 183
Brazil, 48n7
bribe, *See* corruption
bribery, 30, 32, 33, 34, 35, 37, 51, 53, 72, 80, 81, 97t, 99, 102, 114, 116f, 120, 128, 178n6, 198, 207, 223, *See also* corruption
  bribe level, 31
  equilibrium bribe, 22
budget constraint, 24, 25
Bulgaria, 45, 52t, 96n1, 138, 181, 182t, 184
bureaucracy, 2n2, 15, 16, 24, 29, 32, 33, 34, 36, 38, 81, 90, 97t, 102, 111, 112, 113, 113f, 114n17, 120, 127, 130, 131, 149, 153, 154, 170, 183, 195, 197, 199, 202, 203, 207
  probity, 12, 29, 117, 198
  red tape, 11, 21, 32, 33, 33n22, 36, 51, 53f, 73, 80, 102, 113, 114, 120, 128, 152, 171

Index

243

bureaucratic predation, 23, 148, 150, 152, 162n23, 169, 171, 172, 197, 207

Business and Development public foundation (Kazakhstan), 222t

Business Association of the Confectionary Industry (Russia), 214t

business association services
  information on domestic markets, 46, 53, 87
  information on government regulation, 47
  information on international markets, 46
  reputational services, 46

business entry requirements, 51

Business Environment and Enterprise Performance Survey (BEEPS), 10, 42n6, 63, 64, 65, 71, 81, 85, 90t, 96, 96n2, 98, 101, 114, 120, 121, 122t, 125, 190t, 200t

Business Forum (Kazakhstan), 82, 83, 84, 163, 164, 171, 214t, 218t

Business Freedom, 117

business representation, 5, 8, 12, 13, 39, 40n4, 54, 56, 60, 60n17, 63, 77, 78n43, 80, 81, 82, 84, 85, 91, 92, 146, 158, 172, 173, 174, 175, 175n2, 179, 180, 181, 182, 183, 184, 187, 191, 193, 194, 195, 199, 205, 207, 210, 213

business-state interaction, 5, 6, 6n8, 7n10, 8, 13, 29, 39, 41n5, 54, 64, 77, 81, 92, 173, 202, 206, 210

Cambodia, 48n7

capital mobility, 104

capitalism, 6, 6n8, 8, 8n12, 14, 117, 123, 124, 195, 206, 207

Casino Association (Kazakhstan), 83, 214t

Cawson, Alan, 58, 173

Center for the Development and Protection of Small Business (Russia), 63t

Central European Cooperative Initiative, 182t

Central European Free Trade Association, 87

Central Test Laboratory of Quality Surveillance (Ukraine), 151

centrally planned economies, 16, 117, 206

Chamber of Auditors of Kazakhstan, 222t

Chamber of Commerce and Industry (CCI) (Russia), 56, 214t

Chamber of Commerce and Industry of the Republic of Kazakhstan, 214t

Chamber of Commerce and Industry of the Russian Federation, 63n21, 183n12

Chamber of Economy (Macedonia), 186

Chamber of Trade and Industry (Kazakhstan), 218t

Chamber of Trade and Industry (Russia), 188

Chamber of Trade and Industry, Astana (Kazakhstan), 218t

Chamber of Trades and Crafts (CTC) (Croatia), 85, 88, 88n50, 89t

Chamber of Commerce and Industry (Slovenia), 186

Chamber of Craft and Small Businesses (Slovenia), 186

channels
  formal channels, 18
  informal channels, 18, 81, 141

channels of influence, 4n5, 84

charter, 57

charters, 2n1, 71t, 87, 91n52

Chernomyrdin, Viktor, 67

Chile, 48n7

China, 40n4, 48n7, 138, 142n8

Civic Collegium (Ukraine), 77

civic engagement, 4, 106, 184, 204

civil liberties, 55, 72, 80, 106, 107t, 111

Clarke, Simon, 60, 60n17, 174n1, 192, 193

clear rules, 105, 114, 226t

club goods, 23, 37n24, 56, 93, 121, 128, 133, 199, *See also* selective incentives, 23, 37n24

coal industry, 4, 126t, 167, 167n26, 168, 168n29, 168n30, 169, 170, 171

Coase, Ronald, 19, 20

collective action, 4, 5, 7, 14, 15, 19, 21, 29, 32, 33, 34, 35, 36, 36n23, 40, 64, 70, 73, 80, 81, 93, 95, 97t, 102, 103, 104, 106, 108, 124, 125, 126, 128, 129, 134, 137, 139, 140, 141, 142, 143, 148, 155, 159n21, 163, 165, 166, 167, 168, 169, 169n32, 170, 176, 185, 192, 196, 197, 198, 209

collective goods, 23, 36n23, 134, 148, 158, 177, 178n5

collective action problem, 2, 3, 8, 11, 15, 37, 129, 155, 176, 187, 195, 198, 205, 207

Collier, David, 195n26

collusive behavior, 2, 5, 6, 19, 92, 124, 127, 139, 140, 200, 201

Commissions (Coordinating Councils) for Enterprise Development (Ukraine), 77

Commonwealth of Independent States (CIS), 7, 181

communism, 1, 2, 4, 6, 7n10, 66n27, 73n37, 163, 174n1, 181, 183, 206

Index

competition, 4n6, 13, 27, 28, 39, 55, 72, 72n36, 81, 90, 91, 92, 93, 106, 139, 145, 162, 173, 184n14, 186, 187, 200, 201n2

compliance, 11, 17n2, 19n4, 21, 22, 23, 24, 25n15, 26, 28, 29, 29n19, 31, 32, 33n22, 34, 36, 37, 51, 98n5, 99, 102, 114, 114n17, 118, 121, 133, 139, 148, 153, 155, 175t, 177, 178, 198, 208

  cost of compliance, 22, 22n8, 28, 29, 31, 33, 36, 145, 165, 176, 179

  noncompliance, 5, 11, 21, 22, 24, 32, 179n7, 207

compulsory membership, 13, 84, 84n48, 85, 87, 89t, 90t, 106, 107t, 121, 172, 173, 176, 177, 178, 179, 180, 181, 181n10, 182na, 182t, 189, 190, 191, 195, 199

Confederation of Civic Organizations and Employers of East Kazakhstan, 220t

Confederation of Employers (entrepreneurs), Astana (Kazakhstan), 220t

Confederation of Employers of the Republic of Kazakhstan, 218t

Construction Industry Union (Ukraine), 214t

contract enforcement, 18, 22, 49n9, 140, 152, 208

Cooperative Union of Slavonia, 89

Coordinating Council for Employers' Organizations (CCEO) (Russia), 59, 60, 63t, 65, 68, 76n41, 193, 214t

Coordinating Expert Center of Business Associations of Ukraine (CEC), 74, 75, 76, 77, 78, 159, 159n21, 160, 161, 165, 166

  Liapin, Dmytro, 74, 75, 76, 77, 78, 159, 160, 165

  Yekhanurov, Yuri, 161

Copyright and Neighboring Rights Law (1993) (Russia), 138

copyright regulations, 138, 138n6, 139, 140, 140n7

corporatism, 6n8, *11*, 63, 106, 172, 173, 174, 174n1, 175, 175n2, 175t, 176, 180n8, 181, 185, 187, 195, 209

corruption, 5, 11, 12, 15, 16, 17, 17n2, 18, 19, 19n4, 19n5, 20, 20n6, 21, 21n7, 21n8, 22, 23, 24, 26n16, 28, 29, 30, 32, 33, 33n22, 34, 35, 36, 39, 43n6, 51, 53, 54, 55t, 56, 64, 80, 81, 81n44, 94, 95, 96, 97t, 98, 98n5, 101, 102, 107t, 108, 113, 114, 117, 117n18, 120, 121, 128, 129, 131, 134, 140, 141, 145, 146, 147, 148, 149, 150, 153, 158, 160, 164, 167, 169, 170, 171,

172, *177*, 178, 178n7, 198, 204, 207, 223, 224

  petty corruption (administrative corruption), 15, 17, 18, 19, 35

  political corruption (state capture), 7n11, 17, 18, 18n3, 36, 43n6, 72n36, 81, 198

Corruption Perception Index (CPI), 21n7, 55t, 117

cost

  costs of regulatory compliance, 24, 32

  market cost of production (production cost), 24

  transaction costs, 87, 132, 133n2, 145, 151, 152, 199, 204, 211

costless participation, 188, 189

costless transactions, 19, 37

Council of Trade Associations (CTA) (Ukraine), 77

Country Chicken, 142

Croatia, 4, 10, 12, 13, 39, 43, 52t, 54, 55t, 84, 85, 85n49, 86, 87, 89, 90n51, 91, 91n53, 92, 96n1, 106, 107, 130, 157, 158, 159, 170, 173, 181, 182na, 182t, 183, 184, 185, 187, 189, 191n22, 213, 214t

Croatian Airlines, 157

Croatian Association of Credit Cooperatives, 89

Croatian Chamber of Economy, 85, 86, 87, 88, 89t, 90, 91, 157, 183, 183n11, 187, 188, 188n20, 214t

Croatian Employers' Association (CEA), 87, 90, 91, 91n52, 158, 187, 188

  Todorić, Ivica, 90

Croatian Union of Cooperatives, 214t

Croatian Union of Housing Cooperatives, 89

Crowley, Stephen, 60n17, 167n26, 168, 168n30, 174n1, 192

customer, 20, 90, 141, 142, 142n8, 144, 151

Czech Republic, 4, 42, 45, 52t, 96n1, 106, 174, 181, 182t, 184n14

Decree on Stamp Duty (Ukraine), 160

defensive organization theory, 12, 15, 29, 35, 39, 51, 52, 53, 54, 56, 64, 66, 73, 80, 93, 96, 98, 99, 121, 124, 127, 129, 131, 137, 140, 154, 169, 170, 187, 189, 194, 195, 198, 201n2, 203, 204, 207

Delovaya Rossiya (Business Russia), 64, 68

Denmark, 42

deregulation, 11, 202, 202n4, 203

deterrence, 23, 26n16, 28, 53, 102, 108, 128, 140, 170

diversity, 17n1, 39, 41, 42, 54, 62n19, 65n23, 72, 197, 206

Index

245

Djankov, Simeon, 101
Doing Business Project, 48, 52t, 101, 102
Doner, Richard F., 204
Duma (Russia), 66n27, 69, 152, 153

economic competition, 4n6, 93, 139, 145, 162, 186, 200
economic coordination, 8, 8n12, 11, 28, 68, 75, 149, 159, 175, 180, 182, 195, 199, 204, 206, 207
economic efficiency, 4n6, 6, 7, 9, 10, 93, 160, 203, 204
economic fairness, 9, 103, 204
economic reform, 3, 5, 6, 7, 19, 31, 39, 55, 64, 67, 72n36, 73n38, 79, 80, 85, 90, 153, 158, 159, 169, 184, 189, 192, 192n24, 197, 202, 205, 205n7
economic regulation, 21, 31, 34, 97t, 170, 181, 187, 202, 207
Ecuador, 48n7
Egypt, 48n7
El Salvador, 48n7
electronic cash registers (ECRs), 149, 164, 165
Elhov, Valerii, 68, 162
emerging market, 6, 7, 10, 16, 17, 153
employer/producer associations, 3, 8, 62, 75, 137, 146, 161, 180, 185, 193, 195, 196, 197, 199, 204, 206, 207, 215, 216
Employers' Association (Serbia), 185, 193
Employers' Confederation of the Republic of Kazakhstan, 82
enforcement, 4, 11, 15, 21, 22, 23, 30, 31, 31n21, 32, 33, 34, 36, 37, 97t, 128, 138, 139, 140, 141, 145, 145n13, 160, 171, 175, 199, 203, 207, 209, 211
Entrepreneurs' Council (Ukraine), 77
Entrepreneurs' Council of Moscow (Russia), 68
environmental regulations, 19n4, 22, 24, 87, 100t
Eritrea, 48n7
Estonia, 52t, 96n1, 106, 182t
Ethiopia, 48n7
Eurasia, 82, 218t
European Bank for Reconstruction and Development (EBRD), 2, 16, 42, 65, 107t, 117, 118
European Business Association (Ukraine), 79, 214t
European Free Trade Agreement, 87

European Industrial Relations Observatory, 187
European Union (EU), 6, 45, 51, 87, 89, 91, 120, 120n19, 158, 159, 169, 225, 225t
Evraz Group, 169
ex ante corruption (corruption without theft), 17n2
ex post corruption (corruption with theft), 17n2
excludability of goods, 11, 23, 24, 25, 25n14, 37, 70, 70n34, 70n35, 71, 163, 166, 223
extortion, 20, 21, 94, 99, 143, 153, 164, 201n2

factor specificity, 126
Far East Confederation of Businesswomen, 63t
Federal Arbitration Courts of Circuits (Russia), 124
Federal Migration Service, 143
Federal Ministry of Justice (Russia), 124
Federal Service on Supervision in the Sphere of Consumer Rights Protection, 143
Federation of Commodity Producers (FCP), 61n19, 65
Federation of Professional Unions of Cooperatives and Enterprises of Alternative Forms of Property (Ukraine), 73
Federation of Restaurants and Hotels (Russia), 141, 142, 171, 214t
Kindeev, Aleksandr, 143, 144
Fedianin, Anatolii, 130
Figueras, Josep, 169n34
financial services industry, 4
firm, 2n1, 3, 3n3, 5, 10, 12, 14, 15, 16, 19, 20, 20n6, 21, 22, 23, 25n12, 28, 28n18, 29, 30, 30n20, 31, 32, 33, 34, 35, 36, 37, 38n1, 41, 42, 43n6, 43 fig. 3.3, 45, 46, 47, 48, 52, 53, 55t, 56n13, 58, 59, 60, 62, 62n19, 65, 67n31, 69, 70n35, 72, 75, 76, 79, 81, 84, 87, 92, 93, 95, 96n1, 96n2, 97t, 98, 98n4, 100t, 101, 102, 102n10, 103, 104, 105, 105n13, 107, 108, 110, 111, 112, 113, 116, 120, 121, 121n20, 124, 125, 127, 128, 129, 130, 133n3, 134, 137, 138, 139, 140, 141, 142, 144, 147n14, 148, 149, 150, 151, 154, 155, 156, 157, 160, 163, 165, 166, 167, 168, 169n32, 176, 179, 185, 188, 189, 190, 190t, 194, 195, 196, 197, 198, 199, 200, 200t, 201, 202, 207, 208, 210, 211
firm size, 111

246   Index

foreign donor assistance, 74
   foreign-sponsored programs, 74
Fortescue, Stephen, 3, 7, 58, 61n19, 65n23,
   66, 68, 180, 181, 197
fraktsiia (parliamentary group), 69
France, 42
Freedom House ranking, 55t
free-rider problem, 11, 13, 37, 176
Frye, Timothy, 5, 7n11, 17n1, 19, 31, 65, 68, 153

Gaidar, Yegor, 67
Garant legal information service (Russia), 124,
   143n10
Gehlbach, Scott, 25n14, 69
Georgia, 21n7, 52t, 96n1, 182t
Germany, 180n8
Global Integrity rankings, 103, 107t
goods, 9, 19, 19n4, 22n9, 24, 25, 29, 30,
   30n20, 37, 69, 70, 70n35, 71, 79, 87, 94,
   121, 132t, 151, 155, 157, 158, 160n22,
   161, 162n23, 163, 166, 175, 177, 178n5,
   179, 191, 198, 199, 207, 208, 211
GOSTs (Russia), 145
Gourevitch, Peter, 195n26
"Governance Matters" voice and
   accountability score, 103, 107t
government concession, 18, 193, 205
Govorun, Andrei, 6, 59, 65, 66n24, 68n32,
   134n4
Grill Master, 142
group formation, 3n3, 8, 9, 9n13, 11, 15, 36n23,
   96, 105, 129, 140, 141, 167n27, 195, 204
group mobilization, 6
Gryschenko, Volodymyr, 76, 77
Guatemala, 48n7
Guild for the Development of Audio-Video
   Trade (Russia), 68, 214t
   Sorokin, Iurii, 140
Guild of Pharmacists of Astana
   (Kazakhstan), 219t
Guskov, Anton, 156

Hart, David, 167n28
Hauska & Partner International
   Communications, 157
Hayek, Friedrich August, 206
Heinz, John P., 172
Herzegovina, 52t, 182t, 183
Honduras, 48n7
horizontally integrated commercial
   establishment, 2n1, 75, 82
hospitality industry, 137, 142, 143, 144, 145

hostile business environment, 15, 23, 65
Hungary, 45, 52t, 84, 84n48, 85, 96n1, 106,
   180, 181, 182t, 183, 184, 185, 186, 190
Huntington, Samuel, 19, 21, 24, 81

import-export operations, 18, 87
Independent Professional Union for
   Protecting Small and Medium Business
   (Kazakhstan), 222t
India, 48n7
Indonesia, 48n7
industrial conglomerate, 2n1, 200
industrial organization, 4
industrial policy, 8n12, 73n38
industry, 2, 2n1, 6, 14, 25n14, 37, 38, 38n1,
   38n2, 39, 40, 43, 53, 57, 61, 62, 65n23,
   66n27, 69, 73, 78, 79, 82, 83, 86, 90,
   90n51, 91n52, 92, 94, 98, 99, 100t, 101,
   104, 105, 118, 123, 124, 125, 126t,
   127, 129, 131, 133, 137, 138, 139, 141,
   142, 143, 144, 144n11, 145, 150, 151,
   152, 153, 155, 156, 158, 159, 162, 167,
   167n26, 168, 169, 169n33, 170, 180,
   181, 187, 188, 195, 196, 197, 198, 199,
   200, 201, 201n2, 202, 203, 204, 207,
   209, 210, 211, 215
informal economy, 4
information sharing, 22, 69, 72, 87, 103, 162,
   208
information transfer, 8n12, 11, 199, 207
Ingleby, Susan J., 107, 180, 181
inspection, 17, 24, 139, 141, 149, 150, 154
Institute for Business Research
   (Croatia), 157
institutional development, 6, 19, 194, 207
institutional structure, 106, 182
interest-group theory of regulation, 202
interest groups, 3n4, 4n5, 5, 6, 7, 7n11, 8, 9,
   10, 21, 37, 40, 57, 61, 72, 95, 104, 106,
   121, 124, 163, 167n28, 171, 191, 198,
   201, 202, 203, 204, 215
International Intellectual Property Alliance
   (IIPA), 138, 139
Italy, 180n8

joint welfare, 25n14

Kazakh Association for the Protection of
   Copyrights, 222t
Kazakh Association of Business Women, 221t
Kazakh Association of Customs
   Brokers, 220t

Index

247

Kazakh Association of Gaming Business, 221t
Kazakh Association of Independent Consultants and Appraisers (Kazakhstan), 221t
Kazakh Association of Producers of Office Supplies, 221t
Kazakh Brewers' Association, 219t
Kazakh Energy Association, 214t
Kazakh Franchising Association, 221t
Kazakh Tourist Association (Kazakhstan), 221t
Kazakhstan, 4, 10, 12, 13, 14, 17n1, 39, 45, 51, 52t, 54, 55t, 80, 81, 81n44, 82, 82n46, 83, 83n47, 84, 85, 91, 96n1, 130, 153, 163, 170, 182t, 213, 214t, 218t, 219t, 220t
Kenya, 48n7
Khodorkovsky, Mikhail, 205
Kinakh, Anatolii, 73n38, 77
Kostroma Guild of Realtors (Russia), 63t
Krasnodarskii Krai (Russia), 63t
Kravchuk, Leonid, 72n36
Kubicek, Paul, 3, 7, 58, 60n17, 63, 66, 174, 174n1, 181, 192
Kuchma, Leonid, 72n36, 160
Kyrgyz Republic, 21n7, 52t, 96n1, 182t

labor, 3n3, 6n8, 16, 19n4, 20, 22, 24, 46, 59, 60n17, 86, 91, 100t, 167, 168, 168n30, 170, 174, 174n1, 180n8, 185, 192, 192n23, 192n24, 193, 194, 194n25, 200, 206, 209, 209n8
    hiring decisions, 20
    labor laws, 22
    labor organizations, 60n17, 180n8, 193, 209
labor regulations, 24, 48, 49t, 100t, 193
Latin America, 22n10, 41, 180n8
Latvia, 45, 52t, 96n1, 106, 110, 182t
Law on Civic Organizations (Ukraine), 60n18, 75
Law on Collective Agreements (2006) (Slovenia), 186
Law on Employer Associations (Ukraine), 75
Law on Prevention and Limitation of Tobacco Consumption (Kazakhstan), 164
Law on Protection of Competition (2006) (Russia), 67
Law on State Support for Small Entrepreneurship (Ukraine), 60n18
League of Entrepreneurs of Small and Medium Business Left Bank (Ukraine), 214t

League of Trade Merchants (Russia), 70, 148, 164, 171, 214t
Leaseholders' Association (Russia), 57
Leff, Nathaniel H., 19, 21
Lehmbruch, Barbara, 3, 7, 60, 66
Lehmbruch, Gerhard, 173
Lessof, Suszy, 169n34
Liapina, Ksen'ia, 77
licensing regulations, 140n7
Lieberman, Evan S., 131
Lithuania, 42, 45, 51, 52t, 96n1, 106, 182t
lobbying, 3, 4n5, 9, 11, 20, 20n6, 37, 43n6, 46, 48, 53, 55, 66, 67, 67n28, 67n29, 67n30, 67n31, 68, 69, 70, 72, 78, 78n43, 80, 83, 84, 89, 90, 93, 122, 133, 146, 153, 156, 164, 166, 169, 199, 215

Macedonia, 52t, 96n1, 107, 182t, 184, 185, 186, 190
    Chamber of Economy, 186
Madagascar, 48n7
Mali, 48n7
market, 2n1, 3, 4n6, 5, 6, 8, 9, 14, 16, 19, 20, 24, 43n6, 46, 48, 65, 70n35, 76, 78, 79, 91, 94, 101, 112, 117, 122t, 125n22, 130, 131, 132, 133, 134n4, 138, 139, 140, 141, 142, 143, 144, 145, 148, 150, 152, 155, 156, 158, 159, 162, 166, 167, 168, 169, 171, 192, 193, 196, 197, 199, 200, 201, 201n2, 201n3, 202, 206, 207, 211
    market entry, 4n6, 101, 112
Marshall, Tom, 169n34
Mauritius, 48n7
McChesney, Fred S., 20, 21, 32
McDonald's, 142, 142n8
Medfarm (Kazakhstan), 219t
Medvedev, Dmitry, 56n11
membership
    compulsory membership, 11, 12, 13, 40, 41n5, 54, 84, 84n48, 85, 87, 88, 89, 89t, 90n51, 90t, 91, 92, 93, 106, 107, 107t, 110, 121, 151, 157, 172, 173, 175, 175n2, 176, 177, 177n3, 178, 178n5, 179, 180, 180n8, 180n9, 181, 181n10, 182na, 182t, 183, 183n13, 184, 184n15, 184n16, 185, 186, 187, 188, 189, 190, 190n21, 190t, 191, 193, 194, 195, 199
    membership benefits, 28n18
    membership costs, 137n5

248   *Index*

membership (*cont.*)
  membership density, 39, 43, 121
  satisfaction, 46, 48, 72, 89, 90t, 96, 122,
    123t, 184n16, 191
  sectoral membership, 65, 125
  voluntary membership, 11, 13, 40, 89,
    157, 177, 180, 181, 183, 189, 191,
    194, 199
Mesić, Stjepan, 85n49
metallurgy industry, 4, 82, 126t
Ministry of Economic Development and Trade
    (Russia)
  Shipov, Vitaly, 162
mobility
  factor (capital) mobility, 104, 104n12
modernization theory, 15, 105
Moldova, 84, 96n1, 180, 180n9, 181, 182t,
    184n15, 190
Mongolia, 40n4, 181, 182t
Montenegro, 52t, 96n1, 182t, 185
Moore, Barrington, 205
Morocco, 48n7
Moscow Chamber of Commerce and Industry
    (Russia), 214t
Moscow Contractor's Club (Russia), 214t
Moscow International Business Association
    (Russia), 63t, 156, 214t
Myant, Martin, 174

National Association for the Development of
    Trade and Services (UNADTS) (Ukraine),
    164, 166, 214t
  Blyzniuk, Andriy, 166
National Association of Freight Forwarders
    (Kazakhstan), 82, 221t
National Association of International Auto
    Trackers (Russia), 56
National Chambers of Commerce (Moldova),
    180n9
National Council on Social Partnership
    (Ukraine), 146
National Economic and Social Council
    (Croatia), 91
National Energy Association (Kazakhstan),
    221t
National Real Estate Association
    (Albania), 185
Nazarbayev, Nursultan, 81n44, 83, 163
Netherlands, 42
Nicaragua, 48n7
nonmarket forces, 94

nonprofit organizations, 2n1, 58n15, 60n18,
    61n18, 70, 73, 76n40, 82n46, 90, 169
nonrival goods, 23, 25, 30, 37
nonstate economic actors, 5
Northern Kazakhstan Association of
    Pharmaceutical Organizations, 219t
Novosibirsk Producers of Scientific-Industrial
    Products (Russia), 63t

Olson, Mancur, 3n3, 5, 6, 11, 15, 105,
    176, 203
Oman, 48n7
Onishchuk, Aleksandr, 156
Opora, 58n15, 64, 143, 152, 214t
  All-Russian Social Organization of Small
    and Medium-Size Business, 214t
opportunity, 137, 179
Orange Revolution (Ukraine), 72n36, 77, 79,
    80, 205
organizational dynamics, 15, 25n14, 29, 117,
    192, 210

Pakistan, 48n7
Pavlodar Business Association (Kazakhstan),
    220t, 222t
Pavlodar Business Forum (Kazakhstan), 220t
Peregudov, Sergei, 3, 7, 58, 66, 68
Peru, 48n7
Petroleum Union of Kazakhstan, 219t
Pharmaceutical Association of Krivoi Rog
    (Russia), 63t
Philippines, 48n7
piracy, 138, 139
Pleskachevskii, Viktor, 152
pluralism, 13, 39, 40, 72, 92, 106, 173, 174,
    175, 175n2, 179, 180, 184, 184n14, 185,
    187, 189, 194, 195
Poland, 4, 21n7, 45, 51, 52t, 96n1, 106, 181,
    182, 182t, 184n14
political competition, 106
political influence, 39, 45, 72, 77, 83n47, 84,
    93, 167, 168, 169, 200, 200t, 215
political rights, 55t
post-communism, 2, 2n1, 3, 3n3, 3n4, 4, 5, 6,
    6n8, 7, 7n10, 8, 9, 10, 10n14, 11, 12, 13,
    15, 16, 17, 17n1, 18, 20, 22, 30, 35, 37,
    39, 40, 40n4, 41, 41n5, 42, 43, 44, 45, 46,
    47, 48, 48n7, 49, 49t, 51, 52, 53, 54, 55,
    55t, 56n12, 60n17, 67n31, 72, 73, 77, 80,
    84, 85, 89, 92, 93, 94, 95, 96, 96n1, 98,
    105, 106, 123, 129, 134, 134n4, 137, 145,

Index

166, 168, 171, 173, 174, 174n1, 175, 176, 179, 180, 181, 182, 183, 184, 189, 191, 192, 192n24, 193, 194, 195, 196, 197, 198, 199, 200, 201, 201n2, 202, 203, 204, 205, 206, 207, 208, 209, 210, 211

pricing, 4n6

private enrichment, 18

private sector, 2, 4n5, 65n23, 73, 77, 106, 107t, 111, 117, 152, 185, 192

privatization, 18, 66, 73n38, 106, 123, 137, 141, 146, 149, 152, 168, 192

Professional Association of Registrars, Transfer Agents, and Depositories (PARTAD), 152

Pleskachevskii, Viktor, 152

Professional Union for Small and Medium Businesses, Ust'-Kamenogorsk (Kazakhstan), 222t

Professional Union of Small and Medium Businessmen (Kazakhstan), 222t

property rights, 19, 22, 62, 72, 78, 83n47, 84, 102n9, 110, 140, 146, 148, 152, 156, 197, 199, 206, 207, 208, 209, 211

protectionism, 6, 75

selective protectionism, 18

public, 2, 3, 3n3, 4n5, 5, 6, 7n11, 8, 8n12, 14, 16, 17, 17n2, 18, 19, 19n4, 22n9, 24, 32, 36, 55t, 56n12, 58, 67n29, 68, 69, 70n34, 75, 77, 79, 80, 82, 82n46, 83, 84, 93, 100t, 102n10, 111, 112, 113, 121n20, 132, 133n2, 134, 141, 152, 153, 154, 155, 156, 158, 159, 163, 164, 165, 166, 169, 181, 199, 201, 202, 204, 207, 210, 211

public goods, 19n4, 163, 166, 208

public oversight, 111, 112, 113

public policy, 8, 158, 207

public procurement, 18

Putin, Vladimir, 55n11, 56, 64, 67

Pyle, William, 6, 65, 134n4, 197, 198n1, 204

Quality Association (Kazakhstan), 219t

Rabotodavets magazine (Ukraine), 147n14, 148

rational utility, 24, 177

real-estate industry, 3, 104, 153

Realtor's Guild (Russia), 63t

regulations, 4, *11*, 12, 15, 16, 17n1, 19, 19n4, 20, 21, 22, 23, 24, 25, 29, 31, 32, 34, 35, 36, 37, 47, 48, 49, 49t, 67n31, 69, 70, 80,

81, 87, 88, 96, 97t, 98, 98n5, 99, 100t, 101, 101n6, 102, 103, 108, 110f, 112, 113f, 114, 116, 117, 122t, 124n21, 127, 128, 129, 131, 133, 133n3, 139, 140, 140n7, 143, 144, 145, 146, 149, 150, 151, 152, 153, 154, 155, 161, 162, 164, 165, 170, 171, 176, 177, 178, 187, 193, 197, 198, 199, 200t, 201n2, 202, 203, 211

banking regulations, 22, 130

environmental regulations, 19n4, 22, 24, 87, 100t

labor regulations, 24, 48, 49t, 100t, 193

licensing regulations, 138n6, 140n7

safety regulations, 22, 100t, 143, 151, 152, 166

regulatory environment, 7, 12, 16, 20, 21, 23, 31, 32, 34, 35, 39, 48, 51, 53, 54, 62, 68, 96, 98, 99, 101, 101n6, 112, 120, 124, 129, 130, 130n1, 131, 137, 138, 143, 145, 148, 150, 159, 162, 166, 170, 197, 198, 202, 207

regulatory politics, 4

regulatory uncertainty (unpredictability), 5, 19, 20, 32, 48, 49t, 197, 211

Remington, Thomas F., 3n4, 6, 58, 67, 174, 181

rent-seeking behavior, 3, 5, 6, 93, 122, 127, 170, 200, 202, 203, 204

Republika Srpska, 96n1

reservation value, 31, 223

resource mobility, 104n12

resource specificity, 104, 104n12, 111, 120, 124, 125, 127, 137, 167, 169, 197

Road Transportation Act (Croatia), 87

Romania, 51, 52t, 96n1, 181, 182t, 184, 193

RosBank, 130

Rosstat state statistical agency (Russia), 126

Rostov Organization of Private Taxi Owners (Russia), 63t

Rosugol, 168, 168n31, 169

rule of law, 53f, 97t, 102, 108, 110n15, 111f, 116, 118, 121, 197, 198, 207

Russian Association for the Development of Small and Medium-Size Business, 214t

Russian Association of Owners of Trademarks, 214t

Russian Construction Union, 214t

Russian Franchising Association, 60, 152, 214t

Russian Institute for Entrepreneurship and Investment (IEI), 56

Index

Russian Union of Industrialists and
Entrepreneurs (RUIE), 3n4, 57, 59, 60,
61, 61n19, 62, 62n19, 62n20, 63, 63t, 64,
65, 65n23, 66, 66n27, 67, 68, 156, 188,
193, 214t
Russian Union of Insurers, 152
Rutland, Peter, 3, 7, 66, 66n26

safety regulations, 22, 100t, 143
Salisbury, Robert H., 4n5, 66n25, 95, 209n8
sanctions, 3n3, 33, 67, 175, 175t
scandal, 81n44, 95, 156
Schaede, Ulrike, 200n2, 201n2
Schmitter, Philippe C., 173, 174, 175t, 209
Schneider, Ben Ross, 204
Sectoral Association of Recycling Metallurgy
(Kazakhstan), 221t
selective incentives, 3n3, 15, 24, 37, 39, 40,
93, 101n6, 122, 131, 132, 133, 145,
150, 155, 164, 166, 171, 177, 187, 191,
208, 223
self-regulation, 11, 20, 23, 36, 87, 130, 133,
144, 145, 152, 153, 166, 175n2, 183,
184, 201n2, 210, 211
Semenenko, Irina, 3, 7, 58, 66, 68
Senegal, 48n7
Serbia, 52t, 96n1, 107, 182na, 182t, 184, 185
Shokhin, Alexander, 66n27
Shokoladnitsa, 142
Slovakia, 45, 84, 106, 174, 180, 181, 182t,
183, 184, 185, 190
Slovenia, 21n7, 43, 45, 52t, 85, 96n1, 106,
107, 181, 182t, 183, 184, 185, 186, 193
Association of Employers, 185
Chamber of Commerce and Industry, 186
Chamber of Craft and Small Businesses, 186
Law on Chambers of Commerce and
Industry, 180n9, 186
Law on Collective Agreements (2006), 186
snowball effect, 30
social apathy, 4, 15
social-choice theory, 15, 177n3
socialism, 4, 85, 105, 141
Sonin, Konstantin, 69
South Africa, 42, 48n7
Southeast European Cooperative
Initiatives, 87
Soviet Union, 7, 45f, 58
Spain, 48n7
Speed fees, 24
Sri Lanka, 48n7
Stability Pact, 87

Stabilization and Association Agreement
(SAA), 86, 158
standard setting, 8n12, 11, 56n12, 207
state capacity, 18
State Committee for Economic Development
(Ukraine), 77
Stock Exchange Union (Kazakhstan), 219t
Streeck, Wolfgang, 209
SUEK corporations, 169
supplier, 20, 158, 161
Syria, 48n7

Tajikistan, 43, 52t, 96n1, 182t
Tambov Association of Small Entrepreneurs
(Russia), 63t
Tanzania, 48n7
taxes, 14, 17, 18, 19, 19n4, 21n8, 24, 25n15,
31, 48, 49, 49t, 49t, 51, 51n10, 64, 75,
99, 100t, 101, 103, 132t, 133, 147, 156,
160, 161, 165, 170,
188, 211
Tenders Chamber (Ukraine), 214t
The Eurasian Industrial Association
(Kazakhstan), 82, 218t
The National Union of Entrepreneurs and
Employers Atameken (Kazakhstan),
218t
Trade Law (1993) (Croatia), 88
Tragakes, Ellie, 169n34
Transparency International
Corruption Perception Index (CPI), 21n7,
55t, 107t, 117, 118
Tucker, Josh, 204
Tudjman, Franjo, 85n49
Turkey, 42n6, 48n7

Uganda, 48n7
Ukraine, 4, 10, 12, 13, 39, 51, 52t, 54, 55t,
72, 72n36, 73, 73n38, 74, 75, 76, 76n40,
77, 78, 80, 81, 82, 83, 85, 91, 96n1, 103,
130, 146, 147, 159, 165, 170, 174, 182t,
205n7, 213, 214t, 217
Ukrainian Association of Business Incubators
and Innovation Centers, 214t
Ukrainian Association of Leasing Companies
and Entrepreneurs (UALCE), 73, 146
Ukrainian Chamber of Commerce and
Industry (UCCI), 76, 76n40, 79, 150, 152,
171, 214t
Ukrainian Employers' Federation (UEF), 76,
76n41, 77, 214t
Ukrainian Franchising Association, 214t

Index

251

Ukrainian League of Industrialists and Entrepreneurs (ULIE), 73, 73n38, 74n38, 76, 77, 214t

Ukrainian Union of Leasing Companies, 214t

Ukrainian Union of Small, Medium, and Privatized Enterprises (USMPE), 73, 77, 79, 80, 214t

Union of Construction Firms of Kazakhstan, 220t

Union of Employers of Akmola (Kazakhstan), 220t

Union of Entrepreneurs and Employers of Atyrau Region (Kazakhstan), 221t

Union of Entrepreneurs of Arhari village, Amur Oblast (Russia), 63t

Union of Food Producers (Kazakhstan), 220t

Union of Industrialists and Employers of Almaty (Kazakhstan), 220t

Union of Industrialists and Employers of South Kazakhstan, 220t

Union of Industrialists and Entrepreneurs (Employers) of Kaliningrad Oblast, 214t

Union of International Auto Transporters (Kazakhstan), 222t

Union of Manufacturers and Consumers of Packaging Products (Russia), 214t

Union of Producers of Alcoholic Beverages (Russia), 214t

Union of Ukrainian Cooperators and Entrepreneurs, 73

US Agency for International Development (USAID), 157

Uzbekistan, 52t, 96n1, 182t

Verkhovna Rada (Ukraine), 160, 164, 165

vertically integrated commercial establishment, 2n1, 59, 61, 76, 82

Vietnam, 40n4

Volsky, Arkadii, 65, 66n27

voluntarism, 13, 91, 173, 184n14, 187, 189, 191, 194, 195

Waller, Michael, 174, 181

wealth, 81n44, 106

World Bank
  Doing Business Project, 48, 52t, 101, 102

World Business Environment Survey (WBES), 42n6, 43n6, 45, 46, 48n7

World Guide to Trade Associations (WGTA), 40, 40n3, 40n3

Yakovlev, Andrei, 6, 59, 65, 66n24, 68n32, 134n4, 202

Yambaev, Viktor, 17n1, 83, 153

Yanovsky, Victor, 152

Yanukovich, Viktor, 77, 205n7

Yekhanurov, Yuri, 161

Yugoslavia, 84, 85n49, 86, 88n50, 91, 106, 181

Yugur Association of Industrialists, Entrepreneurs, and Agrarians (Kazakhstan), 220t

Yukos, 64, 205

Zambia, 48n7

Zaporozhstal, 76

Zhuravskaya, Ekaterina, 69, 202

For EU product safety concerns, contact us at Calle de José Abascal, 56–1°, 28003 Madrid, Spain or eugpsr@cambridge.org.

www.ingramcontent.com/pod-product-compliance
Ingram Content Group UK Ltd.
Pitfield, Milton Keynes, MK11 3LW, UK
UKHW011319060825
461487UK00005B/190